LISTENING FOR THE HOLY

A LIFE JOURNEY

ROBINSON G. LAPP

Wallace Publishing

Wallace Publishing

ISBN: 978-0-578-24499-0

PRINTED IN THE UNITED STATES OF AMERICA

TABLE OF CONTENTS

Foreword

Aubreyanna L. Gurkin

"Papa. My Great Grandfather"

This is the story of a man with many titles. Every single one of them will be in this book, but I never called him by those titles. To me he was always Papa. My Great Grandfather. The man who built me a castle and helped paint my room pink. The man who I can have a discussion with and not feel like a child. The one person who utterly understands me. Every time I talk to him, I am amazed. Amazed by how alike we are and by how much he has experienced. I have heard every single one of his "long time ago" stories, and I have yet to grow tired of hearing them.

I know for a fact that I do not get my modesty from him, and if you know him, you know exactly what I mean. He is far from perfect, but he does his best to be kind He could not tell you what happens in the latest Marvel movie, but he could tell you what Martin Luther King, Jr's hand feels like.

I hope I did not steal too much of his thunder, but this is the story of Robinson G. Lapp.

FOREWORD

Rev. Dr. Susan Thistlethwaite
President Emerita and Professor Emerita
Chicago Theological Seminary

"If I Had a Hammer."

"Robb! Robb!" I called up to the ceiling of the main room of the Chicago Theological Seminary McGiffert House.

"I'm here, Susan!" Trustee Robb Lapp replied, clearly from within the ceiling.

"Come down!" I yelled, concerned.

My executive assistant had told me when I had entered the President's office that morning that Robb Lapp was on campus and in McGiffert House. I went across the street to find him. Little did I know he was not just "in" McGiffert, he was "inside the ceiling" of McGiffert.

"Just a minute, I'm almost finished," Robb replied. Then he climbed down a ladder having fixed the pesky problem no one in maintenance had been able to find.

And that, in a nutshell, is why Trustee Robinson Lapp received a bronzed hammer upon his retirement as a member of the Chicago Theological Seminary Board of Trustees.

"I had him appointed Chair of the Business Affairs Committee and it was one of the smartest moves I ever made as President and frankly, it was not for his considerable skills with a hammer, impressive as they are. Robb just goes right at a problem, digging down into the source and marshalling the people and the resources needed to fix it.

Autobiographies are interesting when they are about lives well lived, and Robb's autobiography is no exception. But if you want to learn about what Robb calls "secular ministry," you might consider reading from the end to the beginning. And then, from the beginning to the end. The bumps and bruises, the triumphs, and trials of his life as he describes them here have helped him craft an approach to ministry that is nearly unique, and one that should be replicated in ministries around the country. After all, don't we all have bumps and bruises, triumphs, and trials?

Toward the end, Robb writes, "In a very complex and even convoluted life that has focused primarily on an ordained secular ministry totally outside the structure of the church, there is a sense that I have been "counter-cultural" ever since ordination in 1957."

That is the Gospel truth. And speaking of the Gospel, I have worked with Robb Lapp not only as a president with a trustee, but as a professor with a student. In pursuing a second CTS degree Robb recently enrolled in our extensive online curriculum and took my "New Social Gospel" class. It was so helpful to have Robb as a student in that class, as he quietly modeled for the other students what the Social Gospel, the progressive, mostly Protestant movement to unite the gospel and social reform, meant, and he took it further. The "New Social Gospel" is the work of liberation theology that puts the transformation of society at the center of our work in what is called "praxis." Praxis is the unity of theory and practice. That is kind of like having a hammer and knowing exactly what nail you need to hit and why.

Robb does not just advocate for the homeless, *he actually houses the homeless*. I know very few others who have the will and the expertise from decades of work to accomplish that. And Robb accomplishes that over and over and over.

I advised Robb on his CTS STM thesis, *"Hitting the Streets with Jesus – A Spiritual Journey."* Robb comments on his thesis, "I told my story to try to reinforce my denomination's commitment to ordination for secular ministry, with a focus on the world's ills rather than on simply building up the church's institutional security."

I have often joked with Robb that he is one of our younger students, but there is a kernel of truth in that statement. Our younger students, though not just they, want to find a way to do "secular ministry" in the way that Robb has, working to effectively solve social ills at the local level.

I often think of Robb's thesis when I see clergy in #BlackLivesMatter marches with "Movement Chaplain" signs pinned to their front and back. There is a secular ministry right on the news many nights.

Robb is also the very embodiment of what has been tweeted over and over about Senator Elizabeth Warren: #ShePersisted. The hashtag that applies to Robb is #HePersisted through the hard-balls life has thrown at him and at Jan, his beloved wife, through ill health and recovery, and personal tragedy and triumph.

This is also a book about the Holy Spirit, for, after all, #ShePersisted too.

"If we live by the Spirit, let us also walk by the Spirit." (Galatians 5:25) The Spirit persists and Robb listens and acts.

INTRODUCTION

"The Holy" is the mysterious energy and force that creates life, whether that life is an evolving universe, a changing planet, a dinosaur, a bird, a fly, a whale, an ape, or a human being. There is only one Holy behind all the world's religions. Each religion is a sequence of images and metaphors that describe a tribal community's experience of the ultimate truths, meanings, and requirements of human existence. The Holy continues to be alive and well, constantly trying to bring wholeness and functionality into being for the universe, the planet, and every living creature. The Holy is not a supernatural whimsical decision maker. Rather, the Holy is the creative force that makes life possible.

If the world's people as a group fail to do what the Holy calls forth from creaturely beings, one day there will be no more human beings. Our bones will join those of the dinosaurs as new species emerge.

My story is that of a person who has learned over his lifetime that there is an unseen, immutable force which pulls one toward making life work for others, regardless of the cost. I have felt a mysterious tug to distinguish between right and wrong individual and societal behavior.

For whatever reason, I have been called into this lifestyle despite cultural siren calls to the contrary.

As I have struggled with life decisions, especially major ones that define what my life means, the Holy whispers, "Here's what life is calling you to do in this situation."

In life on this earth, we are faced with the need or opportunity to make behavioral decisions many times a day. Some choices we make are good. Some are bad.

A choice is good if it contributes to the welfare of others more than self. A choice is good if it advances justice in the quality of life for one or all human beings, born or yet to be born. A choice is good if it increases one's ability or capacity to do what is right.

A choice can be bad if it is self-serving, taking away from others to benefit oneself. A choice can be bad if it diminishes one's ability to be responsible for herself or himself. A choice can be bad if it is based on the notion that people who are "different" should be excluded.

It is the transcendent Holy that defines goodness and evil, and that invites people to choose to walk in Holy ways. In every moment, a person is challenged with the opportunity to choose a step that fulfills the Holy's vision of good human behavior.

Sometimes, "Oh, what should I do now" challenges are heavy duty and totally unexpected. By the time I was in my Junior Year in High School my life had been dramatically reshaped by two profoundly difficult family events. In each case I had had to decide whether to crumble or to live bravely. Managing to do the latter, and excelling in math and science, at sixteen I was excited about becoming an aircraft engineer and was being urged by my teachers to apply at one of two prestigious east coast technical universities.

But that summer I went to a church youth camp and kept hearing about making a positive difference in people's lives as they search for values by which to live. What a radical change the Holy made in my life in just a week! I tossed engineering and decided to become an ordained Protestant clergyperson.

Subsequently, my fundamental commitments have often put me at risk – socially, racially, professionally, and economically. I never could have imagined the challenges to which I would have to respond. Life has been an adventure of discovery woven through an obstacle course of traumatic blows, incredible challenges, and gracious opportunities.

Life's assignments have come unexpectedly, either as uninvited reversals, or as the results of choices I have made in face of an often-demonic world.

I have learned that I can control only my own behavior. I cannot control anyone else's daily choices. I can only inspire others to take responsibility for their own lives, loving others more than self.

The energy and strength to cope has come from my listening to what a situation needs me to do to make life work fairly for others. Thus, I never have been totally crushed or permanently demoralized by anything that life has done to me.

I share my journey with the notion that one person's walk with the Holy may give light to others.

~~~

SECTION I

1933 – 1945

~~~

HERE I AM!

Chapter 1

~~

EARLY DAYS

A Bit of Genealogy

I CAME INTO the world on March 27, 1933 in the depth of the post-World War I Depression, at Millard Fillmore Hospital in Buffalo, NY. I was named Robinson Gardner Lapp, Jr., after my father, whose name came from his mother, Laura Gardner, and Laura's father, Lawrence Robinson.

My father, a high-school drop-out, was then working in the Township of Tonawanda, NY, making barely enough money to pay the rent and buy meager groceries. Mother, a graduate of Cornell University, was a recently laid-off high school Home Economics teacher.

Robinson Gardner Lapp, Sr., my Dad, was born on March 30, 1908, in rural New York State. Shortly thereafter, his family moved to Williamsville, NY, where Dad spent his childhood and youth. His father, a Baptist clergyperson, was a fire and brimstone Evangelical

Literalist with conservative theological training. My paternal grandmother, Laura Lapp attended a New York State Normal School and was a grade-school teacher before giving birth to two children, the younger of whom, a daughter, died in mid-childhood.

English roots on my father's maternal side date to the 1620 arrival of a Pilgrim named Stephen Hopkins, aboard the Mayflower. Dad's paternal German ancestry and surname came with 18th Century German Mennonite immigrants who settled in eastern Pennsylvania. Most generations of ancestral male Lapp Mennonites were clergypersons.

Helen Dillard Griffin, my mother, was born near Rochester, NY on January 26, 1907. Her lineage was English on both sides. Her paternal Griffin forbearers lived in the Buffalo area. Several generations of men were millers, which was big in Buffalo, as harvested wheat was shipped into Buffalo in steam freighters via the Great Lakes from Ohio and Michigan.

Mother's maternal Dillard ancestors settled in Jamestown in the Chesapeake region of Virginia during the mid-1700's. It being tobacco country, many Africans were an unwilling part of the Virginia cultural mix. It is possible that some of Mother's ancestral family members owned slaves. As the Civil War approached, Mother's Grandfather Dillard, neither a slave-owner nor a supporter of the Confederacy, escaped with his family to Fort Scott, KS, where he set up a general merchandise business. Mother's mother, Irene, was one of several Dillard young adult children.

The maternal Virginia and New York threads came together with the marriage of Mother's parents. Her father, Edwin Griffin, an American Baptist minister who held a Ph.D. from the University of Chicago Divinity School became pastor of the Fort Scott Baptist Church. He, a young widower, and Irene Dillard soon married. Ministry subsequently took the Griffins to Des Moines, IA, then to Maywood, IL, where Mother graduated from High School.

There is a cultural bias story associated with my mother's being unemployed when I was born. Upon graduation from Cornell, she had become a Home Economics teacher in Mexico, New York. Her school district expected its female teachers not to be married. Since their home was in Buffalo, NY, her recent marriage to my father was not widely known in the town of Mexico. It being the Depression, however, she needed to stay employed, as Dad earned a pittance as a surveyor's assistant. Following my conception in the summer of 1932, Mother tried to soldier-on as a teacher in Mexico, NY, but was forced to retire at the end of the first semester in early 1933 because of an abdominal bulge.

A Rural Rental

Home at the time of my birth was a second-floor flat in Kenmore, NY, a suburb north of Buffalo. I do not recall a thing about life as an infant in that apartment, but I am told I was a restless little guy who liked to be pushed around the aging neighborhood in an old baby carriage.

Living on the second floor flat became untenable with the birth of Stuart Dillard Lapp on February 13, 1935. With Dad's salary inching up a bit as the Depression faded, we moved to a rural two-story brick rental located north of Kenmore very near the Erie Barge Canal, in the Town of Tonawanda, and not far from Ellicott Creek, which was named for the surveyor who parceled out that large portion of New York State lying west of the Genesee River. Our house was close enough to the Erie Barge Canal that we could see and hear the throbbing diesel tugboats as they pulled their freight barges along the waterway.

Shortly after dropping out of high school my Dad had managed to land a job working for the Town of Tonawanda as the rod man for the Town Surveyor who laid out new roads and sewer lines. His job as the rod man was to hold a tall measuring stick for the surveyor, and to drive stakes into the ground to mark routes for roadways and utility line construction. My father learned surveying arithmetic and other elements of civil engineering, as well as construction management of land development improvements. He worked for the Town of Tonawanda for a dozen years as the Depression faded into World War II. From the time I learned to walk, I loved going with him to construction sites to watch the giant steam shovels.

As very young children, Stuart and I played both inside the house and out. We were very mischievous. One spring noon when Stuart and I were no older than three and five Mother left us at home alone while she drove to the Township barn to bring Dad for home for lunch. The table was set, and soup was on the stove. As she left, she said, "Now Robin, I'll be gone for a while. You take care of Stuart."

Time passed. I pushed Stuart's stool up to the sink and climbed up to reach the faucet. Stuart stood right next to the stool. I filled a small cup with cold water and handed it to Stuart. Laughing, he threw the water over his shoulder. Then we did it again. Over and over. By the time the folks got home water was everywhere. It filled the dishes on the table. It soaked the tablecloth. It

Happy Team

was running across the floor and down the cellar stairs. When she came back, Mother scolded, "Oh, Robin, how did this happen? I thought I told you to play with Stuart!"

I protested, saying, "Stuart threw the water. I only filled the cup for him!" Each of us was spanked, but I got the worst of it. I was frustrated because I did not think I was more wrong than Stuart. He had thrown the water! When we went to bed that night, Stuart and I waited until Mother had left the room, then laughed as gleefully as we had while throwing the water.

As close as he and I were, some of my memories of Stuart involve jealousy. On the Christmas before we moved from Ellicott Creek Estates, each of us received a used Lionel train. Stuart's had a long engine and fancy light green passenger cars with double wheel trucks. Mine had a shorter engine and freight cars with only single wheel trucks. His would go backward and forward. Mine only went forward. Offended that he had the fancier train, I spent hours arguing with him about which one of us would control the single transformer that operated both trains. The difference between the trains reinforced my jealousy of a younger kid in the family.

Amherst 16

When I was four years old, I started Kindergarten in a city school in downtown Tonawanda, several miles from home. Shortly into to the year I failed to follow the rule about not bouncing a ball in the classroom. Why was there a big ball in the classroom in the first place? Bouncing the ball, I deprived a baby duck of its life and was expelled. Because of the long drive, this suited Mother just fine. But no more Kindergarten that year!

Beginning the next fall, my first three grades in a rural three-room school, Amherst 16, about a mile and a half away from home, were in the same room with the same teacher. I learned all three grades' lessons the first year. How to add and subtract. How to write and spell. How to fool the teacher. After that, I was bored and a disciplinary challenge. When I was in third grade, Stuart became a first grader in the same classroom. Our teacher wisely never let us sit near one another!

The mile and a half walk to Amherst 16, which we did virtually every day without adult supervision, crossed a main highway and paralleled rushing Ellicott Creek.

Winters with lots of snow were a big issue when I was a child. In 1938, one morning when I was in first grade it was snowing very hard. Mother said we should stay home from school. But Dad was unwavering. "You're going to school, by golly!" Dad took our neighborhood kids and me to school in an old black Ford panel truck provided him by the Township for his work as the surveyor's rod man. The truck had no side windows in the cargo area. We kids had to sit on surveying equipment and stakes but got to school safely. Once we were settled in our classroom, we could see from the windows that seriously heavy snow was continuing.

Around noon, Dad appeared at the classroom door and told our teacher he had come for us. "Roads are closing," he told our teacher. "This is a big blizzard. I need to take the Ellicott Creek kids home."

Getting on our coats and leggings we all trudged through waist deep snow to the black panel truck. It took two hours of an increasingly frustrated Dad gunning into drifts, backing and trying again. He could hardly see where to drive. But we all got home. Before it stopped snowing the drifts were as high as the second story of our cozy red brick rental home.

Snow or shine, our teacher made us go outdoors to play on rustic playground equipment. One frozen day, I stuck out my tongue and licked the steel frame of the monkey bars. My tongue instantly froze to the pipe. I could not get it off. Eventually, my teacher brought some warm water and poured it on the pipe and my tongue. My tongue did not enjoy eating for several days.

Another indelible memory is the evening in the Ellicott Creek neighborhood when, at seven years old, it was somehow my fault that Dad's English Setter ran in front of my two-wheeler in chase of a pheasant. Dad had sent me to a neighbor's house to get a gallon of paint. I was carrying it home on my handlebar when Duke shot across the road. I could not avoid him, and when I hit him the bike crashed, and the lid flew off the gallon of paint. White paint got all over the bike, me, the dog, and the road. I did not hear the end of the recitation about my stupidity for days.

Kathy Beats Pearl Harbor

Early on the morning of December 31, 1940, almost a year before the Japanese invasion of Pearl Harbor, Katharine Elizabeth Lapp was born in Children's Hospital in Buffalo, there being no room for another delivery at Millard Fillmore, the family's preferred hospital. This was Mother's fourth pregnancy, a third child having been stillborn a year earlier. Stuart and I were five and seven years old when Kathy came along. Her birth had taken place in a hospital hallway as all the delivery rooms were occupied with other straining mothers.

She was the seventh Katharine Elizabeth on my father's side. Number six, Dad's younger sister, died of pneumonia at age twelve, while number five, Dad's Aunt Katharine, was killed in an auto crash as an adult. But there were high hopes for this baby.

By the time she turned one, Kathy had developmental difficulties. She made sounds but was not forming even simple words. She could not stand or walk until after she was three. She scooted her way along the floor while sitting upright. She never did learn to speak clearly. As an adult she walked with a lurching gait. But Kathy, even as a baby and young child, was a happy, pleasant, and undemanding little person.

I think I may have been the first family member to adapt to the reality of her disability. Hoping for the best, our parents resisted acknowledging and adjusting to Kathy's difficulties. But when she was tested during grade school, and her IQ was only 70, they found new ways to show their love and support.

Closer to Town as The War Begins

As the winds of war escalated with Nazi Germany's imperialism, the Lapp family moved on August 15, 1941 from the Erie Canal neighborhood to a tract house in a developing area in the Township of Tonawanda. It was a new two-story with three bedrooms and a single bath for which my parents paid $6,000!

Less than four months later, December 7th, 1941 was a Sunday. That afternoon, I was with my father at Kenmore Methodist Church where Mother was directing a rehearsal of the annual Christmas Pageant. He and I were watching when another dad rushed up and told Dad we should run down into the basement boiler room where the custodian had a radio. I can still remember the quiet awe with which the several men and I listened to the growing drama of the Japanese bombing of Pearl Harbor. We were there for more than an hour. No one said a word.

Overnight, beginning December 7, 1941, American life changed abruptly. There was a collective nation-wide holding of breath from day one. It only got worse as time passed. No one knew what would happen next, not only on the battlefields and seas of the War, but to life in America and in our neighborhood.

Manufacturing plants of every condition and description were commandeered for war weapon production. Blackouts were a fact of life in north-eastern states nightly for years. Food was rationed. Gasoline was even more tightly controlled. Every eye was focused on the production of planes, tanks, truck, guns, and uniforms. Almost immediately, civilian auto and truck production was halted. There were no new cars built in America for four years.

Men rushed into, or were drafted for, service in the military. Women went into factory work in droves for the first time in history. Because we lived near a national border, every plane that flew overhead took my breath away as I squinted to check the markings on its wings. Kids in every community collected huge piles of scrap metal for re-smelting. Adult daily talk was not of the latest film, scandal, or political maneuver, but rather of the tragic unmerciful tides of war.

The Great Depression with its long lines of hungry men seeking food handouts for their families had been the somber reality. Suddenly, a World War complete with blackouts, unidentified aircraft droning overhead, and raucous nightly air-raid sirens, was the new daily environment.

In addition to being able to afford a modest house, the time came for my Dad to stop fussing with maintaining the 1932 Ford V-8 they had bought as a used car shortly after I was born. After the War started, he was able to find a 1939 battleship gray Buick Special Sedan. This car played an important role in my teenaged years.

Four months before The War started, I became a 4th grader at Philip Sheridan Elementary, and Stuart entered 2nd grade. The next Fall, Philip Sheridan being an annex school with only four grades, I had to ride an ancient school bus farther into town to attend 5th grade at Washington Elementary, while Stuart became a 3rd grader at Philip Sheridan.

Chapter 2

~~

A Dad and Mom

Dad – A Remarkable High School Dropout

As a non-high school graduate, both the financial realities of the Depression and a free spirit kept my Dad from even considering college. After being a surveyor's rodman, when World War II broke out in 1941, Dad was encouraged by a Bell Aircraft engineer to apply for a job at the war plane manufacturing company. Before being interviewed, he sat day after day in his pajamas and bathrobe in our living room, studying the geometry and trigonometry handbooks he had used in his years as a surveyor. Incredibly, he landed an engineering job at Bell Aircraft. His title was Liaison Engineer for Experimental Aircraft. At first, he worked in a factory plant on Elmwood Avenue in Buffalo where Pierce Arrow automobiles had been made until 1933. This is where Bell designed and assembled its early experimental planes. Fleet manufacturing of fighter planes was done in a newly constructed Bell factory in Wheatfield, located near the Niagara Falls Municipal Airport so they could be flown off to war.

As Liaison Engineer, he acted as the technical interface between the design engineers and those shop workers who handcrafted every part for new designs. He became very skilled at interpreting and resolving technical and communication issues between the engineers and the production workers. He spent most of 1942 managing the design of the Bell P-63 Kingcobra as an upgrade replacement for the Bell P-39 Airacobra that had been designed in 1938. Both were single seat fighter planes whose unique features were a mid-fuselage engine and a cannon whose barrel protruded from the pivot center of the propeller. More than 9,000 P-39's were built and used by the U.S., Russia and Great Britain in the European theater. But its altitude and speed were limited. The need for a fighter that would go faster, farther, and higher was evident very early in the War. Hence came the P-63 Kingcobra, a slightly larger, more powerful, upgrade of the P-39. 3,300 of these were manufactured by 1944. They saw stellar service in Europe and North Africa. Dad's P-63 work was completed in late 1942 when the plane was moved from design and testing into production.

His next assignment was a bust. Lawrence Bell, owner of Bell Aircraft, convinced the Army Air Force that a very light, small, fast fighter made with more wood than aluminum would be good for close air-to-air combat. Dad became the lead design engineer for the P-77. There were just too many design problems with the use of wood and an engine not powerful enough for even such a small plane, so the project was scrapped within months. But Dad was quickly assigned work on an early jet fighter.

Mother – A Resilient Wife and Mom

When it had been her time for college, out of necessity, she chose a curriculum that would give her a readily marketable skill. She enrolled in Buffalo State Teachers College as a Home Economics candidate. After two years, her Aunt Clara Griffin, a colorful lesbian with an intriguing partner, and an early female M.D., paid for the remainder of Mother's undergraduate degree at Cornell University in Ithaca.

Toward the end of her studies at Cornell, Mother's father, Edwin Griffin , began a long and painful lurch into senility. He was relieved of his pulpit in Maywood, IL, where Mother had graduated from High School. He and Grandmother Irene were given shelter in a small rural bungalow on a farm in Eden Valley, NY, south of Buffalo, by Aunt Clara. After my Grandfather Griffin died in 1936, Mother and her sister, my Aunt Irene Gould, had responsibility for Grandma Griffin, their mother, who lived another 25 years. Their younger brother Richard also was part of the equation. At least a couple of times he rode his motorcycle to southern California, where he took up residence before the War. Grandma Griffin spent substantial amounts of time living with Uncle Richard in California before and during the War.

Our family attended the Methodist Church in Kenmore, NY, a large stone Gothic structure which was walking distance from the flat where we lived when I, then my brother, were born. How two people who had come from Baptist minister families ended up in a Methodist church is intriguing. The most obvious reason is that during the Depression when people could not afford to drive, Kenmore Methodist Church was right around the corner from the flat where my folks lived. But a more subtle reason is that a denomination new to them resolved their family theological differences that originated from the Baptist homes in which they grew up. Dad was from an evangelical conservative tradition, while Mother grew up in a home where Biblical theology was much less literal. On top of that, Dad was committed to Boy Scouting, and there was an active troop at Kenmore Methodist. For years in the late 30's and into the early 40's Mother directed our church's Christmas pageant, a major production that attracted attention throughout the Buffalo community.

And that is how I got to be a Methodist.

My Grandfather Lapp, who served an Evangelical Baptist Church in Williamsville, NY died of a heart attack in 1937 while calling at a parishioner's home. My Grandmother, Laura Lapp, tried living alone in the Williamsville house they owned. As the War started, Mother insisted that Grandma Lapp come live with us in our new Town of Tonawanda house. Grandma occupied one of our three bedrooms. That put Kathy, Stuart, and me together in a small bedroom. Mother bought an attractive maple bunk bed for Stuart and me, while Kathy slept in a crib squeezed into a corner. We were suddenly a three-generation household.

Mother's role was to run our household, manage the family finances, care for two rambunctious boys, cater to my father's needs in supporting his daily excursions to town for work, give birth to and care for a third child, and keep Grandma Lapp's opinionated vocal interfering to a minimum. I was never comfortable with Grandma Lapp as she was a very rigid person who thought she knew better than either of my folks about how I should behave.

As Kathy's developmental issues emerged, to her credit, Mother never patronized Kathy, nor did she ever give up hope Kathy would someday live independently and productively. But it was difficult to watch Mother silently carry heartbreak over Kathy.

In addition to Christmas Pageants, Mother directed a "Tom Thumb" wedding one winter at our church. My brother Stuart, at 4, was the very solemn groom. A shy church schoolgirl was the literally blushing bride. I was an usher. Mother did a great job. The church was packed the night of the performance. "Tom Thumb" made the Sunday supplement section of the *Buffalo Courier Express* the next weekend.

Chapter 3

~~~

THE LAST TIME I SAW STUART

On the Way to School

FRIDAY, MARCH 5, 1943, started out like most other frigid winter, snowy Western New York mornings for my brother and me. He had just turned eight, and I was almost ten. Dad already had left for the Bell Aircraft manufacturing plant near Niagara Falls. Mother ended her oversight of Stuart's and my breakfast and hurried us out the door, blowing kisses. Stuart and I quickly joined up with neighbor kids Charles and Sue. We continued our way down our street to the Elmwood Avenue corner where I was to catch a school bus to George Washington Elementary, the main grade school in the center of town. The others were to walk three short blocks to Philip Sheridan, a light gray clapboard four-room Washington School annex that went through only the fourth grade. They would have to cross Sheridan Drive, a major highway, to get to their school.

Before my bus came, I walked part way to Philip Sheridan School with

16

Stuart. He was carrying a prized but empty three ring notebook binder our mother had given him. I teased, "Why don't you let me take that binder to Washington today? I need it more than you do. Then, I'll let you take it on Monday." As I grabbed it from his arms, he caved, saying "Oh, okay. But it's really mine. Mother gave it to me first!"

As he went on, I headed back to my bus stop.

Just as the ancient orange and white WOOLEY contract bus wheezed to a stop at my corner, Charles' mother came running down our street in her nightgown, screaming, "My baby! My baby! My baby!" She pushed past me and got on the bus. She continued to scream, "Oh my poor baby. Hurry up! Drive! My poor baby!" As I got on the bus, I was stunned. I could not figure out what was wrong.

The bus headed toward Philip Sheridan to drop off a few younger kids who had already been picked up before my stop. When we stopped at the Sheridan Drive red light moments later, Charles' mother forced the door open, jumped off the bus and ran toward a small body that was lying in the street. I could not tell what I was seeing. I felt faint. Something was terribly wrong. A gasoline truck was stopped in the middle of the road just east of the light. Two cars had stopped. Their doors were open. People were kneeling over two motionless figures in the road in front of the truck. A man in a suit was putting a blue blanket over a third body. No one knelt by it. Though the bus waited only one turn of the light before proceeding, it seemed like we were frozen in time. No one spoke.

The gas truck was light yellow. On the tank was the word RICHFIELD.

I knew in my gut my brother was the unattended figure, but I was too stunned to try to get off the bus and see.

The bus went the block to Philip Sheridan School and dropped off several kids. Those of us going on to Washington stayed aboard. As it did each morning, the bus then made a loop through a more remote rural area and arrived back at Philip Sheridan about 15 minutes later with a few more kids. While we older kids were waiting to go on to Washington, the Philip Sheridan second-grade teacher got on the bus and moved silently toward my seat. Without saying a word, she grabbed my arm and pulled me off the bus. She led me to the school basement. She made me lie on a cot, then left me in the almost pitch-black dark. I was puzzled. I did not know what was going on or why I had been isolated!

After an eternity of less than ten minutes I snuck upstairs. Kids and teachers silently stared at me. I felt very alone. I went into the room labeled BOYS. Inside was a man I had never seen before. He was sobbing quietly. On his jacket was the word RICHFIELD. We looked at each other for quite a while. Neither of us said a word. I left without using the toilet and headed for the school exit door.

A mom I didn't know stopped me, saying, "You can't just leave. School has started." I said, "I am in fifth grade at Washington Elementary. The second-grade teacher made me get off the bus, then took me downstairs. I don't know why." At this point, not a soul had said anything to me about an accident, nor that my brother had been involved. But I knew Stuart was dead.

I started out the door to walk home. The mom, still watching, said, "Wait, I'll drive you." I was shivering. "Okay," I said. We went several blocks out of the way, I suppose to avoid the accident scene. I started to cry quietly. When we got to the corner of my street, I asked her to stop. I told her, "I can't be crying when we got to my house. I don't think my mother should see me cry."

I entered the house alone. Mother and I hugged. Her eyes were red, but her voice was strong and even. She held me close, shook her head while biting her lip, then finally asked, "How did you get here? I supposed you'd still be at your school." As we went to the kitchen I said, "When the bus made its loop out to Military Road and came back to Stuart's school, a teacher made me get off. And somebody's mother just brought me home."

Several women sat at the table at the far end of the narrow kitchen, staring straight ahead, some crying. There was a white oil cloth covering the kitchen table, along with a sugar bowl and brown and yellow salt and pepper shakers. Mother and I joined them. Still, no one told me anything about Stuart's fate. They just talked in hushed tones about what a nice boy he was.

Soon, I heard my father come in the front door. He and my mother disappeared upstairs for a short while. She came back to the table. Biting her lower lip again, she said softly to me, "Stuart won't be coming home. He was killed this morning."

I took a deep breath. I cried, but not for long. Mother looked away. Then she busied herself with getting coffee for people at the table.

I felt very alone. My life lay ahead. Stuart's did not.

My father left the house. I learned later he had gone to what they called a funeral home. Two men from our church went with him to identify Stuart's body. These men decided Dad should not see Stuart. The Coroner accepted the men's word that the body was Stuart's. Stuart had been crushed under the wheels of the truck. He was unrecognizable. Dad also had to make service arrangements at the funeral home. A funeral was to be held at our church on Sunday afternoon.

By evening our little house had been invaded by loads of flowers and casseroles. People, some who I recognized and some I had never seen before, kept coming in. They whispered very quietly. Most, both men and women, cried when they talked with either of my parents.

Without consulting me, my parents made arrangements for me to spend Saturday at a farm belonging to an ex-neighbor and co-worker of Dad's. Prior to the War, we had lived near one another, so I knew the parents and their son Dickie, who was my age. No one asked me if I wanted to go.

The day was a disaster. I was separated from any opportunity to hear my family talk about Stuart. Nothing was said at the farm about Stuart's having been killed. I remember only one scene from that day. Dickie and I were out in the farmyard. It was windy and cold. Nearby was a large two-story white barn. Just beyond was a dormant peach orchard. The leafless trees were multiple sticks against the gray sky. Dickie and I had not played for almost two years. We did not know what to do. He had a BB gun. He let me hold it. I aimed it at a light bulb we could see through an open barn window about 50 feet away. I squeezed the trigger and broke the bulb. "Good shot!" I said under my breath. Dickie's father raced out of the barn. I was still holding the gun. He said sternly, "Robin, why in the world did you do that? You could have hurt someone. Give me that gun!" I said nothing as I handed it over. At that point I wished I had zinged him. I wanted desperately to go home. But all that happened was that it got dark.

I, finally, was taken home after supper. The living room and dining room were full of flowers from floor to ceiling. The stench of cut flowers was overwhelming. People with red eyes were squeezed into every square inch of the main floor of our small house. I started frantically tearing away the flower baskets. I wanted to see what was behind them. I wanted to see my brother. After ten minutes it became clear there was no casket and no brother. I cried. I was angry over being sent away for the day. Knocking over some more flowers, I yelled at my father, "Why did you send me to Dickie's house? I wanted to stay here! Where is Stuart?"

Early the next afternoon, Mother, Dad, my Grandmother Lapp, and I drove the two miles to our church. Stuart's casket was in a large overflow room at the rear of the sanctuary. I was not allowed to go into that room. I could not get near the closed casket I was seeing for the first time. We went into an adjacent smaller room from which we could see the casket and a lectern. I sat between Mother and Grandma Lapp. Dad sat on the other side of my mother. I chose to sit there to join my father in comforting Mother. I gripped my mother's hand. I never heard the words spoken by the minister. There were too many. I did not hear the music. It was too mournful. I did my best not to cry in front of my mother but failed.

After the benediction, we drove to Elmlawn, the main town cemetery, and stopped by a huge leafless elm tree under which was a pile of snow-covered dirt. It was a windy gray day. I learned later that the grave was one of a unit of six my father had hastily purchased the day of the accident. The minister solemnly uttered a string of words. The casket was lowered into the hole next to the dirt pile. My emotions were as frozen as the dirt. I wanted to cry. I could not. I wanted to stay while workers put the dirt over the casket, but we left. We went home. Our little house was filled to the door with people. I wanted to be alone. I went up to my bedroom, but there was Stuart's empty bunk over mine. I went back downstairs. People tried to talk to me. I couldn't say anything. I just felt very alone.

Everything had changed.

Because of the critical need for war workers to remain on the job days, nights and weekends, Stuart's funeral had been squeezed in on Sunday, and Dad was back in Wheatfield on Tuesday, having taken one day to recover. This urgency reflects the life climate in America during World War II which radically changed people's behavior and deepest emotions.

My Father Reaches Out

Monday, the morning after the funeral, dawned overcast and dreary. My father drove me to school. Classmates stared at me and said nothing. When class started, our teacher said, "Robin, would you stand up and tell the class about your poor little brother's accident. Some of the children wondered why you weren't here Friday."

Standing there was awful. I stammered, "My brother Stuart was run over by a gas truck on Friday and I couldn't come to school." I could not think of anything else to say. I sat down. Kids tittered. But I did not cry. I felt miserable and very lonely. I wanted to be invisible. I could not understand why my teacher made me get up and talk.

I went home from school that day on the bus, as though it was a normal day. When I got into the house both Mother and Dad were there. I wondered why he was not at work. But I soon found out. He said, "Let's go upstairs."

I led, followed by my mother then my father. Mother said, "Let's look on your bed." I turned into the small bedroom at the top of the stairs. My bed was the bottom bunk of the set in which my brother and I slept. My sister's crib was still crowded into the room. On my bunk was a large bright red flat metal box. I just stared at it. Mother said, "Go ahead. You can touch it."

It was the biggest Erector set I had ever seen. My first impulse was to think how extravagant it was. I asked guiltily, "What is this for? Why did you get it?" But I was thrilled. I made trucks and cranes and planes with it all the rest of the afternoon. I do not remember supper.

The following Saturday Dad took me to a hardware store in North Tonawanda. I was not sure what the trip was all about. Dad said to the storekeeper, "We are here to buy a few tools."

We found a claw hammer, a set of wrenches, an assortment of wood chisels, a hacksaw and blades, four metal files, wire-cutting and electrician's pliers, several sizes of screwdrivers, a hand saw, two sets of clamps, a hand drill and bits, a folding carpenter's rule, and, last of all, a huge anvil vise. The bill came to just over forty-nine dollars. I was both excited and confused. It felt unreal, as I never had seen my father do much of anything with tools other than the occasional adjusting of something under the hood of our car. "Why are we doing this? What are these things for?" I asked. Dad said, "I just think it's time for you to learn to use tools. I'll show you, and we'll make things together."

We took the tools home. Mother was perplexed. She sighed and shrugged her shoulders upon hearing the cost. We took the tools to the basement and left them on the floor near the foot of the stairs. The next Saturday, Dad and I went to a lumber yard and bought a few two-by-sixes and some four-by-fours. We also got some spikes. We took everything to the already cramped basement. Without saying much about what various tools were used for, or how to use them, Dad fashioned a work bench eight feet long and 3½ feet front to back. I helped him push it against a wall near the foot of the stairs. It wiggled around, as it was attached neither to the cement block wall nor to the floor. This was a problem especially after we bolted the vise to one corner of the bench. We could not do anything about the wiggle before Mother called down, "Supper is ready."

That is the last time I ever saw my father touch any of those tools. His resolve to get closer to his surviving son evaporated. He was handling his loss by becoming even more immersed in his job at Bell.

Is Life A Drudge or An Opportunity?

I turned 10 three weeks later. My life had been thrown into chaos. I was lonely. I was deeply frightened. I did not want to go to school. I became very insecure. I stewed in self-pity. I sulked for attention. I was short tempered. I felt guilty because I had thought Stuart got all the attention in the years before his death. I did not know how to say I missed Stuart. But I quickly saw that my parents were in the same box. Simple emotional survival was a full-time job for each of us. But the days were long. The nights were longer. I was living in a different world.

I was tempted to give up.

How does a ten-year old function when he has just lost a younger brother? How does he cope with the emotionally stressed behavior of his parents and grandmother? How does he relate to peers? In addition to this, how well does he handle the contextual nationwide fear that the world could be destroyed by a senseless war? Will he ever get over being miserable?

I had a very clear sense I was on my own. Within weeks, I began to move on. I learned I was free either to stay in the pit of despair or to focus on the possibilities of each new day. I had the amazingly empowering experience of being energized by worrying about and doing things for my folks and for Grandma Lapp.

I was being introduced to the reality that bad things happen to us even when we have done nothing to deserve them. One must go on. I began to discover that I could choose between better and worse. As I tried to do what seemed right, increasingly positive feelings about myself came from somewhere. The lesson of Stuart's death: Life can hurt like crazy, but do not quit living. I did not know it at the time, but the Holy was telling me that life is both an opportunity and a big job. It was time to look ahead, not back.

It turned out that for me life was defined not by yesterdays, but by tomorrows. I could not change what already was, even those moments when I had behaved selfishly. I could make a difference only in things that had not yet happened. So, I intuitively focused on what was yet to come.

Just following my tenth birthday I asked an older boy who lived in the house behind ours and who delivered *The Buffalo Evening News* on three adjacent streets, "Can I help you deliver your newspapers?" He agreed, giving me the responsibility for the twenty-six houses on my street.

I delivered papers six afternoons a week and collected every other Saturday. I took the money to his house where we counted it on his kitchen table. The papers cost the customers three cents each, of which I got a third of a cent. I earned $1.00 each two weeks! This job gave me a way to do something important each day.

Gradually, my neighbor boy added streets, one at a time, to my route. In less than a year I had his whole three-block route, and gradually added two more long streets. At age 12, I was delivering 120 papers each day. Since I was now in charge of a whole route, the paper's supervisor came to our house for the money.

Buffalo winters were snowy and bitter. I carried heavy bags of papers three miles each day and did not get home before dark in winter months. But, delivering in the snow, often deep, did not bother me as much as collecting.

It took no time at all for me to realize that people were lying to me about having paid prior bills when they had not. They would say, when I rang their doorbells, "What do you mean, you're collecting? I paid you just last week." So, I began carrying date-cards which I carefully punched, with the customer watching, each time I was paid. A few then began to accuse me of not punching their cards. Not liking to be yelled at when I skipped deliveries to these deadbeats, I usually left papers whether I had been paid or not. Gradually, most of them came around and sheepishly began paying for their papers.

I had that route for more than four years. When I let it go to several other boys in 1947, I had built the route up to 275 papers. Before I stopped, I had been paying some of these other boys to deliver. I spent most of my time collecting. This was Economics 101 for me.

In retrospect, this paper route was a life saver. It got me out of the house after school, and away from Grandma Lapp. It was the first time I had ever really done something totally independent of my family. I walked many miles one step after another, alone with my reflective thoughts.

One thing still stands out vividly. To get to some of my streets, I had to cross the intersection where Stuart had been run over. Every day the accident replayed itself in my heart.

"Walking one step after another," I began to learn to cope with life as it happens. I liked my emerging independence. I discovered I was not afraid to try new things.

The War - Context For Everyday Life

Mid-war, the outcome was far from clear. For everyone, fear lay behind every other emotion of the daily round. However, life did not stop. If anything, there was a viscerally felt acceleration of urgency and common bond in the daily round. Surviving the War became everybody's job. No one knew when or how it would end. Assuming life would someday return to normal, our days were known as "The Duration."

People became more aware of what was happening in Normandy, North Africa, Iwo Jima, Wake Island, Berlin, Guam than they were about what was occurring in their own neighborhoods.

Dad's Secret War Work

Military secrecy shielded Dad's transfer to a new project in early 1943. Even my mother did not know Dad had been assigned to the team designing of one of America's first fighter jets, the Bell P-59, which pioneered design solutions later incorporated into Lockheed's famed P-80. The P-59 was a single seat, low-winged plane that had a jet engine mounted on each side of its fuselage. This being a new concept, there were many engineering challenges that led to much design experimentation. But enough progress was made that for combat testing, the United States Army Air Force ordered 80 production machines, designated the "P-59A Airacomet" in June 1943. Dad continued to work on P-59 design issues for another year. During this period, it was becoming obvious to the Army Air Force and to his colleagues that Dad had extraordinary skills in solving engineering problems in a manner that would facilitate development of producible designs.

As soon as the limited 80-unit production of the P-59 Airacomet jet was essentially complete, Dad was assigned at year's end to an even more secretive project that had begun in mid-1944. By then the Germans had already built and flight-tested the Messerschmitt Me 163 interceptor, the worlds' first rocket powered pilotable military aircraft. It was now time for the U.S. to pursue development of a rocket propelled plane.

Thus began a sequence that led to Dad's notoriety in the military aircraft design industry. A dialogue between Bell Aircraft and the Army Air Force over the possibility of the U.S. building a rocket propelled fighter was begun in mid-1944. Representing Bell, Dad flew many times to Wright Air Force Base in Dayton, OH, to participate in the envisioning process.

In March of 1945, the U.S. Army Air Forces Flight Test Division and the National Advisory Committee for Aeronautics (NACA) contracted with the Bell Aircraft Company to build three XS-1 (for "Experimental, Supersonic", later simply called X-1) aircraft to obtain flight data on conditions in the transonic speed range. As Chief Project Engineer, Dad managed the design and fabrication process.

During the part of the War that came after Stuart's death, Dad was gone both literally and mentally most of the time. That left Mother at home trying to make life work for a precocious pre-teen son and a slow-learning younger daughter.

In May of 1945, the war in Europe ended with "V-E Day." As the war in the Pacific wore on, the saving of American lives became the justification for use of newly designed atomic bombs to kill 265,000 people in two days in Hiroshima and Nagasaki in August of 1945. Then, on August 15, 1945, when Kathy and I were with our Mother and Dad at a Kenmore Methodist Church Adult Class picnic in Ellicott Creek Park in Tonawanda, a block from where we had once lived, news came that Japan had surrendered.

The War shaped the culture for years. I have never since felt so estranged from the inner souls of others, and yet so much at one with them at the same time. You never had to ask what was on someone's mind. Elements of the War always were there.

The most immediate societal change was the ending of the use of stamps for the rationing of food and gasoline during The Duration. The War was over!

What About School?

After Stuart was gone, I completed 5th Grade at Washington Elementary in Kenmore. It was a drag. I liked my teacher even less than I had when she had made me tell about Stuart's death on the Monday after it happened. She had begun fussing about my failing eyesight. I could not see her handwriting on the blackboard. She seated me in the front of the room and made fun of me to the delight of the other kids. After I got glasses, she would not let me return to my desk in the rear of the room. But I successfully completed the year.

Continuing to feel lonely both at home and at school, my 6th Grade teacher did something very caring. Early in the school year we were studying the Medieval era in Europe. As part of the course, we had a week or two of building castles out of sheets of cardboard for the structures and big round oatmeal containers for the turrets, using papier mache to hold everything together.

When we had finished the first castle my teacher asked me if I would like to come to school early and make another one. Would I! Weeks and weeks later, I had gone to school very early most mornings and, by myself, had built two empty classrooms full of castles. That gave me something meaningful to do. Again, I was learning how to walk on my own after Stuart's death.

I finished Washington Elementary with commendable grades. In the Fall of 1945, as the War was ending, I entered 7th Grade at Kenmore Junior High. The school district had a policy of placing students in classes based on their performance and apparent intelligence. The Fall semester classes were called "B" terms, while the Spring classes were "A" terms. There being ten 7th grade classes, the highest achieving group was called "10," while the slowest kids were in group "1." So, that Fall I was in classroom 7B-10

For most of 7th Grade I was pretty much a loner, and not particularly interested in engaging socially with a peer group. We had different teachers for each course, so it was a new experience to change classrooms several times a day. At first, I was more interested in technical courses than in language or social studies classes. But I liked going to school more than anything else I did that year.

The Will to Go On

By War's end, though most of it was subliminal, an awareness of what life was calling on me to do and be was beginning to emerge. Going to school was my most important daily activity. I kept being amazed by what I was learning. In terms of spiritual growth, I was the kind of kid who looked forward to tomorrow's possibilities with hope, not despair. I was beginning to sense that I, not my parents, had control over my behavioral decisions. Their role was to seek to inspire me to make good choices. I saw that I could make a difference in what was transpiring in my relationships with others. Bottom line, it was up to me to figure out what to do from moment to moment. I was experiencing the Holy as the ground of hope and the call to accountability. And every day was a new day to which I looked forward.

SECTION II

1946 – 1954

WHAT WAS MY LIFE
MEANT TO BE?

Chapter 4

~~~

DAD'S SKIING ACCIDENT

New Year's Day!

IN DECEMBER, FOUR months after V-E Day, I finished the first semester of 7th Grade and was ready for the Christmas Holiday break. It had been less than three years since Stuart's death.

Celebrating January 1, 1946, Dad took me and three other boys skiing on a farmer's countryside hill in a rural area south of Buffalo, NY. Mother, not a skier, had stayed home to cook New Year's Day dinner. The oldest and biggest kid, 16-year-old Garland, was the son of a neighbor whom Dad knew from Bell Aircraft. Thirteen-year-old Bobby, a childhood friend from Ellicott Creek days, knew little about skiing and did not really want to learn. Then there was my 9-year-old cousin, Donny Gould, who sledded but did not ski.

It was a very cold and overcast afternoon. There was lots of crunchy white snow on the roads and hillsides. After parking our gray 1939

Buick Special along a country road adjacent to some downhill farmland, we found a slope that suited everyone but Dad, an accomplished skier. We would ski to the bottom of a gentle 200-foot slope, then go back to the top using the herringbone steps Dad was teaching us to get back to the top. It was not challenging enough for him, but he had selected that farm hillside for us kids. After a couple of hours, when we all were thoroughly soaked and suitably frozen, Dad said, "It's time we headed back."

He was out ahead of us as we skied along the top of a slope adjacent to the road toward the car. While we were catching up, he abruptly turned left and flew down a steep but not very long hill. At the bottom, a boulder under the snow tripped him and he fell butt first onto the boulder. I saw him lean forward as he let out a haunting cry of pain and moved one arm. I threw off my skis and raced down the hill, followed closely by Garland. Dad cried out, "Ohhhh! I can't move. Ohhhh! I think it is my back. Robin, help me. O God, it can't be!"

Garland leaned over to pull Dad up. "No, don't pull me," Dad said, almost in a whisper.

My mind was churning a mile a minute. I knew someone would have to go find help. Garland was the biggest and strongest of us boys. I said to him, "You better stay here with Dad. Get down next to him and brace him. Try to keep his hands and face warm."

I did not know what else to do to help Dad. I was frightened by his groaning. I reached into his parka pocket for the car keys and said, "I'll go find help. I'll be back as fast as I can."

I struggled back up the steep slope. I said to my friend, Bobby, "You stay here and wait for the rescue crew I hope to find. But just stop anyone that drives by and ask for help."

A Driver at Twelve!

Four years younger than I, my chubby cousin Donny, who lived on a farm not too far away, was never much fun. Even around his house, he whined a lot. Worrying about cry-baby Donny, I told him, "Get in the car. We'll have to go look for a farmhouse."

I never gave any thought to whether I could drive the pre-war Buick. I was fascinated by cars so had watched Dad use the clutch and shift the gears. My biggest problem was that I did not know where to find a farmhouse. After about a mile I spotted a white clapboard house on the left. When I stopped there Donny began crying. I said, "You'll just have to stay in the car." He cried some more. I left the car in the drive and went to the door. Not seeing a doorbell like we had in town, I knocked.

Finally, a woman opened the door a crack. I was very nervous but said, "My father is hurt. We were skiing over on the Gap Road and he hit a rock and can't get up." She left me shivering at the door and went for her husband who peaked out shortly, complaining loudly about people who skied on his land without asking permission. I could not fix that. I interrupted the farmer's rant. "Do you have a telephone?" I asked.

After looking at me, then at the car in their yard, they finally let me in. The farmer asked the phone operator to dial the volunteer fire department, He abruptly handed me the phone, which I took in my mittened hand. A man finally answered. I said, "My father is hurt. It's very bad. He can't move."

"What happened?" the guy asked somewhat disparagingly.

I started, "We were skiing…"

"Oh my God," the unfriendly voice said. "You mean we have to come out there somewhere on New Year's Day to find some guy who should have known better?"

Growing desperate, I said, "Come on, mister. It is my dad, and he is really hurt. Can you send somebody?"

"Well, where are you?" I had to hand the phone to the fuming farmer so he could give directions.

After describing the location, the farmer handed the phone back to me. The guy at the other end said, "I hope I can find somebody to come out there," and hung up.

I picked up the phone again and asked the operator to ring my Uncle's phone number." Uncle Chester answered.

"Why are you calling me," he asked. "What has happened to Donny?" "It's not Donny," I said. "It's my Dad. He's hurt in the snow and can't move."

"What do you want me to do about it?" he groaned into the phone. "I've just had hernia surgery, and I can't help!"

"I think you should come get Donny. He's scared and he's crying." I handed the phone back to the farmer, who told Uncle Chester where Dad was.

As I left the farmhouse, I thought the farmer and his wife might accompany me back to the hillside and help. No such luck!

Back at the scene, I ran down the hill and told Dad help was coming. Appearing ready to pass out, he said, "I can't move. I have no feeling in my legs. It is cold out here! I wish they'd hurry up and get here."

Garland, who had been born and had lived in Georgia, was freezing, too, but I told him he had to stay next to Dad. Donny was still crying. Bobby looked like he had seen a ghost, and just stared at me. My next job was to look for the rescue crew.

Uncle Chester arrived. Because of his surgery, he couldn't get down the hill. He told me he had called my mother. Before leaving with Donny, he just stood in the road and grumbled piously.

I waited. And waited. And waited.

Finally, three or four men drove up in an old ambulance. None wanted to go down the hill to help Dad. They wanted Garland and me to bring him up to the ambulance. I told them, "Dad can't move. And he's too big for two boys to carry up that steep hill." Then I asked quizzically, "Isn't that your job when someone is injured?"

Slowly, they retrieved the stretcher from the back of the ambulance. Begrudgingly, they struggled down the hill with the stretcher. I will never forget the blood curdling scream Dad let out when they picked him up and forced him out straight on the stretcher. This crude field first-aid may well have completed the job of severing his spinal cord. I learned from Mother the next day that Dad's fourth and fifth lumbar vertebrae were crushed and that, indeed, his spinal cord was severed.

It was already dark when the ambulance headed for the Sisters of Mercy Hospital in Lackawanna, fifteen or twenty miles north. Bobby, Garland, and I stood there alone on the hillside in the dark. For the first time, I realized how cold it was.

Meanwhile, Mother, upon hearing the tragic news from Uncle Chester, had rounded up Garland's father and the neighbor across the street, who had enjoyed too many New Year's Eve drinks, to come get us boys.

They did not arrive at the scene until after the ambulance had left. Garland went home with his father. Our neighbor unsteadily drove Bobby and me back to Tonawanda in the '39 Buick. At age twelve, I realized I was a better driver than this hungover man. After dropping Bobby off, we headed for my house.

On the way to our house, our neighbor told me that Mother had headed for Sisters of Mercy Hospital. The house was dark when I went in through the one car garage. Kathy and Grandma Lapp were already in bed. I was cold, and suddenly nervous for the first time. I noticed a pot of uncooked, darkening potatoes sitting on the basement stairway. There would be no New Year's dinner that night.

During the night Dad was transferred by ambulance from Sisters of Mercy Hospital to Millard Fillmore Hospital in north Buffalo. He would not leave Millard Fillmore for nearly eight months.

In January, he had several surgeries to clean up splinters of his vertebrae and to splice surgically removed ribs into his backbone to reconstruct it. The internal fire of his spirit sank so low he nearly expired. This injury was a huge emotional challenge for him as he had been very athletic. Then he began to realize that though he would never be "normal" again, life still had meaning. With the encouragement of his physicians and several really caring nurses, as well as Mother, he came to believe he was loved, appreciated, and could still make a difference. Even before beginning physical therapy, as soon as he could be in a wheelchair, he began visiting patients who had lost their wills to live. Many rallied and found hope as he told his story. When he was released from the hospital seven and a half months later, several of his caring nurses cried to see him go. He was able to walk out with crutches, wearing steel hip-to-foot leg braces.

Dad was very much the invalid for months after he got home. Stairs were difficult. Mother had to help him into and out of bed, taking off and putting on his leg braces. From that day on, everything about our homelife revolved around his learning to live with his handicap, both physically and emotionally.

In my moments alone I began to realize that I had saved my father's life. I had learned that I could stay calm in a crisis and that I could be a leader when no one else knew what to do. This gift came from beyond me. The Holy was calling, "Be strong. Care for others."

Chapter 5

~~

PLANES WERE MY WORLD

Dad Goes Back to Bell Aircraft

WHILE HE WAS in Millard Fillmore Hospital for those long 8 months there was serious speculation as to whether he would ever return to work at Bell Aircraft, or anywhere.

Immediately upon my father's being hospitalized, Mother was hired at the beginning of the second semester in early 1946 for a position teaching Home Economics in the Kenmore Junior High School. She had long wanted to return to the career she had left behind when I was born. She taught at Kenmore Junior High for the Spring semester. During the remainder of my 7th Grade, she and I walked the mile to the school together each day. Every weekday afternoon she would leave school and go directly by bus to the hospital. She hardly ever got home until after I had gone to bed. Essentially, my homework having been done at school, I was on my own after school, delivering newspapers, and joining Kathy and Grandma Lapp for supper.

However, by mid-1947 Dad started back to work, first on a part-time basis, on the supersonic X-1 plane project. It was not long before he was back in his role as Chief Project Engineer. In simple concept, the X-1 was a "bullet with wings and a pilot's seat", its shape closely resembling a Browning .50-caliber machine gun bullet, was known to be stable in supersonic flight. For a variety of weight and flight characteristic reasons, as production models were developed, Bell engineers determined that the X-1 should be carried aloft partially inserted into the belly of a B-29, one of the most utilized bombers of the War. When the bomber reached its near-maximum altitude, the X-1 would be dropped either for a test glide back to base or for a powered flight that would use all its fuel before gliding back to base. On October 14, 1947, the X-1 became the first plane in the world to fly faster than the speed of sound.

In the late '40's Dad frequently had to fly to Wright-Patterson Air Force base in Dayton, OH, and to various test sites around the country. Tough work for a guy with his physical challenges, but he did it!

Planes Fascinate Me

From the beginning of the War, Dad's world was full of airplanes. I quickly became fascinated, constantly scanning the skies for glimpses of planes. Dad even took me to the Buffalo Municipal Airport to watch early piston-engine DC-3 airliners landing and taking off. I learned everything I could about how heavier-than-air machines could fly.

During the War, auto manufacturing plants made airplanes. With several such companies in the Buffalo area, I learned to identify various fighter planes as they were being flight tested. Fuselage components of large Curtis C-46 Cargo planes were being carried on flat-bed truck trailers from a factory to the Buffalo airport for final assembly. While delivering newspapers, I often encountered these huge plane fuselage sections at the intersection where my brother had been killed. I kept trying to imagine how they would be fitted together.

Sensing my interest, my father often took me through security at the Niagara Falls Bell plant to watch the building of piston engine fighter planes and early jets. He took me into the experimental engineering department where I got to sit in the pilot's seat of jet fighters and a couple of the manned-rocket planes being developed. I even met three famous Air Force test pilots. It was breath-taking!

On a Saturday after he had gone back to work, Dad and I went to the Bell airfield where there sat a contraption I had never seen before. It was a canopy-less open-seat two-person helicopter. I was given an extensive ride that included dipping below the top Niagara Falls ridge over which Lake Erie splashes down into Lake Ontario. I have never forgotten the thrill of that morning.

My mechanical sense of how parts could fit together to accomplish specific tasks was being whetted as I moved into my mid-teens. Dad spoke frequently of my becoming an engineer.

To Texas on My Own

It was June of 1947. I had turned 14 in March. Because of my interest in aircraft my father had connected me with Stan Smith, Dad's supervisor at Bell, who loved gliders and sailplanes, and who had been a contestant in the post-war 1946 National Soaring Contest held in Elmira, NY.

For months I had been helping Stan rebuild a gull-winged sailplane, which initially had been known as the "Yankee Doodle." It was a one-of-a-kind model, built before the War as an experimental predecessor to the Army Air Force's Laister-Kaufman two-place training sailplane. We were using a hangar at a private airfield near the Niagara Falls Bell factory for our project.

Stan must have liked my work. One Saturday, he casually asked, "Would you like to be part of my crew, and go to the national contest in Texas?"

I could hardly believe what I was hearing. "I'll have to ask my father," I blurted. "And I'll have to get someone to deliver my papers."

I first tried the idea on my father. He just smiled. Perhaps Stan had asked him for his thoughts before approaching me.

When my mother heard about the trip she asked, "Do you really think you could handle being gone from home for four weeks, traveling with people you don't know, to a part of the country where you've never been?"

"Of course," I said. "And I'd really like to do it. I am not worried about being away that long. All I have to figure out is who will deliver my newspapers."

The trip was going to take a month as the contest was scheduled for three weeks and the round trip to Wichita Falls would consume another week. I was to be part to be part of a team that would drive the sailplane, by now named the Excess Two (after the Bell XS-2) to and from the contest. To save himself some time-off from work, Stan caught an airliner.

Stan hired two fellows who knew nothing about flying or sailplanes to do the driving. Since I knew how to disassemble the Excess Two for putting it on its 30-foot-long trailer, and how to reassemble it and manage it behind a towplane, at 14, I was the crew chief. My mother was anxious about my driving two thirds of the way across the country with two fellows none of us knew. But she agreed.

The annual National Soaring Contest was held at Sheppard Air Force Base in Wichita Falls. This contest was the first National Contest to be held anywhere other than Elmira, NY, where flight durations and distances were limited because of local weather conditions. Soaring officials wanted to see how much longer and farther sailplanes could go in the more favorable soaring conditions usually present in west Texas.

These National Contests were gatherings of top pilots and their sailplanes, a few from countries other than the U.S. Over an approximately three-week period, daily points are awarded based on who comes the closest to performing that day's assignment. The pilot with the most points at the end of the contest is declared the National Champion. Typically, there are three types of races. One is to see how fast a plane can fly from the contest site to a designated airport. The second is to see how fast a pilot can fly to a designated turn-around site, then back to the home field. The third, on free flight days, awards points on the total distance a plane flies that day, with bonus points being given for landing at a location declared in advance.

During a contest, because a sailplane has no motor, a pilot's ground crew must drive the car and glider trailer to the sailplane's landing site, load up the plane, and return to the contest home field, hopefully in time for a little sleep before the next morning's pilots' meeting.

At the Wichita Falls contest, the flying began by mid-morning, as soon as the sun's heat on the ground caused hot air to rise, creating thermals. A contestant's crew would leave Sheppard Field as soon as it was clear its plane had left the immediate vicinity. Two-way radios were a rarity in those days, as batteries weighed too much to be carried in sailplanes which need to be as light as possible. We tried to maintain visual contact with our sailplane throughout what was often a six to eight-hour flight. Since my crewmates had little interest in what we were doing, it soon became my job to use our one set of binoculars to track Stan. The planes often flew ten thousand feet above the ground, so it was a real trick to distinguish one sailplane from another.

During contests, pilots often did not find airports at which to land. They had to land on open fields or even on little used roadways. Occasionally I would ask an already-landed pilot, "Have you recently seen Stan Smith's dark blue plane?"

Mostly, the answer was something like, "No, son, the last time I saw him he was blazing due west. And that was at least an hour ago." So we would drive on, looking in open fields on both sides of the road hoping to find him shortly after he landed. Once we found Stan, we would rush him and our sailplane back to Wichita Falls to prepare for the next day's contest.

On one of the free-flight days, Stan declared Kiowa, KS as his goal. When he showed us on a map, I saw that it was all the way across the area of Texas north of Wichita Falls, across the widest part of Oklahoma, and a short distance into Kansas, to Kiowa. I said to myself, "We'll never make it."

But Stan did!

A few days later, Stan declared Tucumcari, New Mexico, as his goal and almost made it, flying farther than anyone else during the whole contest. On the Tucumcari flight we did not reach Stan until sometime after midnight. We were driving west along U.S. Highway 66 not seeing a trace of other vehicles for miles at a time when we came upon a man sitting in the middle of the road. It was Stan, who sat in the road so he could better see snakes, tarantulas, and scorpions. We were on our way back to Wichita Falls within thirty minutes. Arriving at Sheppard well after daylight, we were grateful for the announcement that it would be a non-contest day because of the outstanding distance of our flight.

We had a big sailplane that was not as fast as a few of the custom midget post-war gliders. They won most of the short out-and-return days that were awarded points for speed, so we did not win the overall contest. However, we were high in the standings, and were honored for the longest flight of the contest.

This taste of the West was intriguing. Most Buffalonians had not traveled west by car in those days, so I became an instant neighborhood celebrity with many tales to tell. It was hard for a fourteen-year-old to discern and describe, but the Texas culture was different from anything I knew in Western New York. Westerners smiled and said hello along their streets. Yet a deeply rooted strand of ethnic, race and class-oriented bigotry did not feel right to me.

Going to this contest was thrilling. I had done a major project away from home on my own for a month and had experienced life in a part of the country never visited by anyone else in my family. What was I learning about myself? I could risk moving into the unknown! A message from the Holy?

Sometimes Dad was Hard to Live With

The handicap of no longer having full control of a body of which he was proud did nothing positive for an already fiery temper. My father's explosive disposition kept me guessing. One pleasant summer day in 1948 when I was fifteen and still without a driver's license,

Dad had called a fellow worker for a ride to the Bell plant. His '39 Buick, the one I had driven the day of the ski accident, wasn't running right. He thought it might be the carburetor. When I got home from school, I took wrenches, a screwdriver, and a pair of pliers from what had become my basement workbench. I pushed the car out of our single-bay garage and stopped it just outside on the drive. I opened the hood and removed the carburetor. I sat on the concrete garage floor and took it apart. Springs, gaskets, little bolts, and big parts exploded everywhere. The intake valve was covered with dried residual gasoline. I carefully cleaned it and all the other parts. I was about to start trying to put it back together when Dad arrived home from work.

What happened next astounded and even frightened me. He was angry beyond rationality. "What in the world do you think you're doing? Now I'll have to get a new carburetor. We could have had this one fixed!"

He clomped on into the house, his braces clicking. I did not dare go in, even though it was supper time, and I was hungry. I put the carburetor back together, installed it, easily started the car, and drove it back into the garage. All Dad said was, "You're late for supper!" Mother quietly warmed up a plate for me.

The next Sunday, while we were sitting in the car waiting for Mother to go to church, Dad said, gunning the engine, "I'm glad we were able to fix the carburetor without taking the car to the shop."

Hmm? I thought to myself, "What's this WE business?" But I didn't say anything and was grateful the displeasure was over. I took it as an apology and felt better.

Liberated by a Driver's License

Even though I knew how to drive a car, I was dying to get an actual license that would legalize my interim driving. In New York State, a fifteen-year-old kid could get a temporary license that allowed daylight driving. Then, at sixteen, the licensee, whose license became permanent, had adult privileges. That's what I craved.

In those days, school driver-training classes were pretty much limited to classroom coaching on driving laws, and to brief trial drives around the blocks near our high school. However, I often drove an old stick shift Pierce Arrow back and forth across the small airfield where I was helping Stan Smith with the reconstruction of his sailplane.

My mother took me for the New York State driving test. I passed on the first try. I was licensed to drive! The next trick was getting my dad and mom to allow me to take the family car on occasional in-town outings. This was the final step in my discovering the breathless liberation of being able get myself from one place to another in a car, without having to depend on another for a ride. It was even better than the emotion I felt when I learned to ride a full-sized bike. Driving a car was another step toward my becoming responsible for my life.

In a very subliminal way, I have continued to enjoy the freedom to control going where and when I wish or need to go. The independence represented by driving was a significant piece of my emerging self-identity.

Athlete?

As the son of a high school football star, I was encouraged, almost expected, to be an athlete. My father took me to fall high school football games to generate interest. He liked my playing hockey with neighborhood boys on a nearby pond. He even bought me some box-ing gloves for Christmas one year.

Not being excited about sports in which I had to bang into other guys or get knocked onto the ground, I held back.

But then, one day during a high school gym class, our teacher, who also was the track coach, had us run six times around an imaginary square for a total of one mile. Much to my surprise, and to the notice of many classmates, I completed the circuit in six minutes, faster than most. This led to my being on the track team, the only high school sport for which I ever qualified. When I joined the team, the school "loaned" me a pair of hand-me-down running shoes. I trained at the school's quar-ter mile track all fall and did relatively well in the spring's competitive meets. Tickled that I was finally doing some he-man stuff, my father coached me on sprint starts. All the following summer, I practiced with a friend on the school track. I finally ran a 4:30 mile. Having achieved this with a degree of smug self-satisfaction, I then dropped off the team because I chose instead to work in a local laundry to make money for college. Coach was disappointed. So was Dad. But being on the track team gave me my first taste of peer-related self-esteem.

Becoming Comfortable with My Identity

My high school experience through my Junior Year was one in which I felt pretty much out of the popular mainstream. Younger than virtually all classmates, I was a skinny physically clumsy kid who had significant trouble with acne.

Though I could not see it at the time, a personality style had been evolving through my years from ten to sixteen. In terms of my relation-ships with other kids, I wanted them to like me. But I did not do things

48   SECTION II: 1946 – 1954

just to gain acceptance from them. While I enjoyed daily engagements, honored boundaries, and accepted others' foibles and cruel remarks mostly about my face, I did what I wanted to do, or at least felt that I ought to do. My psychic energy came from within. I was not absorbed by trying to impress my peers.

The exception to my not needing to be empowered by others were my parents. While making my own choices about daily behavior and major commitments, I was always sensitive to the question of whether they approved of what I was doing. So, there were boundaries for my behavior that reflected their sense of right and wrong in the treatment of other people. It was not acceptable to be unkind to others, to be lazy, or to be demanding about my own wants. It was clearly the fact that I was loved, safe, and cared about that made my home a warm and inviting place. But, in looking back, even at home I was strongly independent, always trying to make my own decisions.

Going to school and paying attention had become my highest daily priority. In Sr. High, I began to have a great sense of fulfillment in excelling in math and science courses. I was getting 97's to 100's on my New York State Regents tests in the science and math sequences, making me one of the three or four top students in these courses in my large public high school. I was fascinated by American history and ancient world history. I did less well in English grammar, scoring in the high 80's and low 90's. That should have told me something about career selection, but providentially it did not.

In my Junior Year in high school, I was assigned the task of writing a term paper whose subject was to be an exploration of the field I intended to enter. It was an effort to get students thinking about college. On my paper's yellow folder, I had drawn "ENGINEERING" in large block letters. A couple of my teachers told me they thought they could help me get a full scholarship at such notable universities as Carnegie,

Rensselaer Polytech, and MIT. I was feeling like I knew what I wanted to do and be when I grew up.

By the end of my Junior Year, I had decided that I would become a chemical or aeronautical engineer.

As I went through Junior and Senior High, the death of my brother and the traumatic, disabling injury of my father were unanticipated emotional and physical challenges for both Mother and me. As my father recovered, Mother and I became co-conspirators in the enterprise of making a go of life, each in our own way and in face of our separate challenges. This whole time was painful and hectic for me, partly because I had to deal with a needy little sister and a rigid grandmother any time I was home. Mother and I solved household problems pragmatically. We laughed together when life hurt a lot. She would say, "Well, Robin, you just have to pull up your socks and keep walking!" We silently affirmed one another in our separate walks in the darkness. We shared each other's burdens in caring for my sister Kathy. To have a fellow traveler enabled each of us to go further and more confidently than we might have done alone. God was speaking to each of us through the other.

Chapter 6

~~~

I FELT MY BODY GET
UP AND WALK

Even I Was Surprised

DR. PARKER PALMER, in his book, *Let Your Life Speak*, wrote: "Before you tell your life what you intend to do with it, listen for what it intends to do with you. Before you tell your life what truths and values you have decided to live up to, let your life tell you what truths you embody, what values you represent."[1]

Without any forethought along the lines of Parker's words, I had an out-of-body experience that, in just one week, started me on a lifetime journey of listening carefully to the dynamic calls of eternal truth, the voice of the Holy.

---

1   p. 3 Parker J. Palmer, *Let Your Life Speak*, ©2000, John Wiley & Sons, Inc., A Wiley Company, 989 Market Street, San Francisco, CA 94103-1741

This event occurred in the summer of 1949, between my Junior and Senior years of high school. It transformed my life forever.

Our family attended a large Methodist Church in Kenmore, NY. I attended church school, became a Boy Scout, and eventually participated in the church's junior and senior high youth groups. When I was 14, during Christmas vacation, I rode a train to a national Methodist youth convocation in Cleveland, Ohio, attended by 10,000 kids. I slept with 3,600 new friends in the main manufacturing area of a bomber plant in Berea, OH.

Thus, it was not so far-fetched for me to go to Silver Lake, the Genesee Conference Methodist youth camp, in the summer of 1949 when I was sixteen years old, I faithfully attended the classes and discussions, but mostly I liked the recreational activities and free time. The week's featured daily speaker was the Senior Minister of the Methodist Church in Kenmore of which I was a member. He had played a significant support role with my father and mother during Dad's long hospitalization three years earlier. His theology was essentially the "power of positive thinking." Though I couldn't see how my vigorously affirming a supernatural power would bring my brother back or make my father walk without crutches, I was inspired by his certainty that there is a God out there that cares about human existence.

There was to be a closing worship service on Friday night. After dinner that night I walked by myself around the campus to fill time. At the last minute I had to use the bathroom. While I was in the men's room the strangest feeling began to sweep over me. I could not identify it. I felt like I was floating. I tried to ignore the feeling, and walked into the large assembly hall, finding some of the other kids from our church. We sat toward the back. The kids around me were chattering quietly, but I sat there in pensive silence.

The service started. The choir sang. A leader prayed. I paid little attention.

But, suddenly, when the minister read a verse from the Book of Isaiah, I focused. He said, "Also I heard the voice of the Lord saying, 'Whom shall I send, and who will go for us? Then I said, 'Here am I; send me.'"[2]

"Here am I! Send me…Here am I! Send me," kept hauntingly reverberating in my head. I did not hear anything else until the sermon started.

It was about totally committing one's life to God by becoming a minister, the most holy vocation one could choose. When he finished his sermon he said, "And now, as we enter into a time of silent prayer and reflection, if you are moved by the power of God, calling you for ministry in his church, you will come forward to this prayer rail and dedicate your life to God's work."

During the silence I felt my body get up. What was this? Without my choosing to, my body was walking down the aisle. Two other kids also were walking toward the chancel. It was the most other-worldly experience I have ever had. I felt my body kneel at the little rail up front. I felt my minister's hand on my shoulder. I heard him pray for me, "Dear God, accept Robin as he commits his life to your service. Bless him and anoint him with your love. Amen." Campers sang a hymn, and the service was over. There was a spontaneous hushed silence. Then people began to leave.

Outside, even kids I did not really know spoke to me respectfully. A couple of girls cried. Several adults congratulated me. My emotions were a mixture of shock and elation. I had no idea what this meant or

---

2   Isaiah 6:8 – p.728. The Holy Bible. Authorized King James Version. The World Publishing Company. Cleveland, Ohio. New York City.

what I was supposed to do next. By the time I went to bed that night my overriding thought was that I had made an adult decision, and that I would never change my mind.

When I got home the next day, my parents asked me how camp had gone, and whether I had liked it. Almost reluctantly I said, "I have decided to be a minister." When they asked me why, I responded, "I have decided I want to use my life to 'help people'. I think I can do this best as a minister." 'Helping people,' though a vague generalization, was my full picture of what it would mean to serve God.

Neither said much, but Mother seemed pleased. Dad, a little perplexed, asked, "Are you sure this is what you really want to do?"

"Yes," I said.

I have never looked back.

For me, the emotion of that moment was something akin to trying on new clothes. I did not know how well they would fit, or whether I'd really like them. But I felt like I was walking on air. I felt a certainty that came from beyond anyone or anything I knew. I had suddenly gained an identity that felt right.

That night, in an old assembly hall at an even older Chautauqua-like church camp when I was sixteen, it was exceptionally clear to me that I had been touched by the Holy. God seemed authentically real for the first time. Though I had no blinding view or definition of God, I thereafter had no doubt that God had come near. In many moments of difficult challenge that had begun with my having to deal with the tragic death of my brother my course has been sustained by the intensity of that divine touch.

At the time, I had no idea that encouraging people to walk with Jesus in solving their life's problems was anything other than helping them achieve the good life promised by the American dream – personal freedom, success, wealth, and power. Turns out that true walking with Jesus is a life-changing pilgrimage that creates a counter-cultural lifestyle. This church camp moment was the beginning of my awareness that knowing there is a God is much more an intuitive feeling than a scientifically provable fact.

Living a New Dream

So here I was at sixteen, experiencing a third major pivotal event. My brother had been killed when I was nine. My father had become a paraplegic when I was twelve. Now God wanted my life! And I was only in High School.

As I went to Kenmore High for a final year that fall, I began seeing my life through different eyes. A poignant moment came early in the school year. As I sat in my homeroom one morning before classes started, the man who had been my chemistry teacher the year before, came into the room. He came straight to my desk and knelt on one knee by my desk. He spoke softly so others would not hear. But there was a hush as everyone stared at us. He said, "I have been doing research on scholarships available from Rensselaer, MIT, and Carnegie. You would do really well at any of them. I think I can get you a full scholarship."

Hating to interrupt him, I said, "I have decided to go into the ministry. Thank you very much for thinking of me, but I will need to go to a Liberal Arts college or university." His response, in addition to frowning, was, "Are you certain that's a good decision? You have such good grades in math and science, you would do very well in a technical field."

The first period bell rang, and he stood up and left, saying, "Well, think about it." This teacher never spoke of these colleges again, but he remained friendly through the year. On the night of my graduation ceremony, he shook my hand and wished me well.

With my whole senior year yet to go, I had to decide what changes I might make in my course load. I really wanted to take physics and trigonometry as previously planned. I was fascinated by learning how and why things work in the natural world. I was analytical by nature, and really liked science and math. But I also knew that English and other liberal arts courses would be important if I was ever to think critically and communicate clearly in ministry.

There was another factor at play. Though I had not yet started the process of choosing a college, I knew I needed to earn significant amounts of money to pay for my education.

While in mandatory study halls in the 10th and 11th grades I had frequently been sent to the Assistant Principal's office because I was walking around talking to the other kids instead of sitting and studying. As I started my senior year, I was taking five courses, including two electives I did not need for graduation. One hour of study hall each day was a requirement. This hour was the most boring of my day. Needing to complete only three more classes to graduate, I hatched a very unorthodox plan. Part way through the first semester of my senior year I approached the Assistant Principal, and said, "I have an idea that could help both of us. How would it be if we jiggled my 2nd semester schedule so that I could take History, English, and Physics in the morning. That would give me enough credits to graduate. Then, you could sign me up for three study halls in the afternoon." He frowned.

I continued, "You could then excuse me from lunch period and the three afternoon study halls so that I could work to make money for college." The Assistant Principal smiled, then said, "We've never done anything like this before." I could tell he was secretly delighted at the prospect of getting me out of my study hall antics. He said, "Well, let's try it."

So, at the beginning of my final semester at Kenmore High, I was able to begin working 40 hours a week at Dates Laundry where I already worked part-time, eating my sack lunch while walking the mile to work. During daylight hours I worked the retail counter. After hours, another young guy and I cleaned and painted the dry-cleaning machinery in the big production room. Working full time got me out of the study hall conundrum!

Shortly before I graduated, Dates Laundry opened an experimental satellite outlet in a shopping center near my house. Having just turned 17, I was by far the youngest of some twenty-five clerks in the key Buffalo location, but my supervisor asked me if I would become the manager of the new store. I did, with his clear understanding that I was going to college in the fall.

The lesson from my Silver Lake church camp experience: "Pay attention. You never know when something will turn out to be one of the brightest, most significant turns of your life.

In addition to internalizing a claim that had been made on my soul, the church camp experience brought another learning. I had been freed to make decisions whether they pleased those around me or not.

This non-conforming behavior has characterized my entire ministry.

If one can distinguish between ingrained religious beliefs and inexplicable experiences of God's continuing personal mandates, by the time I left high school I had only begun to glimpse organized religion as not fully capturing God. For most of my college career I focused on attempting to prove philosophically the existence of God. God was in my life, but I wanted it to be somehow scientifically provable, not simply experiential.

God taps people on the shoulder or in the heart in unexpected and uncontrolled ways. Historically, in the Christian Church, the concept of "call" has meant God is nominating a person for work in the church. In a much broader sense, I was in the early phases of an impulse from the Most Holy awakening me to minister to all human creation, not just to those in a humanly contrived institution.

A Dictionary for Christmas

Once I had decided to enter the ministry, I turned to the task of choosing a college. It needed to be a liberal arts college. I also thought it would be good if it were a school related to the Methodist Church. Where to go? How to choose?

In one of those coincidences that lasts all one's life, for Christmas in my senior year Mother gave me a *Webster's Collegiate Dictionary*. As I opened it, she said, "Your father and I thought this dictionary would help you throughout college." I quickly discovered four pages in the back section that simply named and gave cities for American colleges and universities. This dictionary is now worn and faded, but those four pages still have twenty-one faint pencil checkmarks next to schools I thought I should consider. I picked seven, and then wrote for catalogues. Examining each one carefully as it arrived, my first choice for further investigation was Ohio Wesleyan University, a highly regarded Methodist college in Delaware, Ohio, which I then visited that spring with a friend from our church, along with his parents. Both Mother and Dad seemed pleased it was a Methodist school.

Neither had any objections, and each said, "It's up to you. We'll help you financially as much as we can, but you will have to work during the summer and school year, as well as use the money you've already saved." Late that spring I applied and was accepted. It was that straight-forward. I never applied to any of the other colleges, which were spread out in the northeast, from Iowa to New England.

I didn't become Robb until after a Spring, 1950, visit to the Ohio Wesleyan campus. Up to then I had hated "Robin," and my family re-sisted my being called "Bob", my dad's handle. "Rob" was okay, but my family members did not pick it up, though most of my school friends did. While visiting Ohio Wesleyan, I learned that the student body president was a fellow named Donn Miller. That was good enough for me. I arrived back in Tonawanda as "Robb."

Chapter 7

~~

OFF TO OHIO WESLEYAN

How I Do is Up to Me!

IN SEPTEMBER OF 1950, my parents drove me to Delaware, Ohio for my first year at Ohio Wesleyan University. I was not to see them in Delaware often. Because of the many issues they faced, my parents were preoccupied with daily survival. My father's ego and physical needs made most everything pivot around him. Mother quietly kept family life moving. She invested a great deal of energy in her public-school teaching, which became the core of meaning for this phase of her life.

I had made virtually all the decisions related to selecting and attending Ohio Wesleyan. And I was free to choose all my coursework, and extra-curricular activities. I felt sorry for classmates whose parents smothered them with overactive involvement.

My first campus residence was one of the World War II U.S. Army Air Force barracks that had been moved to the campus toward the end of the War to house U.S. Army Air Force cadets who were stationed at Ohio Wesleyan for academic training. A compound of perhaps a dozen barracks, each having eight double rooms, had been placed in an open area of the campus. By 1950, the fall of my arrival as a seventeen-year-old freshman, the barracks were occupied by civilian male students. Two faculty families also lived in this compound. The room rent being less than for housing in private homes in town, I chose to live there. By their second year at Wesleyan most men lived in fraternity houses. For all their four years, most women lived in college owned dorms. A few lived in co-op houses.

Ohio Wesleyan had two distinct types of students. One group, the majority, did not have clear vocational goals but embarked on exploratory curricula in search for something to do when they "grew up." Their families thought college would be a good next step in their maturation. Students in the other group came in pursuit of specific careers. Many of these were students preparing for some form of religious or social service.

It being a Methodist college set in the geographical center of one of the then most Methodist states in the union, a slight majority of students were from rural and urban homes in Ohio.

The others, those from out of state, represented population centers in northeastern states. These students chose Ohio Wesleyan, not because it was a safe religious college relatively close to home, but because its academic offerings were well regarded in the tier just below eastern Ivy League schools. People who wanted to become doctors, scientists, professors, musicians, authors, as well as clergy persons and social workers, attended Ohio Wesleyan with the intent of going on to graduate school.

Many students were from either New York City or Washington, D.C.

A few were from Europe, Asia, Africa, and South America. While almost all Ohioans were white Protestants, non-Ohioans included blacks, Jews, Catholics, and persons for whom English was a second or even third language.

When I started at Wesleyan, I was planning to attend Boston University School of Theology, a Methodist seminary, where I already had pre-enrolled.

My initial major at Ohio Wesleyan was Religious Studies, organized specifically for students considering ministry and graduate studies at a seminary. But I ended up with a triple major in Religion, Psychology, and American Literature. Three non-major elective courses gave additional shape to my sense of the world. For the first of these courses to mean anything, one must know that I absolutely cannot carry a tune or play any musical instrument. However, I enrolled in a semester-long music appreciation survey course, complete with compulsory classical music listening labs. I aced the course, getting a higher grade than a friend, the daughter of the head of the Ohio Wesleyan Music Department, which always has tickled me. She was not pleased. Contemplative listening to music is one of the things that keeps my motor running.

A second fluke was my year in American Political Science, an elective. It might as well have been a required psychology course. It ended up being a study of why society functions the way it does with competing subcultures having different societal agendas. It also provided helpful insight into the strong ego required for playing in politics. This course inadvertently gave me a critically needed frame of reference for helping people improve the fundamentals of their societal lives and governance.

Perhaps the most opportune accident of my college academics was my enrollment in a year of Geology, an option for fulfilling the two semesters of science courses required of all students regardless of degree major. It was formative in my understanding the intricate details of natural evolution and the formation of Earth, a prerequisite for any clear thinking about the nature and being of God. My fundamental conclusion in pondering the nature of God was that God, like we humans, cannot break, or operate outside of, truths of the natural order. This insight is at odds with the faith of many Christians, including my home church minister.

In addition to the fine liberal arts education I received, two social involvements gave fundamental shape to my life. One was my participation in a fraternity, Beta Sigma Tau, and the other was my meeting a serious-minded girl from New England. These two experiences got me beyond the social immaturity I felt when I arrived in Delaware.

My First Civil Rights Activism

Beta Sigma Tau was a fraternity formed after WW-II primarily by veterans who could not stomach the traditional white biases of older national college fraternities. Beta Sigma Tau was the only fraternity on campus that would seek and accept Jews, Muslims, Christians, Blacks, Whites, Asians, and Hispanics.

I visited Beta Sigma Tau three times during rush week. Without visiting any of the other fourteen campus fraternities, I became a Beta Sig pledge. I was not sorry about this decision. It became a harbinger of many subsequent social justice commitments I would make.

Our fraternity house was located right on the edge of the black ghetto of Delaware, OH, away from the mainstream aggregation of white sororities and fraternities. Our "house" was three buildings. An ancient brick two story home that contained sleeping rooms, a kitchen, two dining rooms and a living or daily gathering room, stood proudly at a corner across from a block-square city park. A modest house that contained only sleeping rooms was right behind the main house on a side street. Next to the main house was the "Annex," a small brick structure that had once served as the Delaware city jail. This was our social hall, the scene of many Saturday date nights.

In a setting in which intramural sports were very important, Beta Sigs couldn't do much with football, baseball or basketball, but we got the volleyball trophy almost every semester. To the chagrin of the mainstream jock fraternities, we also were awarded the fraternity scholarship cup virtually every semester.

At the outset of the second semester of my junior year, I was elected President of the fraternity. Shortly into the semester there was a social explosion in the fraternity. The latent racism, by which the whole American culture has been warped since day one, erupted.

Following a typical weekend when many couples had enjoyed dancing and socializing in the Annex, a rumble began to spread through the fraternity. By midweek it was at fever pitch, and by Friday it was a full-blown crisis. The poisonous allegation was that a popular white Beta Sig had entered the Annex around mid-evening the prior Saturday, when most of the couples there were black, and exclaimed, "My God, what is this, Little Harlem?"

In the turmoil, what did the Holy need me to do next?

I called an emergency meeting of all members and pledges for Sunday evening. My intent was to encourage an open and full discussion, both of the incident itself, and of less tangible concerns about our functioning as an inter-racial, multi- ethnic collection of young men. This turned out to be more easily imagined than executed. Anger and defensiveness permeated the living room of the main house as virtually all members were present. No one really wanted to be there. There was whining about classwork, and about missing social time with girlfriends. But I said, "We're going to stay here until we get this issue talked through, even if it takes all night!" Groans, but no one left.

I started by revisiting the precipitating encounter in the Annex. "I have heard that one of our white brothers went into the Annex last Saturday night and said, 'My God, what is this, Little Harlem?' I also have heard that most of those who happened to be there that night were black. We need to talk about this."

The first person to speak was the white fellow who had made the precipitating remark. "I don't know what all this fuss is about. I was just trying to be funny," he asserted.

A respected younger black man responded, "All you white guys are racists. You're the majority in Beta Sig, and you always do things your way. The black men often do not feel welcome or comfortable, but we don't have any choice in fraternities. Look, all the chapter's presidents since incorporation have been white." I gulped silently.

Another black student exclaimed, "The New York Jews are more respected here, and have more voice than we do!"

A Siamese student said, "I feel the same way the black guys do." A Malaysian student added, "I have experienced the same ethnic rejection, but we have to live with it."

Painful allegations and confessions continued to emerge, mostly involving usually unexpressed race-generated emotions. The meeting started at 7:00. By 10:00, I was worried that the philosophical principles that held us together would fly apart and the fraternity would disintegrate.

But, still, I would not let anyone leave, pressing for what we should do about the realities being shared.

Anger and resentment began to dissipate. We started to explore the need for radical honesty in our calling one another on the inappropriate use of racial stereotyping. By midnight we were openly listening to one another's personal stories of dealing with our various racial and ethnic identities. There being enough blame to go around, the meeting ended with renewed commitments to making the fraternity work. Hugs and handshakes were shared as members went off to bed. It turned out to have been the most identity-reinforcing "house meeting" that Beta Sigs ever had in my entire time on campus. Whew!

Another fraternity story began simply enough with an incident on a late Saturday night at a roadside restaurant between Delaware and Columbus, the Ohio Capital twenty miles to the south. A couple of the black fraternity brothers and their dates stopped there for coffee and dessert on their way back from an evening in Columbus. They were refused service. On a subsequent night, others had the same experience. On a third occasion, a small racially mixed group of us went there to test the restaurant's policy. We were given seats, but the staff served none of us. Time for action! On the next Saturday night, most of the fraternity brothers went to the place for what became one of the early sit-ins of the nascent national civil rights movement. The restaurant caved after three nights of our sitting there and agreed to serve people of color.

Encouraged by this experience, we faced another racial issue that was alive and well in Delaware. Black men, both students and "townies", could not get a haircut at any of the three men's barber shops in town. The fraternity came up with a complicated strategy. We printed tickets good for haircuts in Delaware. We then sold them to supporters throughout the community, including many male faculty members.

After we had sold thousands of dollars in tickets, we recruited a barber who was willing to cut the hair of black men, and who was able to rent and open a fourth shop with the money we had collected. He eventually became the most successful barber in Delaware, and black men no longer had to go to Columbus for service.

That interracial institutional progress is possible became real when my successor as Beta Sig president was a black student.

Chapter 8

~~

JANET WALKS INTO MY LIFE

I Instantly Knew We Could be Friends

A SECOND TRANSFORMATIVE personal experience occurred at Ohio Wesleyan: Though she does not remember our first meeting, Janet Richardson Wallace literally walked into my life at the outset of my sophomore year. The moment came on the Sunday afternoon before classes started, when each fraternity held an open house for new campus women. Of course, I was out front of the Beta Sig house to scope out the girls. I scrutinized each group of women under the guise of being there to welcome them to our modest facilities. Jan was walking up with a group of Cosmodelphians, the women's ideological social counterpart to Beta Sigma Tau. So, it was natural they would have come to our house first.

As they walked up, Janet smiled a hello at me. I stepped over to her and said, "Hi. My name is Robb. I'm a sophomore and I am a Beta Sig. Where are you from?" She blushed a little, and responded, "Littleton, New Hampshire. And my name is Janet Wallace."

I asked, "Where are you living here at Wesleyan?" She said, "Our group is in one of the co-ops, Hartupee. I've been here only three days, but I thought I should look around before classes start." We did not say much else before she and her group faded back across the park.

I must not have made much of an impression that Sunday afternoon, as it is her fervent conviction that we met for the first time the next Friday night at a student religious group. Though we immediately became casual friends, it was a year before I got up the courage to ask her for a date.

Janet Wallace was the second oldest of any of the children born to the five brothers and two sisters who had grown up on a northern Vermont dairy farm. The farm, which was one of the few continuing milk producers in that region, had been purchased by Janet's great-grandfather at the conclusion of the Civil War. Throughout its Wallace decades, the farm's hillsides were populated by herds of Jerseys.

As her first year at Ohio Wesleyan went on, I learned she was a totally unaffected, somewhat tentative, certainly cautious, eighteen-year-old. Her father was a Methodist Minister who had recently married Lillian Kelly. Jan's mother had died five years earlier. At the beginning of Jan's senior year in high school they all had moved to Littleton, NH where her father was to serve the Littleton Methodist Church.

Jan was a second-generation student at Ohio Wesleyan, her father and late mother both having been graduates. Ohio Wesleyan was considered a safe place for young women, so here she was. All women except "townies" were required to live in college-owned dorms or co-op houses. For economic and societal reasons, Jan had selected Hartupee House, one of the two co-op houses.

Though we did not date until the next Fall, almost every day we met on campus between classes for quick chats. Meanwhile, each of us occasionally dated others.

As soon as I got to Delaware in the Fall of Jan's sophomore year, I called her. That summer I had bought and fixed up an old pre-war Ford coupe. Having a car on campus curiously reinforced my courage. The college administration had closed Hartupee at the end of Jan's freshman year. Jan and the rest of her house mates were moved down Oak Hill Street to Hayes House, a newly opened co-op. Hayes House, named after Rutherford B. Hayes whose birthplace was Delaware, was a spacious clapboard three story house that had just been vacated by Ohio Wesleyan's president. When I called, Jan was in the bathroom preparing to dip her head into a sink for a shampoo. She momentarily paused to learn whether the call might be for her! When she got to the phone I said, "I bought a car this summer. Would you like to go to the Dairy Queen with me?" She instantly agreed. The shampoo could wait. Our first date!

Thereafter, we spent most of our free time with each other. We went to school events, mostly lectures or concerts in Gray Chapel, as well as an occasional sporting event. There were casual date nights each Friday and Saturday at the Beta Sig house. We often ended up there. Before Halloween, on a date following a football game, I gave Jan my fraternity ring, symbolizing our going steady. My parents had driven to Delaware that weekend to meet the woman I was dating. They seemed appropriately pleased. I was in the hopelessly-in-love stage.

Jan was able to totally melt me with her loving eyes. These were moments I had never experienced. I was in seventh heaven. But imagine my shock when she returned my fraternity ring a few weeks later! She quite simply and straightforwardly told me, "We are moving too fast." She continued, "I'm not very old. I haven't dated much. My parents have said I am here to get an education, not a husband! I'm afraid my decision to accept your ring was too hasty." I was perplexed, perhaps even confused. Being hurt by one I loved did not feel good. What to do? We continued to meet between classes, but we did not date. It suddenly occurred to me that if Jan wanted more experience dating, I should encourage guys whom I knew to be honorable and decent to date her. Several went out with her over the next few weeks. To show Jan I was surviving, I had two or three dates with Pat, a very nice Wesleyan girl from my high school in Kenmore, NY, though my heart was not in it.

When school closed for the Christmas break, I drove home to Tonawanda, taking Pat and a couple others who lived there. But Jan also rode with us as far as Buffalo where I dropped her off at the bus station for the remainder of her trip to New Hampshire. As she got out of the car, trying not to let Pat see, I gave Jan a wrapped Christmas present. Inside was a soft pink sweater. Then, I wistfully watched her disappear into the station.

The holiday was painful for me. Though we were not dating, I missed Jan immensely.

A Rescue Flight to Idaho

As soon as I walked into our house my father said, "Grandma Griffin is stuck in Twin Falls, Idaho. She and Aunt Maude thought it would be a lark to sleep in the hay mow at Maude's family's farm. That soft hay was too much for Grandma's back. It looks like her Osteoporosis has progressed to the point where a couple of her vertebra have disintegrated."

My Father handed me tickets they already had purchased: a round trip for me and a one-way for Grandma Griffin. It was obvious I would not get to vote.

When I arrived at the family farm in Twin Falls, Maude's son asked me, "Since you don't leave with Grandma Irene until tomorrow, would you like to see what this part of Idaho looks like

The Snake River was not far away. I stood at its southern edge watching the icy water flow from east to west in a deep gorge. And, I had never seen such a cloudless deep blue sky. I could see thousands of square miles, and only an occasional structure. It was breathtaking! This reinforced my infatuation with the grandeur of the west.

Next day, the trip home turned eventful. Getting Grandma Griffin up the sloping aisle of a DC-3, a small plane with a tail wheel rather than tricycle gear, was a trick. We flew from Twin Falls to Cheyenne to Denver, where a howling blizzard had the airport under siege. We finally left Denver the same day for Chicago, but did not outrun the storm. Upon landing at Chicago's Midway Airport, we were bundled off downtown by bus to the Palmer House for the night, an ancillary service which airlines provided in those days.

Next morning, we were bussed back to Midway where I had to arrange for my grandmother to lie on a cot in the terminal's first aid room all day while the snow continued. We finally took off and arrived in Buffalo about thirty hours later than originally scheduled.

As difficult a time as I gave my parents about losing precious time for writing a term paper that I had been putting off until the holidays, I secretly enjoyed this adventure, both the flying and the exposure to yet another wondrous part of the West. Throughout the trip, however, I longed for a revival of my relationship with Jan.

Maybe There's Hope

The day after I returned from getting Grandma Griffin, I was alone in the kitchen with Mother while she picked up after dinner. Sitting on the floor, I confessed my stress about Jan. Mother didn't give any direct advice. She just kept asking questions. "Well, do you think Jan likes you?" "Why are you working so hard to get other boys to ask her out?" "Do you think she is so focused on her studies that she doesn't feel she can take time for dating?" "What do you think she would do if you asked her out again after you get back to school?" I felt affirmed. I no longer entertained thoughts of not being good enough for Jan.

While focusing on my term paper, the remainder of the Christmas holiday passed quickly, and it soon became time for me to round up my passengers and get back to Delaware. Jan arrived at the Buffalo bus terminal, where we picked her up. As she climbed into the car, Jan handed me a small package. After arriving in Delaware, I opened it. There was a lovely pair of authentic deerskin gloves from northern New Hampshire. Hope springs eternal!

On the first Saturday back in Delaware, she and I were slated to appear together on a faith-based campus radio program. Before the Christmas break, I had asked her for dates three times since she had given me back my fraternity pin. The third invitation was for a classical concert on campus which had not yet been held. I had determined not to ask again; three times was the polite number. I drove her to the radio station. As we somewhat silently waited for our appearance, she grew serious and asked me, "Is it too late for me to reconsider your invitation for tonight's concert?" One of the most pivotal moments of my entire life!

We were in my Junior and her Sophomore years. From that radio station moment on, though we both had many independent responsibilities, we spent as much time together as possible. And my grades, which had slipped during our separation, went straight up!

Jan was a student assistant at Delaware's Asbury Methodist Church while carrying a full-time class load. She also had a job hearing and grading oral book reports from students of one of the English professors.

I worked for one of the two local undertakers, mostly assisting with funerals, and serving as night clerk. And, in return for meals, I managed the food service team at the Beta Sig house. And I soon had my hands full as the fraternity's president.

Mutual Commitment

Our relationship went well through that winter. Then! Saturday, March 21, 1953, was a warm and sunny day. I joined Jan for a daybreak bird walk with her Ornithology class. We had a Philosophy class together later in the morning. Around noon we packed a lunch at the Beta Sig house and went for a picnic at a park along the Olentangy River. We lingered most of the afternoon, absorbing a glorious spring day. After dinners at our respective residences, we headed for a basketball game. We never went into the arena but sat outside talking.

On Saturdays, the normal curfew was 12:30. We were in front of Hayes House by 12:00. We sat in the car holding each other closely. On a whim, she went in and signed out for one of her four annual 1:30's. Around 1:00, on March 22nd, I said to her tentatively, "Sometime, I'd like to give you my fraternity pin."

She asked, "Oh, when do you think that might be?" Emboldened, I responded, "Well, it could be tonight."

She said, "I could be persuaded." She accepted it! We agreed it had the same meaning as an engagement ring. That night she wore my pin on her pajamas and had to point it out to roommates in the morning.

Then, on March 5th, 1954, at noon in broad daylight, amid a churning crowd of students in front of Slocum Hall, the school library, I gave Jan an engagement ring containing my Grandmother Lapp's diamond.

It was in a simple white gold setting that Jan and I had selected over the Christmas break at a jeweler's in Tonawanda, NY. Now we were formally engaged! One of the most exhilarating moments of my life!

Special Guests at the Beta Sig House

Before I graduated, Eleanor Roosevelt came to campus to deliver a speech one spring Friday evening in 1954. She always travelled by train, and most often was accompanied by one of two personal secretaries. An American Literature Professor, the faculty chair of the event, planned a welcoming dinner at her home. She had invited several prominent faculty members to join them. When it came time to meet the train, this Professor took along Ola Fashola, a Nigerian student and member of Beta Sigma Tau, to demonstrate how liberal and internationally committed she and the school were. After meeting Mrs. Roosevelt and her secretary, the entourage got into the car, the Professor and the secretary in front seats, and Ola in the back seat with Mrs. Roosevelt. On the way to the hotel where Eleanor was to stay, Ola asked her, "Would you like to come to dinner tonight at the Beta Sigma Tau house, the fraternity where I am a member?"

Perhaps assuming this was the plan, Eleanor graciously accepted! Ola then announced that a fraternity member would pick her up at 5:30. The Professor was horrified, but kept her cool, and did not contradict Ola. She ultimately served her faculty guests without the presence of their honored guest.

Meanwhile, Ola rushed to the fraternity house to tell "Ma" Smith, our cook, that Eleanor Roosevelt was coming for dinner. When I showed up after class, fish sticks were already out on the counter. Ma decided the fish would not do and sent me to the market to get 40 pork loin chops.

Speaking of Ma Smith, as a middle-class white boy who had not yet begun to understand "systemic racism," it seemed perfectly normal that Ma, a black woman, was our cook. However, in working with her every day, I began to understand the dynamics and injustice of systemic racism in America which forced blacks into servitude roles. This was a pivotal turn. I was hearing the Holy.

Ola told me he promised Mrs. Roosevelt that someone would drive her to the Beta Sig house. I put in a hurried call to Jan, saying, "You won't believe this, but I have to pick up Eleanor Roosevelt at the Hotel Delaware at 5:30. She's coming to the Beta Sig house for dinner. Can you sign out and meet us at the house?"

Ola and I picked up Mrs. Roosevelt. She looked a bit puzzled at being picked up in an older Ford Tudor driven by a student. But she graciously smiled her toothy grin, saying, "Mr. Lapp, how kind of you to meet me here!"

Before we sat down to dinner, Mrs. Roosevelt perched carefully on a scruffy couch in a corner of the living room, next to Jan. Looking around the room and seeing no faculty members or other dignitaries, Eleanor then commented to Jan, "It's so nice to be here with another woman!" From the look on her face, it was clear she did not quite understand why she was being entertained in a nondescript interracial fraternity house rather than in an official University setting. However, it was a perfectly delightful dinner, with Eleanor answering all kinds of questions from the assembled brothers, mostly about her current public service activities.

After the meal, Jan and I took her to campus for her speech, then to the Student Union for a reception. With never a troubled word to me, the distraught Professor took Mrs. Roosevelt back to her hotel.

I marveled to myself that the Secret Service would be allowing her to travel around the country without protection.

On an earlier occasion, Dr. Ralph Bunche, then Ambassador to the United Nations, had joined us for lunch at the Beta Sig house following a similar spontaneous invitation from one of our members. But some of the members thought the most exciting visitor was Duke Ellington, who came to the house following a campus concert. It turned out he knew Ma Smith from an earlier incarnation of her life in Chicago. They hugged, and the Duke kissed Ma on her cheek.

Boston Seminary Comes Next?

Throughout my days at Ohio Wesleyan, I was pre-enrolled in Boston University School of Theology, a Methodist seminary of significant repute. A tangential motivation for pre-enrollment was to secure an educational deferment from the Korean War draft, for which I became eligible toward the end of my college Freshman year. I was a borderline

Conscientious Objector. By pre-enrolling in the Boston seminary, I simply avoided the corollary issues such a declaration would have precipitated. My main mission, however, was to attend seminary to become an ordained Methodist church pastor.

Then came one of those moments which seemed innocent enough at the time, but which transforms one's trajectory through life. During a religious emphasis week toward the end of my Senior year at Ohio Wesleyan, Jan and I were the campus escorts for Dr. Cushman McGiffert, President of Chicago Theological Seminary ("CTS"), a seminary of the Congregational Christian Church. Over ice cream sodas one evening before he was to speak, he asked, "Robb, you have said you're committed to becoming a minister. Can you tell me more about this?"

I started a bit awkwardly, "Well, I attended a Methodist church camp in the summer between my junior and senior years of high school. Though I was planning to become an engineer I felt an intense call to full-time ministry, whatever that would come to mean. Here at Ohio Wesleyan, my goal has become one of studying the variety of ways in which people approach life.

"I plan to attend Boston University School of Theology in the fall. My interest is focused on helping people figure out how to get along with themselves and each other. Particularly because of my experience in leading an interracial fraternity here on campus, I think I would be good at that. I think I know what it is to walk through difficult times. I think I am aware of the pain of being black in a majority white society. Besides that, I think I can assist people whose lives are in the ditch. My intent for seminary is to learn how to help make life work better for folks than it is to become a theological academic."

McGiffert responded, "You'd be interested to know that Professor

Seward Hiltner teaches at Chicago. As you may know, he is internationally respected for his ground-breaking work in pastoral counseling. At CTS, we could help you gain skills that would prepare you to help people deal with their personal issues."

As our sodas disappeared and it became time for us to take Dr. McGiffert to his evening campus appearance, he asked point blank, "Robb, would you do me the great personal favor of visiting CTS before you fully commit to attending Boston University School of Theology?"

I looked at Jan. Her face said, "That could be exciting."

Jan and I drove to CTS one April day that spring. After meeting with Dr. McGiffert and being shown around the seminary, we decided it was the place for us. I soon applied to and was accepted at CTS.

One's pilgrimage and spiritual journey through life is most often the story of transformative moments and events one does not see coming.

An Ohio Wesleyan Graduate

On June 7, 1954, my parents, my sister, and Jan sat in the Ohio Wesleyan stadium bleachers and watched me receive my B.A. degree before we all headed for home in Western New York. Jan and I were to work that summer in the upstate Methodist Church camp at which I had decided to be a minister.

My Ohio Wesleyan window had started when I was an awkward seventeen-year-old. And here I was, at twenty-one, with a liberal arts degree, a fiancée, acceptance at a first-class seminary, and a significant commitment to racial justice!

By the time I graduated, I could hardly wait for each new morn. I had the spiritual confidence that, on balance, life is good, to be embraced. There was something about the transcendent allure of the unknown Holy that was reaching out to me with a "you can do it!"

My time at Ohio Wesleyan showed me that I had the skills and style to consistently handle the challenges life was throwing my way. As an interracial, interfaith fraternity president, I had been a campus leader. As an engaged man, I had conquered the world of dating. And, I had done well academically. I was enrolled in a prestigious graduate school. My job was to make life work for people. That was what I was meant to do.

SECTION III

1955 - 1961

IN OUR TWENTIES ALREADY!

Chapter 9

~~~

A LONG ENGAGEMENT

Summer Work at a Church Camp

THE SUMMER AFTER I graduated, Jan and I worked at Silver Lake, the Methodist church camp in western New York where I had experienced my life-changing call to ministry as a high school Junior. I ran the Snack Shack, the ice cream and soda time-out center of the camp, while Jan operated the bookstore in a side room of the Snack Shack. Each of us also led recreational and social activities with our campers every day.

But we faced a significant dilemma. Should I go on to Chicago Theological Seminary, leaving Jan at Ohio Wesleyan for her senior year, or should I try to serve a rural Methodist church near Delaware for that year? Jan's folks had insisted that she graduate from college before she married, so marriage that year or even living together were not options.

Jan's instincts and good judgment won the day. She persuaded me to go on to CTS while she finished her degree at Ohio Wesleyan.

Robb Goes to Chicago - Alone

At the end of the summer, after five days back in Delaware, OH, Jan and I stood by my car in front of Hayes House and hugged and kissed before I headed for Chicago, very unsure of what lay ahead. Having visited CTS so briefly in April, I really did not have a feel for the place where I had enrolled for three years of graduate study. And, I had no sense of what it would be like to live on Chicago's very urbanized south side. Nevertheless, I felt twinges of excitement about the new chapter of my life that lay ahead.

In mid-afternoon I drove up in the front of the buildings Jan and I had visited earlier in the Spring. The act of going to Chicago, a city with which I was totally unfamiliar and to whose culture I was a virtual stranger, to a seminary not of my denomination, left me with uncertainty. But I had a strong sense I was doing the right thing in the right place at the right time.

I pulled into a lone parking space right in front of Davis Hall, the dormitory portion of CTS's main building on 58th Street. I saw a guy about my age and size peering out the entrance door. So, I tentatively exited the car and ventured toward the red brick building. The mystery person opened the door wide and thrust out his hand. "Bill Hobbs," he said. "Welcome to your new home!"

Bill introduced me to Clyde Miller and Donald Sevetson who were standing behind him. All four of us were entering as first year students. They pitched in to the task of moving my stuff into the building. My room was right next to Clyde's, on the third floor. Bill and Don were in rooms on the fourth floor of the dorm.

The main seminary building in 1954 was a block-long brick four story structure on University Street with the Davis Hall dorm at the east end, classrooms and administrative offices in the middle, and the library and Graham Taylor Chapel at the west end. The walk from the Chapel past the offices and classrooms to the dorm was a long beautiful carved stone walled hallway with a brick floor, and windows opening to a garden on the south side. It was called the Cloisters. I found myself stopping here in reverent silence two or three times each day, searching my soul, or contemplating a next class assignment.

My First Year at CTS

When I arrived at CTS, my agenda was to prepare for parish ministry in the Methodist Church. My sense of parish ministry was that its goal was to help congregants achieve positive mental health and social maturity, something life offers all people. I saw a functional connection between religion and psychology and wanted to pursue this.

In addition to working individually with people on their spiritual growth, I was looking forward to leading worship, to assisting congregants in their efforts to be faithful loving people, and to guiding the church's engagement with its community and world. I thought I was interested in pastoral counseling, which I imagined could be central to pastoral ministry. I was not considering any form of institutional or military chaplaincy, retreat center management, or Methodist hierarchical administration.

Heading for parish ministry, I was aware that I would be sharpening my theological perspective and my understanding of the Bible. But I had not remotely begun to imagine how such courses might challenge the theology I was embracing as I entered CTS.

As did most first year students, almost all of whom were males in those days, I signed up for a Bachelor of Divinity degree program which had a slate of required courses including Church History, Hebrew Bible and New Testament, Constructive Theology, Christian Thought, and Homiletics. There was clear flexibility in the choosing of various electives through which I could explore my specific human service interests.

I gradually discovered that at an effective seminary one appropriately reexamines every part of his/her theological pilgrimage: Beliefs about the ultimate meaning of life. An understanding of sin and evil. Sense of vocation. Value commitments. Concepts of God. Personal relationships. Loyalties. Place and boundaries within ones cultural and national setting. Interpreting the Bible. An effective seminary experience is much more than a simple gathering of professional tools and classic dogma.

In seeking to focus my seminary education, I liked the looks of an academic elective series in the Religion and Personality Department, whose main professors were Seward Hiltner and Ross Snyder. In my first year, I tried a course with Hiltner, who was known for his applying contemporary psychology to the pastoral work of the clergy. The course focused on human psychological dysfunction and repair. It did not click for me, primarily because his focus was on sickness, not wellness, in an individual's life. It was a lot like what I imagined one would study in pursuing a graduate clinical pastoral counseling degree, which I did not want to do.

One Bachelor of Divinity requirement was a first-year on-the-job field placement in a church setting, along with reflections and evaluations done in a formal course. Passionate about helping children and teenagers become responsible adults who care about a better world, I wanted to try a Christian Education setting. I was very fortunate in being assigned to the Union Church of Hinsdale, in a suburb west of Chicago.

As it happened, this was my first-year CTS classmate Don Sevetson's home church, and he, too, chose it for his field placement. We were assigned to lead the Jr. High Youth Group, with which we met each Sunday night for most of the two semesters of our first CTS year. We also observed the church school operation on Sunday mornings.

An ancillary benefit of being in Hinsdale all day Sunday was that Don and I were invited for dinner each week by his mother.

During that first year I drove from Chicago to Delaware twice, once for a Fall weekend visit, and once to pick up Jan for the long drive to Littleton for the Christmas vacation. We were getting more and more excited about our upcoming wedding!

Jan came to Chicago for Spring break, and we were interviewed by two different Methodist churches for jobs in Christian Education and youth work after we were married. We were hired by First Methodist Church of Western Springs, a Chicago suburb on the Burlington commuter line. Jan was to be full time Director of Christian Education, and I would be part-time Youth Minister while in seminary for my second and third years. We were offered a modest combined salary, plus a place to live. We were to start our ministry in Illinois just three weeks after our wedding in New Hampshire!

Chapter 10

~~

TIME OUT FOR A WEDDING!

June 11, 1955

JANET RICHARDSON WALLACE and I were married in Littleton, New Hampshire, on June 11, 1955, ten days following the end of my first year at Chicago Theological Seminary, six days after I was ordained as a Local Deacon by the Methodist Church at the Genesee Conference Annual Meeting in Rochester, and five days after Jan's graduation from Ohio Wesleyan. The sites for these events were, in order, Chicago, IL, Rochester, NY, Delaware, OH, and Littleton, NH. This breathless sequence, by road, was a harbinger of our future.

Jan's father and Alan Francis Geyer, a Beta Sig fraternity brother and future editor of *Christian Century*, conducted our wedding ceremony in the white clapboard Littleton Methodist Church on Main Street. Jan and I each nervously, but successfully, recited the Methodist Book of Worship vows we had memorized. After the ceremony, we were proper guests at a reception attended by church members whom Jan, and particularly I, did not know.

As soon as the ceremony was completed, the photos taken, and the last bites of cake eaten, Jan and I rushed off for our honeymoon, a week's stay at her parents' cottage on East Bear Island in Lake Winnipesauke.

As we got to the lake, Jan was wearing a beautiful turquoise pastel going-away outfit, and I was still in my navy-blue suit. We had had to reserve and hire a boat to get to the island. It was an ancient, open launch that cruised at least a knot per hour, piloted by a man of nearly the same age and hustle as the launch. Here we were, sitting in a small craft not much larger than a dingy amidst suitcases and boxes of supplies, in our fancy duds, motoring slowly past many who just stared and a few who smiled and waved.

We made and ate a light supper before we hopped into bed. Jan had a sexy new nightgown for the occasion, but the cabin was cold, so she found an old pair of her father's flannel pajamas in a rickety dresser for our wedding night!

I had been to the cottage with Jan and her parents once before we were married. There was much to explore on the island. On our first morning Jan said, "Let's hike up through the woods to the chapel where the family goes every Sunday while here."

She wanted me to appreciate the vacation lifestyle she had experienced on Bear Island as a youngster and teen.

That week, we walked past nearby cottages that lined the way to the main dock where the mail boat stopped twice a day. We went past a cottage owned by Dr. Stan Hopper, a renowned professor at Drew Seminary, to collect sparkly drinking water from a remote spring, one of many that feeds Lake Winnipesauke. We canoed to several of Jan's haunts. A cove called Sandy Beach was particularly inviting.

In the evenings, it was cool enough to light fires in the cottage fireplace.

We had a whole week of establishing initial patterns of relating as married partners. In keeping with our similar family traditions, Jan prepared the meals, made the bed, and picked up the cabin. I started the fire, emptied water from the canoe and fixed anything that did not work. It was a good week, ending months of frenzied anticipation and hectic schoolwork, and beginning the joint venture of married life.

The week ended with her parents coming to inspect the place to be sure we had not wrecked it. Her father asked critically why the bricks above the fireplace looked so clean. I responded, "Several nights we lit a fire. One night the flames got a little aggressive and burned years of soot off the bricks."

He asked disapprovingly, "Did you use up all my firewood?" I answered, "No. I actually added to the supply by collecting downed wood up the hill." His only response was, "Well, you could have burned the place down!"

Though I did not know Bill and Lillian Kelly Wallace at all well, my initial impression was that they were insecure, cold, and judgmental. My experience of "family" with my parents was one of knowing home was a safe place infused with warmth. For as long as my in-laws lived, I felt their judging scrutiny. Though not severe nor abrasive, their subtle stiffness kept both Jan and me on guard any time we visited. I always thought that my father-in-law was a good and decent person, but I never felt close to him. I certainly never shared with him any of my personal quandaries, or issues with ministry.

I was glad when it came time for all four of us to squeeze into the ancient motor launch for the ride back to the mainland. And I was even happier when we left New Hampshire the next day for the drive back to my home in the Town of Tonawanda, NY, and eventually, to Western Springs, IL where we were to live for at least the next two years while I completed my degree at CTS.

Jan had grown up with an intense desire to please her family. In her relationship with her father, she was not a rebel, but more one who should fulfill his expectations. Jan felt that her mother, who died when Jan was 13, was sharp tongued and harsh in judgment, perhaps not a happy person. When her mother died, Jan felt that it was her responsibility to care for her father, particularly emotionally.

Jan was not a big risk taker. She came from a cautious family. But a subliminal part of her soul quietly longed for liberation from New England and her past. Jan became her own person early in our relationship.

We came to see ourselves in a family joint venture in which we each had mutual voice.

We Move to Western Springs

Two weeks after our wedding we pulled up in front of an older house in Western Springs, IL, carrying everything we owned in our very used Ford station wagon. It being early post-war in a major metropolitan region, First Methodist Church of Western Springs, our new employer, had had great difficulty locating an abode for its new staff team. The church found a house whose owners were out of state for the summer. There, we were to share everything but a bedroom and bath with a young couple and their infant daughter, who also were there on a short-term rental.

Many young families that had been formed in the decade following World War II had become members of First Methodist Church. Jan and I were overwhelmed by the number of children and teenagers. The church sanctuary building was a "first unit," built with the expectation that a large classroom facility would be constructed on an adjacent lot owned by the church. Only the worship sanctuary and a basement social hall, along with two offices, existed when we started there. The church rented a nearby grade school for Sunday morning classes.

Jan's role was to recruit church-school teachers, train them, and support them in their Sunday morning activities. She often called on teachers in their homes. She also was responsible for organizing and leading a two-week Vacation Church School. As Director of Religious Education, Jan did a great job.

At the outset, in my part time Youth Director role, on Sunday afternoons I met first with Jr. High kids, then with those in the Sr. High group.

MINISTRY TEAM – WESTERN SPRINGS

I soon learned that action games and the singing of church camp folk songs were key to getting both age groups to feel comfortable talking about their lives, dreams, values, and challenges.

Emergency On-The-Job Training

Because our first child, Robyn, was expected to arrive halfway through my third year in seminary, I took two classes during the prior summer.

One sunny afternoon, just as I was arriving home from the city, I heard the big siren atop the nearby volunteer fire department station wailing urgently. I didn't think much of it as I went into our apartment, a flat over a delicatessen on Western Springs' main street. The phone was ringing. It was Rev. Jack Mettler, the Associate Minister of the Congregational Church calling to say that Scott, a teenager from my Methodist youth fellowship, had just stabbed a woman from his church in her shop across the mainline Burlington Railroad tracks from our apartment. The senior ministers of both our churches were away on their summer vacations. Jack Mettler and I were going to have to handle this! My first task was to call on Scott's parents to find out what happened, and how they were doing. Jan was getting an early taste of ministry with Robb.

Scott was an only child. When I arrived at their house, Mom was there, and Dad was on his way home from his office. Their son was in custody. As their story unfolded, I concluded the boy had some form of serious emotional illness, of which his parents were not particularly aware.

Though the shopkeeper survived, she had savage wounds about the neck and chest. Within hours after the stabbing there emerged a subtle victim and perpetrator conflict between the two congregations, with the Congregationalists blaming the Methodists for the incident.

During the summer hiatus, the Methodist and Congregational Churches were holding joint worship services, with Rev. Mettler and me leading on alternate Sundays. The coming Sunday happened to be my turn. Jack, and I decided to jointly lead that Sunday's worship. We interwove scripture readings with briefly stated interpretations. Their point was the combined message of not jumping immediately to judgment but being first to forgive. The service ended the blame game, at least publicly.

Over the next few weeks, with Scott in custody, I helped his family and the court understand the best consequence for the crime would be treatment in a residential therapy center, rather than incarceration in a correctional facility. We successfully lined up a place in central New York State, to which the judge committed Scott. I did not hear much from the family after that, as mom and dad soon moved back east to be closer to their son.

In this event I learned that a minister, no matter what else he or she is doing, is called upon to mentor people out of the deep holes into which they have accidentally fallen or have dug for themselves.

Here Comes Robyn

Jan's paid career in Christian Education ended when I was in the middle of my final year at CTS. Before daylight on January 10, 1957, the morning after she had been delivering Church School teaching manuals in a snowstorm, Jan realized she was in labor.

Robyn was in her hospital basinet before the end of the afternoon. In those days, dads did not get to be in the delivery room or to hold their newborns before their release from the hospital. However, I was allowed to see Jan while she was still in the delivery room. Her doctor ushered me to her bedside. A searing life memory was generated the moment I did not immediately kiss her. Abruptly pushing my head to her face, the doctor almost shouted, "Kiss her, dummy!" I felt so small! Jan was pale and a bit limp, but as I kissed and hugged her she smiled. We were the anxious and totally inexperienced parents of Robyn Elizabeth!

Our early days found us reading Dr. Spock incessantly. But we did not have a clue one frigid morning in our aging flat when we almost suffocated Robyn. We thought she was crying because she was cold.

After placing her basket near a not-so-hot steam radiator for a while, we turned on the gas oven and stuck the head end of her basket right at the open stove door. Coughing and thrashing replaced whimpering. Realizing the fumes were suffocating her, we grabbed her out of the basket just in time. We instantly learned that holding and caressing can solve lots of problems.

When Robyn was born, Jan retired from her role as Director of Christian Education of the Western Springs Methodist Church. For the remainder of my third year, I picked up her duties while still serving as Youth Minister and finishing a graduate degree.

Chapter 11

~~

EARLY THEOLOGICAL JOURNEY

THIS IS THE story of how my religious beliefs evolved from childhood through my experience at Chicago Theological Seminary. I grew up in a home that included my Fundamental Baptist Grandmother Lapp, and two parents who managed their conflicting independent Baptist Fundamentalist and more liberal National Baptist family heritages by joining a Methodist Church, where I attended both Sunday School and morning adult worship. Next, I attended a Methodist Liberal Arts College whose religion classes focused on a Supernatural God. Finally, I attended a theologically liberal Protestant mainline seminary. The transitions were dramatic, but I ended up with a theology that made real the Holy power that creates life on this earth.

Grandma Lapp "Saves" Me

An evidence of the religious disparity within our household occurred one day when no one other than Grandma Lapp and I were at home. I was a grade school student. She took me upstairs to my bedroom and had me kneel next to my bed. Then she made me repeat after her a prayer in which I asked God for forgiveness for my sins and told God of my acceptance of Jesus Christ as my personal savior. Then she blessed me for becoming a Christian. Later, she smugly told Mother that I was now a Christian.

That whole thing made me very uncomfortable.

In the years following Stuart's death, Grandma Lapp kept telling me that "God has a plan" for everyone's life, and that "things happen for a reason." I had to conclude that Grandma's belief meant that Stuart had not been a good enough person for God to protect and save him. I could not accept this. I already believed that premature death is a fateful accident, not the will of God.

Grandma Lapp also portrayed God as a supernatural being not subject to the rules of the natural order. God could do miracles that fly in the face of reality, as in reaching down and lifting a child out of the path of a skidding gasoline truck. Fervent praying by a true believer could generate miracles that defy the natural order of things. However, I could not accept the thought that Stuart's death was part of some divine scheme. How could a supernatural being who is said to love everyone single out certain ones for tragic demise?

The Minister of the Methodist Church in which I grew up was an unabashed advocate of the Power of Positive Thinking. Stated simply, our Minister preached that God, a supernatural being, created the universe, and has run it throughout human history. God is a self-aware agent outside the natural order who selectively intervenes on behalf of individuals and nations. Christians are the good people, the ones upon whom, and upon whose enterprises, God smiles the most beneficently. God is the Great Rescuer. Being faithful means having positive thoughts about ways in which this God answers prayers. If one prays long enough and hard enough, God will fulfill one's desires. Religious fealty is about "doing good so as to do well." Being a faithful person is what a good American Christian would strive to do, primarily to be on our culture's success track. And, at the end of life we would "be with God," whatever that means, provided we had held the right beliefs and had lived "good" lives. This all seemed more reasonable than what Grandma Lapp was telling me in that it affirmed good behavior rather than punishing one for bad behavior. But God was still a supernatural power who could defy the way things work in the natural order.

As for the Bible, it was a true story of the way in which things really happened in the days in which they happened. Yes, it was factual that there had been a flood, a parting of the Red Sea, and a face-to-face encounter between God and Moses on a mountain. And it seemed reasonable that a young couple had had a baby on a holy night, though a virgin birth was unimaginable to me. Loyal believers were the ones committed to the notion that Biblical passages all were true, whether based on fact or fantasy. So, the earth was created in five days, and people on the sixth. That must have been the way it happened – the Bible says so.

Being religious meant believing the Bible and praying that God would get you through the tough stuff, getting you into Heaven for your loyalty.

Theological Transition Begins at Ohio Wesleyan

When I got to Ohio Wesleyan my theological journey took an unexpected twist. Somehow, I got onto the tangent of whether I could philosophically prove the existence of a supernatural God, an intentional power outside the natural structures of the universe. I felt I would be heroic if I could do that. At a minimum, to do so would be what I needed for ministry. I could explain to people why they need not doubt the existence of God. This was an intellectual conceptualizing, rather than a life-experiential approach. One could talk and think about God as being "out there," not affecting our behavior unless we acknowledged His existence. However, all my cerebral attempts failed to prove the existence of a supernatural power whose behavior had no boundaries.

In college, I did not get to the matter of how people know there is a power out there because they have experienced that power's love, or its call, or its commissioning for caring, or its message of hope in difficult times. That people "just know" the reality of the Holy because their souls have been touched was not a concept I had spent any time pondering. At the time, it did not occur to me to think about whether knowing God is an experience or an intellectual exercise. But I was beginning to sense that some transcendent force was pushing me to distinguish between right and wrong, both personally and societally.

There is something about the concept of human freedom to make bad or self-serving decisions that calls into question the concept of an all-powerful, manipulating God. God does not plan or direct one's life. One is free to either join or defy an eternal transcendent call to service and accountability. And this human freedom is where heroic and tragic events come from, not from a God who punishes and rewards.

Except for two Geology courses at Ohio Wesleyan, four undergraduate years of religion, philosophy, psychology, and literature did little to restructure my youthful view of God. Courses in Physical and Historical Geology had made details of evolution very clear for me, raising deep questions about the Biblical perspective of how and when creation occurred, and even raising the question of whether God is a Divine Power that exists outside of the natural structures of the universe. However, what I learned about the radically changing face of the earth during geologic eras, the characteristics of solar systems, and, most particularly, the ever-evolving forms of life through the eons, has become the framework of my understanding of God. This gave me a basis for my later view that all religions are communally contrived metaphoric human interpretations of a universal divine imperative that defines and calls forth meaningful behavior in the stewardship of creation and all its living beings. The world's many differing religious narratives depend on the claims of various tradition's prophets. But there is only one God.

While in college I did not get totally out of the box that declared all evolutionary steps to be the manipulative work of a supernatural God. I also never thought to question whether we human creatures are truly the final and highest form of life in the ultimate unfolding of the evolving universe, the inference behind most interpretations of scripture.

However, during my four years of college, I realized that I was much more interested in the pre-Easter Jesus than in the Resurrected Christ. The stories and parables of Jesus were much more compelling than any fear of eternal condemnation from which I could be rescued by belief in a Risen Lord. So, I just did not even try to figure out how a risen dead man could make a difference to me, particularly in the time after I would no longer be alive.

In the big picture, as I finished my B.A. at Ohio Wesleyan, I was enthusiastic about my call to ministry, and confident it was the right direction in which to be headed. Though I hadn't gotten there yet, I was beginning to be free to question every narrative paradigm of the meaning of human existence.

Theological Transformation at CTS

So, I arrived at CTS with a Sunday School understanding of a supernatural God, a college experience which raised questions about literal

Biblical concepts of Creation, and a beginning understanding of an historical Jesus who frequently confronted both Temple and Societal status quos. I had not begun to think about the doctrines of creatureliness, sin, evil, and salvation. More important, I was just beginning to perceive that instead of objectively proving the existence of a supernatural life-controlling being, true faithfulness could be a matter of listening for a still, small voice that calls out the ultimate meaning and purpose of human existence. At first, I did not see life as a spiritual journey, walked as a joint venture with a Holy that infuses all of life with hope.

CTS started me over in my theology and in my interpretation and understanding of holy scriptures. Professors introduced me to the concept of Christian Doctrine. They taught me critical thinking. They moved me from certainty to uncertainty about the religious beliefs I held upon arrival. I heard for the first time that there is a narrative connection between human experiencing of what is Holy and the evolution of the Judeo-Christian story. Brand new to me was the insight that the Bible could be full of not literally true stories that are myth or metaphor for the ultimate realities of human existence. And, most of all, I got a glimpse of what Jesus, Teacher and Activist, saw as the holy claim on human existence, a hope for the highest and best behavior from any human being.

In my first year at CTS, I took the required Hebrew Bible course. My professor was J. Coert Rylaarsdam whose eyes twinkled mischievously each time he was about to offer a profound insight about a Biblical author's intent. It was in this course that I had my first exposure to the concept of religion as myth, that is, stories that are metaphors about the ultimate meanings of life. In another early course, Robert Grant, a New Testament scholar, added very helpful insights into how to read the Bible as stories people told one another in various cultural settings to give witness to their experiences of the Holy. In these Biblical courses I began to learn to think critically about narratives and to probe for their meanings. Literal interpretation and proof-texting were not in the curriculum.

Jesus

Undoubtedly the single most important theological and doctrinal learning of my seminary days was the difference between the pre-Easter and post-Easter Jesus. The early Temple outsider who taught in plain and often revolutionary language by way of loving the dispossessed and lost, and who confronted empire and power whether in temple or social governance, lived out of a vision of the coming of the Kingdom of God. Jesus' willingness to be crucified for his witnessing to God's truth about life tells us everything we need to know about God's call to sacrificial giving. A gift from God, Jesus would die ***because of*** our sins, not to ***rescue us from*** our sins. But through Jesus we learn that the Holy loves all of us, no matter what right or wrong we manage to do or be.

My calling became that of approaching life and human situations as one who strives to imitate the secular Jesus in changing people and the world, more than of trying to use dogma and doctrine to attract people to the faith. I was beginning to understand the difference between the living Jesus and the incarnate Christ. That Jesus was described as having become the Christ was a declaration that Jesus was a perfect manifestation of the will of the Holy.

What Christianity was becoming for me is the compelling story of how God brought into this world a revolutionary who started his ministry by inviting twelve ordinary men to help him show God's love for everybody, both in individual encounters and in his transforming narcissistic-driven cultures. Jesus was a radical, born in poverty, who modeled sacrificial living on behalf of the broken and dispossessed.

God

I began to analyze life experiences from the perspective of an intuitive awareness of God's transcendent presence, both in my life and in the fabric of all human existence. A God who engages with humans as a life co-creator was becoming profoundly real. By the time I graduated from CTS I was committed to the notion that knowing the Holy is basically existential. Though centuries of "proper" Dogma help set boundaries, one cannot know God's authenticity via an intellectual construct only.

I came to believe that the ultimate purpose of a religion is not to make life better for oneself, but rather to make life work for all.

Human history is the story of how the power of doing justice and loving mercy generates positive social change. Emerging new communal structures that make life work better for all are the work of a caring Holy power that gives meaning to human existence. This gives us hope that truly functional new tomorrows will follow history's functional brokenness.

We hear the Holy as we are moved to discriminate between good and evil, between justice and injustice, between life and death, and as we are inspired and energized to believe in, and to work for, the glory of the common good. God is that "something" that causes people to choose life, not death, in our battle to make survival possible for all. God's acts and influences change continuously from person to person, time to time, and situation to situation. God's love is constantly giving each human specimen on earth a sense of worth and belonging, strength to do what is required of her or him. However, God reaches out to all people despite their behavior. The Holy knows that until one expires there is always the chance that he or she can become more sensible, just and loving. That is the energizing dynamic of forgiveness.

Thus, "God," who also can be described as Life-Creating-Energy, provides courage for all people to have hope for more just and merciful experiences in their personal and contextual lives.

God is not an all-powerful supernatural being, but rather an anointing holy spirit moving silently across the waters of life. The job of theology today is to demystify the historic experiences of the ages, and to create new metaphors for ultimate reality, as the Holy Other addresses the ambiguity of human existence.

Bible

Though there were likely, or surely, people named Abraham, David, Joseph, Moses, Mary, Joseph, Jesus, Peter, and Paul, the words, *myth* and *metaphor* best describe the Bible's stories. Even the most scientifically far-fetched events, like Jonah surviving in a whale's gut, the virgin birth and a physical resurrection are meant to convey a specific metaphoric insight about ultimate reality or the mysteries of human existence. The personal and communal life experiences of the Jews and early Christians shaped the Bible. The Bible also includes a very intricate record of Hebrew law, which must be understood in historical context. Nearly half of the Hebrew Bible is composed of poetic and musical interpretations of life. The entire Jewish-Christian Bible is testimony to centuries of calling that creative energy out there, "God."

Because Jesus was an outspoken and troublemaking Rabbi (teacher) who did not intend to start a new religious tradition, the Disciples and the "Jesus people" recalled Jesus' teachings and parables to convey the life-truths they had learned from God through Jesus. These are recorded in the New Testament.

The Bible is a compelling record of understandings of many myth images of The Holy, including, most particularly, visions of what the Holy expects from human creatures.

From the Resurrection and the making of Jesus into the Christ, the Incarnate Son of God, the human ticket to Salvation, the story becomes one of mythmaking by later saints who were trying to develop an institution for the control of human behavior. This is where Literalist Evangelicals are divided from Liberal Progressives. While Evangelicals have a book of facts that outline what one must do to be saved, Liberals see the Bible as addressing and wrestling in mythical form with the temporal and creaturely ambiguity of human existence.

Literalists use the Bible to foster and reinforce their social biases. To distinguish between societal right and wrong, Liberals try to understand the realities of life through careful study of the history of the times in which various Biblical passages were written to describe human reality. Literalists use their secular predispositions, such as those relating to patriarchalism, race, sexual identification, to declare what Biblical passages mean, while Liberals use the creating love of God as reflected in the Bible to reach for a community that reflects the Kingdom, no matter how hard it is or how hopeless it often seems.

Freedom of Choice Pivotal to Saintliness

Now I get to the reason why religions have developed throughout human history. Unlike other creatures, whose behavior, good or bad, is primarily instinctual, human beings can choose between good and evil. The bottom-line purpose of a religion is to motivate people to do what it takes to create societal community that supports life for all. Like animals, people are innately selfish, making them want to serve their own interests and needs. Those who can get beyond themselves in making life work for others are saintly, beloved by the Holy. So, a religion's laws, worship rituals, parables and paradigms are meant to create and reinforce workable community.

The early Hebrew Bible narrative of the Fall became imagery to explain how a good and loving God could possibly create an imperfect species. It boils down to the truth that human creatureliness and finitude are what distinguish humans. According to the narrative, humans were perfect creations by God, but who quickly, because of their own freedom to make choices, negatively pursued self-serving goals. In one strand of the Fall, it is interesting how patriarchalism within early Hebrew thought blamed the Fall on the seductive behavior of women, rather than on the carnality of men.

Religion is all about trying to manage human creatureliness. Such work is the dynamic behind every effort to create societal governance. This reality of human finitudinal imperfection has become the central driver in my ministry.

Increasingly, Christian theology's intricately stated doctrines of creation, man, fall, sin and evil, atonement and resurrection, salvation, resurrection, eternal life, eschatology, and heaven, hell, and eternal life, do little to motivate human saintliness. People today are way more interested in what their self-serving behavior can do for them than they are in whether they will go to Hell when it is all over. Experiencing the love and care of others does more to heal self-serving lives than does hearing the preaching of historic doctrines of human sin and evil.

Chapter 12

≈

PREPARING FOR YOUTH MINISTRY

AFTER A FIRST year during which I had taken basic courses required for any Bachelor of Divinity along with Dr. Hiltner's course on clinical pastoral counseling, I felt a calling to explore specializing in Youth Ministry. Not interested in clinical pastoral counseling, I found myself much more attracted to helping kids become functional, responsible adults. It was the beginning of my commitment to inspiring people live more for others than for themselves. I was instinctively inclined to help both individuals and groups see visions of what they could do to make the world more hospitable for human existence.

While I was completing my first year at CTS, Dr. Ross Snyder, Professor of Christian Education in the Religion and Personality Department came into view. In my second year, I tried a course with him.

Snyder was a bit of a mystic, and described life in contemporary, poetic terms. For him, the mysteries of the Holy were intuited during the daily challenges of life, rather than in a series of discernable objective facts or within the structure of historic dogma. I once wrote for him a short piece entitled, "Men as Trees Walking." He loved its imagery because of its incarnation of life. Ostensibly, his courses were in Christian Education, Youth Ministry, and adult faith transformation. But, under it all, he introduced me to the concept that experiencing the loving, calling touch of God, rather than the philosophical defining of God, is where people find meaning in their faith journeys. I learned that enabling people to grow in their experiential understanding of God's action as a creative and loving life force is the ultimate mission of ministry.

Snyder and two other professors, Perry LeFevre and Phil Anderson, led me to analyze individual and collective human experiences with the question, "Can we learn anything in this moment about the Holy?" We hypothesized about God's role in current events, in relationships, in tragic turns, and in history. This was fundamental to developing my faith in a living God of justice and mercy. Being in a functional relationship with God clearly makes one's life more challenging, and the outcome more fulfilling. I came to realize that at the times of my brother's death, my father's paraplegia, and my sister's developmental disability, I had begun to internalize the role a loving God plays in generating human courage. My dealing with the intricacies of leading an interracial, interfaith community in college had strengthened my soul.

I decided to select Ross Snyder as my thesis advisor. My B.D. thesis was entitled, "A Study of Structures of Value as Reflected in the Relationships and Important Experiences of Eight Junior High Young People." The document was even longer than the title...almost 175 pages! My eight subjects were members of the junior high youth group at First Methodist Church of Western Springs.

These young teens were surprisingly open about the pains and joys of their peer relationships. I initially thought that emerging value structures would guide kids in their selection of friends, as well as in the kinds of experiences they would seek. In long weeks of interviewing each participant three times, I learned that I had it backward. The most driving force in the lives of mid-teenagers is not any set of societal or religious values, but rather a craving for acceptance and belonging. Generally, kids were driven by what they had to do to be part of some in-group. One boy revealed his severe sense of isolation, expressing deep anger toward judgmental peers, rather than examining his own behavior in light of larger social values to which he had been exposed. For most, peer acceptance was far more important than caring about life's ethical issues.

I wrote about how, to get to higher values in human existence, kids need to be walked through, and reflect upon, inter-relational experiences with others, rather than being lectured about universal aphorisms of right and wrong.

This finding was an insight into the challenge that lay ahead for me in the mission of getting people to move toward adopting values that are driven by reflections on ultimate reality and on what is good for the whole human family. Faith development grows out of wrestling to engage oneself with the Holy. And the Holy is at work trying to get people to behave altruistically, serving the interests of others and the common good of all. How staggeringly distant this theory was from the words of eighth graders! And, perhaps, from many people who consider themselves to be Christians!

As I graduated from CTS in 1957, I saw the Holy, not as a being, but as an unseen life force that calls forth loving and just human behavior. I was beginning to understand that Christianity is more about loving neighbor than about correct theological beliefs. Being a Christian means commitment to, and imitation of, Jesus. I was ready to take a run at youth ministry to tell this story and to lead others in living it. It was that simple.

Two Young Fellows at a CTS Graduation Ceremony

Besides developing a practical theological belief system that was way different from that with which I arrived at CTS, I had another life-changing moment at my June 1957 graduation. Chicago Theological Seminary's Graham Taylor Chapel was somber in its dimly lit formality. Tones from a classic Baroque organ signaled the entry of brightly hooded faculty and serious-minded graduate candidates. As I stood at the end of the line-up of candidates waiting to enter, I noticed a man I had never seen before. Standing alone in the hallway, he looked shy, and slightly uncomfortable. I dropped out of line and approached to greet him. "Robb Lapp," I said, extending my hand. "Martin Luther King, Jr.," he responded, just as cool and unassuming as that, as he clasped my hand!

I had known that he would be present to receive an honorary doctorate, but I did not know that this was to be the first he would receive. He did not seem to be in any hurry to enter the chapel, so we stood and visited as the service began. I knew about the Montgomery bus boycott, and of his reputation as an outspoken leader of the emerging civil rights movement. I knew that he was a Baptist Minister. I was impressed that he was being honored both as an activist, and as a contemporary theologian. After I shook his hand, I commented on the courage it takes to call out the Establishment for its racist behavior. He smiled the smile of one who knew I had no personal experience of the oppression and discrimination common to a black man. He didn't respond with any tales of the social issues he was confronting. Instead, he asked what I planned to do after graduating.

Suddenly, we were just two young guys talking about the challenges of ministry in a culture that enables injustices of racism and human greed. It was a serious exchange. His eyes betrayed an intensity of courage and an authentic intelligence. After a few minutes, we decided we should join the others in the chapel.

Faculty, graduates, and families filled Graham Taylor Chapel. Jan had retreated to the hallway between the chapel and the Library, trying to calm Robyn, now a fussy 5-month-old child. A seminary administrative employee and descendent of Ozora Stearns Davis, a CTS president in the early Twentieth Century, assisted Jan in the hallway.

At the time I was there, CTS was part of a seminary federation with a consolidated faculty that also included the University of Chicago Divinity School, Disciples Divinity House, and Meadville Theological Seminary. I received two diplomas, one from both the University of Chicago Divinity School and another from Chicago Theological Seminary.

So ended my three years of graduate study. The most meaningful part of my three years had been the opportunity to re-examine the building blocks of my faith and life. Those years had also included the joys of early married life, two years of youth ministry in a suburban Methodist church, and the birth of a daughter.

Graduation was a milestone ceremony that celebrated another step in my listening for the Holy. But who then knew through what valleys of the shadow of death I would be called to walk?

Chapter 13

~~

ORDINATION AS A METHODIST

Seven Years in the Making

WITHIN MINUTES FOLLOWING the 1957 CTS Friday evening graduation ceremony, Jan, Robyn, and I left Chicago for the 500-mile all-night drive to Tonawanda, New York, where, on the next afternoon, I was to be examined for ordination to ministry by the gatekeepers of the Genesee Conference of the Methodist Church.

It was already daylight Saturday morning before we arrived in Tonawanda. I was to meet later that day with the presiding Bishop, several District Superintendents, and a handful of other officials for an interview to determine my fitness for ordination as a Traveling Elder of the Methodist Church. Because the ordination ceremony was to be conducted there the next day, the meeting was held in the Kenmore Methodist Church in which I had grown up. Thirteen other candidates were to be examined that afternoon. When it came to my turn, I sensed an edge of uncertainty among the examiners because I had not graduated from a Methodist seminary. I was asked a few questions about CTS professors and classes. They wanted to know about my work at the Western Springs First Methodist Church where I had recently been asked to continue serving upon my graduation and ordination. I wanted to be ordained in the Genesee Conference, my home Conference in Western New York, because I thought I would soon be returning for ministry there.

When it came to the question of my purpose for seeking ordination, I answered, "Because I want to help people." That was it. Nothing about theology. Nothing about Methodist polity. Nothing about the role of church in society. Nothing about my leadership experience. The assemblage voted unanimously that I should be ordained, and the interview was over. Next candidate.

On Sunday afternoon, in front of a cast of hundreds of observers including my proud parents and grandmothers, I was ordained. During the ceremony of laying on of hands I held in my right hand a Bible, given me for the occasion by the Genesee Conference, with my left forefinger on a verse from the 6th Chapter of Isaiah:

> *And I heard the voice of the Lord saying,*
> *"Whom shall I send, and who will go for us?"*
> *Then I said, "Here I am! Send me."*[3]

The service was suddenly over, and I was The Rev. Robinson G. Lapp, a Traveling Elder of the Methodist Episcopal Church, the title given to ordained seminary graduates who could then serve a Methodist church anywhere in the world.

---

3   Isaiah 6:8 – p.715. The Holy Bible. Revised Standard Version. Thomas Nelson and Sons. New York

Western Springs Ministry Continues

After my CTS graduation and ordination, I became the full-time Assistant Minister of the Western Springs church. My main role was that of working with dozens of kids in the Junior High and Senior High Youth groups. I also learned a great deal about local church parish ministry. The Senior Minister often included me in worship leadership. He also coached me in preparing and preaching some of my first sermons. I found that sermons can help shape worshippers' responses to the call of the Holy. I also began doing meaningful amounts of pastoral visitation.

That year I led the development of a large educational and fellowship wing of the church building. I was able to translate the church school's need for classrooms into a large two-story structure for the congregation. When finished, it reinforced the church's ability to grow and serve the community.

A funny story. While the Sr. Minister and his family were on their annual month-long summer vacation, I became officiant at a wedding, marrying a young church member and her fiancé. A minister's need to be inventive arose on the day of the wedding when I was handed their license. It had been obtained in the next county to the west. In Illinois, people had to be married in the county in which their license was issued. As one who tries to follow the rules, I had to decide what to do. The solution was that we went ahead with the ceremony in front of at least 120 guests in the church in Cook County, but when it came time to pronounce the couple husband and wife, I filled in with words about the celebratory nature of the occasion.

While people were gathering for the reception, the bride and groom, the best man and maid of honor, the bride's parents, and I hopped into two cars and drove quickly across the nearby county line into DuPage

County. In the middle of a neighborhood street, we jumped out while neighbors mowing their lawns looked on. Using the traditional language, I pronounced the couple husband and wife, added a hands-on blessing, then had the witnesses properly sign the marriage certificate in the correct county. We jumped back into the cars and hurried to the reception, where our brief absence had been noted by only a few.

Such are the unexpected challenges of parish ministry!

Chapter 14

~~

EDGEWOOD PEOPLES CHURCH

An Interdenominational Parish

NINE MONTHS AFTER I graduated, Phil Anderson, Dean of Students at CTS, called me in Western Springs and asked, "Would you consider moving to East Lansing? Edgewood Peoples Church is looking for a Youth Minister, and I think you are the most qualified person I could recommend. They hope to have someone by July 1st."

While I had not anticipated leaving the Western Springs church just yet, the prospect of even larger youth groups and more church responsibilities was intriguing.

Phil told me that Edgewood Peoples Church was an interdenominational congregation created by the Presbyterian, American Baptist, Methodist Episcopal, and Congregational Christian denominations. It was organized in 1954 as an annex outgrowth of the large Peoples Church of East Lansing, located directly across from the campus of

Michigan State University. Edgewood grew rapidly, and by 1957 it needed a second minister to work with children and youth.

With Jan in the late stage of a second pregnancy, I went alone to East Lansing to interview. I conditionally accepted an offer to become Co-Minister of Edgewood Peoples Church. My acceptance condition was that I would have to be appointed to this position by my Illinois Bishop to maintain my standing as an ordained Methodist Elder. The fact that one of the four participating denominations was the Detroit Annual Conference of the Methodist Church led me to believe that I would have little trouble being appointed to the ministry at Edgewood.

A year earlier, I had been appointed by the Bishop of the Illinois Rock River Conference, to serve another year at the Western Springs Methodist Church. But after deciding I wanted to serve Edgewood Peoples Church, I was faced with persuading the Illinois Bishop to appoint me to an interdenominational position in Michigan, outside his jurisdiction, something infrequently done in the Methodist Church. He reluctantly did so.

A Boy Child!

After we agreed to go to East Lansing, our next child, Stuart, was born on May 31, 1958. The next morning, when it was clear Jan and Stuart were safe and healthy, I left them in MacNeal Hospital in Berwyn, IL, deposited Robyn with our Sr. Minister's wife, and drove to East Lansing to check out a rental home the church had selected as a second parsonage. I got back in time to take Jan and Stuart home from the hospital.

Jan wanted to know all about the East Lansing house. There was not much to tell. It was tiny! Two bedrooms. A living room. A small eat-in kitchen. And an outdoor side entrance hallway that was just large enough for a washer and dryer.

We arrived in East Lansing, bag and baggage, in late June with an old washing machine that had been given to us in Western Springs, but no dryer. This is an important piece of intelligence, as we had two kids in cloth diapers. We had to pull down the stairs, climb to the attic, and hang diapers to dry, which took a day and a half in the humid climate. The first appliance purchase of our marriage was an electric dryer whose placement limited access to the pull-down stairs.

We lived in this little blue house for only a year. But one of my clear memories is of the cramped kitchen. When Stuart became an toddler, he put a hand on to the side of our 20-inch oven/stove. He burned his palm so badly that a blister the size of a ping pong ball quickly arose. A quick trip to the doctor led to treatment and the wrapping of his entire hand in a large white bandage. The next day, Jan found him fishing in the toilet with his bandaged hand. Later to become a swimmer and coach, this toilet episode was the first of Stuart's many fascinated explorations of a body of water.

Co-Minister

As we began on July 1, my title was Co-Minister of Edgewood Peoples Church, but I was obviously the junior not only in age and experience, but also because Truman Morrison, the other Co-Minister, was a brilliant preacher and worship leader. Despite our titles, Truman was the Senior Minister.

Though I was responsible for the church school, teacher recruitment and training, and working with the Christian Education board, my opportunity for innovative ministry came with the junior and senior high youth groups. My having concentrated on Youth Ministry while at CTS was very important. Particularly in writing my thesis I had learned how to communicate deep life thoughts with kids in contemporary secular terms.

Eleanor Morrison, Truman's wife, a bright and gifted Christian Educator, was extremely helpful in making the church school experience exciting and fulfilling for many families. For example, we organized parent groups, based on the ages of their kids, to discuss what we were teaching, as well as to talk about issues germane to child-developmental stages. Eleanor also developed a community weekday preschool that met at the church.

I was also the Edgewood minister involved in the process of designing and constructing two additional church school and youth activity rooms. I learned about coaching church committees in the process. It was a good thing that I had learned how to design and construct church school space in Western Springs!

Pastoral Care

I had occasion to do significant amounts of pastoral care and small group leadership in neither of which was Truman particularly engaged. One Sunday morning, just as worship and church school were beginning, I received a phone call from a frantic mom. Through her crying spasms I learned that her young grade school daughter had just been hit by a car in their neighborhood while out riding her bike before church. I told my teachers that they would have to get along without me, and immediately raced to this family's house, fully expecting to accompany them to Sparrow Hospital in Lansing. When I entered their living room, several family members were siting, crying softly. I instantly realized that the accident had been fatal. I spent several hours listening to their stories and trying to make helpful comments. I closed with a prayer of committal for the girl, not into the ground, but into God's loving care. It must have been meaningful, as I was later asked to conduct the memorial service for this dear child.

The loss of my brother Stuart when I was a child came back to me when I was working with this family. I listened carefully, tried to be compassionate, and assured the family that the death was an accident, not an act of a judgmental God. I also included the victim's sibling in my conference with the family. My having been excluded from the family scene and preparations the day before Stuart's funeral led me to include children in such family sessions. For a child, the pain of not knowing what going to happen next is worse than the pain of seeing and hearing what is transpiring. Death is real. Attempting to protect loved ones from that truth and reality is quite often an attempt to be dishonest with oneself about the harsh finality of the event.

I learned that if I am doing the counseling and support with a family when there is a death, it helps if I lead the memorial service. It is a way of identifying publicly with the pain of the loss and reinforcing hope for the future. Stuart's death is in my heart every time I work with a family that is grieving a loss.

Youth Ministry

After I began working with the Edgewood junior and senior High kids, I was staggered by the number of home visits I was asked to make when parents wanted to talk about issues with their kids. I was grateful for what I had learned about the trials and stresses experienced by Junior High kids in writing my B.D. thesis at CTS.

I dubbed the Junior High group of seventh and eighth graders, "Club

78." We met for a couple of hours in the afternoon each Sunday. For warm-up, we did brain-teaser games, then did skits and held discussions that helped the kids deal productively with family and school issues facing their age group. At least twice a year we went on weekend retreats at one or another nearby camp. Club 78 grew to be some 120 kids.

The senior high group which met in the early evening was even larger. We had many kids whose families were not part of the church, though quite a few parents began participating in worship because their children were excited about their experiences in our youth group. Again, meetings were a mixture of socialization activities and serious discussions. We dealt with matters of faith in the context of school and interpersonal challenges. I led senior high retreats two or three times a year, which lasted from Friday evenings through Sunday afternoons.

My approach to most issues was bluntly straightforward. Once, when invited to speak at a female health-ed. class at the high school, the dialogue turned to sexual relations. The teacher asked me to comment on how a girl could handle sexual advances in a dating situation. I said, "The only thing I know that really makes sense for teenagers is for the girl to be sure she keeps her pants on, and for the boy to keep his hands out of those pants." The teacher gasped. She must have thought I would support pre-marital sex.

At Edgewood, I was into the beginnings of what was to become a non-traditional secular ministry. My emerging role was not to help people be successful and comfortable with their personal pursuits, but to lift up the vision of reclaiming the Biblical vision of reaching out to others in building the Kingdom of God. I already could see that the church must be counter-cultural, and that being a Christian meant advocacy for transforming the American Way of Life into a meaningful structure that gives every soul an opportunity for survival. So, even though I was later to be involved as an "infiltrator" in secular non-church-authorized ministries, I was already seeing the need for ministry to be a profession of asking and living the hard questions, something I had not experienced earlier in ministry.

"Any More Grampa"

One day in October of 1959 Mother called me in East Lansing. She was deeply concerned about Dad's health. Specifically, he had a bad burn on the side of his left knee. Having little feeling in his legs because of the skiing accident, he had burned himself with a heating pad. Mother said he had no energy and that his face looked puffy. He had had a heart attack before I graduated from high school. I now suspected he was having a heart or circulation related problem. I rushed home to Tonawanda, New York, where I learned from Mother that his general practitioner had run out of ideas of what to do for him.

I called his doctor and asked, "Do you suppose they could do anything for him at the Mayo Clinic?" After a long pause, he responded, "You can call up there and see if you can make an appointment for your father." I was shocked that he did not say he would call. I thought a physician would have greater entrée. It was a long shot, but I reached a heart specialist. He listened to my description of Dad's symptoms and agreed to an appointment in Rochester, MN before Christmas. Dad flew to Rochester and learned that he had a damaged aorta. While he was still there an appointment was made for insertion of an artificial aorta, a very new surgical procedure, in April of 1960, the earliest it could be scheduled. In those days aortic replacement was a difficult experimental surgery. Today, it's done routinely in every heart trauma hospital in America.

After his diagnostic appointment in Minnesota, Dad flew to East

Lansing for Christmas. Mother arrived with my sister Kathy two days later for a holiday celebration that had been planned the previous summer. I thought Dad seemed lethargic, both mentally and physically, but he enjoyed being around Robyn and Stuart. Mother, Dad and Kathy left before New Year's Eve for the day's drive back to Tonawanda.

On January 21st, Mother called again. She said tersely, "Dad is back in Millard Fillmore Hospital and is failing rapidly." Literally racing the 100 miles to Detroit, I flew to Buffalo, making it to his bedside before the end of the afternoon. Dad's aorta had ruptured. He was bleeding to death internally. I silently reflected, "Poor Dad has but a few hours at most." Having been there throughout the preceding night and all during the day on which I arrived; Mother was exhausted. I walked her out into the hall and suggested, "You should go home and at least lie down. If the end becomes even more immanent, I'll call no matter what time it is."

At 5:45 in the morning he was gasping for breath. There was nothing more any attendants could do for him. I was alone in the room with him. I called and told Mother to come as quickly as she could.

Hoping that Dad could hold on until she returned, I started a little charade.

"Dad," I said, "Mother is in the car and is backing out of the driveway."

"Mother is on Delaware Avenue, almost to Kenmore Avenue."

"Mother just got a green light at Hertel." "Dad, keep breathing."

"She's looping through City Park now."

Dad gasped! … gasped! … gasped!

Winging it, I said next, "I see the car pulling up next to the hospital. The snow piles are making it hard for her to park."

Within four minutes Mother walked through the dim doorway.

Without taking her coat off, and without any other words, we three immediately took hands.

We prayed together,

> "Our Father, who art in heaven. Hallowed be thy name. Thy Kingdom come. Thy will be done on earth as it is in heaven. Give us this day our daily bread. And forgive us our trespasses, as we forgive those who trespass against us. And lead us not into temptation but deliver us from evil. For thine is the kingdom, and the power and the glory. For ever and ever. Amen."

Then he immediately breathed his last breath. He died of a ruptured aorta on January 22, 1960, at the age of 51. I shed effusive and sad tears right on the spot. So did Mother. But our tears subsided before long. Much needed to be done that day.

By 8:30 in the morning I was driving Mother back north along Delaware Avenue to Kenmore. We started to pass Bury's (what a great name!) Funeral Home, which had handled several family funerals beginning with that of my brother Stuart. We decided there was no time like the present, so we stopped to "make arrangements." The unctuous undertaker on duty that morning, upon greeting us and hearing our story, said, "Oh, I'm glad to meet you, but I'm SOOO sorry it's under these circumstances."

Mother laughed as I blurted, "Under what the hell other kind of circumstances would you be likely to meet total strangers so early on a Friday morning?"

We held a proper church funeral. Dad was buried between Grandma Lapp and my brother Stuart in the six-pack plot in Elmlawn Cemetery he had purchased the day Stuart was killed. The next evening, Jan and I took Mother out for a simple dinner celebration of her 52nd birthday.

When Jan and I got back to East Lansing, we told Robyn, then barely three, that Dad had died. She looked at us for a few moments, shrugged her shoulders, and said, "Any more Grampa." That was it.

Reflection about Dad

In his career, Dad's crowning achievement was the designing and building of the Bell Aircraft X-2, which came after the X-1A project which he also led.

In 1953, Air Force Test Pilot Charles "Chuck" Yeager had piloted the X-1A to a new record speed of Mach 2.44 (1,620 mph). That X-1A now hangs in the Smithsonian Air Museum in Washington, resplendent in its original orange paint.

The X-2 was even more sleek and could fly faster and higher than the X-1A. I had the experience of watching a test flight of the X-2 at Edwards Air Force Base in Southern California. After being carried aloft under a giant B-50, the rocket flew out of sight in an instant, before coming back and landing at the Edwards field. I met Captain Ivan Kincheloe, the pilot who became famous for these test flights. Kincheloe and all the others had an unspoken reverence for the project, for the X-2 and for one another. While I would not call it holy ground, the venture, which consumed the energy and attention of everyone present, was certainly revered.

BELL X-2 – EDWARDS AIR FORCE BASE – 1956

I gained a clearer picture of the job Dad had been doing since the beginning of the World War II. It was obvious he was highly respected.

This X-2 project was so spectacular, as well as so meaningful to the Air Force, it led to a LIFE magazine special air-age feature on June 18, 1956. Filling a central page was a head shot of Dad with the note, "Designer of the plane, R. G. Lapp, watching it in action."

Dad was a tremendously creative and inventive guy – making a life out of thin air, with no formal education, no prior aircraft design experience, and little engagement in his parents' ministries. He was his own person right out of the box.

He threw himself into everything he did. Whether it was moving on in spite of the tragic death of a child, recovering from a debilitating back injury, visiting dispirited people in Millard Fillmore Hospital, believing his disabled daughter would eventually become normal, learning skills for which he had no formal training, building pioneering jet and rocket planes, fishing and motor boating, pushing me to pursue the same interests and abilities he had, he lived his life on his own terms.

I never truly saw him as the male after whom I wanted to model my life. He was a jock; I was not. He had a very quick temper that I never thought was fair, either to Mother or to me. Particularly after his ski injury he had what I considered to be a very simplistic and unrealistic view of God. God was a personal valet who could do what Dad commanded if he prayed fervently enough. Throughout, his focus was on himself, almost to the total exclusion of everyone else in the house. His affirmations of me were always tentative and conditional. He was someone with whom I learned to cope and even to admire, but we never reached the mutually respecting adult-adult relationship that is so desirable in mature father-son situations. Nevertheless, I deeply honored him for his professional accomplishments and personal physical triumphs. And I admired him as a person possessed of incredible ingenuity for overcoming odds. But it was always from a distance. I was proud of him, but he was tough to live with. The truth is, I yearned for many years, even after his death, for an unconditional affirmation from him.

Nevertheless, I loved him very much. He was my Dad.

Mother Had to Continue

After Dad was gone, Mother taught for several more years at North Tonawanda High School. Her Home Economics courses at first were those of traditional cooking and sewing, but as more and more girls were having babies, both in and out of wedlock, Mother added household management, meal planning, and childcare to her classes.

But Mother's biggest challenge was Kathy's need for help.

Just prior to Dad's death, continuing to structure her life, Mother imagined that Kathy could become a nursing assistant. Mother found Lincoln College, a junior college in Illinois that specialized in training young adults with learning disabilities. Kathy was then enrolled in a medical curriculum. My parents drove her there for the fall semester. Then, when our father died that January, she flew home for his funeral. She never returned to Lincoln. This is when a major schizophrenic break occurred. The reality was that in addition to being developmentally disabled, she was chronically mentally ill.

Summer Work Trips

My major contribution in the Edgewood Peoples Church's senior high youth ministry was the development of Summer Work Trips. When we moved to East Lansing, Bill Hobbs, my closest CTS classmate and friend, and his wife Barbara were serving the Congregational Church in Jackson, MI, less than an hour to the south.

In 1958, while Bill and I were brainstorming how to teach young people the Holy value of caring for others, we hatched the idea of a "work trip." A work trip would provide kids with a fantastic opportunity for self-discovery as well as for reinforcement of the Christian core value of self-sacrifice.

We would go somewhere as a group, live modestly, perform helpful works at our destination, relate to the people we were helping, and have seminar conversations and brief worship experiences each day. Where to go, what to do? For some reason, probably because I imagined it to be the frontier west where things could be done differently, we contacted the Colorado Congregational Conference. We were told that the people of the Silverton Congregational Church, the oldest continuing Congregational church in Colorado, needed help refurbishing their parsonage so they could attract a resident minister.

Silverton, Here We Come

Bill and I agreed on Silverton, thinking nothing of the fact that it was high in rugged mountains at least 1,300 miles away from East Lansing and Jackson. Kids from both our churches would go.

How to get there? I found a very used yellow Chevrolet school bus that had already had a second career as an intercity mail carrying vehicle in central Michigan. It cost $500. The Edgewood church custodian had been an auto mechanic earlier in his career. It did not take him long to see that the worn six-cylinder G.M. gas engine would not make it to Colorado and back. We found a rebuilt replacement engine. He and I worked evenings in the Edgewood parking lot to install the new engine.

At a pre-trip meeting at the church, the work campers and their parents gathered for a final briefing. The kids would be allowed one suitcase, one sleeping bag and one pillow each. The pillows would be used on the bus during the day drives which were expected to be long. Their other belongings, along with many boxes of food to be consumed en-route, would be carried in a utility trailer pulled by my GMC Carryall. There were all kinds of questions at this briefing, but the one that staggered me came from Cindy's dad. He asked, "Are any adults going on this trip?" I kept my cool as I answered, "Yes sir, a minister from Jackson, his wife, my wife and I will be directing the trip and mission work." Though he frowned, he had nothing further to say. Cindy did well on the trip!

We left the church before daylight on July 1st, headed for the Congregational Church in Iowa City, Iowa, where I had arranged for the entourage to sleep on the floor of an activity room. When we arrived at about 5:00 p.m., Barbara Hobbs, Jan, and a third counselor turned to preparing dinner in the church kitchen. That third counselor was the single mother of five young children whose husband had been tragically killed some months earlier in a car-train accident. Though she needed the trip just to be quiet and away from home, we were accompanied by her two youngest children. She quickly became the chief cook and food manager. The youth group kids, as they would for the next three and a half weeks, bedded down following a brief sharing on the day and a closing prayer.

On the second day of the trip, we reached the Congregational church in Hastings, NB, and on the third day out, we camped in the First Congregational Church in Colorado Springs, CO.

As July 4th dawned, we headed west into the high mountains. Before we reached the top of Monarch Pass in our worn school bus, it became clear that all the drinking water in the ten-gallon milk can located by the front door was going to be consumed in replenishing boiling radiator fluid. I had to stop about every ten minutes to refill the radiator. Then, on the way down the western side of Monarch Pass I realized that the bus brakes would burn if I did not creep down-hill in the lowest gear possible. We finally reached Montrose and headed south towards Silverton. When we reached Ouray, we were faced with the Million Dollar Highway, famous for its multiple roadside cliffs and steep mountain sides. We slowed to a crawl and ground our way toward Silverton. I worried we might never get there. But by twilight we had found the Silverton Congregational Church. The church people had made several community arrangements for our hospitality. Our females were to sleep on the floor of the church sanctuary among the pews. The males were to stay on the floor in the nearby town library. Several blocks away was an old hotel whose manager agreed to let us use a shower in the hotel basement. We arranged a daily bathing schedule with girls first, then the guys.

Our work consisted mostly of painting the inside and outside of a two-story frame parsonage which stood next to the white clapboard church building. Bill supervised the exterior painting. The three adult women prepared the meals and painted with the kids. I did modest upgrading of the kitchen and its adjacent bath, the only bath in the house. No problem. At least it was not outdoors.

Church people tried to join us in our daily work, but July was the height of the tourist season, so most days we were on our own. Each noon we all took time off to serve as supporting cast when townies dressed as cowboys met the antique narrow-gauge steam-powered excursion train from Durango. There were lots of gun shots into the air and much threatening shouting, all in fun. Late in the afternoon, when work tools and brushes were cleaned up for the day, we went on sightseeing excursions. After dinner, we sat on the church floor sharing personal meanings of the day and reflecting on New Testament passages about Jesus calling people to discipleship.

Bill and I hoped their experience of their doing work tasks in response to God's call to love others more than self would be far more convincing than reading the Bible to them. This turned out to be very transformative. Most of the kids have spent their lives making a difference in their personal and professional relationships. Bottom line: Faithfulness to God is more what you do than about what you believe. What you believe is your business. What you do is God's business.

As a special treat for the visiting work campers, one day several towns-people rounded up a small fleet of WW II and early post-war open Jeeps. We all were taken over a very precipitous trail from Silverton to Telluride, which was then just an abandoned old mining town. It had not yet become a resort and ski area. Bouncing over big rocks, we hung on for dear life, but it was very exciting.

On our trip back to East Lansing we had just left Silverton on the Million Dollar Highway when our bus was forced too close to some overhanging rocks by a large sheep-hauling truck coming the opposite direction. I could not stop before all the windows on the right side of the bus were broken or knocked completely out. The kids sitting next to the windows were surprisingly calm, more irritated than frightened. I was chagrinned by my inability to avoid the accident. We were in an open-air conveyance the rest of the way home. But that was the least of our problems with the bus. The old original transmission bell housing cracked in such a way that the starter fell off. For the final three days the kids had to get out of the bus and push it every time we wanted to start the engine. They thought it was great sport, and the activity extended an already close camaraderie. It also broke up the monotony of long stretches of two-lane highway in those pre-interstate highway days.

We finally got back to East Lansing safely on a sunny Saturday after-noon. What an exhilarating trip! Was it worth the effort? Yes, in two ways. First, we accomplished a meaningful piece of work in Silverton. But second, and more important, it was a life shaping experience for most of the participants. The idea that some of life's most meaningful moments come as we make sacrifices for the benefit of others was new to some and reinforced for others.

Mother had agreed to care for Robyn and Stuart, then ages two and one, at her Tonawanda home. At the end of the work camp Jan and I drove from East Lansing back to Tonawanda to retrieve the kids. My folks had rented a cabin on the north shore of Lake Erie in Canada to which we then all went for a vacation. It turned out to be the only time Mother, Dad, Kathy, Jan, our kids, and I ever spent any quality time together as a family. Most of the week was spent playing on the beach and in going to town to wash diapers. Not relating closely to the kids, the highlight for Dad was his catching of a super-large Lake Trout.

To give Jan a bit of a break, one afternoon Mother took Robyn on a diaper washing run to town. They returned with clean diapers and a small paper bag of cookies. Robyn had sampled them on the way back to the cottage. Upon arriving, she started around the circle, handing each of us a cookie. When she got to me, she looked in the bag and said with alarm, "No more cookies. Where yours?" Mother was tickled beyond words, as there had been more than enough cookies when they left the bakery.

Southern Union College

During summer of 1960, we undertook a similar adventure. This time, the destination was Southern Union Junior College in Wadley, Alabama. Some of the same adults and kids who had gone to Colorado excitedly participated a second time. Our purpose was to make additions and repairs to buildings on this tiny UCC-related campus which had a racially mixed student body. Unlike Silverton, we had dorms for sleeping and bathing, and an institutional kitchen for meal preparation. Jan, who was beginning the second trimester of her pregnancy with our third child, and Barbara Hobbs spent most of their time in the kitchen, while Bill Hobbs and I led two work crews.

The most intriguing part of this experience in northeastern Alabama grew out of the emerging civil rights unrest in the south. Mostly because there was not much news about it in northern media, we were not aware, prior to our arrival, of the extent and intensity of the ongoing resistance activities. Sit-ins, Freedom Rides, store and transportation boycotts, and civil disobedience had become part of everyday life. While there were no blacks in our entourage, Klansmen and other white local townspeople were exceedingly suspicious of our group of Yankee do-gooders. A Southern Union Sociology professor, realizing the danger to which we were exposed, joined many of our evening study-reflection sessions. At the outset he gave us safety pointers, mostly involving our remaining on campus, particularly at night, and our walking in groups wherever we went. In later sessions our professor host gave us invaluable insights into Southern culture and its many forms of racism. Our kids had a hard time believing what they were hearing. Though we were under careful surveillance by the locals, there were no attacks or incidents. But, because of the tenseness of the situation we never had any face-to-face exchanges with Wadley blacks or teens.

On our return trip to East Lansing, the old Chevy bus had so many problems it was laid to rest when we finally made it home. Later that summer I was able to find a discounted brand-new Ford bus that had been ordered by a New Jersey school district, then rejected because it was not what the district thought it had ordered. We paid $5,000 for it, and I picked it up from the factory in Wayne, Indiana.

And Here's Karen

Karen was born on January 9, 1961, the day before Robyn turned four. She arrived in Sparrow Hospital in Lansing, MI. As soon as I had Jan safely into the Delivery Room, I rushed home to check on Stuart who, that afternoon, had sustained a forehead cut that required stitches. We had left him and Robyn with a Dutch Exchange Student who was living with us. Gratefully, Stuart was sleeping and was okay.

I soon returned to Sparrow Hospital. In those days, fathers could not be present in labor rooms or hold their newborns. But, because it was 3:00 a.m. when Karen was dried off, a nurse snuck Karen into Jan's room as I sat there. The nurse let me hold Karen, still a thrill. The next day I hosted Robyn's fourth birthday party.

Both before and after Karen was born, Jan was eternally grateful that her Uncle George and Aunt Martha Wallace, and their daughters Sylvia and Myra, lived in East Lansing. George was a noted Professor of Ornithology while Martha taught graduate-level math. Sylvia was away at college, and Myra was still living at home. Jan isn't certain she could have survived without the help of Martha and Myra. Many were the nights that one or both came to the parsonage to help put three preschoolers to bed. Martha also was a fine seamstress. She made beautiful snowsuits for our two "big kids."

During the Spring of 1961 I used the new school bus to take kids to High School sporting events in which East Lansing High School students were participating. This activity attracted even more young people to participate in our Sunday youth group faith explorative discussions.

Pine Mountain Retreat Center

In early summer of 1961, I had my youth group on the road again, this time to Gorham, New Hampshire, where we worked on building a Taize retreat center atop Pine Mountain. Our Gorham host was Dr. Douglas Horton, a prominent Congregational denominational leader and Harvard Theological Seminary professor. Living in Randolph, near Gorham, Horton was a major player in the formation of the United Church of Christ. He was the vision and energy behind the development of the Pine Mountain Retreat Center. Horton was involved with our kids through the entire work effort. "Dr. Doug," as the kids came to call him, had engaged a local schoolteacher to be project manager for the construction of the retreat center. He was delighted to have our help.

For the New Hampshire venture, Jan stayed in East Lansing with our 6-month-old daughter Karen and, of course, three-year old Stuart, and four-year old Robyn. Neither Bill nor Barbara Hobbs was able to accompany us either, but we had 3 kids from the Jackson church as well as over 30 from Edgewood. In some ways this was our most successful trip. We accomplished significant amounts of construction work on camp buildings and an access road. We also had many wonderful campfire discussions of faith, mission, and God's claim on people's lives with Dr. Doug who joined us nearly every evening.

Several of the kids who were by now on their third work camp had become excellent mentors for newer, younger recruits. Our travel to and from New Hampshire was uneventful but for the loss of a clutch in an older truck we had purchased for hauling food, suitcases and sleeping bags. I enjoyed driving the new Ford bus, which was safer and much more comfortable for the kids.

In addition to these Work Trips and to the leading of the large Sunday afternoon youth groups, my ministry at Edgewood included many family camps and youth retreats. They provided participants with the opportunity for concentrated and extended discussion and reflection of their personal and spiritual journeys. These events reinforced and strengthened other elements in the ministries of Edgewood.

Edgewood Peoples Church and the East Lansing community turned out to be an exciting and stimulating place to live and work. And I was beginning to find "out of the box" ministry to be a meaningful response to what the Holy was calling me to do and be.

Chapter 15

~~~

OOPS, NO LONGER A METHODIST

A Bishop Failed to Reveal the Entire Truth

THE BACKGROUND FOR this story is that the Methodist Church is hierarchical, that is, run from the top down. Bishops are essentially the ones to whom clergy report. The standing of ministers is reviewed annually, and appointments to specific ministries are renewed or changed by a Conference's Bishop at each year's Annual Meeting. Because I was serving in Michigan by appointment of the Northern Illinois Bishop, my assignment was inconsistent with normal practice.

Before we were to leave for the Summer Work Trip to Colorado, in June of 1959 I was summoned to attend the Annual Meeting of the Rock River Conference in northern Illinois, where I held my ministerial standing. On a very hot Saturday afternoon, I sat in the minister's office in Rockford's Court Street Methodist Church. The Rock River Conference Bishop and the Chicago District Superintendent already were there. For some reason, the Bishop of the Michigan Annual

Conference of the Methodist Church was also going to be present. As we waited, I wondered why the Detroit Bishop would be at the Rock River Conference meeting in Illinois when he typically would have been in southern Michigan during this season of Methodist Annual Conference meetings. Why did he want to see me?

Once both Bishops were in the room, with precious little introductory prologue, my Illinois Bishop said, "Rev. Lapp, as you know, it's not normal procedure for a Bishop to appoint a minister to serve in another Bishop's jurisdiction. I really want you to be serving a church in northern Illinois. We need additional young clergy here. Besides, the Michigan Bishop has asked that you no longer serve at Edgewood." I immediately sensed there was a back story I was not getting.

The first word out of my mouth was, "But…" I went on, "But, I have just gotten started at Edgewood. In less than a month I am taking 36 senior high kids and adults to Silverton, Colorado, for a youth work trip. The plans are all in place. The kids are counting on it!"

Searching for a compromise solution, I suggested to the Michigan Bishop, "Why don't I simply transfer to the Detroit Conference? Then you could reappoint me to Edgewood Peoples Church." Curiously, neither warmed to that solution. My Illinois Bishop said, "I am thinking of a church that would be a good place for you to try a solo ministry. It's not too large, and the people are used to having young seminarians."

Hardly hearing him, I instead was thinking about how the Methodist Book of Discipline might relate to my dilemma. I said, "Another way of allowing me to continue my ministry at Edgewood would be for me to go into 'Supernumerary Status,' which, as you both know, is a category that gives a clergyperson a leave of absence from Conference assignments for up to five years."

The Michigan Bishop looked puzzled and took his Book of Discipline with him as he left the room, obviously to check the veracity of what I had just said. When he returned, he told the Illinois Bishop he did not want to do this. We went back and forth for about 45 minutes, during which both Bishops became increasingly agitated. Finally, they agreed that I could spend one more year in the Edgewood appointment, but would then have to leave East Lansing and commence serving a church in the Illinois Rock River Conference. My Illinois Bishop, who was holding my Elders Orders certificate in his right hand, thrust it back to me, and the meeting was over. I never saw either Bishop again.

A year later, having been summoned again, instead of attending the Rock River Conference meeting to argue my case, I simply wrote a letter to the Illinois Bishop stating that my ministry at Edgewood was vital to many junior and senior high kids, and that I would not accept appointment to a church in northern Illinois. Assuming it likely that I would be terminated as a Methodist Elder, I enclosed my Deacon's Orders and Elder's Orders certificates.

Shortly after, I received an envelope containing both Orders on each of which had been typed, "Voluntarily terminated, - June 20, 1960," and signed by the Illinois Bishop.

I had just lost my ordinational standing in the Methodist Church! Legally, this meant I was no longer ordained, could not administer the sacraments of the church, and was not eligible for appointment to a Methodist church. For some eerie reason this did not bother me, even though the first 27 years of my church identity and family pride had just been trashed. I didn't immediately recognize it, but this arbitrary action by Methodist officials opened the door to my participating productively at every level of a liberal denomination, the Congregational Christian Church, to which I had been introduced while in seminary.

Later that same summer, I learned that the Michigan Conference of the Methodist Church was planning to abandon its covenant as part of the Edgewood Peoples interdenominational church venture and start a new Methodist Church just down the street. Apparently, the Michigan Bishop had been worried all along that my having nearly 300 junior and senior high kids in Edgewood youth groups would deter Methodist efforts to start a new church in East Lansing. I finally understood why the Bishops were so determined to get me out of town. I had lost my ordination in the process of confronting a Methodist Bishop who was quietly undermining the very existence of the interdenominational church (partially Methodist) of which I was Co-Minister. But I decided that it was more important to pour my energies into the day-to-day rounds of ministry than it was to mount a challenge to the unethical behavior of a couple of Bishops.

I never felt like a victim, but more like a young bird that was becoming more certain of its wings. My ejection was another of those events that dramatically affected the course of my life.

By the next year, I had been accepted and given ministerial standing by the local Association of the Michigan Conference of Congregational Christian Churches. In 1961, that Conference voted to confirm its membership in the newly formed United Church of Christ, an historic national merger of the Evangelical and Reformed Church and the Congregational Christian Church which had occurred in 1957. So, when I came up for air, I was a minister of the United Church of Christ!

I had retained my integrity. And I was still Co-Minister of Edgewood Peoples Church!

End of the Edgewood Road

While at Edgewood I had the good fortune of working with Truman Morrison, one of the most intellectual preachers I ever have heard. He was a good fit for a church in a university community. His sermons revealed extensive exposure to contemporary theology. His starting point often was not a Biblical passage but rather a current issue that he examined from a Biblical perspective. Though sometimes it seemed to me his explorations were vastly esoteric, listeners most often went on mental journeys that helped them tell up from down. More than anything, I learned to be brave in preaching, and risk going beyond safe platitudes and traditional Biblical interpretations.

Even so, because of my emphasis on the youth and educational ministries of the church, which led to significant amounts of personal pastoral counseling with the kids and their families, I privately questioned Truman's overall ministerial style. He made few pastoral calls. He did not do much with church boards and committees. He was so cerebral, people perceived him to be personally remote and distant. He was more about belief than action. While I tried hard to fill in the blanks, even taking the lead in constructing the addition to the church building, I found myself chafing for an opportunity to lead a church. Rather than do anything to undermine or contradict Truman, I quietly yearned for an opportunity to be the senior or only minister of a congregation.

At Edgewood Peoples Church, in developing the Youth Work Trip program I had developed new ways in which a church could make a difference in the world. I was hearing the Holy.

SECTION IV

1962 - 1971

TRANSFORMATIVE MINISTRY

Chapter 16

~~

A New UCC Church in Arvada

MINISTERS DO NOT often accept calls to churches that have no building and no members. But that seemed to be what made sense to the Holy Creator.

It all began in the Fall of 1961 when I received a phone call from Dr. Robert Inglis, Colorado Conference Minister, I immediately recognized his name, as he had helped Bill Hobbs and me locate the church in Silverton to which we took our Youth Work Camp in 1959.

Dr. Inglis said, "As you know, your friend Bill Hobbs is here in Colorado starting a new congregation in Aurora, a Denver suburb. He has told me about your work in East Lansing and has said you are an innovative guy. Would you consider applying for the job of starting a new congregation in Arvada, Colorado?"

My first question was, "Where is Arvada?"

"It's on the west side of metropolitan Denver, nestled against the Rocky

Mountain foothills," he said. He continued, "I'd really like to meet you. I'll be in Chicago next weekend, and I could drive over to Michigan." We arranged to meet at a church in Grand Rapids where I would be attending a youth retreat with my senior high kids. On the appointed day I saw a distinguished looking grey-haired man standing in the hallway. I guessed it was Dr. Inglis, so I introduced myself. An hour later we had agreed that Jan and I would fly to Denver over Thanksgiving weekend, 1961, to lead a candidating worship service in Arvada.

Jan and I slipped off to Colorado, unnoticed. We stayed overnight with Dr. Inglis and his wife. Next morning, he drove us west through the city to Arvada. I preached a sermon in the old Enterprise Grange Hall which still stands at the intersection of 72nd Avenue and Simms Street. In attendance were several people interested in starting a new Congregational congregation. Also present were members of the Conference's New Church Start Committee.

There having been no hitches in the worship service, we went back to the Inglis' home for a meeting of the New Church Start Committee. After an interview by fifteen people, Jan and I were sent out of the room. Five short minutes later we were called back. Dr. Inglis said to us, "After serious deliberation (I laughed to myself), the committee would like to ask you to move to Arvada to lead a new church start."

Wanting to go through it with Jan one more time, I said, "Thank you very much. Jan and I will discuss this tonight after we go to our room. We'll let you know tomorrow morning."

Jan and I spent time later that night and in the early morning weighing the pros and cons of such a major move. Among other considerations, we had three pre-school children. However, we convinced each other that we should accept, and did so at the Inglis' breakfast table.

Now what? Curiously, I was not intimidated. But I was not overly self-confident either. I was energized by the challenge.

The news that I was resigning my position at Edgewood Peoples Church did not go over particularly well. Eleanor Morrison, Truman's wife, who was very involved with the church school and with our weekday preschool, tried to make me feel guilty, as though I was breaking some kind of covenant that included life-long permanence. Others were more charitable, but my remaining days at Edgewood felt chilly. I was given two going-away gifts, a used manual typewriter, and an old Ditto machine, both with the good intention of helping to get the new church started.

Easterners Move "Out West"

Trying to moderate moving costs, on a very cold January morning in 1962, I headed west with 3 ½ year-old Stuart and a small U-Haul trailer filled with my books and other compact but heavy office items. Thirteen cases of Jan's home-canned fruits and vegetables were in the back of our station wagon. Jan and the two girls were to fly to Denver two weeks later. On the first night Stuart and I spent $7.21 for a motel room! The next frigid night we spent in a motel in Fremont, NE. For a second time I carried all thirteen heavy cases of canned goods into a motel so they would not freeze. Stuart was so excited to be liberated from his heavy snowsuit and clothing that while running around the room naked he skidded on the slick bathroom floor and flipped into the tub which already was filled with warm water. What a surprised but pleased little boy!

We arrived in Denver during rush hour on Friday night, and located Bill and Barbara Hobbs' home on Peoria Street in Aurora. All the mounting tension of moving to a new setting that had few definitions began to dissipate as Stuart and I were embraced by Bill and Barbara. The next morning, we reloaded and headed for Arvada, on the other side of Denver. Stuart and I were to stay, of all places, with Earl and Virginia Rau for the week until Jan and the girls arrived. I was uncertain about staying there because of something that had happened at the end of our candidating weekend in November.

Late on that Monday afternoon we had been dropped off for dinner at the Rau's home. Earl was the apparent emerging leader of the small gathering group. In a few minutes, on a pretense of needing to go get a bottle of milk, he asked me to ride along with him. Part way to the store, he stopped the car and said to me, "You did an acceptable job in your sermon yesterday. But if I ever hear you speak favorably from the pulpit about N's or Mexicans, you won't last long in this church." Trying to be both honest and conciliatory, I said, "Earl, I hope and pray that you will one day regret what you just said. As a representative of Jesus' ministry on earth, I will say and do what I feel I need to say and do in this new church. Our loving God does not discriminate, and I believe you have the courage to come to agree. Now, start the car." Not another word was spoken until we were back at the house. The next morning Jan and I flew back to Lansing. The conversation with Earl had left me more than a bit anxious, but Stuart's and my stay with them went smoothly.

After I had been asked to lead this new church start, the Conference, with consultation from people in the new group, had purchased a brick ranch tract house in what was then the western-most developed area of Arvada. It was to be the parsonage. It had a living room that could handle group meetings, and a large basement, half of which eventually would be finished for church school, youth groups and adult meeting space. My study was to be a room in the basement below the kitchen. The parsonage wasn't quite completed when Jan and the girls arrived, so we lived for several weeks in a nearby apartment.

Here the Lapps were in Colorado in an icy January to serve a church that yet had no formal members. I had never led worship and preached every Sunday. I had never organized a new church. I had never been the minister responsible for the managing of all the affairs of a congregation. I knew more about Methodist Church history and polity than that of the Congregational Church. Though the group had arranged for use of the Enterprise Grange Hall on Sundays, I did not know how worshipful it would feel. Everything else had to happen in the parsonage or in parishioners' homes. We had little idea how this would work out.

My first sermon was entitled, "The Irrelevance of the Church," revealing my hope that people would be inspired to risk for a servant fellowship. Nine weeks later, during Lent, reinforcing my calling to follow a pre-Easter Jesus, my sermon was "The Man Bold Enough to Fail." People were very responsive, and soon began to bring neighbors to the Grange Hall services.

Being the only minister, the one who could be praised or blamed for everything, was a new challenge. I had not yet reached my twenty-ninth birthday! Writing a relevant new sermon each week was a trip.

Before long, we had organized a choir, formed a church council, assembled a youth group, started a Sunday School, and created the beginnings of an organizational infrastructure. On weekdays I called on people who had attended our worship service for the first time on the previous Sunday. I also called frequently on the people who had already become active participants. Many of these visits became informal pastoral counseling sessions.

For the first two and a half years, while a new facility was being built, Sunday nursery and preschool classes as well as all our committee meetings were held in the parsonage. Raising three children, to say nothing of doing so in a house that was constantly subject to congregational inspection, was very stressful for Jan. No wonder she said the church was her fourth child!

In preaching, I tried to address everyday issues of living in our culture and society. Worshippers listened carefully to what I said in sermons. I was a Progressive Christian. The people ran the gamut from Literal Fundamentalists to Liberals. Nevertheless, the new church in Arvada was an early precursor to what one day would be called "The Emerging Church," and it drew many people.

After only a few months, our people began their very first mission outreach. During the Cuban missile crisis, they assumed responsibility for the relocation to Colorado of a male Cuban refugee. They found him a job, a place to live, and provided financial assistance. A year later this refugee needed medical and legal help when he fell and injured himself. Working with him helped create a mission identity for the congregation.

Early on, we had long discussions about what should be stated in our church covenant. Upon adoption, we called it the Covenant of Intention, and repeated it in unison in every worship service:

> *"Seeking unity in the fellowship of Christ's church, and confessing our need for the continuing guidance of the Holy Spirit, we covenant with God and with one another to walk together in God's ways, known or to be made known, whatever this shall demand of us."*

In moving toward our chartering service, in which the Denver Association of the Congregational Christian Church would formally recognize and give standing to our congregation, we had to create a name for our new church. Because this recognition service was scheduled to occur in March of 1963, it would happen shortly after the Colorado Congregational Conference had become part of the United Church of Christ. So, we named ourselves First United Church of Arvada.

The congregation, with a few delightful senior exceptions, was composed predominantly of younger families with children. Before the Church Center was completed, we were holding Church School classes in the Grange Hall basement, at the parsonage and in several member homes. Families had to depart for Sunday worship more than a half hour before its commencement so they could drop their kids at our various class locations.

In addition to her role as mother and wife, Jan was very clear about her additional identity as "the minister's wife" while we lived in Arvada. As a preacher's kid in the 1930's and 40's, she had gained an insider's view of the role of a local minister's wife. It was a full-time job. In the early 60's a clergy spouse, usually the female, most often did not have a career of her own and was expected to be an unpaid part of the clergy team. Always feeling vulnerable to what parishioners and others thought of her, Jan, nevertheless, was hugely supportive of the new church start.

The children of both the Arvada City Manager and Arvada City Attorney, along with their parents, became active in our new church. The parents were close friends and had seven children between them. The eldest child of the City Manager had Cerebral Palsy and was confined to a wheelchair. But she came to every youth group meeting, usually with her next younger sibling, another girl. The youth group met in the parsonage basement activity room, so I had to struggle the handicapped girl down and up the stairs each week in her wheelchair.

On a snowy day outing to a park in Evergreen, the kids were enjoying short toboggan runs down an incline. The disabled girl wanted to try it. I thought I could hold her and make the run. I put her on the toboggan in front and sat behind her with my arms wrapped solidly around her. In her excitement she could not control her body, and as we went down-hill she stiffened out straight, shrieking gleefully. This reflex forced me backward and down so that I could no longer control the toboggan or see where we were going. No mishap! We did not do it again, but she was thrilled to have done something the other kids were doing.

When the church first started, congregants had a substantial interest in reaching out to the unchurched of the community. We organized the "Fishermen's Club" whose members made door-to-door calls inviting people to visit our Grange services. Over 250 calls were made with numerous folks coming to participate.

I quickly saw that economic, career, domestic, and child-rearing stresses within the congregation led to many cries for help. I learned something about counseling that I had not expected. As most of my counseling sessions were somewhat informal and even spontaneous, with one adult at a time, a pattern emerged. I would be told of all the ways in which a counselee's mate or teenaged child needed to change one or more behaviors. I was asked repeatedly to see the imagined perpetrator of the counselee's problems, and to ask him or her to change. A significant number of the people I was counseling did not want to change anything in their own lives or behavior. They wanted me to perform magic that would change a mate or child. Further, I learned that this yearning for such change was something most thought God could fulfill. No matter how many Progressive theological sermons I preached, many congregants, when in crisis, reverted to their childhood religious perceptions of a supernatural God who would miraculously change others upon request. Yet, I tried to support folks in their trials.

One of the early members of the congregation was a fellow named Bill

Haefele, who attended his first worship service in the Grange Hall on Easter Sunday in 1962 right after we had started. In addition to being very engaged in the life of the church, he became a close personal friend. He was the son of German immigrant parents who had settled in South Bend, IN. They were deeply involved in a German Evangelical and Reformed church there. He called me Herr Pfarrer. Because Jan and I had only one car, Bill would pick me up at the parsonage each Sunday morning, and then spend the next half hour setting up the Grange Hall for worship. He was the only usher, and during the service he would stand at the back to greet latecomers.

Bill's wife Pat was a faith-seeking Roman Catholic who attended our worship with increasing regularity over the years. They had two rambunctious boys who were in Church School virtually every Sunday. Later, they had a third son who was slightly developmentally disabled. Mental illness followed for Pat, and eventually she divorced Bill. During one of Pat's hospitalizations, I called on her. I was let into her locked room which had a tiny window in the door. When I finished visiting with her, I tried to leave the room, but the door was locked. After a while I started knocking on the door. An attendant whose shift had started after my arrival peeked through the small aperture and smiled condescendingly. It was an hour later, when they brought Pat's supper, that they realized I was trapped.

La Foret – A Spiritual Home

La Foret is an amazingly effective church camp and retreat center. Located in the woods of Black Forest, a large rural area and community just east of the U.S. Air Force Academy near Colorado Springs, it is a ministry of the Rocky Mountain Conference of the United Church of Christ.

I never will forget my first encounter with La Foret. It was on a gloriously beautiful Sunday in June of 1962. Riding southbound from Denver down the Valley Highway (I-25) for the first time, I was going to serve as a counselor in a Sr. High Youth Camp at La Foret.

As the week rapidly evaporated, there were the dining hall meal-time fellowship and singing, the softball games, the morning watch private prayer sessions, the intense personal discussions on life values and directions, the safe haven for sharing dreams and doubts, the pool, the odor of warm pine, the dry, clear air, and most of all, the worship in the historic chapel. I felt I was in an inviting place where many of the shreds of cultural pretense were peeled away so that both kids and counselors could see one another in the context of God's deeper claims on their lives. During that week I did not know what La Foret would come to mean in my ministry, but it was the beginning of a lifetime of engagement.

La Foret was originally the summer estate of Mrs. Alice Bemis Taylor, a descendant of the wealthy Judson Bemis, founder of the Bemis Bag Company of St. Louis, MO. Mrs. Taylor and her husband Frederick Morgan Pike Taylor became one of Colorado Springs' most important founding families. In December of 1943, the Bemis-Taylor Foundation deeded the estate to the Colorado Congregational Conference, predecessor of the Colorado Conference of the United Church of Christ.

It is such a serene, natural setting! Many lives are transformed there. Profound experiences of the Holy, and reflection on its meaning for one's deepest identity occur there night and day. Countless numbers of young men and women have been called to the sacred task of Jesus' ministry at La Foret.

La Foret has played a significant role in the lives of the Lapps throughout the decades. Our children have attended many summer camps and weekend retreats there. Jan and I have led summer camps there. We have spent time alone there in silent contemplation, listening for the Holy. It is a place that has fed our souls with hope.

March on Washington

In August of 1963, I flew from Denver to East Lansing, MI, to officiate at the Saturday wedding of a young couple who had been members of my Edgewood Peoples Church youth group. On the way there, I took a redeye to our nation's capital for the Peoples' March on Washington. In the days leading up to the March there were threats of violence, predictions of heavy police involvement, uncertainty about travel, and congestion in the streets. News reports declared King was not to be intimidated. I flew into Baltimore. On the plane were several others from Denver, mostly black community leaders. We and others from around the country took the same bus into Washington. The driver did his best to register his disapproval of the Peoples' March by continuously jamming on the air brakes and throwing us out of our seats. Though no one was injured, we got the driver's uncivilized message.

Shortly after daylight, our entourage walked to the square surrounding the Washington Monument. It was encircled by police and National Guardsmen standing shoulder to shoulder with rifles at the ready. I politely asked two of them if we could get past them to sit on the grass near the Monument. They nodded and let us through. The morning went like a church picnic, though, like me, most of the men wore suits, and the women were in party or church dresses. People with lunches shared with those like me who had come empty handed. People sang and talked as the throng grew. Contrary to the expectations of President Kennedy, virtually every one of us was committed to keeping the March peaceful. By the time we were lined up for the March there were over 100,000 people in and near the Washington Monument square. Others joined in from side streets as we walked. When we got to the Reflection Pool at the Lincoln Memorial, I was among 250,000 of my closest friends, the largest crowd, many of them black, ever to have gathered peaceably or otherwise in Washington.

King did not speak softly, nor seem the shy guy I had met in Chicago, as he eloquently outlined his dream for the America that could be. Echoes of "I HAVE A DREAM" still resonate in my soul. I was participating in a powerful expression of the authentic countercultural character of prophetic Christianity. I was inspired and moved beyond words. As I stood next to the reflection pool in front of the Lincoln Memorial, I was in absolute awe not only of the single-mindedness of a silent, focused group of 250,000 people, but also of the passion of Dr. King.

As soon as King finished, I rushed to Washington National Airport and caught a plane to East Lansing for the wedding I was to perform. The girl's father, an MSU professor, was not pleased that I had flown to Washington using part of the ticket he had purchased for my getting to the wedding. Racism creeps out most unexpectedly!

Building a "Church Center"

Trying to help the new congregation understand that a church is not a building, but rather a people of God in action, we started working on a "Church Center." We had to find a site and hire an architect. Because of a "comity agreement" among several mainline denominations in Colorado, we were assigned a geographic area within which we could locate our new Church Center. This comity area also defined the boundaries within which we could make calls and distribute literature from house to house. The problem was that the Methodists and Presbyterians, who had existing churches in Arvada, had selected their areas prior to the entry of the Congregationalists into this agreement.

Thus, most of the existing neighborhoods were spoken for. As a result, our boundaries on the northwest side of Arvada included almost as many head of feeder beef as people. A substantial portion of our comity area was undeveloped farmland outside the Arvada city limits.

There was a four-acre tract just south of the Grange Hall at 72nd Avenue and Simms, right across the street from the Grange Hall. Its owner, a faithful Roman Catholic, felt good about selling a portion of his little farm for a Christian church.

We selected a prominent Denver architect who had designed the major engineering school buildings on the University of Colorado's Boulder campus. Our building's roof line was reminiscent of the angular roofs he created for the engineering complex.

Sitting in the worship space, one is immediately aware that there is no way to see out of the sanctuary. I wanted people not to be able to look out at grazing cattle or passing traffic during worship. The symbolism was that of leaving the world to focus on spiritual renewal, then re-entering the daily round to make a difference.

At the outset of construction, the contractor laid out and poured the foundation 25 feet too close to 72nd Avenue. He asked me to go to the city to get a variance. I told him he would have to go as it was his mistake. I do not know if he ever went, but the building was not moved south. If 72nd Avenue was ever to be widened to four lanes, the north face of the building would be right at the edge of the roadway!

Because the site was nearly at the flood plain level of a small nearby creek, we needed a substantial amount of fill dirt for the parking area. One of the church members was a concrete flatwork contractor. He was willing to loan the church an older dump truck. An excavation contractor was installing a large water line a mile to the south. I noticed that many truckloads of dirt were being hauled off. I said to this contractor, "I'm the minister of a church just up Simms at 72nd. We are building our first worship center. We'd love to have some of your excavation dirt to fill our parking area which is presently too low. Could you fill our truck any time it showed up in the line of trucks next to the excavation?" He looked quite surprised but warmed to my query, primarily because it would reduce the number of truckloads he'd have to pay for. Several of our church men, but mostly I, hauled many loads of that wonderful fill dirt to the church site.

NEW CHURCH START

We had a dedication worship service for the completed building on a weeknight just before Thanksgiving in 1965. The sanctuary was a compelling place to gather. It truly felt like a quiet retreat from the world where one could reflect on his or her life and recommit to caring for others out there in the often-unfair world. A high school carpentry teacher member fashioned a Communion Table and matching pulpit. A wooden cross dominated the tall interior front brick wall.

Members and newcomers loved the new Church Center.

Skill sets for which I had no training were shaping my ability to make a difference in the Holy's human community.

Jan and I continued our ministerial leadership of the Arvada church for two years beyond the opening of the building.

Through the course of attracting a congregation of some 150 adults, leading worship in our new Church Center, leading Junior and Senior High Youth Groups, and doing lots of pastoral counseling, I served on the Board of the Congregational Conference of Colorado as it became the new Colorado Conference of the United Church of Christ.

For mission outreach, as the Center was dedicated, the church created a major service program assisting struggling, underprivileged Hispanic women at the Denver Inner City Parish. We also made our Center available to local community service groups.

In my five years as Minister of First United Church I had many fulfilling high moments in leading worship, in loving congregants, in mentoring kids, in developing community mission activities, in completing an innovative church building, and in being a partner in a delightful family.

Chapter 17

You Could Be Shot!

People in our church were generally supportive of my passion for social justice. Even though most were not ready to engage, they seemed quietly pleased. This was not entirely the case on March 14, 1965, the Sunday when I announced simply at the end of the worship service that within the hour, I would be leaving to join Martin Luther King, Jr. in Selma, AL. One of the church members literally muttered aloud "Martin Luther Coon." Another cried out ominously, "My God, Robb, you could be shot!"

However, there was one surprise. Earl Rau, the member who had cautioned me upon my start in Arvada not to speak on behalf of people of color, stood at the rear of the Grange worship room waiting until everyone else had left. He approached me, threw his arms around me, and shed more than a few tears. This was a miraculous transformation that had its initial roots in a seemingly unrelated event that had occurred when Stuart and I were staying at his home upon first arriving in Arvada. Earl's father suddenly died unexpectedly, and I was able to be a helpful pastoral presence through the funeral and subsequent days of grieving. My logical, affirmative preaching about the injustices of racism had not hurt, either.

In March of 1965, there was an ongoing intense ruckus in Selma, Alabama, around voting rights for people of color. More truly, it was about America's pernicious and persistent racism. In Selma, on Sunday March 7th, a mostly black group of 600 tried to cross the Edmund Pettus Bridge on the east side of town, on its way to Montgomery to demonstrate for the right to vote. By direction of George Wallace, the highest elected official of Alabama, State Troopers and local police ordered the marchers to turn around. When the protesters non-violently refused, the officers shot tear-gas, and beat the marchers with billy clubs. Over fifty people were hospitalized, including Student Nonviolent Coordinating Committee leader, the Rev. John Lewis, who, with the Rev. Hosea Williams, represented the Southern Christian Leadership Conference and led this first march from Selma.

Two days later, on Tuesday the 9th, in downtown Selma, Jim Reeb, a Unitarian minister from Boston, was beaten to death by three men who were never convicted. Dr. Martin Luther King, Jr., already a Nobel Peace Prize holder, immediately issued a passionate nationwide call for clergy to come to Selma.

I had to go! The Holy was speaking. For the rest of the week, I told no one in the church other than my wife what I was going to do.

All together there were sixteen other brave souls, black and white, men and women, with whom I rendezvoused in east Denver early that Sunday afternoon, the 14th, after several of us had led worship that morning in churches we served.

We drove 3 cars straight through to Selma, arriving mid-day on Tuesday. My car pulled a trailer loaded with food and clothing for besieged Selma black families. It was a very dicey drive, as the closer we got to Selma the more we were followed closely by police cars whose officers' rifles were visible. In one small town I was so busy watching a very close police car in my rearview mirror that I went through a red light. I was sure I was fried, but we were not even stopped. The officers apparently were glad to get us through their town without incident. My apprehension grew.

Our next sense of the trouble ahead in Selma mounted in a restaurant in Tennessee on Monday night. As the seventeen of us entered the main dining room, the other patrons, all white, got up, left their dinners, and stared at us through the lobby doorway. Eerily, we soon were the only diners left in this large room. After having ordered our meals, I noticed through a large window that there was a full string of cars, some of them with stars painted on their doors, circling past the window. Then I realized that the black minister sitting across from me, back to the window and next to a white woman, was not eating his dinner. When I looked caringly into his eyes, he said, almost whispering, "You're white, Robb, I could be shot in the back." I don't think any of us digested that meal. Following the Tennessee dinner, during which we were bombarded with several racist remarks, we continued our trek south.

The next morning as we approached the north edge of Selma, I was shocked to see in open fields over 250 state highway patrol cars, STATE patrol cars! It quickly became obvious that the officers were not there to protect us outsiders!

Upon our arrival at Brown Chapel, the protest headquarters, all seventeen of us were told we would be able to sleep at the home of a black woman in town, for whom having whites in her house was obviously a new experience. Floor was bed for most of us, and we were grateful. Her house felt like a haven in a climate of hate.

After choosing spaces on her floors, we went back to Brown Chapel for our assignments. Hosea Williams, King's chief field lieutenant, was speaking to a disparate group of ministers. To instill courage for that night's work, he was firing up the small crowd. He singled out a group of white ministers, among whom were three of us from Colorado. He told us, "You need to stay here at Brown Chapel as the center of to-night's action in all of Loundes County is right outside our front door. Your job will be to stand along the curb facing the armed police, keep-ing the entire crowd of protesters from stepping into the street. There will be about 100 of you. You may be here all night." Williams then told us, "The patrol commander has sent us word that anyone stepping or falling off the curb into the street will be shot."

We white ministers went out to the street in front of Brown Chapel. We talked among ourselves about how best to protect the milling crowd. One could not avoid the sight of the shoulder-to-shoulder row of city police and state patrolmen, all armed, some with rifles, facing us right across the city street. I had never seen anything like this, nor had I ever been the object of contempt of so many armed officers. I simply could not believe that public servants, especially those employed by a state of the United States of America, could get away with this kind of behavior. But there they were!

So, we lined up on the curb, locked arms, and faced the officers. Talk about holding one's breath while being bumped and jostled from be-hind! I shuddered at the look in the eyes of the officer who clearly had me in his gun's sight. I was nearly knocked into the street three differ-ent times. The cops were playing with us, tauntingly. That night I got a very ugly taste of what it means to be black in America.

That same night, no one, including King, knew whether or when another attempt to march to Montgomery would occur. While they continued to strategize, on both Wednesday and Thursday I traveled with a small racially integrated team into the back woods of Loundes County to go from dilapidated shack to dilapidated shack to encourage black adults to go with us to the Court House to attempt to register to vote. No one agreed to go with us to the Court House. Fear is a very strong driver!

On Wednesday night, four of us men and women agreed to hold a prayer meeting with some of the rural black Americans whom we had met that day. One of them led us to a tar paper shack deep in the woods where others were already waiting. It was a flimsy dark structure. We could barely see one another even though several people had brought candles or flashlights. One could see out through cracks where the tar paper had separated. It grew very dark outside. I suggested we start by going around the room to share stories of our life commitments and struggles with racism. The words from both visitors and residents were candid, heartfelt, and very moving. This sharing united us in human togetherness as God's children facing a common evil. Suddenly, through one of the cracks of this highly flammable structure we could see a torch moving past. Then another, and another, until we were being encircled, I am certain, with the intent of setting the shack on fire, so as to either burn us all to death or to frighten us into exiting so we could be beaten. We briefly talked about what we should do. Rather than run out in panic, I urged the group to sit quietly, not flinching, sharing prayers for our pursuers. We kept talking and praying until these racist mobsters slunk home. Whew!

Something else happened later that night. As we got back to the house where we were staying, we seventeen shared stories of our various activities of the day as we sat on the floor in the cramped living room. I grew cold. So, I excused myself and went out to my car for a sweater.

As I started to open the rear door, I noticed a car, its motor running, sitting under a street-light up at the corner, about three doors away. I could see three or four white men in it, and they all were watching me. Then I saw the glint of a rifle barrel as it was being leveled toward me. As I flipped over the hedge in front of the house, I heard a gunshot, as a bullet hit the tree right behind where I had just been standing. Back in the house, I could not speak. I was beginning to understand the cruelty of the racism that was, and still is, deeply rooted in the American culture, nationally, not just in the South. Such a helpless feeling! But I was still alive.

With most of the Colorado crew needing to be home to lead worship on Sunday morning, we reluctantly left Selma late afternoon on Friday. I got back to Arvada well after dark on Saturday night after a harrowing week and had to lead worship the next morning without preparing a sermon or bulletin! So, my sermon became an extemporaneous recitation of my experience. The people of the church, not quite knowing how to express their emotions, held a food shower for the Lapps. Following the service, I learned that King had just successfully led a very large group across the Pettus bridge and was heading to Montgomery. Risking our lives, folks from around the country had made the difference.

Then, as though nothing out of the ordinary had happened, next day I went with the church architect to a construction supply yard to select bricks for the new Church Center.

As the Civil Rights Movement came into full bloom, one of the activist threads with which Dr. King had to cope was the rise of the Black Power movement, some of whose leaders called for and espoused community violence as the only possible means of arriving at a just resolution of America's racial crisis. While Dr. King strongly counseled that only peaceable demonstrations and interracial dialogue would work, riots developed in many American cities, and many understandably fed-up blacks, as well as resistant whites, armed themselves for confrontations.

When King was assassinated in 1968 in Memphis, I felt the deep shock of a Christian who suddenly is reminded again of the theological paradox of how the collective sins of some people become a societal evil in a world in which the Holy loves all people. King was driven by the same call as that Man from Nazareth who had lost his life confronting societal illnesses.

Without realizing it at the time, this traumatic Selma adventure was the beginning of the end of my days as a local church minister. It was not that I was criticized for demonstrating against racism, though there was some of that. It was more that I had a growing conviction that the Holy was calling me to work on society's transformation of its racist structures.

In reflecting on these harrowing Selma experiences, I have come to realize that I gained a deeply important perspective on my existence as a human being. In seminary I had learned of the Judeo-Christian insight that as God's beloved beings, we are nevertheless finite creatures whose lives are terminal. This means that one's existence in the present life on earth will end with death, a very, very profound existential realization, no matter what one thinks of an afterlife. In Selma, for the first meaningful time, I came face to face with the possibility of my own death. That I was at peace with this allowed me to be fully committed to risking my life in doing justice and loving mercy. I am not afraid to die.

I can think of no contemporary individual who has embodied the wisdom and courage it takes to be an accountable member of the human family more than did Martin Luther King, Jr. My several encounters with King have been a source of strength, both in helping me choose my battles and in giving me the endurance to stay the course. To be willing to pay the ultimate price on behalf of the whole human community is the essence of understanding, and committing to, the meaning of the life of the "man from Nazareth." The Holy was speaking to me through Dr. King.

A thread of what was to come next for the Lapps began with our participation in the Jefferson County Human Relations Council. This was a group of volunteers, mostly church people, who sought activist ways to improve white, black, and Hispanic relations in the western suburbs of Denver. The Council later evolved into the Jefferson Action Center, concerned primarily with poverty and service to marginalized people. But in the 60's the issue was discrimination in housing and "red-lining" by lenders and realtors. One of the participants, Pat Schroeder, went on to become a long-serving and effective member of the U.S. Congress.

My involvement with the Council, along with notoriety that had come from my Selma adventure, led to the next chapter of our intense lives.

Chapter 18

~~

THE HOLY DOES NOT
EMBRACE RACIAL INJUSTICE

Metro Denver Fair Housing Center, Inc.

I WENT TO seminary to become a minister. Ministers work in churches. However, I heard the Holy whispering other visions for my ministry. The living pre-Easter Jesus, a revolutionary in the streets, was becoming my model for responding to God's call. Being a Christian, as well as a minster, is a life of seeking to be a co-creator with God in the building of just communities, apart from which functional societal relationships cannot work. Much of God's work goes on outside the church. So, following creation of the First United Church of Arvada, I found myself ministering "in the street."

Not soliciting it, during Lent in 1967 I was asked to become organizing Executive Director of the Metro Denver Fair Housing Center, Inc. ("MDFHC"). MDFHC was an incorporated non-profit creation of the Denver Religious Council on Human Relations. Having been formed by metro area church leaders and citizens of good will, the Fair Housing Center had very little money and one clerical person. But with my years of commitment to racial justice, dating back to my college fraternity, I accepted the invitation to become Executive Director.

Jan and I immediately began a search for a house in Park Hill, a Denver neighborhood in which many black families were living, particularly north of 26th Avenue. We knew that living south of 26th would not make nearly the statement it should. The press took note when the new MDFHC Director bought a house surrounded by black families. It was the first house we ever owned, having lived in church parsonages theretofore.

On my final Sunday in Arvada, following worship, Jan and I were celebrated and wished well. As a going away gift the congregation held a community open house and initiated a student scholarship fund named for us.

A *Denver Post* article about my leaving the Arvada church said, "Lapp has become a familiar voice in the community. In addition to frequently voiced concern for city government, he served as chairman of the Arvada Ministerial Association during 1966. He is presently chairman of the Jefferson County Human Relations Council, and chairman of the Housing Committee of the Denver Congress of Racial Equality."

There were a couple of church members who clearly thought it was time for us to leave because I had not gotten their mates to love them more. However, Jan and I felt blessed and supported by most of the folks we were leaving behind.

The transition from church to street ministry took less than 24 hours. Before dark that same Sunday, I was on a plane to St. Louis, MO to see the very recently burned-out Pruitt-Igoe high-rise Federally subsidized apartment building. It had become a decrepit warehouse inhabited exclusively by poor black residents, causing substantial community unrest. The city evicted remaining residents and dynamited, then burned, the structures. I learned first-hand of the disaster that can occur as poverty-stricken people of color are forced to live in untenable segregated inner-city housing.

As I boarded my return flight, while feeling that I was doing the right thing, I realized that I had jumped from a church parish ministry role into perhaps the most radically controversial community change role the Holy hope for humanity could have called me!

None of the following courses were offered by my seminary: Institutional Management and Staff Development, Working with a Volunteer Board, Hiring and Firing, Transforming Systemic Racism, Foundation and Government Fund Raising, Speaking to the Press, Financial Management, or How to Avoid Being Shot. Turned out, I needed all these skills along with an intuitive confidence that the Holy would sustain me through the toughest of days.

At the outset, the work of the Center was seen by its Board to be that of working with black families who were financially able and willing to be pioneers in risking their social survival in becoming functional members of white majority neighborhoods. The acronym, NIMBY (Not in My Backyard), symbolized the white community mentality which the Center was created to overcome. The Center saw a strong need to confront brokers of the region's Boards of Realtors who often found ways to dissuade black home buyers from even viewing available properties. For support in persuading brokers to do what is right, a close link with the Colorado Civil Rights Commission had to be established. Under the leadership of James Reynolds, a fearless black leader, the Commission was becoming a major force in the state's fight against racism.

Energy for this open housing movement in Denver centered in the Park Hill neighborhood east of Colorado Blvd, a white community into which blacks were moving. People of good will in Park Hill wanted to be open to integration, but they did not want black in-migration to result in white flight and a depreciation of their property values. At its best, this commitment to integration resulted in cooperative open housing. At its worst, it was taken by African Americans to be just another incarnation of white supremacy. 26th Avenue became an invisible line in Park Hill, north of which the area was expected to become majority black, and south of which there would be symbolic racial mixing. One of the underlying reasons for drawing this imaginary line, which few admitted, was that housing north of 26th generally was modest in size and cost, while south of 26th houses were larger and more expensive. Economic differences between people of color and whites were not often acknowledged or faced.

Naively, through a failure of a predominantly white board to understand both the economic and psychological impacts of being black in a white culture, the initial mission of the Center had been to encourage and assist black middle and upper-middle class African Americans to move into scattered white neighborhoods throughout the metropolis.

Very little thought was being given to the larger problem of societal economic discrimination against blacks which gave rise to economically marginalized ghettos. As MDFHC was beginning its work, there was substantial racial societal unrest in Denver, though we were not having the big race riots seen in other metropolitan areas. However, in Denver, anger-generated hostility and distrust was the theme among blacks, while fear-generated self-righteousness was stock in trade for many whites. Issues within and about Hispanic sub-communities had not yet risen to similar boiling points.

The Denver black culture was focused in an area just northeast of downtown Denver known as Five Points, spreading to the east for several miles into the north part of Park Hill. Life for blacks in this section of town was not all bad. Black families felt safer in black neighborhoods, engaging in mutually supporting one another. However, among other disadvantages, neighborhood public schools which were majority black generally did not provide quality educations, and the drop-out rates were significantly higher than in schools in predominantly white communities. Economically, many African Americans were not faring as well as their white brothers and sisters in metro Denver. And the crime rate was visibly higher than elsewhere in Denver.

Fundamentally, the call for racially integrated housing in metro Denver was part of the larger issue of the need for equality in income, education, public assistance, and participation in governance.

My initial work as Executive Director was to raise funds, to grow a functional staff, and to make the Fair Housing Center a catalyst for integrating neighborhoods throughout metro Denver. Dick Young, an attorney, and white Park Hill resident, became President of the Fair Housing Center. With his support we landed a three-year Ford Foundation grant.

Dick was an insightful and tireless proponent of open housing for the entire metropolitan community, not just the Park Hill area. But at the outset, open housing was essentially limited to middle and upper-middle black families.

In the Center's early days, seeing their mission as being centered on freedom of choice for African American families, early board members totally ignored the housing and social woes of the Hispanic community, an even larger group in Denver than the black populace.

When we started, there existed, sub-rosa, extensive resistance within the real estate brokerage industry, and lots of redlining. In addition to working with black families who wanted to purchase homes in other than northeast Denver, our staff did extensive "shopping" of for-sale housing. White couples would contact brokers and ask to be shown selected houses that were for sale. Then a black couple would do the same. In every instance in which our "shoppers" got opposite responses about homes, we went to the Colorado Civil Rights Commission with complaints that ended up exposing discrimination on the parts of agents or home sellers. In doing this, we opened the way for black families to move to southeast and southwest Denver, as well as to the outlying suburbs of Littleton, Englewood, Arvada, Golden, and Aurora.

Mission of Center Transformed by Reality

It took less than six months for the Center to learn that moving into white neighborhoods was not a top agenda priority for most black Denver families. While the initial small staff team, through publicity and advertising, was able to attract several progressive, self-confident middle-class black households as they walked through the often-negative realtor and financing maze to purchase homes in non-traditional areas, we soon realized that the largest housing issues facing black families were economic. Not being able to afford anything better, many folks were living in substandard, even unsafe, houses and apartments.

Others, if they did wish to move, could not afford even modest units in scattered white neighborhoods.

This gave rise to our focus on housing rehabilitation and on construction of affordable apartments. The first senior associate I hired was Shedrick Devers, a black real estate broker. He took the lead in forming the Housing Development Division and became its Director. Over time, the Center's Housing Development Division purchased several hundred vacant, vandalized homes, rebuilt them, then sold them to minority families under HUD's Section 202 (h) very-low-interest program. We also teamed up with Archbishop John Casey of the Catholic Archdiocese of Denver to build 300 new apartments in clusters of around 60 each in dispersed locations of the metro area using HUD 221(d)(3) financing. The Archdiocese provided seed money and we did the development, construction, and management of the apartments. It was a good working relationship, and we never had any serious opposition to locating small groups of these units in basically white neighborhoods.

I accompanied Shed Devers on many searches for vacant and vandalized houses. One day, upon opening an unlocked front door and starting to step into the darkened hallway, I plunged feet first into the basement. The house had been gutted by vandals and there was no first floor inside the entrance. No injuries. Shed and I laughed as we returned to the office.

As Shed and his team got going with housing rehab and new development, I began to see that the human services and political action dimensions of our work needed more attention and senior leadership. A quick nationwide search led to the hiring of David Herlinger, a housing activist and community organizer from Pittsburgh. Dave moved with his young family into Park Hill. The thrust of his emerging Community Services Division was, on the one hand, to assist individual families find decent affordable housing, and, on the other, to mentor the adoption of statewide legislation that would improve housing justice and racial integration, often as a means of reinforcing quality public school educational opportunities for all.

The terms of our first Ford Foundation grant were broad enough to cover staff members both for assisting middle-income integrative moves, and for helping black families move out of substandard, unsafe housing in their still segregated neighborhoods. We made enough difference in the community that we were able to land additional Ford Foundation grants over time. But for the specialized work of the Housing Development Division, we were awarded a Model Cities renewable grant from the U.S. Office of Economic Opportunity ("OEO"), whose Director, Sergeant Shriver, later visited our Center. Over time we also received funding from the City and County of Denver as well as from other governments in the metro area.

As in other major American cities, in Denver there were cadres of African Americans whose anger over both blatant and subtle racism justified their violence in pursuit of change. The emerging Black Power movement was fed by generations of black suffering at the hands of the white power structure, and by a sense that change was not occurring quickly enough.

Violence simmered and frequently boiled in northeast Denver. In Park Hill, it usually took the form of fire-bombs. Over and over, especially on hot summer nights, Jan and I would hear the sirens of fire trucks responding to Molotov cocktail-caused house fires in the neighborhood. Thinking about the pain involved for participants, I often could not go back to sleep after a fire truck roared by. And there were frustration-motivated shootings throughout Five Points.

It soon became obvious to me that increasing justice in housing would not resolve America's systemic racism. But our work was a vital step in the right direction.

During this community racial tension Jan and I were serving as Directors of the week-long Conference Family Camp at La Foret in 1969. I had asked The Rev. Reuben Sheares, a member of the national staff of the United Church of Christ, and his family, which included three young children, to spend the week as our Program Resource team. It is important for two reasons to know that the Sheares were of African ancestry. First, the campers all were white, and I wanted them to experience intimately the leadership of an African American family. But, as a coincidence, this Family Camp was held the same week that I was under intense fire from a divided Metro Denver Fair Housing Center Board in Denver. Each day I had to drive the 75-mile trip to Denver to respond to press, staff, and Board members. At night, after I returned to La Foret, through Rev. Sheares, the Holy whispered to me to stay the course, difficult as it was. My soul survived the next two years as director of this controversial civil rights program.

We were able to secure enough grant and government funding that after three years we had fifty employees and occupied the entirety of a small office building in east Denver. Our operation was one of the largest and most focused open housing efforts in the whole country.

We worked hard to develop a positive relationship with the Denver Board of Realtors. A senior broker from one of Denver's largest real estate firms became a long-term member of the Center's Board.

After our first two years we had continued to experience resistance from the real estate establishment. One of its hostile false charges was that we were working as unlicensed real estate agents. Wanting to defuse this argument, I hired a well-known real estate licensing teacher and had all Center employees, except for our moving-truck drivers, take an extensive

Colorado Real Estate Commission course after-hours at night. We then scheduled everyone for the state brokerage licensing test. There were almost 50 of us in the testing room, along with other license seekers. Some of the broker hoorah quieted down after every one of our staff members passed the test. But I had to announce that no Center employee would act as agent in a home sale. We insisted on members of the real estate industry getting their commissions as usual. This sequence worked. Brokers and agents increasingly respected our work.

In my work on the streets, I learned the power of a clipboard. I discovered that if I carried a clipboard and ballpoint pen as I trespassed to look at a possible redevelopment property, witnesses thought I was a city official. I was never confronted by a neighbor, owner, or police officer. This methodology also worked when I accompanied a minority family in a housing search. Sellers' brokers and agents usually assumed I was from the Civil Rights Commission and refrained from discriminating in the showing of properties.

The *Denver Post* published a long article in the January 1969 Sunday Perspective Section about dispelling negative myths regarding the Center. It described the history of the center as well as the work we were doing to provide both decent and integrated housing especially for modest income black families. The article concluded with the words, "This could lead to a generation which would have greater experience in integrated living."

Perhaps the most significant legislative contribution made by the Fair Housing Center was its leadership in lobbying the State Legislature to form the Colorado Housing Finance Authority (known later as CHFA). The mission of this body was that of providing financing for affordable housing throughout Colorado. Dave Herlinger eventually became Director of the Colorado Housing Finance Authority, a post he held until his retirement.

Several young MDFHC staff idealists who became involved in community change efforts went on to play community leadership roles. One became President of the Denver Board of Realtors. Another served as a renowned City Councilman as well as a member of the Denver School Board. A third became Director of the Colorado State Division of Housing. Another became head of the housing department of the City of Jacksonville in Florida.

People in other cities in Colorado, like Pueblo, Colorado Springs, Grand Junction and Fort Collins, began to take note of what we were doing in metro Denver. They kept asking us if we had come help them with their racial housing issues. As a result, MDFHC formed a separate non-profit named Colorado Housing, Inc. Though it was harder to get public funding, Colorado Housing, Inc. was able to hire an executive director and a small staff to work in these outlying cities.

Jane Who?

One of the most amusing moments of my entire tenure at the Center came after we were well known throughout the community.

By way of background, MDFHC had several large flatbed trucks that I had been able to get from the U.S. Government Service Administration surplus pool. We used them for assisting lower income families in their moves from substandard to better housing. We had the trucks painted the same forest green we used in all our signs and promotional materials. The Fair Housing Center name and equal-sign logo was emblazoned on the doors of each cab. We also procured a bus through the same government surplus disposal procedure. It, too, was painted green, with name and logo writ large on each side. We used the bus to take groups of ghetto residents through non-traditional neighborhoods for looks at options. I took a public beating from several housing developers over this strategy.

On the afternoon of this humorous event, I was sitting at my desk when I received a call from the Governor's office. The chief of staff was mightily excited. He exploded, "Do you know that Jane Fonda is on the back of one of your trucks in front of a peace rally being held on the lawn of the State Capital building?" Even over the phone I could hear the speaker system booming her antiwar presentation for all the world to hear. Suddenly endowed with extra fast thinking, I asked, "Are you able to tell where the power is coming from for that acoustical system. "Well, let's see...oh, there's a long extension cord coming into the Capital," he responded. Realizing we both had similar problems, I said, "I won't call the police if you don't." "Okay," he said.

A Housing Services Division staffer, Rev. Dick Peterson, a social activist by nature, and later a leader in the Board of Realtors, had arranged for the use of our flatbed as a speaker's stand for this peace rally. As soon as we could extricate our truck, we did, but not before the local media had taken many shots of Ms. Fonda on the truck bed in her anti-war protest. Of course, the Center received extra publicity as images of our name and logo were on most evening news stations. Before I went home that day, I received a very nice call from Jane Fonda thanking me for use of the Center's truck. We talked of her anti-war protest leadership, which I told her I strongly supported.

Fired!

After pouring my heart, soul, and body into one of the more effective fair housing efforts in the nation, I was fired by the Fair Housing Center's Board in April of 1971! Because this event was so painful, requiring such spiritual strength to stay the course, I share here details of the termination.

The termination sequence began five months earlier, when I fired a black employee.

In our community service work, we had offices in several strategic neighborhood offices to which people came for help with their housing issues. This neighborhood service program was part of Dave Herlinger's responsibility as Director of the Community Services Division. Our office in the heart of the Five Points neighborhood of northeast Denver was headed by a fiery young black man named Charles. He was an outgoing guy who worked as hard at self-promotion as he did at assisting clients. Though I did not know it at the time, Charles was one of the really outspoken leaders of the Black Power Movement that was sweeping the country and emerging in Denver.

One day in December, as the holidays approached, I stopped by Charles' office to check in and to show interest in his work. I quickly noticed a loaded Uzi hung on the wall behind his desk chair. The Center had a no-guns policy. I asked him to tell me about the Uzi and why he had it in his office. He smiled and said, "I need to protect people here in Five Points." He then took it down and pointed it at me.

I recoiled. "See," he said, "I can get you to do what I want."

I took a deep breath then told Charles to remove the gun from the premises. He said, "No one can tell me I don't have a right to carry a firearm." Without thinking through a strategy for dealing with this complex cultural issue, I simply fired him on the spot, even though I was not his direct supervisor. Next day, Dave Herlinger, Charles' supervisor, was displeased. He thought Charles was an effective housing worker and defended him for protecting himself in a tough neighborhood.

My impulsive act of termination festered for several months, mostly with rumors generated by Charles. Gradually there was an increasing notion in both the black and white communities that I was a racist. Looking back, I did not yet quite understand the deep meaning of white privilege in our systemically racist society.

Almost immediately, Charles and fellow Denver Black Power activists started circulating the word that I was a White Racist. I began getting calls from Board members and community supporters of the Center. This background noise kept rumbling until the night I was fired. It was a terribly uncomfortable time for our entire family. We did not feel safe even in our home.

On the first Sunday in February 1971, I walked the block from our house to Park Hill Congregational UCC, a significantly racially integrated church, for morning worship. Jan and the kids had been afraid to join me. I sat by myself toward the rear of the sanctuary.

About halfway through the service, just as our minister started his sermon, there was a very noisy ruckus in the entry area behind the sanctuary. As I turned to see what was going on, the first of a large group of black adults burst into the sanctuary in a demonstration parade that went up the side aisle where I was sitting, then across the front by the pulpit and worship center, and back to the rear going down the other side aisle. Many carried large placards high above their heads. I was the target. They started around the sanctuary a second time. There were over 90 demonstrators. It had been organized by supporters of Charles. I had never seen anything remotely like this in a Christian church. Neither had the Minister.

I immediately knew what was going on. I jumped up and ran out to the front sidewalk in hopes of drawing the group out of the sanctuary. As the protestors followed and gathered around me, shouting, and waving their fists, a Denver Police car screamed around the corner and stopped right in front of the church. It was followed by at least six other patrol cars whose officers jumped out, some with hands on their guns. They immediately started telling the crowd to disburse. I worried that this demand could lead to a street riot.

I signaled the officer who appeared to be in charge. He pushed through the crowd and stood in front of me. I said to him, "This is about me because I fired one of them from a civil rights community service job. To keep this event peaceful, all of you fellows should disappear. I will try to talk this through with them."

Reluctantly, the cops all went to their cars and drove off.

For the next 45 minutes I listened to charges of White Racism and descriptions of all the horrid things that would happen in Denver if I did not rehire Charles. "We're tired of being pushed around, and we're not going to put up with it any longer." At the end, I smiled and said, "You've given me lots to think about. Thank you."

Gradually, they began to drift off, but I had singlehandedly averted a street riot. As they left, I walked around the block toward our house. I was astounded to see there all the police cars with officers sitting in them. I told the lead officer that I had successfully gotten the crowd to disburse. So, they all left too.

Jan was totally frantic when I walked in. She cried tears of relief and asked, "Where have you been. Church was over an hour ago, and seven police cars have been right here on our corner. Are you okay?"

Sometime after I told her what had happened, she said, "You missed the news that Apollo 14 is circling the moon and will land soon." That news took my mind off the morning drama for at least 30 seconds.

Even though the Holy was telling me I was doing the right things, I felt very uncertain, but stayed the course.

The Board was No Help

As often occurs when action begins to be taken to overcome a societal injustice, both proponents and defendants become much more vigorous and outspoken. The emerging civil rights movement of the 1960's gave rise to whites snidely declaring that injustices were being overstated, while blacks were rioting in the streets because nothing was truly changing.

In very a subtle way, this polarization was affecting the Fair Housing Center Board. Committed whites wanted to show black colleagues how unbiased they were, while black members realistically saw the whites as the power elites. This reality led to white board members pleasing black members by agreeing that I was a white racist.

Into early March I had hoped the Board members would face the stressful impacts of the larger racial inequities in order to keep the operation going. But at the March board meeting it was becoming quite clear that the Board would give in to community pressures to end the conflict by terminating me. The net result was that getting rid of me was easier for the Board to do than to deal with the larger cultural issues.

Prior to the end of the year 1970 I hired a government management consultant who knew Denver politics quite well to evaluate our situation and work to bring functional resolution. He was very supportive and tried to bring peace, but by the March board meeting he concluded that I should be prepared for termination in the near future. He had done all he could.

Those early months of 1971 were awful for Jan and me. Essentially, through unconditional loving, we kept each other going. Jesus never said it would be easy.

April Board Meeting

Prior to the April Board meeting the *Denver Post* announced that my future would be decided that night.

Just before that last meeting, my consultant met with me one more time to help me prepare for my termination. He said, "You know, Robb, immanent hanging clears the mind. Stay calm and stay the course. You are not a White Racist."

On the night of the meeting, when I arrived at the Center's main office building there were crowds of people outside. Most were black. As I walked pensively into through the main door, I saw that the lobby and the hallways also were crowded. I quickly correctly guessed that Charles and fellow Black Power advocates had organized this show of force. I was relieved that I saw no Uzi's. Heading toward the large conference room, I had to navigate through the crowded hallway, heading for the board meeting. As we jostled along, a young man dropped a pistol. Feeling like I was still in control of my own behavior, I picked up the gun and handed it to its apparent owner, asking, "Oh, did you drop this?" He took it and thanked me.

When I got into the board room, most of the board members were already seated. Shed Devers also sat at the table. The room became packed, standing room only. It was clear that the Chair would proceed with all the standing visitors present. When the young man to whom I had handed the gun realized I was his target, he looked at me with awe! As the meeting progressed, I saw other pistols.

When the meeting started, the Chair said, "We all know why we're here this evening. Robb, do you have anything to say before we proceed?"

My first words were, "Immanent hanging clears the mind. With a clear mind, I have some advice for the future work of the Center." Then I set forth a statement of things needed to keep the Center on course.

There was little discussion among the Board members before I was told I was finished and could leave the meeting.

I went to my office, cleaned out my desk, took a deep breath, shed a few tears, and went home.

After I left the room Shed Devers was asked to assume the leadership role.

Later, at about midnight, our home phone rang. It was Denver Archbishop Casey, who had been a strong supporter of the Center's work, wanting to assure himself that I was okay and that my soul was intact.

After this firing, the Center was no longer the same. It was no comfort that once I was gone the new staff leadership of the Center soon lost most national and local funding and shuttered the operation.

Reflection

By way of analyzing what had happened, because of my absolute commitment to the equality of all people in the Creator's eyes, there were two underlying societal truths that I did not totally grasp.

The first societal reality I had not recognized was that I was blinded by my philosophical commitment to the truth that all people are equal.

I did not see that the negative educational, economic, and cultural African American experience in America, and in Denver, put African Americans at a fundamental disadvantage, and thus not able to compete with whites. In my commitment to racial justice, I thought blacks were free to exercise their human rights. All they had to do was exercise those rights.

In my commitment to peaceful solutions to societally unjust realities, I saw Charles' Black Power demonstrations as both illegal and immoral. I simply did not recognize that societally things were so bad for Black Americans they felt a legitimate need to take to the streets, even with guns.

As Director of the Center, I expected all our employees to be honest, to come to work, to do their assigned jobs, to be committed to the principle of open housing for all, to live within the rules we jointly developed, to work within the parameters of group decisions we made about strategy, and to behave honestly and ethically. I failed to cut anyone any slack because of race or gender.

The second societal reality was that I was not fully aware of the power of white privilege in America. Just being white makes one a racist. I did not yet understand America's systemic racism. No matter how devoted to human equality a white person may be, she or he is subject to racial mistrust. I was the privileged White Man in Charge.

What I did not see was that a white liberal does not fully understand what it means to be black. Despite all the personal risks I had taken, and all the honorable achievements the Center had made, because I am a descendant of northern Europe, I am part of the discriminating, oppressive majority. I just missed it.

A better way to have handled this would have been to assemble a racially mixed group of fellow workers to sit down and talk through the dynamics of what was occurring. This group process could have led to a peaceful determination of consequences, including possible termination, for Charles, but then his humanity would have been treated with respect. But I was not wise enough to do this.

In final analysis, what good did the Fair Housing Center do? In Denver, by the turn of the 21st Century, freedom of choice in neighborhood location for all people was a reality for those who could afford it. Nevertheless, because white racism and economic forces still limit freedom of choice today, many minority folks continue to be more comfortable living among persons of similar racial and ethnic backgrounds. In its brief life, the Center was one of the major forces in creating a foundation for the residential diversity the Denver community knows today. In retrospect, I am comfortable that I had to pay a personal price for walking with Jesus.

A White Family's Life in a Predominantly Black Neighborhood

As a family, while we were doing what was right from a social justice perspective, there were many days and hours that we did not fit into the mainstream culture. Life was challenging for all of us. It would be fair to say that particularly Jan and our children arose each day with very insecure emotions in their guts.

The ones in our family who paid the greatest personal social price were our three children. On a Friday afternoon, they left a suburban school in Arvada. On Monday morning, they went to Hallett Elementary, a 95% black school in northeast Denver. Naively believing that all people could just naturally get along with one another, we had not properly prepared them for being in the racial minority. In various ways, they each experienced social out-casting as they struggled to make new friends. I must tip my hat to each of them for keeping her or his equilibrium and cool in a difficult situation!

Jan also faced an unfamiliar environment when we moved to Locust Street. Her first assignment was as a mom whose three kids went from racial majority to minority over a weekend. There was lots of stress for her as our children coped with the social changes accompanying our move. Before long she was a respected participant in the mostly black neighborhood elementary school PTA.

When Robyn and Stuart got to middle school in Park Hill, ironically, they were bussed many miles south to predominantly white Hampden Middle School. Eventually, they were subjected to so much bullying on the bus, particularly on the way home, that Jan picked them up every day. In my role as director of a civil rights effort that saw racially and economically integrated housing communities as its main goal, I found a certain hollowness in the Denver School System's bussing effort. Integration in the classroom did not sufficiently address any of the fundamental problems of segregated housing, or of racism in America. But it was a genuine effort to improve the quality of education for black kids.

Jan was amused by what happened one day when it was rumored there would be a race riot at our older kids' predominantly white Hampden Middle School. Robyn went to class because she did not want to miss the excitement. Stuart and a black friend were apprehensive, so they stayed home that day and shot baskets in the friend's driveway. As it turned out, nothing of note happened. But mothering during those years was more than a full-time job.

What was it like to be white family members living in a predominantly black neighborhood? Bottom line, it really did not seem much different than in other places we had lived. As it can be for anyone living anywhere, we had some wonderful neighbors and some who ignored or avoided us. Though it was modest like the rest of the houses in our block and in the blocks to the north, we were living in a sturdy brick one-story that was quite accommodating for a family of five. Conversely, the homes on Monaco Parkway, the street right behind our house, were generally grander, much larger houses. Some of them were owned and occupied by well-known black sports figures. The people who lived on either side of us and in the house immediately across the rear alley from us were very nice to us, caring about how we were doing without ever mentioning race.

In the bigger picture, however, living in a racially mixed community was a continual walking on very uncertain ground. In short, we could not tell whether blacks trusted us white folks, or not. This also was true in our exchanges with whites, who, deep-down, did not want to be faced with issues of their own subliminal racism.

It is hard to overstate the overwhelming sense of hurt and failure that beset me following my termination as Director of the Fair Housing Center. For months, not a waking moment went by without introspection. What had I done wrong? How could I support my family? Why had people I trusted and admired turned on me? Why had I lost the support of the Board? It was all so personal. These swirling feelings clouded my thinking about the form my ministry would take next. I did not yet see the larger picture of institutional and cultural racism as having anything to do with my dilemma.

However, throughout this entire very difficult and unpopular assignment, I found that the harder one works for equal opportunity social justice the more one is spiritually energized. A mysterious life force fires one's courage. I was called to stay the course. I was not going to give up!

Jan was a huge influence in my nontraditional ministry. I absolutely could not have made it, had I not been married to a woman who, even though she thought she was marrying a parish minister, learned to heal my wounds and inspire my courage. Though our relationship could not be described as classically patriarchal, our early family roles were typical of the times. Even though we saw ourselves in a family joint venture in which we each had mutual voice, Jan's early role clearly was that of "chief cook and bottle washer." My early family caregiving was that of sharing in joint family decisions, and in providing the where-withal for family economic survival.

For Jan, early marriage was a collage of babies, summer youth work trips, parsonage life, homemaking, and service as "the minister's wife." By the time we were living in Park Hill and experiencing the dramas of a life in civil rights, Jan could begin to come up for air. The kids were in school. She did not have parishioners to worry about. I was deeply engrossed in creating and managing a civil rights operation in whose details she was not involved, but to whose mission she was to-tally committed.

To get her soul out of the fret mode while I faced daily mayhem, she became part-time secretary at Park Hill Congregational Church, of which we were members. Though she knew little about electric type-writers and copy machines, she was great on the phone because she is a warm and caring person. She also was able to support a newly arrived minister both because she knew all the people, and because she knew first-hand what ministers should be doing.

By this time, I had come to realize that Jan is neither a person of many words nor one who overanalyzes the dynamics and possible effects of events that occur in her life. With a grace seldom seen, Jan solemnly adjusted to those life happenings over which she had no control. Her boat just did not rock easily.

Perhaps it is that she's a New England native. Perhaps it is that she grew up in a strict home. Perhaps it is in her genes. Jan's personality style is very "proper," even rigid. She has a comprehensive built-in list of the right and wrong ways to do things. She is sensitive about the way people see her. She has very high standards for herself and her family. An amazing characteristic is that she lives out those standards, apparently without stress. She has gone a whole lifetime on two glasses of wine. She has never tried a cigarette. She has been maritally faithful, as have I. Our house has always been picked up and is tastefully appointed with ever changing objects d'art. As a successful "straight-arrow," she expects similar behavior from all of humanity.

She has boundless compassion. She is upset when people are wounded by others or by circumstance. She expects everybody to be fair in all their actions and is personally offended by miscreants she reads about in the paper or hears about on the news.

So, she was taken aback when I was fired after four dramatic years. She could not believe that I was called a racist on the front page of the *Denver Post*. But Jan spent little time fretting over the illogical injustice of the condemning act of an ethnically diverse board. Her main issue was the future of the family.

Chapter 19

~~~

LIFE IS TOUGH WITHOUT
AN INCOME!

AFTER I WAS fired, I needed another job. Quickly! Because I had "left the ministry" in taking on the fair housing challenge, my parish ministerial colleagues viewed me as having abandoned my ordination. Since my work had been notorious and controversial, I was even asked to forfeit my standing as an ordained UCC minister. Apparently, there were church folk who were opposed to racial equality and integration. I flat could not get an interview for service as a pastor in any available church in Colorado or the West. My dossier was returned from a campus church in Montana, without even being considered.

Also, because I had been publicly critical of a then US Senator from Colorado, Gordon Allott, on the issue of open housing, I was quietly quashed for a job in any Federal agency although I knew government housing and War-on-Poverty programs inside and out.

For six long months after my termination, I had no income, and we lived with the intense uncertainty of what would happen next. In addition to looking for a meaningful job, I tried to invent one in Denver. Because there was a mayoral election coming up, I thought that if I handled it correctly, I might be appointed by a new mayor to serve as Director of the City of Denver Housing Authority. The candidate I was supporting was a fellow I knew fairly well. He was a true visionary and member of one of our Denver UCC churches. So, I volunteered to work with him quite often in public appearances and other campaign work, even driving a campaign bus up and down Denver streets. The mid-June night he lost by a thin margin was major handwriting on the wall. The Lapps were toast economically!

Home to Mother

Despite not finding a church or community-change opportunity in the West, I found hope in the Holy's vision of making life possible for all beings. After my Denver mayoral candidate lost, in July I flew from Denver for an interview for leadership of a fair housing group in High Point, North Carolina. As soon as I got back to Denver, with a possible job offer, we put our Park Hill house on the market. It sold immediately.

Stashing our entire cache of belongings in storage, including warm clothing we would not need in North Carolina, we headed east to my mother's house in Tonawanda, NY. We drove our two cars, with three kids, a dog and five suitcases. As we headed northeast on the Colorado highway through Fort Morgan and Julesburg toward Nebraska, my eyes flowed with tears of regret and pain when I looked back over my left shoulder at the line of Rocky Mountains receding into nothingness on the western horizon.

We landed at my mother's house totally broke. At least we had a place to sleep.

We moved children, suitcases, and dog, into my mother's small home on Hampton Parkway in the Town of Tonawanda where I had lived when my brother had been killed. Mother was wonderful. She told Jan to treat the place like her own, and to take charge of all family activities. Mother said she would stay out of the way and would come and go independently, eating with us if she was there at mealtime.

Our three children were comfortable with Mother. She had had several meaningful engagements with them as they were growing up. When they were preschoolers, before Karen was born, Robyn and Stuart had stayed with her in Tonawanda while Jan and I took the East Lansing High School kids on their Work Trip to Silverton, CO.

A few years later, we all went on a camping trip to Yellowstone. I had constructed a relatively crude but sturdy tent camping trailer that was not capable of sleeping three adults and three young school aged kids. Mother cheerfully declared she would have no trouble sleeping in the back of our car. This went on for four nights. The children were delighted to be with Mother to see Old Faithful erupt.

Another summer Mother came to Denver and then took all three kids to Los Angeles to visit her brother, Richard Griffin, and his family. Richard's five children were not significantly older than our three. They lived in a tiny house. I am not certain where any of the extras slept, but they had a great time, even taking in Disneyland.

And now, at ages 14, 13, and 10, our children were ready for another adventure with their Grandma Lapp.

From Teacher to Community Volunteer

Mother had stayed busy after Dad died in 1961, continuing to teach at

North Tonawanda High School. Then, in the summer of 1966, Mother was 58 when she finished a master's degree in Home Economics that she was taking at the University of Syracuse. She wanted to be certain she was keeping up with the Home Economics curriculum required in the rapidly changing American culture.

At that time, I was still minister of the First United Church of Arvada and our kids were young grade schoolers. Because Mother was worried about being away from my sister Kathy while in Syracuse, Jan and I drove the family from Denver to Buffalo during our vacation that year so we could care for Kathy. We were not present when Mother received her master's degree, but Kathy was safe and happy. We visited Mother only briefly one afternoon in Syracuse. But we got to show the kids several thrilling natural sights in Western New York. Niagara Falls and Letchworth State Park were especially interesting to each of them. Another 2,000 miles later, we were back in Arvada. I suppose that was what we could call a working vacation.

As Mother continued to teach, Kathy's schizophrenic episodes became more intense. So, she ended up as a patient in the Buffalo State Hospital numerous times.

While she was still teaching, Mother began to spend Saturday mornings at a United Methodist Church in north Buffalo teaching young black mothers how to sew. Shortly, she realized that if these mothers had some form of day care they could find jobs to supplement, or liberate themselves from, welfare payments. So, Mother made a deal with the church for space, then formed a 501(c)(3) nonprofit that quickly became a packed day-care operation. At first the Center was not licensed for meal service, so Mother carried lunches in the trunk of her car to the church each day. Eventually, a local community woman was elected president of the board and Program Director, and Mother left, feeling it was better that an outside, older white woman, not hover.

When Mother retired from teaching, she was 62. Not one to sit around, next came a Meals-for-Seniors program at her own church. She involved herself in a volunteer operation that prepared lunches for neighboring seniors to enjoy at Kenmore United Methodist Church. Again, the innovator, she quickly realized that the neighbors who really needed meal help were home-bound. So, Mother began quietly taking meals out of the church each noon for delivery to disabled folk. Obviously, other volunteers soon figured out what she was doing but did not join her. One icy noon she fell on the sidewalk near the church and broke her arm. That ended the meal-delivery routine.

But her fall did not end Mother's concern for homebound people who were not eating properly. Hence, the Kenmore-Tonawanda Meals on Wheels program was born. Mother organized it, raised funds from area churches, town and city councils and community do-good organizations, recruited volunteer delivery drivers, hired cooks, planned the menus, and ordered the food, founded the Board, and got another 501(c)(3) nonprofit exemption. Her biggest coup was getting use of the kitchen, cafeteria, parking lot and associated facilities of a closed Town of Tonawanda public grade school. Ken-Ton Meals on Wheels became one of the largest such programs in New York State. It is the epitome of what one woman can do in inspiring a cohort of volunteers for an urgent community activity.

What a role-model! I see her as living a life in response to God's call to care for others more than self. Each of us understood the other very clearly and would do anything legal and loving for the other.

Kathy Finds Romance

During one of Kathy's longer sojourns in Buffalo State Hospital, she became acquainted with Victor Murray, another patient who also was both developmentally disabled and mentally ill. In the summer following my Selma protest work, we stopped in Tonawanda on our way to New England where we were to visit Jan's family. To see how the rear of the house was holding up, I stepped out into Mother's back yard where, leaning against a shed, was the scruffiest guy I had seen in years. He looked furtively at me, then ducked around the corner of the shed.

Going quickly into Mother's kitchen, I said, "I just saw a bum by the shed."

Smiling, "Oh," she said, "that must be Vic." I looked at her blankly. "Victor Murray," she said. "Kathy met him at Buffalo State, and he keeps hanging around here."

"Where does he stay at night?"

"I don't know. He has relatives on a farm southwest of Buffalo. Maybe he stays there sometimes."

The relationship evolved. Over the next couple of years, Vic came often to Mother's house to see Kathy. As time passed, each was in the Buffalo State Hospital Psych Ward, Kathy more often than Vic. The drama was a huge emotional burden for Mother.

In mid-December 1967, shortly after I had become Director of the Metro Denver Fair Housing Center, Mother called and said, "Robb, honey…" This salutation almost always meant something was up and I was about to be asked to do something I could not possibly have imagined. "Robb, honey…could you come the week before Christmas and marry Kathy and Vic?" I blurted, "What!?" "Yes," she said.

Though my perspective was that Mother was just taking on one more disabled person who would need both physical and financial care, she saw it differently. Mother's view was that having a companion would be good for Kathy. If Kathy wanted to have a husband, she should have that opportunity. Besides, Vic would occupy Kathy so Mother could catch a few breaks. So, I flew to Buffalo on a loaded pre-holiday plane.

We had a fine wedding in the 800-seat main sanctuary of the Kenmore Methodist Church where I had been ordained years before. Dwarfed in the magnificent arched chamber were Kathy, Vic, Mother, a friend of Mother's who took photos, and me, the officiant. Kathy wore a pretty street length white dress, and Vic was in a rumpled, ill-fitting suit with tie akimbo. No one from Vic's family attended. In fact, none of us ever met any of the Murrays.

Mother quickly recognized that she could not stand having Kathy and Vic living in her house, primarily because of their inability to organize anything or to pick up after themselves. Mother solved this problem by purchasing a small used house trailer located in a nearby trailer park in the shadow of the south Grand Island Bridge along the Niagara River. Kathy and Vic were close enough for Mother to keep her eye on them, but out from under foot.

After Kathy and Vic were living in their trailer, Mother called and said, "Robb, Kathy is pregnant." By this time Kathy had become obese, so I wondered how anyone could allege pregnancy. "O My!" I blurted. "Has she been tested by a physician?" Mother said, "No. Maybe I can get her to do that at Buffalo State Hospital." The "baby" turned out to be a large abdominal tumor that was successfully removed.

Each time I visited Mother, the inside of the trailer had become more of an unkempt disaster, while Vic grew increasingly surly. Gradually, the trailer became dysfunctional as the result of total lack of care by its occupants. Solution: Replace it with a somewhat larger, somewhat newer trailer in the same park, which Mother did.

So, when we arrived at her house following our forced retreat from Denver, Mother was running the Ken-Ton Meals program and checking daily on Vic and Kathy who were living in their nearby trailer, for which she was paying.

Here We Are in Tonawanda

My High Point interview in North Carolina turned out to be "for show." They had no serious intent of addressing black housing discrimination or racial justice issues. After receiving an offer, I was torn because we desperately needed employment. But pondering only one night and day, Jan and I decided we should not go to High Point.

As soon as we got the kids enrolled in local Tonawanda schools, I started further job searching. My goal was to stay in the field of racially open housing. I soon flew to Philadelphia to interview for the position of Executive Director of the Housing Association of Delaware Valley. A few days after I was back in Tonawanda, I was offered a second interview in Philadelphia. I was also offered an interview for an open housing job in Phoenix. But I did not do either of these interviews because, in the meantime, I had started working temporarily as a consultant for an emerging New Town project in Rochester, NY.

We soon needed the stored coats and sweaters we had left in Denver! Western New York is very cold and snowy in the wintertime.

The family's flight from Denver and retreat to a safe place in Tonawanda became a major dividing line between our past and future. Jan and I were thirty-eight. Our three children were not yet in high school. While Jan and I each knew our Holy call was to keep the faith in making life work better for people we did not know, we had no new substantive assignment. But all five of us were filled with hope and expectancy that each tomorrow would be a positive adventure.

Upon reflection, many life events had occurred in this fourth decade of my life. Jan and I were raising three young children. I had had to choose a new Protestant denomination that would reinstate my ordination. That denomination called me to start a new congregation that could make a difference in its community. I then was fired as ED from an activist antiracial non-profit and went eight months with no income for the family because of community controversy relating to systemic racism. But the Holy kept whispering, "Each tomorrow is filled with human need."

SECTION V
1972 – 1980

CREATING COMMUNITY

Chapter 21

~~

What is a "New Town"?

GANANDA WAS THE name of a large proposed real estate development in Wayne County, east of Rochester, NY to be located on some 10,000 acres of rural dairy farmland. It was to be a planned "New Town," one of several around the country whose early funding was provided through loan guarantees made by the U.S. Department of Housing and Urban Development under Title VII of the Urban Growth and New Community Development Act of 1970. A New Town is a real estate development project which creates all the elements of a complete community including residential, commercial, schools, medical facilities, police and fire protection, utilities, roadways, and employment opportunities. Typically, it is created on an undeveloped portion of a countryside land area. Columbia, MD, Irvine Ranch, CA, and Reston, VA are famous model New Towns initiated in the two decades after World War II.

When the Lapp family arrived in Tonawanda, an old friend, Paul Barru, had just resigned as Senior Minister of Twelve Corners Presbyterian Church in Rochester. I had met Paul in East Lansing years earlier when he was attending Edgewood Peoples Church where I was Youth Minister. When I met him, he was a nominal Jew who had just sold the Tastee Freeze franchise rights for the entire state of Michigan. Inspired by the preaching of Truman Morrison, Senior Minister at Edgewood, Paul became a Christian and eventually attended Harvard Divinity School in Boston after completing a liberal arts degree at Michigan State University.

After we had moved to Arvada to start a new UCC church, Paul, having completed his B.D. at Harvard, moved with his family to Glenwood Springs, CO where he was ordained and installed as Minister of First Presbyterian Church. Continuing our relationship, I participated in that worship service. Paul and family often stayed with us while living in Glenwood Springs. When I was Director of the Metro Denver Fair Housing Center, the Barrus moved to Rochester, where Paul had been called to the Twelve Corners Presbyterian Church pulpit. Stuart, a lawyer who was a prominent member of that church, had initiated acquisition of land east of Rochester for a New Town, and was assembling investors. He had asked Paul to join him to work on development of community services for the New Town, by this time named Gananda. Paul resigned his ministerial position at the church to work with Stuart on the Gananda project.

Upon the Lapps' arrival in Tonawanda, not yet knowing of Paul's church resignation nor his work on Gananda, I reached out to him. Paul excitedly told me about his new venture. He invited me to come to Rochester to meet Stuart and to talk about the project. Much to my surprise, I left that meeting as a temporary consultant. As I had already done HUD projects twice, Paul and Stuart asked me to assist them with an application for a HUD Title VII Loan Guarantee for the development of Gananda.

It was 100 miles from Tonawanda to Rochester. For several weeks,

I drove forth and back each day. That drive home at the end of the day was time for quiet contemplation and reflection. Weary as I exited Rochester each evening, I felt renewed by the time I was back in Tonawanda. Here I was, working as a consultant for the New Town project of Gananda! Was I helping the Holy create functional human community on earth?

A Young Family Moves to Rochester

After several months of commuting the 100 miles from Tonawanda, Jan and I initiated a search for a house in the Rochester area. On our second weekend of looking, we made an offer on a clapboard-sided two-story in Penfield, a suburb just north of Rochester. It had separate bedrooms for each kid, as well as a back yard that bordered on what we dubbed a babbling brook. Once we had closed, we called the storage company in Denver where we had stashed our earthly belongings in July. The Mayflower truck was scheduled to arrive in Penfield within a week. We were in such a hurry to move out of Mother's house in Tonawanda, we decided to camp for a few interim days in the new house. Days grew into weeks before the trailer van showed up. The driver had been having engine trouble with his tractor and had stopped at his home in St. Louis to get the motor replaced. We all survived!

That Fall and the next brought some very special Saturday mornings. We discovered a cider mill just east of Penfield. I thoroughly enjoyed taking Karen there to watch the apple pressing, eat donut holes, and buy unpasteurized cider.

In the course of time, assuming we would be in Penfield at least through the kids' public-school educations, we joined Mountain Rise United Church of Christ in Fairport. One of the minister's sons took a puppy love interest in Robyn.

While we still were members of Mountain Rise, the minister left the church for another pulpit. I somehow heard the Holy say, "Do something beyond the traditional in a local church interim situation," so I suggested that the church try not hiring an Interim Minister while searching for a replacement. I said I would handle the Sundays when the Sacraments were scheduled, as well as special holiday services. My notion was that lay members of the church could preach and lead worship the rest of the time. The scheme worked quite nicely, but whenever it was my turn, I frantically wrote my services on planes to or from somewhere. Various lay members did very well with their sermons, finding significant new spiritual self-awareness as they assembled their thoughts.

A meaningful lifelong relationship continued at Mountain Rise with a woman named Jeanne. While I was a kid in Kenmore Methodist Church, friends of my parents had a baby named Jeanne. She was ten or so years younger than I. I babysat Jeanne when I was in high school. Later, she babysat our children when we were visiting in Tonawanda. After becoming the mother of three boys, she lived near Mountain Rise UCC and was a very involved member and musician. We were good friends, and I appreciated her support as I volunteered.

Parenthetically, years after we moved from Rochester, I was invited back to Mountain Rise to preach on Pentecost Sunday. Jeanne undoubtedly was behind the invitation. There having been late rumors that Mountain Rise was suffering a bout of middle-age malaise, I entitled my sermon, "What Mountain Rise Needs is a Good Fire." I waxed eloquent about God burning the old and allowing fresh starts. After the service, a man I did not know introduced himself as Paul Hammer. I almost fainted. Paul was a widely known New Testament scholar and Professor at Colgate-Rochester Seminary. He rescued me by saying it had been the best Pentecost sermon he had ever heard. Jeanne was amused.

The Gananda Project

An exciting prospect for ministry began to come into view as I became acquainted with the mission of the project. The whole point of a "New Town" is to create a community in which people of all races, economic backgrounds, and ethnicities who crave transparent local governance could live and work together. I began to think of a New Town as that kind of egalitarian human community and matrix of relationships as would be envisioned by the Holy. Conceptually, a New Town could be consistent with Jesus' radical notion that a powerful few in a community should not control the many.

I immediately saw that there were competing personal priorities among those involved in the "dream" stage of this project. The investors were in this for economic gain, or for increasing the size of their local markets. Paul Barru valued the idealistic vision of a fair and just open community. Stuart was willing to agree to anything to achieve his goal of creating a New Town project. He seemed to want veto power on all decisions, and often did not fully disclose independent steps he was prone to taking.

I felt that my underlying role as a minister in a secular setting was to confront the inappropriate ways people were treating one another, and to create an institutional management structure that would be open and fair, encouraging productive creativity.

But my initial assignment was to walk the project through the HUD Loan Guarantee process that would lead to adequate funding for creation of an idealistic community that would serve the best interests of many people.

The composition of the Board of New Wayne Communities, Inc., was an important factor in how the project unfolded. The Chairman of the

Board was a prominent Rochester attorney. Board member investors included both an architect and a contractor from Pittsburgh, the owner of a large Rochester Chevrolet dealership, a Xerox corporation executive, a very wealthy woman whom Stuart knew from Twelve Corners Presbyterian Church, and this woman's father, owner of a world-renowned manufacturer of dental and medical office equipment. It also included Donald, a small-time real estate broker and farmer who lived in adjacent Wayne County, east of Rochester. Central Wayne County had about 10,000 acres of farmland that Stuart thought could become the future New Town of Gananda. Donald was a corporate partner because Stuart had him making contingent land purchase deals for which he would not receive his commission until project funding was completed.

There was no majority shareholder. Stuart was the prime mover and the largest single shareholder of New Wayne Communities, having arranged shares for himself based on the work he had done in conceiving the project, recruiting investors, and supervising Donald in the acquisition of land options.

I immediately saw that there was little organization, and that preliminary efforts to prepare the HUD Loan Guarantee application had been scattered at best. To start, I helped Paul characterize the future community in documents to be used for early publicity and public support. But soon my top priority became the preparation and submission of a HUD Loan Guarantee application.

Stuart had already created a preliminary working relationship with a Columbia, MD, consulting group, Land Ventures, Inc., each of whose principals had worked for James Rouse, developer of Columbia, a pioneering New Town near Washington, D.C., and in many ways, father of the New Town concept. The Land Ventures group included a land planner, a development manager, a construction supervisor, and a non-practicing lawyer. When I arrived, it was clear that Land Ventures, Inc., was salivating over the prospect of becoming the operational developer of Gananda.

Then there was Jack Jones, a real estate attorney with the firm of Piper Marbury in Baltimore, who had worked on large real estate projects including Columbia, and who had been brought into the effort by Land Ventures, Inc. Jack turned out to be the most helpful and creative contributor of the Maryland contingent.

My role on the HUD Loan Guarantee application involved coordinating the work of all the players, even though I was not "the boss." Because the HUD application had to include evidence of control of the land parcels we were to purchase with the guaranteed loan, I also had to focus on Donald's completion of contingent purchase contracts. While we already owned several farms and other tracts, we needed exercisable options for purchase of additional dozens of parcels. For all practical purposes, I quickly because the unofficial development team leader.

For the loan application, in addition to a financial plan, we needed to have detailed land use plans. The Land Ventures team led that work. HUD required that we get design approvals from Wayne County and from the Townships of Walworth and Macedon, which I did.

One of the most unique things about planning a New Town is that of creating all the institutions and programs that will serve the populace. Paul, and another minister employee, made a major contribution in this societal conceptualizing.

Keeping in mind that I am not an engineer or a land planner, I had two weeks to prepare the Environmental Impact Statement, a task that typically takes land planners and engineers months. In the next few days, I gathered data and wrote scientific sounding phrases that described how the building of a New Town would preserve and protect the geological character of a rural area filled with Ice Age glacial deposits called moraines. I also declared that the "moderating influence" of Lake Ontario would make Gananda habitable for residents in a deeply snowy climate.

On one frantic day during those two weeks of drafting the Impact Statement I flew with a local engineer in a small, chartered plane to Cleveland to consult with an environmental specialist. On the way west our plane's wings were icing up in a frozen drizzle. I had had enough flying experience in my glider days to know that we were in deep trouble. The copilot used an onboard system to break up the forming ice as we flew, and we ultimately made it safely to the airport. I was reluctant to start back to Rochester that night but had to. We made it with less trouble than on the outbound flight. When I took my draft to D.C. just days later, my HUD gatekeepers coached me on needed changes, which I gratefully made. No one at HUD commented on my lack of professional credentials. However, the Environmental Impact Statement was accepted, approved, and made part of the application packet!

At the end of a business day in December 1971, I was preparing to fly to Washington D.C. where I was to submit to HUD the next morning all the land purchase options, contracts and deeds that were required for the HUD Loan Guarantee application. It was a stack about eight inches thick, all original documents. Having to run to the men's room, I set the stack on the top edge of a large square waste basket next to my desk in my second-floor office. When I returned a couple of minutes later, the waste basket and papers were nowhere to be seen. I did not even look for the janitor but gulped and raced down to the dumpster in the alley. Digging frantically through the recent deposits I found the precious documents strewn about and stained by coffee grounds and liquid. I did not even get to wiping off the sheets or reassembling them until after I was on the plane to D.C.

That was one of the few nights I stayed overnight in D.C. I normally flew back to Rochester each night even when I had meetings the next day at HUD or in Columbia, MD., because the flights were less expensive than dinner and lodging in Washington. Shortly after the meeting in which I delivered the worst looking set of legal documents ever assembled, brown stains and all, New Wayne Communities, Inc., was approved for a $22,000,000 Loan Guarantee. Then came the tedious work of negotiating the HUD Project Agreement and preparing the Loan Guarantee Indenture. Lots more flights to D.C.!

Successfully securing the HUD Guarantee had been my top priority for several months. Only a few applicants, of which there were many around the country, received an award. I was thrilled.

But another issue was just below the surface for the Gananda project through these early months. How was our project to be managed?

The solution? Staff members joined together and formed Wayne Management Corp. which then entered into a contract with New Wayne Communities, Inc., to manage the project. That management contract included profit sharing terms. Stuart would continue as President of New Wayne Communities. He would also be a partner in Wayne Management, Inc., along with Jack Jones, Paul Barru, and me. Land Ventures, Inc., as a corporation, was also a partner, receiving small interests for its four principals.

Paul was named Director of Marketing and Ancillary Business Operations. While I did not seek it, I reluctantly accepted the position of Chief Operating Officer of Wayne Management, Inc., accountable to the team of sundry partners. Amazingly, as the person least experienced in real estate development, I was the unanimous choice! The successful Loan Guarantee and my open leadership style got me into this fix.

It seemed like we were ready to start creating our New Town.

Family Members Adjust to Rochester

Jan found living in Rochester an inviting experience. Her full-time job was managing our housekeeping and working with our three kids. She loved all the fresh fruits and vegetables that grew in Western New York. Not only did she use them for family meals, but she also canned many for the winter season.

The kids had started school in Tonawanda when we first arrived at Mother's after our sad pilgrimage from Denver, and then transferred to schools in Penfield shortly after we moved there in 1971. Robyn was in 9th Grade. Stuart was in 8th Grade and Karen was in 5th Grade. Given their grade levels, each was in a different school that first Fall.

Socially, Robyn was very engaged with her school peers as she worked on her emerging identity. She was increasingly interested in boys and was a good student. As a family member, she was very independent.

Stuart was more even keeled and significantly less dramatic. When we first got to Penfield, Jan drove him back to Tonawanda on Saturdays to finish the football season with the team he had joined when we first arrived from Colorado. He was better than Robyn at living within family and school boundaries. He too was a good student. He had decided before we left Denver that he should become a lawyer.

Karen, just entering her teen years, was becoming our "Steady Eddie."

Though Robyn and Stuart kept Karen out of many activities, and while Robyn frequently harassed her, Karen invented her own independent lifestyle. While she was not as much a socializer as Robyn, she handled her relationships with other kids very well. And Karen was our third good student, perhaps the best!

Just before Christmas in 1972 our family drove from Penfield to Concord, NH for the funeral of Jan's father, which was on a Sunday in the Methodist Church of which he and Jan's Stepmother were members. The next day I had to be in Washington D.C. for a final meeting on the HUD Project Agreement.

Gananda Falls Apart

In the first sixteen months of New Town creation, The Wayne Management Corp. team had accomplished a tremendous amount, including the pivotal awarding of the HUD Loan Guarantee. As 1973 dawned we had all our land parcels lined up or already purchased. We had found a bank that would loan us the $22,000,000 covered by the HUD Loan Guarantee. Road, water, sewer, and drainage infrastructure had been designed. Development approvals had been received from the Wayne County Townships of Walworth and Macedon in which Gananda was to be located, and from the Genesee Regional Council of Governments. The first school had a site and design. We had completed construction of a Community Center that was to be used at first as a sales and marketing facility. We had assembled a staff of competent people. We had our first home builders lined up. With good publicity, there was an air of expectancy in the Greater Rochester community. We were ready to break ground and make Gananda a reality.

But it was all for naught.

Two events, totally out of the control of Wayne Management, Inc., the operating corporation I ran, ended up destroying the project.

The first of these two unfortuitous turns began surreptitiously when the owners of the parent corporation began to scheme on how to break the operating agreement with Wayne Management, Inc. This plotting included a search for another contract development entity. No one on the Wayne Management, Inc. team knew anything about this. If they hired a contract development manager company, they would not have to share profits with Wayne Management, Inc.

The second unexpected turn became clear as I worked on the Indenture and Deed of Trust committing various land parcels as security for closing the $22,000,000 loan.

After we closed the Project Agreement with HUD, to sell the bonds that would net the $22,000,000, we had to complete the Indenture and Deed of Trust. This step required committing various land parcels as security both to HUD and to the as-yet unknown purchaser of the bonds. As I looked at the land ownership documents in detail, I discovered that Stuart had covertly and intentionally confused the land collateral. Apparently, Stuart was trying to manipulate the loan security process to guarantee that neither Lincoln Rochester nor HUD could foreclose and kill the project.

Next day, viewing Stuart's actions as misfeasance, I went to see the Attorney who was Chairman of the Board of Wayne Communities, Inc., the owner corporation. He did not seem alarmed and went on to make disparaging remarks about the Wayne Management, Inc. team. I did not "get" the point of the negativity right off the bat. It soon became clear that the Rochester Good Old Boy network had closed ranks, and that Stuart would be protected in his deceit. Nice behavior for two attorneys!

Shortly after my session with the parent corp. Board Chair, I was called to a meeting in his office. Present were several of the investors. I was introduced to a fellow who was in town from Tennessee. The Chair proceeded to ask me to give this man a briefing on the legal and financial status of the project. Through off-hand comments and eye-contact among the visitor and various owners, I quickly sensed that he had already been hired as the contract developer of Gananda. Because the owners had not been open with my Wayne Management. Inc. team, I said as little as I could. However, right on the spot I was relieved of keys to both my office and my leased car. I had to call Jan to get a ride home!

So much for whistle blowing!

The development management agreement between New Wayne Communities, Inc. and Wayne Management, Inc. was toast!

As a bright spot on my personal horizon, one of the Land Ventures, Inc. partners had already left the Gananda project to become an employee of The Woodlands Development Corp, another HUD Title VII New Town, near Houston, TX.

Jack Jones, our Maryland attorney partner represented the Wayne Management, Inc. team in negotiating a closeout. He was able to secure a small severance for Paul and me. But here I was without a job for the second time in two years, this time for blowing a whistle on an act of misfeasance by a lawyer.

Turns out that my personal sense of loss was a far smaller disaster in the eternal scheme of things than something else that happened shortly thereafter. The land security debacle and the termination of the operating agreement with Wayne Management, Inc. that had been a condition of the HUD Project Agreement, led to HUD's placing the project

214   SECTION V: 1972 - 1980

in default and foreclosing on the land. Gananda was not to become a New Town. That made everyone a loser.

The rest of the story of Gananda is unremarkable. While originally designed to be a city with upwards of 90,000 residents, not far north of Palmyra, where Joseph Smith received the Book of Mormon, the collapse of HUD funding led to the disintegration of a consolidated effort to develop a New Town. Over time, though the general area continued to be called Gananda, development was piecemeal, with various builders developing small disparate tracts of housing. Any of the egalitarian benefits that would have accrued to residents of Gananda were it a "New Town" planned community, were lost.

Reflection

In this Rochester outside-the-box street ministry I got a first-hand taste of the human craving for power, money, and control over others that has driven empire builders since the beginning of time. Any effort to make the rich richer at the expense of the many is frowned upon by the Holy. This experience reinforced my commitment to walking with Jesus no matter what the personal cost might be.

Moving to Rochester from Denver felt like having been exiled from a culture in we had chosen to live. We did not leave Denver because we wanted to. We were simply run out of town. In Rochester we did not seem to "fit" in the social milieu. It seemed closed and unfair. Life was based very much on who one "knew," and not so much on what one "could do." It was claustrophobic.

But, especially for Jan and the kids, there was an emotional sense of having been liberated from a very stressful life in Denver.

On the plus side, the deciduous forests and wooded areas I had grown up with were embracing for me. Small truck farms with ancient buildings were what I had grown up with. Drives along the Erie Barge Canal, the Niagara River and Lakes Erie and Ontario were nostalgic. But in the end, it was like visiting another planet. There was nothing of the West in the local fabric. The saying that one can never go home felt very real to me.

In some of my psych courses in college and seminary I had learned that grieving is a prerequisite to good mental health. By the time my father died when I was twenty-seven, I was able to practice existentially what I knew intellectually. I could grieve. Jan got it. She would say to me, "Go ahead. Cry. It's okay to have feelings." Her quiet observations about my uncertainties came off as deep support.

In leading the monumental effort to secure a HUD Loan Guarantee, I learned that I had skills in finance, management, community building, and sharing the love of God in the secular community.

So, what did this have to say about my faith journey? In my innermost reaching for strength, I continued to find myself doing what I had first done when my brother was killed and again after my father became disabled. Keep breathing. Put one foot in front of the other. Be mindful that in his pre-Easter behavior on behalf of love and justice, Jesus modeled the cost of sacrificial living. Despite the brokenness that accompanies every facet of creation, I am grateful for each day in which I continue to be a player! One does what life requires of him. And the Holy blesses one with courage.

Chapter 22

~~

TEXAS? REALLY?

AFTER SEVERAL PAINFUL months in Rochester trying to figure out what was next, I received an out of the blue phone call from Bob McGee, the Land Ventures partner with whom I had worked on the Gananda project before he moved to a new job in Texas. He said he was in Houston working for Mitchell Energy and Development Corporation on the creation a New Town to be called The Woodlands. All I knew was that it was the largest of the ten Title VII applicants and that it was owned by a large mineral extraction company.

Bob was calling me to explore the possibility of my working with him on The Woodlands project! He told me that The Woodlands, north of Houston, had just been awarded a $50,000,000 Loan Guarantee from HUD under Title VII of the Urban Growth and New Community Development Act of 1970.

I asked Bob what staff position he was calling about. He said, "There isn't one – yet." Bob did not even have approval for hiring some-one. But he said, "No one here knows as much as you do about how to manage a HUD New Town Loan Guarantee and Project Agreement."

I agreed to fly to Houston on the coming Monday after leading worship at Mountain Rise UCC on Palm Sunday.

The corporate offices of Mitchell Energy and Development Corporation ("MEDC"), owner of the land that would become The Woodlands, were in the prestigious One Shell Plaza office building in downtown Houston.

Nothing but piney woods existed on the 50,000-acre site of The Woodlands New Town north of Houston, so the development team was temporarily located in One Shell Plaza. I met Bob there on the Tuesday morning after Palm Sunday.

As my interview with him concluded, he said he would have to ask both the President of The Woodlands Development Corporation ("WDC"), another fellow from Columbia, and George Mitchell, principal owner of MEDC, about hiring me. Bob was confident he would be authorized to make me an offer. I was excited by the prospect of being part of the creation of a New Town that might become a reality.

After my interview with Bob, not knowing whether I would be invited to join the WDC team, I spent the next day visiting the site of the future New Town and looking around at a few residential areas north of Houston imagining where the Lapps might live.

I flew back to Rochester on Wednesday evening. The next day, Maundy Thursday, at supper time, just as I was on my way out the door to again lead worship at Mountain Rise UCC, Bob McGee called to ask if I could be in Houston the following Monday for an interview with George Mitchell.

Oops. We were planning to spend Easter with Jan's brother Bill's family in Atlanta, GA. However, I told Bob I could fly from Atlanta to Houston early on the Monday morning after Easter.

Jan's brother, Bill Wallace, was enrolled in the Center for Disease Control for a Master of Public Health, a second medical degree, having finished his M.D. in Vermont. With high spirits for the future, we five Lapps drove from Rochester to Atlanta on Good Friday and Saturday as scheduled. Before daylight on Easter Sunday, we all trekked up Stone Mountain for a Sunrise Service.

At the crack of dawn on Monday I flew to Houston from Atlanta. Bob accompanied me in the interview with George Mitchell. After an hour, Mitchell looked at Bob, then said to me, "If we were to ask you to work with us, would you accept?" "Yes," I said, secretly relieved, "if you think I could contribute to your project."

Without our having discussed a specific position or role, George Mitchell told Bob to hire me. However, it was obvious that he wanted me because of my previous experience at Gananda in working with HUD's New Communities Division which had given me more actual hands-on negotiating relationship with HUD than any existing Mitchell employee had.

The Mitchell corporate interrelationships were intricate and confusing, something that would later create a problem with HUD. Bob had been set up as "Vice President and General Manager" of the Woodlands Development Corporation so that it would look like someone was managing the specific development defined by the HUD Project Agreement. But most of the real estate staff was committed to the creation of income producing commercial projects that were to occupy developed land within The Woodlands. After we left George's office, Bob said, "Why don't we just say that your job is to be my assistant."

Fundamentally, I was pleased, as I thought I could influence the creating of a communal life in The Woodlands from the perspective of just and fair human relationships. Whether it was to turn out to be a good step in the Lapp family's life was not yet answered, but I was taking my third shot at secular ministry. In the big picture of what I heard the Holy calling for in human community, I thought this was the right thing to do next.

The project, located in south Texas and being developed by a very strong and profitable corporation, the incarnated revolutionary Jesus' largest challenge would have been human sin and evil. In south Texas, greed and self-interest drove everything. Racial discrimination in the form of open hostility was a huge social and political issue. Real estate development was destroying the natural environment. Far away jobs with long commutes were creating major family domestic discord. Schools were mediocre, serving the interests of upper income whites in predominantly rural settings. In summary, the largest single human need to be addressed in The Woodlands was for it to achieve open, accessible, fair governance, with schools and services that enhanced the ease with which people of all backgrounds could live together and be comfortable within their own souls.

What Was I Hired to Do?

I walked into the One Shell Plaza corporate headquarters in downtown Houston just two Mondays following the interview at which I had been hired, having flown in from Rochester the night before. I sought out Bob McGee, who found a temporary office for me and proceeded to describe details of The Woodlands planning and development to date.

The Woodlands Development Corporation's role was to own the tens of thousands of acres destined to become The Woodlands, to do the New Town's physical infrastructure development, to sell completed lots and parcels to builder/developers, and to create all the community service entities such as governance and school, hospital, and fire districts.

Mitchell Development Corporation of the Southwest ("MDCS"), WDC's sister subsidiary, was the Mitchell entity that would purchase commercial tracts for the construction and ownership of office buildings, plazas, golf courses, country clubs, and other for-profit structures and spaces.

Many of the employees of both real estate entities were people who had been hired from Columbia, Maryland, the most successful New Town to date in America. So many had come from that project that they were known in-house as the "Columbia Mafia." Len Ivins, a key player on the Columbia development team, had been recruited as President of both subsidiaries to manage the work of both MDCS and WDC, something which I eventually came to view as a conflict of interest.

All eyes were focused on the creation of amenities that would be in place on Opening Day: a golf course, a dramatic Inn and Conference Center, a Country Club, a truly inviting Visitor Center, and a lakeside mall containing shops and an upscale restaurant. These all were business ventures of MDSW intended to be financed with funds other than those borrowed under the HUD Loan Guarantee agreement.

Land development infrastructure, roadways, subdivisions, water, sewer and drainage facilities, a Swim and Athletic Center, an entry parkway, and hiking and bike paths were the responsibility of WDC. Supervision of the execution of the development terms of the HUD Project Agreement was also a WDC responsibility, but not yet assigned to anyone. Community Governance was to be done through an Association, instead of a local municipal government structure, but there were no detailed plans for its creation.

After Bob left me in my temporary office with no specific job description, I sat there realizing I would have to figure out what to do to help the project. After a couple of days, I started carrying my handy clipboard into the offices of all the senior managers in both the real estate corporations, and even a few in the parent corporation. I took notes on what they said their jobs entailed. No one refused an interview. I said to each of them, "I'm new here. Could you tell me what you do, what your responsibilities are, to whom you report, and how your work relates to the roles of other senior people?" I took lots of notes. Because I yet had no clear job title, and had been hired upon direction from George Mitchell himself, I think I intimidated a few of them. But every one of them gave me thorough answers, some of which did not make much sense, or which revealed subtle power conflicts existing among the players.

The bottom line was that I discovered no one was paying any attention to the creation of a transparent community governance structure that would serve the tens of thousands of people who would become residents. Further, as I analyzed the corporate situation, I also realized there was no functional coordination among the disparate parts of the organization and, particularly, that no one was charged with execution of the operating relationship we had with the U.S. Department of Housing and Urban Development which had given us the $50,000,000 Loan Guarantee.

No one knew much about, nor had much interest in, the specific community development commitments and financial management requirements contained in the HUD Project Agreement. No one was managing The Woodlands' human service and societal commitments recited in the HUD Project Agreement. No one was getting roadway permits from the County. No one was worrying about police and fire protection. No one was developing functional working relationships with the local school districts. No one was working on the formation of The Woodlands Community Association, the proposed community governance vehicle. No one was coordinating the sale of land to churches or creating an interfaith cooperative effort. No one was recruiting doctors or thinking about a hospital. No one was forming water, sewer, and drainage taxing districts to pay for and manage delivery of basic utility services. And no one was arranging for government grants for roads, subsidized housing, or recreational facilities.

Not yet having an assigned job description or perceived role, I envisioned a role that would give me an opportunity to "make a difference" in the quality of life for our future residents. I saw an opportunity for shaping a secular ministry from the ground up.

I created my own job description. Since no one else was worrying about "community" in the social sense, I thought I should take on the task of creating all the governance and community service entities for The Woodlands. And I could be the project's manager of the Project Agreement relationship with HUD in Washington, D.C. I could form a team with experience in local government and human services to turn a real estate development into a true human community. Because I would represent The Woodlands in our contractual relationship with HUD, our team would have to have a clear internal working relationship with the financial and legal departments of all the Mitchell corporate entities. I thought that such a team could become the Community Development Department of WDC. Its corporate status would equal that of the Land Planning, Engineering, Construction, Sales and Marketing, Architectural, Finance, and Legal Departments of the inter-corporate real estate division.

From the outset my goal was to create a racially and economically integrated community with multiple employers, transparent governance, top schools, recreational features including small lakes and miles and miles of bikeways, an interfaith religious community structure, shopping, and top-notch medical services, including a hospital. After describing to Bob McGee how we could provide these needed community development activities, I suggested, "Why don't you get me appointed as "Vice President for Community Development," a title more consistent with my notion that how people live with one another is even more important than how the land they live on has been developed. He agreed. I had a role and job title!

It is not often that a person gets hired for an undefined senior corporate position that he then gets to design. A good opportunity for a Christian street-infiltrator!

Where to Live?

On my first day in Houston, I rented a temporary apartment and selected a leased car. For several weeks I looked around for a neighborhood location in the metro area that would be good for the family and convenient to both the Mitchell company's downtown office and The Woodlands site in Montgomery County 30 miles to the north. I concluded we could manage somewhere along FM-1960 on Houston's north side. I selected a house in Oak Creek Village which we ultimately bought but never really liked. Jan flew to Houston the next weekend and agreed to my selection, despite the horrid orange carpet in the family room. More memorable that weekend was our visit to the historic battleship, TEXAS, anchored in Galveston Bay, where we also found the adjacent San Jacinto Inn where they served great seafood, beginning with an appetizer of all the shrimp one could consume, leaving little room for an entree.

Jan flew back to Rochester and started packing for our move. Her ingenuity played a role in getting our Rochester house sold. The contract for sale of our Penfield house had been signed by a man whose family was moving in from out of town. His spouse had not seen the house. When she showed up, she grew angry with Jan, accusing her of misrepresenting the house, and saying it was not anything like her husband had described to her. Not Jan's problem. But the buyers abruptly cancelled their contract. Jan told the buyer he would forfeit his $1,000 earnest money deposit. She called the Rochester newspaper, and reran the house-for-sale ad. A second buyer came that weekend, liked the house and signed a contract. Jan handled all the negotiations and the closing. I was impressed, as she had very little experience in such dealings. Then, she packed up family belongings, organized our furniture, and hired ATLAS VAN LINES for the move!

Now that school was out, with her older siblings excluding her from daily socializing, twelve-year-old Karen grew bored. She told Jan she missed me and wanted to be with me. Jan suggested she fly to Houston "to take care of Dad." Not without difficulty, toward the end of June Karen flew unaccompanied from Rochester to Houston. She was to change planes in Cleveland, but her second-leg flight was cancelled. The airline phoned me in Houston, but somehow the call was routed to the office of George Mitchell. George's puzzled Secretary called me, giving me an airline phone number in Cleveland. Two hours of scrambling later, Karen was on a substitute flight which delivered her safely to the Houston airport. She and I stayed several nights in our newly purchased unfurnished house in Oak Creek Village, having borrowed a card table and two folding chairs, but no cots, from a neighbor. I took her with me to business meetings, mostly at the downtown Mitchell office. It made her feel important to be doing this with her father.

Jan, Robyn, and Stuart arrived at our new home north of Houston on the Fourth of July, just in time for a neighborhood picnic at the pool house/community building in our subdivision. The moving van had not arrived yet with our things, so we camped in an empty house for what seemed like an eternity, but was only two weeks. Texas was a new culture for all of us. And a new climate! Being outside was like being in an oven. Jan's 40th birthday was the day after they arrived. I took her to a nearby restaurant which turned out to be a bust. But Jan was exhausted by events of the previous two months, and quickly forgot the crummy meal.

Each subdivision along FM 1960 had at least one community swimming pool, and most of them had kids' swim teams. Stuart and Karen quickly became stars on the Oak Creek Village swim team. Jan spent summer Saturdays driving them to area meets. Jan also took the lead in enrolling all three in schools for fall classes. She was chagrined to learn that Robyn, who was to be a Junior in Spring High School, would not have access to an orchestra, as the most upscale music program was a concert band. It included no violins! Robyn quickly learned to play a glockenspiel for the marching band, and a xylophone for the concert band. Stuart, an entering Sophomore, became very proficient on the euphonium and played in marching bands all the way through high school and college. Karen, a 7th Grader, like her Dad, was not musically proficient, but enjoyed other school activities.

Jan Becomes a Social Worker

After we moved to Texas in 1973, the longer we lived in the Oak Creek Village house the more Jan realized that she yearned for something important to do. She did not really know what it should be. I knew I could suggest options but could not tell her what to do. This was something she needed to work out on her own. It could not be a future I designed or even suggested. It was more a matter of her "hearing" how life wanted her to contribute to the larger human good.

I urged her to find a counselor that could evaluate her skills and help her prioritize her interests. This she did. Jan opted for a field that could utilize her creative ingenuity and fulfill her desire to directly assist people in need. Learning that the Texas Department of Human Services did not require an MSW for social work, she quickly landed a job as a Social Worker.

Her first assignment was as a Work Incentive Program (WIN) worker in Houston. Her responsibility was to arrange for day care and other assistance services for single parents so that they could enter job-training programs. She was away from home for long hours each day, as her morning and evening drives in notoriously crowded Houston traffic extended her workday to over ten hours.

Not long into this effort she had the brilliant idea of asking Karen, a seventh grader, to fix dinner each weeknight. Jan and Karen wrote out dinner menus for the week and bought all the necessary ingredients on weekends. Jan taught Karen the fine art of reading cookbooks, of braising meat for pot roasts, of baking cakes and cookies, and of preparing vegetables. Karen did a great job and become a fine cook.

Jan's transition from mom, wife, and homemaker to professional social worker in the workforce was an identity shift for me, too. I became much more involved in the details of working with our kids and managing household affairs.

Chapter 23

~~

GETTING THE
WOODLANDS STARTED

MY FIRST YEAR and a half at The Woodlands is best seen through the lens of the October 19, 1974 Opening Day. Tons of money and hundreds of people were thrown at this date. However, the two Mitchell real estate subsidiaries were able to keep everything focused on the need to have a dramatic visitor experience in place on opening day.

On the day I started, The Woodlands was a totally undeveloped 50,000-acre pine forest.

A land use Master Plan had been created. The first area was to be called The Village of Grogan's Mill. Financial, planning and construction teams were in place. We needed to complete the infrastructure for the first village of an emerging city, along with initial housing and public spaces, in just eighteen months.

Because much of my initial work included meeting with Montgomery

County officials for approvals and services, I leased a construction trailer and lodged it in the woods just west of Interstate 25 near an exit named, believe it or not, Robinson Road. I was the first Mitchell management employee to have an office on the New Town's property!

Earth moving equipment started roaring back and forth past my trailer creating roadways, a golf course, sites for a Conference Center and a commercial mall, and a site for fifty small townhomes. Excavation for small body of water, to be called Lake Woodlands, was started near the commercial mall and Conference Center site.

As soon as construction workers could get to these developed sites, work began on the mall, to be called the Wharf, The Woodlands Inn and Conference Center, a large Visitor Center to house the sales and marketing team, and two office buildings for staff.

During the rush toward Grand Opening, in addition to negotiating required local governmental authorizations, I had to develop a working relationship with the U.S. Department of Housing and Urban Development staff in Washington, D.C. Lots of flights!

Forming a Municipal Utility District

From time to time all eyes focused on me, as I was the one who was going through all the necessary protocols to establish the first Municipal Utility District, a quasi-municipal entity with bonding power and the authority to deliver services for a fee. It would develop and manage the water, sewer, and drainage facilities for the Village of Grogan's Mill. I also had to negotiate an intricate deal with the San Jacinto River Authority for a deep canal which would handle run-off drainage toward the Gulf of Mexico in very wet, nearly sea-level topography.

To create the first utility district, which would serve the entire first phase commercial development as well as the first homes that would be built, I had to have resident voters. That led to my getting the MDSW staff to build a townhouse neighborhood at the intersection of Grogans Mill Road and Millbend Circle. There were 50 units. The first two of them had to have occupant voters before Opening Day. What a push! On the day I was helping the first family move in, a paving truck got stuck in the mud in front of their townhouse. Someone brought a bulldozer to extricate it. With one mighty tug, the dozer yanked the front right off the dump truck. Until well after dark we carried the family's stuff around the remaining truck carcass into their nearly finished townhouse.

What About Community Governance?

Instead of an incorporated municipality, a Community Association was to be the governance and service agency for the New Town. Prior to my time, staff had worked a deal with the City of Houston that provided for The Woodlands to be in an "Extraterritorial Jurisdiction," a term of art used in Texas to describe a city's legal relationship to unannexed land. When land was in a city's Extraterritorial Jurisdiction, no other municipality could annex it. The agreement with Houston included the commitment that Houston would not annex The Woodlands for a prolonged period, at least twenty years.

I saw that no one was working on the actual formation of The Woodland's Community Association ("WCA"). Writing its Covenants, essentially the By-Laws, needed to be done before people started moving into The Woodlands. So, I asked the WDC planning and legal staffs to prepare the Covenants. As the project came to its Grand Opening, we were ready to appoint Board members, hire staff, and initiate operations.

Not a local government that could collect taxes, the Association levied monthly fees to provide community services. At the outset, the WCA Board was composed of WDC employees. The initial plan was for WDC to control community governance until the New Town's development was essential complete. I became Chair of the WCA Board. From the day the first resident moved in, the Association was an important player in the creation of true human community.

Swim and Athletic Center

In addition to many hiking pathways throughout the Village of Grogan's Mill, a large recreation complex was needed. Since it would be owned and operated by The Woodlands Community Association, it was my team's job to get it designed and built. It was a wonderful facility with an indoor gymnasium and swimming pool. In its adjacent outdoor yard, we built an Olympic pool with a set of high diving boards. We were able to open the complete grand complex by 1975. Our son Stuart became a lifeguard at the outdoor pool and diving facility. The Center was a major attraction for people moving to The Woodlands and helped create community among the residents.

Public Safety

As with other projects in the months before Opening Day, there was an additional issue on which no one was working. There was no Public Safety service. I saw that it could become yet another mission of The Woodlands Community Association.

For fire protection, as soon as there were unpaved roads under construction, I bought a large used pumper fire truck. I had an open shed put up at the end of one of the dirt roads to serve as The Woodlands' first fire house.

WDC already owned and operated an ambulance for construction workers. By arranging for WCA staff to run it, I initiated a rescue service for visitors and early residents, as well as for construction workers.

Before the Grand Opening, for police protection, we relied on the Montgomery County Sheriff's Department. State law did not provide for creation of a police department by a residential Community Association.

Early on, the U.S. Postal Service began delivery once we installed neighborhood gang mailboxes in all our residential neighborhoods.

Public Schools

As for public education, there was more than a little concern in existing school districts that WDC would try to reduce their boundaries and establish a new Woodlands district. Very early on, I went to see governing representatives of the Conroe Independent School District ("CISD"), the district covering the first lands being developed. I calmed the worries as we began negotiations for new CISD schools in The Woodlands.

Early on, I worked with the CISD to build a high school in The Woodlands. McCullough High was to be located on land we donated to the District southwest of the future site of Lake Woodlands, a large artificial lake that was both a community amenity and part of the drainage system we were creating in conjunction with the San Jacinto River Authority. Part of the deal with the District was that we would build a westerly extension of Woodlands Parkway with a bridge over the creek that would be dammed upstream to form Lake Woodlands to reach the school. HUD being HUD, it took the government many months to agree to a grant for this vital road construction. My argument was, "What is a Title VII New Town without a first-class high school?"

When the grant finally was awarded, we rushed through the final road permitting and construction, and had a ribbon cutting at the new bridge the night before buses started driving across it to deliver entering sophomores to McCullough High School. Our daughter Karen was a Sophomore who then attended McCullough for its first three years.

Continuing My Ordination as a UCC Minister

One of the church institutional challenges I had as a member of The Woodlands development team was that of continuing my standing as an ordained minister of the United Church of Christ. To maintain one's ordination in the United Church of Christ, one's ministry must be regularly reaffirmed by one of the denomination's many regional Associations. While I viewed my work in community development as a valid form of ordained ministry, the Houston Association of the UCC did not, since The Woodlands was not a UCC project.

Early on, Jan and I had joined First Congregational Church of Houston. Its Senior Minister was a fellow graduate of Chicago Theological Seminary. He appreciated my non-traditional ministry. He was interested in seeing me retain standing as a UCC minister. He recommended that I become a member of the Board of Settegast Heights, a 300-unit low-income apartment project, sponsored by the Houston Association of the South-Central Conference of the United Church of Christ. Once I began serving on the Settegast Heights board, the Association affirmed that I was "in ministry" and could keep my ordination in good standing.

Grand Opening Day

October 19, 1974 was a very pivotal day in the early creation of The Woodlands. On that day we opened for business. There were concrete main roads with entrances at two Interstate 25 exits. There were five subdivisions complete with lots, streets, water, and sanitation services, all ready for new homes. There were the 50 townhomes I had needed for formation of the first Municipal Utility District. There was an Inn and Conference Center. There were stores, a restaurant and two office buildings. There was an inviting sales center. There was a golf course complete with a lake. A New Town had opened its doors!

That night, after all the visitors had left, some 400 staff members of the two Mitchell real estate corporations held a grand celebration and dinner.

Much had been done. But creating a truly functional human community still lay ahead.

Chapter 24

~~

LIFE WITH HUD

WHEN I FIRST started working at The Woodlands there was no functional working relationship between The Woodlands Development Corporation and HUD, our loan guarantor and Project Agreement partner. Things were not going smoothly. The parties were not talking to each other. It was immediately obvious that this needed to be corrected.

The Project Agreement had been signed just shortly before I got there. HUD had not begun to deliver the early construction grants that had been contemplated in the documents. WDC was not starting infrastructure construction as quickly as projected. HUD was beginning to be frustrated that MDSW was spending so much money and time on higher end amenities, to the exclusion of housing and facilities for modest income families. On the Mitchell side, senior Mitchell Energy and Development people were worrying that real estate activities were distracting the company's gas and oil efforts. There was significant bad communication between Mitchell's energy people and the New Town staff.

For much of the year prior to the Grand Opening I was back and forth to Washington D.C. trying both to land promised grants, and to make HUD staff comfortable. After I established a working relationship with HUD's Assistant Secretary for New Town Development, things began to fall into place.

Because of my being responsible for execution of the terms of both the HUD Project Agreement and the HUD staff's subsequent requirements, I had an intangible unarticulated authority in the work of both MDSW and WDC.

The HUD Default

Opening Day was a marketing success, with hundreds of people coming north from Houston to see what we had wrought. However, we were no more than open when I came on a fact that threatened the whole project and all its financing. In the rush to get the MDSW facilities open, particularly the Inn and Conference Center and golf course, Len, our corporate President, had used over $10,000,000 of HUD-guaranteed money for upscale development that was outside of the scope of the Project Agreement. Because it was my job to assemble detailed financial reports to HUD, I was the one who recognized this use of funds as being illegitimate. Giving not more than a few seconds of thought to my two previous firings, I made an immediate lunch date with George Mitchell. I took along a colleague from the land planning department as a witness to my second whistle-blowing adventure.

At lunch, I took a deep breath and said to George, "You need to know that The Woodlands Development Corporation has misapplied HUD funds. The Project Agreement provides that we would use HUD guarantee money for roads, water, sewer, drainage, and certain social infrastructure. Len, in the pressure to reach opening day, has used

$10,000,000 of the $50,000,000 for the golf course and Conference Center. When HUD figures this out, it will declare a default, shut us down, and demand that the whole $50,000,000 be repaid."

George, who always talked like a machine gun, talked even faster. He said, "Robb, catch the next flight to D.C. and work things out with the Secretary!" The lunch was over. This time, for confronting an employer with the truth, I had not been fired!

My accompanying lunch witness who did not really know what the meeting was to be about, told me later that he almost swallowed his fork when I told George the cold truth. I took this fellow back to The Woodlands and headed straight for the airport, not even taking time to go home for a clean shirt or toothbrush. While on the plane I devised a strategy that I thought would work.

Next morning, meeting with senior HUD staff, I honestly admitted to them that in the rush to opening, about $10,000,000 intended for land development had gone into the Inn and Conference Center and even a golf course.

After describing openly to HUD officials what had happened, I said, "I will see that whatever we owe our HUD loan guarantee account will be quickly repaid."

In my effort to appear totally transparent, I next boldly suggested that the HUD staff could review The Woodlands financial records from day one. "Well," one of them asked, "how would we do that? We're not sending anyone to Texas."

I responded, "I'll get the paid construction invoices sent here. You can look at the invoices right here in D.C."

"Okay, let's do that," said my key HUD contact.

Then I called The Woodlands Chief Financial Officer and asked that he immediately ship all the original invoices and payment vouchers for every development expenditure since the Loan Guarantee had closed. By this time, it was clear my role gave me respected authority in the company, so the accountants went to work. After dozens of boxes were unloaded into a HUD conference room days later, I told the HUD staff to feel free to go through them and sort out what funds should have paid for what. They must have trusted my $10,000,000 estimate because not a single box was ever opened. But this process took six weeks, with my negotiating our commitment to use non-HUD funds for a list of specific future infrastructure items costing $10,000,000 for which the HUD money otherwise would have been used. I ended up being credited, both at HUD and in the Mitchell parent corporation, for getting this mess untangled.

Though it was known both at HUD and in the corporate management structure that I was an ordained minister, I tried very carefully to not use that reality as a foil or defense. Nevertheless, my transparency, delivery of commitments in all dealings, and passion for an openly governed community gave me serious credibility in both camps. This came from the Holy's claim on my risk-taking in doing what was right.

Improved Government Relations

Shortly after the Grand Opening, Bob McGee and several other senior managers, all who had come from the Columbia project, left the company. George Mitchell had already terminated Len, the subsidiary company President the day after my sounding the alarm. Though I never knew exactly why the others left, I presumed that parent corporation officers had demanded additional terminations. At the same time, The Woodlands V.P. for Government Relations, an older and celebrated local, died. Thus, in the aftermath of the Grand Opening of The Woodlands, as Vice President of Community Development, I was responsible for everything related to governance and community services.

To generate more transparency and sense of mutual control, I negotiated with HUD the creation of what we called the "Annual Budget Control Document." It was an agreement for specific HUD-approved development activities that would occur at The Woodlands in each next year. Under the Project Agreement, we had to get HUD's approval for any expenditure of debenture funds and current grants before work began. So that there would be no confusion, the Annual Budget Control Document included all the intercompany transactions as well as the WDC land and public facility development expenditures. For all my future years at the project I was the creator of the Annual Budget Control Document for The Woodlands. I prepared huge budget spread sheets using a hand calculator for several years, until a young fellow in the accounting department came up something called a computer. I gave him what I wanted to include in my budgets, which he completed after-hours as a personal favor.

It was my role in preparing these annual revenue and expenditure budgets that gave me significant influence in managing the whole operation, regardless of reporting structure. Colleagues also cared a whole lot about my corporate role because I negotiated federal grants each year, which over time amounted to many millions of dollars.

Chapter 25

~~~

LAPP FAMILY VISITS LIBERIA

IN THE FALL of 1975, with Jan and me both working full time in community human service roles, and with three teenagers still in school but moving into young adulthood, we decided to go to Liberia as a family to visit Jan's brother's family for Christmas. It was a wonderful experience for all of us, as we each gained a clear feel for a Third World view of America.

Liberia, located on the southwest corner of Africa's horn on the west coast, is unique in African history. It was part of the region from which natives were captured by traders and shipped off to western hemisphere countries, particularly the U.S., where they became slaves. Liberia was formed as a distinct country in the 19th century as a place to which freed American blacks were repatriated, not necessarily willingly, prior to the American Civil War. As a result of Liberia's American heritage, the primary language is a form of pidgin-English. The returning immigrants were treated very negatively by indigenous residents, but the African American returnees controlled the government of Liberia from its inception until 1980, when there was a bloody military coup d'état.

Jan's brother, Dr. William T. Wallace, Jr., was serving the Methodist Medical Missionary in Liberia. In his first two three-year terms, he, his wife Marilyn and their three children, Bill III, Susan, and Sandra, lived and worked in a back-country mission outpost in Ganta deep in the bush of eastern Liberia. At the end of their second term, in 1974, they had spent a year in Baltimore where Dr. Bill earned his Master of Public Health degree from Johns Hopkins University.

Then, in the summer of 1975, in his third three-year missionary term, Dr. Bill worked as a consultant for the Liberian Ministry of Health and Social Welfare in Monrovia. His mission was to upgrade and modernize Liberia's health delivery system and to develop a functional hospital in Monrovia, Liberia's capital city. The Wallaces lived in Monrovia, where we were to visit them.

Since there was going to be a Christmas dinner pot-luck be at the Monrovia Methodist missionary compound, Marilyn suggested we bring fixings from the U.S. On the flight Jan carried a ten-pound bag of potatoes, and I had a large frozen turkey on my lap.

When we entered the terminal's only passenger room, we spotted Marilyn, who blurted the sobering news that Dr. Bill was very sick in bed with Hepatitis, which, we learned, is far from rare in West Africa. It can come from a variety of sources in the tropics, including polluted water. One can try to prevent the disease by being vaccinated. Since it also can travel from person to person, Marilyn took us all to the hospital to get shots.

On our first morning in Monrovia, Jan, Marilyn, and I left six kids to entertain one another, and rode a city bus to Waterside, an open-air market near the seaport. The bus was a meaningful first exposure to the culture and economy of a West African nation. The heavy aroma of human bodies filled the air. Clothing, though colorful, was modest, and compared to well-fed Americans, most people were very spare.

Marilyn, Jan, and I were the only white people on the bus. The locals were polite to us. Some stared. Some were rude to one another as they jostled for position, getting off and on the bus. The relative poverty was obvious everywhere. The streets were filled with pedestrians, most of whom carried bundles, some on their heads. Ever present beggars cried out in need, their uncared-for physical disabilities quite obvious.

As tourists, not identifiable missionaries, we were sucked up to, but silently disrespected by numbers of Liberians, particularly those not connected to the Methodist mission. I guess I had expected, probably naively, that we would be accepted as fellow human beings, neither put on a pedestal nor distrusted. But on the buses, along the streets, and at Waterside, we were stared at and whispered about. I sensed it was because we were white rather than because we were foreigners.

On Christmas Eve, all of us, except for the convalescing Dr. Bill, went to a service at the Monrovia Methodist Church, a crude structure that did not have any glass in the rough window openings. It was great! Up front was the traditional stable crèche scene, complete with a live black baby Jesus. But after the arrival of the angels, shepherds and wise men, there was an additional parade, mostly of children and teens, offering music and dances representative of the indigenous culture. It was an ingenious mixture of a European understanding of Jesus' birth and a West African vision of the celebration of new life. Seeing this cultural adaptation of a Christian story gave me further insight into the inter-connectedness of Jesus and culture in communities around the world. In America, we often so equate democracy and economic prowess with Christian values that we forget our religion should be fundamentally countercultural.

The Christmas day celebration on the Monrovian mission station was unlike anything we ever have experienced either before or since. The meal was served on the beach which was covered with oil tar balls that had washed ashore from tankers purging their empty holds as they left a nearby terminal. Having Christmas dinner on hot sand was eerily pleasant. It was not a cold winter's day. Instead, the sun was blazingly hot. We looked out, not across a snow swept field but over a rolling Atlantic Ocean. We were outdoors, not around a hearth. Dr. Bill, by now strong enough to sit up, was in a folding chair on the sand. Children ran around throwing tar balls. Almost ethereally, we were imposing a New England turkey dinner on an equatorial environment. You can take the Americans out of America, but you cannot take America out of the Americans. As people in other countries struggle for their own identity, it is often difficult for them to understand varying cultural strands of Americans and America. But on this Christmas day the locals enjoyed the spectacle as they walked up or down the beach.

The next day, everyone except Dr. Bill squeezed into a UN Volkswagen Microbus, complete with a UN driver, for which Marilyn had arranged, to go to Ganta. Getting sleep in the small house where we were staying was a bit of a trick with very noisy nocturnal fruit bats screeching as they hit the screens.

Seeing the "hospital" and a few of its patients was more than sobering. We noted that when family members brought in an ill or maimed child or adult, they slept on the floor next to their loved one. And patients did not have private or semiprivate rooms. The patient care rooms could best be described as a cross between a dormitory and a camp site.

While in Ganta we ventured into the rural bush to visit a nearby leper colony. It was heart wrenching to see what the disease did to fingers, limbs, and faces. But some of the most beautiful thorn carvings were made by people who could hardly hold their knives and scrapers. We bought a complete nativity set and later, in Monrovia, found a large calabash gourd from which to fashion a manger.

GANTA - LIBERIA

Before leaving Monrovia, Jan and I went to the American consulate to see the face our homeland presents to a subordinate nation. It was not pretty. As were most of the Methodist missionaries, most of the consulate staffers were white. This stood out as being abrasive in the local culture. The baggage of white superiority was carried by the agents we met. They asked if we were "Peace Corps." They seemed not able to believe that whites could simply be tourists.

The trip lasted just over two weeks. It had been great to see the Wallaces and to learn first-hand of the work they were doing. But it was a very sobering experience. We had seen America from the outside. And we had been exposed to living conditions lived by well over half the earth's population. This experience, which occurred on our only overseas trip, gave me new insights about the American culture. I cringe when our foreign policy and behavior looks and feels like an arrogant, if not belligerent, misuse of power. Despite all our attempts to aid other nations, we often are seen by others as bullies serving America's economic and political self-interests. We must sound to non-Americans as puffer-bellies who squander the world's natural resources while polluting and overheating the earth, and while behaving militaristically. Because we have been strong enough to seek peace on our terms, it is no wonder so many in the world resent us while we live self-congratulatory lives. My citizenship has become that of a person who supports leaders who attempt to negotiate human differences with an even hand.

In terms of what the trip did for my view of the American culture, the incongruity of imposing a generally European religious tradition on a variety of people whose stories of ultimate reality are very different has made me aware of the dangerous link between Christianity and the imperialist soul of America. Culturally, Americans are very self-absorbed and self-serving. We honor wealth and fight for personal success, however defined. Religiously, we believe in a God who rewards those who look out for themselves. Paradoxically, the God incarnated in the pre-Easter Jesus of Nazareth is very countercultural. This God calls us to sacrificial living for the benefit of the "least of these," the powerless, the infirm, the hopeless, and the lost. But our culture views the good life as just the opposite. Success is the freedom to do what we want, to live where we are safe, to be served by the economy and the government, and to have control over all the events, forces and people that impinge on our self-interest. This trip made me an uneasy American.

Chapter 26

~~

A Home in The Woodlands

FROM THE OUTSET, it had been our intent to move into The Woodlands once new homes were being built. In 1975, Jan and I spent many hours picking a lot and deciding on a house plan we liked. We decided to buy a Mitchell employee-discounted wooded lot located at 2710 Timberjack Place in the Village of Grogan's Mill.

We hired a local home builder who had a house plan we liked. While our house was being built, we purchased one of the early houses near the Swim and Athletic Center, for a short interim stay. The first owner had installed a nice below ground pool in the backyard. Jan and I enjoyed it almost every muggy night that Fall!

Our new house in The Woodlands was built on a densely wooded lot that backed up to a golf course. Because of the thick woods, we could not see the course but occasionally we could hear shouts when someone made a good shot. Our house had a master on the first floor, and three bedrooms and an activity room on the second. It was a great place for our three kids while each transitioned from high school to college. The kids had the upstairs pretty much to themselves.

Shortly after we moved to The Woodlands in 1976, Jan transferred to the Conroe office of the State Department of Human Services. Her new job was to provide emergency services and support to people in economic crisis. Jan solicited funds and food to aid people in need. After having Jan often send people to his church for assistance, the local Catholic Priest gave her a checkbook. He counted on her to give small sums of money to people who needed food or help with rent. She also collected significant amounts of food, some of which she kept in her office for the drop-in trade. Jan thoroughly enjoyed this job as it allowed for substantial innovation in reaching out to the community's forgotten poor, many of them black.

Robyn and Stuart had already graduated from Spring High School before we moved, while Karen became part of the first graduating class of the new McCullough High School in The Woodlands. Each had learned how to drive. Each selected and began attending a college.

Robyn Goes to Stephen F. Austin

Robyn's independence came to full flower as she finished high school and launched into the intriguing world of trying to run her own life. We had it in our minds that she should attend a liberal arts college, perhaps one associated with the United Church of Christ. Oberlin and Carleton were on that list. She made a different decision. After visiting Oberlin College in Oberlin, OH, and Carleton College in Northfield, MN, she chose Stephen F. Austin, a state university in nearby Nacogdoches, TX, at least partly because she'd be nearer to a boyfriend. Stephen F, as it is known in Texas, is a good school with strong teachers. In fact, Dr. Sylvia McGrath, Jan's first cousin, and head of the History Department at Stephen F, had been valedictorian of her graduating class at Michigan State University. Her husband, Dr. Thomas McGrath, also a very capable educator at Stephen F, was a Forest Pathologist. The point, from the perspective of parenting, is that Robyn's choice represented an emerging independence.

She started her freshman year in the Fall of 1975 but was not certain about her intended major. However, after two years Robyn lost interest in Stephen F and went to Brooks Institute, a photography school in Santa Barbara, CA. She ended that effort, too. When she needed money to fly home from California, I was pleased that I had the courage to tell her to figure out how to get train fare and that we'd meet her at the Houston station when she called.

After returning to The Woodlands, Robyn worked for a while as the Radio Dispatcher in the WDC Public Safety trailer before becoming a guest services worker at The Woodlands Inn and Country Club where she met David Patten. Apparently, there would be no more school for her, at least at the time.

David was a cool guy with similar interests in arts and literature. But he had one characteristic that made heterosexual marriage unrealistic. David was openly gay. Frank conversation with Robyn did not deter her. I therefore supportingly officiated at their wedding ceremony in First Congregational Church in Houston on May 27th, 1978. I liked David. He was very responsible and caring. I think the marriage was more Robyn's idea than David's. But Jan and I were learning to watch, hoping to be able to embrace our children's decisions.

This marriage fell apart when David's partner moved in with Robyn and David in 1980. By then she was working for Continental Airlines as a scheduler and freight agent at Houston Intercontinental.

Stuart Goes to Southern Methodist University

In late 1975, while he was still in his senior year at Spring High School, Stuart flew to Delaware, OH, to visit Ohio Wesleyan University, Jan's and my Alma Mater. He wanted to be a lawyer and thought an undergraduate Liberal Arts degree was the place to start. I could tell from the look on his face as he walked down the jetway upon his return to Houston that he would not be going to OWU.

It was cold and snowy in Ohio when he visited. That is all it took to dissuade him. Later, someone told him that Southern Methodist in Dallas had Methodist connections. He applied and was accepted.

Stuart excelled as a student at Southern Methodist in Dallas, majoring in Pre-Law. During the summers he worked at The Woodlands, first as manager of the small recreational boat operation on Lake Woodlands, and later as a lifeguard at The Woodlands Swim and Athletic Center.

When Stuart was an SMU student, on a fall Friday morning in 1979 a car pulling a horse trailer drove up in front of our house. Stuart and two friends piled out. Stuart told Jan they were on the way to a football game at Tulane in New Orleans. The critter in the horse trailer was the team mascot, a mustang named Peruna. As Mustang Band members, the boys had gotten permission to take Peruna to New Orleans for the game.

To give Peruna a break, the boys led him out of the trailer and tied him to a tree in the front yard woods, where they tossed him a partial bale of hay. Jan had in the refrigerator some leftover lasagna which she heated for the boys' late morning breakfast. She laughed when one of the boys asked Stuart, "Do you often eat lasagna for breakfast?" One of the carryovers from Jan's first incarnation as a homemaker and mom was that we always had a reliable stock of leftovers.

Jan and I were proud parents at Stuart's SMU graduation in 1980. My mother joined us for that celebration. By the time he graduated, he had been accepted at the Bates School of Law at the University of Houston.

Karen Also Chooses Southern Methodist

When McCullough High School opened in the Fall of 1976, Karen was in the entering Sophomore class. She was among the top students, graduating ninth in a class of over seven hundred students. Jan and I were excited by her accomplishments and very joyful as she crossed the stage at her graduation in the school's first Senior Class.

With her older sister and brother already away at college, Karen found having jobs after school and during summers worked well for her. During her senior year at McCullough High, she was a clerk at the Jamails supermarket located in the Wharf Mall at The Woodlands. After graduating she worked as a lifeguard at the pool in Oak Creek Village where she had been a member of the swim team when we lived there. She worked there again the next summer, this time also helping Stuart coach the Oak Creek Village swim team.

Unlike her sister and brother, she did not make a big production out of choosing a college. Through Stuart, she had become acquainted with Southern Methodist University, and she thought it would work for her. She applied and was accepted. Her major was, not surprisingly, Business Administration.

Of our three children, Karen was the most organized and the one who had the strongest control over daily life challenges. In many ways, she incarnated Jan's strict distinguishing between right and wrong behavior. But she did this very quietly. She was clearly her own person.

Prior to Karen's starting at SMU, when Stuart was going to or from SMU I had driven him either all the way to Dallas or to Houston's Hobby Airport, which was an hour and a half from our home in The Woodlands. Once Karen had matriculated at SMU it was simply easier to let them drive together in a car that we were not using. That car eventually became Karen's.

THREE COLLEGE STUDENTS AT HOME

Chapter 27

≈≈

MAKING THE WOODLANDS WORK

After the Grand Opening

FOLLOWING THE GRAND Opening of The Woodlands there was much to do to make the WCA a strong force in creating a sense of community. Hiking and biking pathways through the woods had to be built and maintained. The Swim and Athletic Center had to become operational. Community Governance had to be established. Trees and other vegetation along roadways had to be cared for. Administrative and program staff members had to be hired and trained. Public Safety services had to be developed. And the whole operation had to be financially managed in a responsible fashion.

From the Grand Opening through the rest of my tenure at The Woodlands, I was President of the WCA. It turned out to be one of the most fulfilling roles I played at The Woodlands. The Holy kept whispering that the human race must live communally.

Residents watched WCA closely because we levied owner fees for facilities development, community services and general administration. Appropriately, property owners were very interested in the uses of their funds.

At first, all seven WCA Board members were WDC employees. We announced all meetings to the public and held them at times that were reasonable for residents to attend. Before long, it became obvious that we should have resident participation. I soon asked residents of the first village to recommend candidates. We then appointed two residents to serve on the board. This number soon grew to three to give voice to more segments of the community while keeping control in the hands of WDC. Even though resident directors would be in the minority during the New Town development era, there was serious interest in winning positions at the table. For the remainder of my time at The Woodlands, the public board positions were hot commodities for which we held annual community elections.

After we had community representatives, I tried not to arbitrarily exercise the authority of developer control, though I held the majority vote. We discussed items long into the night trying to come up with solutions that could be supported by the resident representatives. For all practical purposes, the residents generally achieved their goals. Questions involved guidelines for use of public facilities, expenditures and design for new community facilities, street parking and other rules, police, and fire service, use of the then state-of-the-art CATV, architectural design standards, and a host of other issues.

As the corporate officer most responsible for WCA decisions and services, I received many phone calls from residents, whether in my office or at home. I shudder what to think it would have been like if we had had internet email and smart phones in those days.

Fire & Rescue Department

During the pre-Grand Opening construction window, we had had an ambulance and a fire truck in a temporary shed. As homes were built and residents began moving into The Woodlands, I organized a volunteer fire-rescue crew and bought a second fire engine. My first public safety employees were dispatchers who were housed in a construction trailer near the temporary sheds where the trucks and ambulance were parked. Before long I was able to hire a paid chief, who turned out to be both competent and caring. We bought more fire trucks and a new ambulance as time went on.

Police Protection

To gain better policing I soon negotiated a deal with the Montgomery County Sheriff. If we paid for officers' salaries, police cars, and radios, the Sheriff agreed that he would assign deputies to patrol only in The Woodlands. At the outset we had two cars and sufficient officers to cover The Woodlands 24/7. Though this was the structure of the agreement for my entire incumbency, this arrangement became very difficult to manage.

The first Sheriff with whom I worked was an insightful, flexible fellow who did everything he could to make this arrangement work. The next Sheriff essentially did everything he could to create dysfunction between his deputies and my WCA management team. Gradually, both this Sheriff and his deputies totally resented the WCA's keeping tabs on them and their activities inside The Woodlands. They hated it that I had a two-way radio in my car on which I could listen to calls as they unfolded.

The agreement with the Montgomery County Sheriff led to a satisfactory public safety program but required constant attention. There were soon enough officers to have a command structure. A difficulty was that the senior officer reported to both me and the Sheriff. This clearly created frequent conflicts of interest and was a tenuous arrangement at best. On the one hand deputies were authorized by law to respond to incidents anywhere in the County. On the other hand, the WCA was paying for the cars, deputies' salaries, and all operating costs for the entire operation in The Woodlands under an agreement that said the assigned deputies would work only in The Woodlands.

An example of this tension occurred one day when there was an incident on the frontage road across the Interstate outside The Woodlands. Though not specifically called to the scene, one of our assigned deputies left The Woodlands to join other deputies at the scene. He totaled the patrol car we owned while racing the wrong way on the frontage road. Fortunately, no one was injured. But I never could get the Sheriff to pay for the car.

Nevertheless, people in The Woodlands were appreciative for the public safety services they were getting.

A Public Safety Building!

Very soon after Opening Day I landed a federal grant for the construction of what became an impressive public safety building. On one side it had space for the Sheriff's deputies. On the other side was the fire and rescue equipment, and lodging space for fire fighters. The building was designed so that the dispatch office was above and off to the side of the large room that housed the fire equipment. I did this so that dispatchers could see volunteers arriving, and emergency equipment leaving during emergency calls. I had police and fire offices in the same building because I saw emergency services as involving both units in mutual support. The Sheriff's deputies never saw it that way. They kept to themselves.

Over time we hired paid fire/rescue personnel to supplement the work of volunteers. We devised a system of having the volunteers respond directly to incident scenes, and having the paid staff respond with appropriate equipment.

A humorous little story makes it clear my day job wasn't enough work. Early on, volunteers drove our ambulance to scenes and to hospitals in Conroe and on FM 1960. But not for long. For some reason there were numerous problems with the driving of the ambulance, though not with the on-board emergency medical care. So, I took on the job of responding to the station and driving the ambulance for most night calls. Some nights I was out as many as three times. It was bizarre to be a senior management guy in a suit during the day and a rescue volunteer in casuals at night. It was also exhausting. But driving the ambulance felt like a caring volunteer role.

Houston Open

In 1974, when The Woodlands was barely a community, the Houston Golf Association and The Woodlands Development Corporation entered into a ten-year agreement to hold the Houston Open on one of our courses. We had tens of thousands of visitors crawling all over The Woodlands each year. I quickly learned that the most efficient way to manage the necessary public safety was to ride with my Fire Chief and patrol through the community. Whenever something untoward happened, we would establish incident command and guide responding police and fire units on routes through tangled traffic.

There always were many celebrities in The Woodlands for the Houston Open. One year, while patrolling, the Fire Chief and I were momentarily in our corporate office building at ten in the morning when I heard a pounding on an entry door. A man and a woman were seeking entry. Each held a drink cup. Because I supposed they needed a restroom, I let them in. Sticking out his right hand, the guy said to me, "Hello. I'm Ed McMahon, and this is Miss Vicky." Being congenitally unimpressed with celebrity, I had no clue. But I welcomed them and waited to secure the door after they left. My Chief exclaimed, "Wow, do you know who that was?" I said, "No. I just know it was a tipsy man with an even more tipsy woman who probably is not his wife." In amazement, the Chief said, "Ed McMahon is the guy who says, 'Heeere's Johnny on the Johnny Carson show." "Oh," is all I said.

Why Not Lease Corporate Cars in Montgomery County?

In early days, when I was trying to gain the confidence of the Montgomery County Commissioners Court so that we could get support and government approvals, I had a thought. The various Mitchell companies regularly leased annually upwards of 400 cars and trucks. Why not get them from Montgomery County instead of Houston dealers? This turned out to be an excellent idea. The resulting good will gave us lots of leverage in getting respect for our New Town.

Montgomery County Hospital District

I was very concerned about medical care. The closest doctors were ten miles north, in Conroe, or twelve miles south, along FM 1960. We envisioned having a functioning relationship with hospitals and doctors of the famed Texas Medical Center. The first thing we did was to make free office space and administrative support available to a young M.D. who agreed to open a practice in the Grogan's Mill Community Center. In the beginning, we even subsidized his income. He turned out to be very popular, and had as patients a high percentage of early residents.

At the outset, I thought we would simply get a branch of one or more of the Medical Center hospitals to open in The Woodlands. As I cultivated relationships with their administrators, this seemed possible. But it was not that simple. The county hospital in Conroe wanted us to facilitate the opening of an annex in The Woodlands. After prolonged negotiations that involved both Houston and Conroe medical interests, I came up with the concept of a hospital district that would include Conroe as well as The Woodlands. Voilà, the Montgomery County Hospital District was formed. The Woodlands Medical Center, Inc., the nonprofit I had formed to facilitate the opening of the medical clinic, eventually was integrated into the Hospital District. Then I arranged for the Woodlands Development Corporation to contribute a tract of land to the Montgomery County Hospital District for construction of a local hospital. Gradually other hospitals, mostly from the famed Houston Medical Center moved branches into the Montgomery County Hospital District.

Federally Assisted Housing

As I prepared Annual Budget Control Documents for submission to HUD, and in using development plans to leverage Federal program grants, I focused on the issue of societal integration. People both at The Woodlands and at HUD gave lip service to economic and ethnic integration for The Woodlands, but parties on each side were waiting for the other to commit.

I found a way to motivate the Mitchell real estate team by telling management colleagues that I thought I could get funds for subsidized housing if they would commit to contributing land at below market prices and developing the projects. And I said to people at HUD that I thought I could get assisted housing in The Woodlands if only HUD would support it through designated allocations of housing program funds. Neither side could resist. Our first project was 300 plus units of senior housing apartments near the elementary school in the Village of Grogans Mill. This project was racially integrated from the outset. For the next several years, I arranged for lower income housing financing from HUD as part of each annual development agreement.

The Woodlands Religious Community

Partly because of the lobbying of a Lutheran minister, and partly because of George Mitchell's commitment, an unusual concept had emerged early in the planning for The Woodlands. Prior to there being any land sold for churches, this Lutheran minister formed The Woodlands Religious Community, Inc. ("WRC"). Its intent was to foster interfaith cooperation in serving residents of the New Town. WRC was able to use the Sawmill Center in the Village of Grogan's Mill for worship and activity space. It became the Interfaith Center. Inevitably, the founding Lutheran minister involved me as an advocate. One of things I did in helping judicatories that wanted to start churches in The Woodlands was to urge them to support WRC, and to use the Interfaith Center as a place for worship before their sanctuaries were completed. Later, I persuaded WDC to sell church sites to participating groups at discounts. I tried to locate these sites near school or office buildings so that we could get multiple-use parking. As a result, most religious traditions were able to locate in The Woodlands.

Jan and Robb Organize Shepherd of the Woods UCC

The South-Central Conference of the UCC wanted to start new congregations in the northern part of the Houston metropolis. After Jan and I moved to The Woodlands, what was to become Shepherd of the Woods UCC began holding informal worship in our living room in 1978. Outgrowing our house, the Shepherd of the Woods congregation moved to the Woodland Religious Community's space in the Sawmill Community Center, where Jan became the pianist. One Easter Sunday, in the Interfaith Center, the only instrument available was an electronic organ that another church had brought in for an earlier service. Sight unseen, Jan, a pianist, sat down and played the organ very well.

Soon, our group had grown enough to call our first full time minister.

Next, Shepherd of the Woods UCC bought a site in The Village of Panther Creek, near the site of the future Panther Creek Community Center and adjacent to a grade school. The church and school shared off-street parking. When the UCC bought this site, it was in a remote western section of undeveloped forest. Jan and I had left The Woodlands by the time construction of the new church building was completed in late 1981. Unfortunately, once the building was finished, a couple of poor ministerial selections led to the demise of the congregation and the sale of the building.

Our lives were very full while we lived in The Woodlands. We both were gone long hours. Church work was our primary extracurricular activity. We had little social life. But each day we tried to exercise by walking on the extensive new community pathway system. Except for many yo-yo returns of our kids, we were empty nesters for the last two years we lived in The Woodlands.

Corporate Management as Ministry

At our weekly management meetings throughout the years, I sat at the end of a long table opposite George Mitchell who sat at the head. Apparently because of the positions I took on community service issues, he came to see me as a moral beacon on many justice and transparency questions that arose among staff members. Whenever a question of strategy or corporate integrity arose, he first would glance at my eyes and body language before entertaining comments from others. Mitchell also called me at home or in Washington D.C. many nights to ask for details of my negotiations with the Dept. of Housing and Urban Development.

I always thought it was interesting that my colleagues at Mitchell never forgot that I was a clergyperson, although no one ever addressed me as "Reverend." However, Mitchell people, as well as those with whom I negotiated, gave me the benefit of the doubt on issues of fairness, honesty, transparency and caring. This may be one of the reasons I was able to broker so many pivotal agreements.

Chapter 28

≈

TIME TO LEAVE THE WOODLANDS

EVEN AT THE Woodlands, I kept learning who I was meant to be. Following my graduation from seminary almost everything I did I had never done before. This also was true about my becoming a husband and father. It was like watching myself from outside my being.

I had always been on edge in my church pastoral roles, particularly in Arvada. Essentially, I often told people what they did not want to hear. There always was a subtle undercurrent of, "We're on the wrong path with you if you don't make us comfortable and happy."

At both the Fair Housing Center in Denver and Gananda in Rochester, in confronting the dynamics of the American culture in its racism and striving for economic power, I felt the pain of sacrificial risk-taking.

My "at will" employment in each of those settings never felt very secure. However, The Woodlands became a time of my being respected while pursuing social justice ministry.

At The Woodlands I knew how my person worked. I saw how I acted and reacted. I had confidence in who I was. My commitments had played out in real life, time and time again. When I chose to leave this team, I knew I was doing the right thing, and I knew the humanness I was taking into the future.

After eight years in Texas I had come to the realization that the time of my major transformative work in The Woodlands was coming to an end. I was no longer creating a community development style for the corporation. I was increasingly being asked to manage a departmental staff whose work had essentially become routine. The Woodlands Development Corporation President, my boss, was making arbitrary decisions and not valuing input from his senior managers. His being President was mostly about him, not the project or the new community.

I had completed establishment of a governance structure that would serve The Woodlands long into the future. We had new schools, a municipal utility system, a hospital district, parks and open space trails, police and fire departments, and a community association that would one day become a township government with a city manager. It would become a community that could work for everyone.

Jan was first to think that I should leave Mitchell Energy, and that we might return to Colorado. The ending of our time in Texas was a process that unfolded over several months, as it took a while for me to embrace the idea that I could walk away from a very meaningful secular ministry. In truth, I wasn't recognizing that I was emotionally and spiritually burned out and that I needed a period of restoration. But I came to think that returning to Colorado would help me regain clear perspective and a refreshed soul. It was time for me to go into the mountains to pray.

For a couple of years prior I had been thinking somewhat off-handedly that I would like to build a house myself. One day, while we were walking along a tree lined pathway in The Woodlands, Jan said suddenly, "If we're going to build a house, we can't wait until you're 65. You need to do it now." The seed was planted!

While we were thinking about this, we took a quick vacation in Hawaii using our daughter Robyn's Continental Airlines employee family discount for flights and housing.

The day spent visiting the shrine-like assemblage in Pearl Harbor was both sobering and deeply moving. We both felt a deep chill as we stood over the sunken battleship Arizona. Realizing how many lives had been lost right at the spot where we stood took my breath away. I was swept back to the Sunday afternoon of December 7th, 1941, when I sat in the basement of the Kenmore Methodist Church listening to the news reports of the Japanese bombing of Pearl Harbor. In many ways, standing over the Arizona was a sacred moment. The Holy was saying, "War is not the way to fix things."

While in Hawaii it did not take much imagination to picture my leaving Mitchell Energy, and Jan's leaving the Texas Department of Human Resources. It was exciting to picture our buying land in the mountains west of Denver on which I would build a passive solar house with my own hands! I was nearly 48 at the time.

In the fall of 1980, we decided we would move to Colorado. Prior to saying anything to anyone in The Woodlands, Jan and I flew to Denver in early October 1980, and spent three intense days looking at mountain property options. A tract overlooking Gross Reservoir in Boulder County on what would eventually be named Tunnel 19 Road seemed the best choice, but it would require the purchase of three parcels from two separate sellers. This site was located just north of Tunnel 19 of the Denver and Rio Grande railroad which runs from Denver through

Grand Junction and Salt Lake City to San Francisco. The railroad and all its tunnels had been built by David Moffat at the outset of the Twentieth Century. Our future driveway could cross over Tunnel 19 some 200 feet above the track. We signed contracts to purchase the three tracts. A Sabbatical retreat was at hand!

We also made an offer on an existing nearby mountain house to have a place to live while we were constructing our new house, which, of course, had not yet even been designed. This home purchase offer was not accepted, so we later bought a house in Arvada, just around the corner from the parsonage where we had lived from 1962 to 1967.

Not trusting the President of The Woodlands Development Corporation, I waited until I received my promised bonus for 1980 before I announced my resignation. On March 27, 1981, my 48th birthday, I met with him. Though I had done him many favors, including taking him to the Conroe hospital late one night when he fell off a ladder at his home, he was not pleased as we negotiated our separation.

On one of my trips back to The Woodlands, the President had confiscated my company car, even though I had committed to working for the WDC for the next several months. I was frustrated. Jan's enthusiasm for my leaving Mitchell Energy was reinforced!

I was either at The Woodlands, or in Washington D.C., or in New York City, off and on all spring and summer of 1981, closing the Indenture created for the HUD Project Agreement and the $50,000,000 loan. It was the end of August 1981 before I concluded such traveling, but I had walked WDC's deal with HUD from initiation to fulfillment. There was a Title VII New Town!

Moving Back to Denver

Once I had formally resigned, by late March we were ready to move to Arvada. We rented a U-Haul van and a large trailer to tow behind the van. While loading we discovered we did not have enough room to carry everything. Jan took a deep breath and said, "Well, I suppose I could pull a second trailer behind my car."

We made quite a parade going across west Texas. It took us two days to get to Arvada. Jan managed the second trailer and enjoyed the company of Snoopy, our mongrel dog, who our kids had left behind as they went off to conquer their worlds. As we arrived in Arvada, our friend Bill Haefele was standing on the front porch of our new house waiting to help us unload.

Two Daughters Move to Colorado

Knowing that Jan and I were moving back to Colorado, after Robyn divorced David Patten, she requested that Continental Airlines transfer her to Denver. She soon was assigned to the off-airport site of the Continental freight depot in north Denver. We were pleased that she would be joining us back in Colorado.

Robyn's freight agent work was in a service warehouse at Stapleton Field. At first, she rented an apartment, but she soon moved in with a boyfriend in a community north of Denver.

As Karen completed her second year at SMU, she told us she was not going to return to SMU for a junior year. She simply said, "I'll just move to Colorado when you do."

While Jan and I thought Karen's leaving SMU might be a negative, we were pleased that she, too, would be moving back to Colorado. We would be able to have a supportive working relationship with her as she stepped into the world of living on her own.

Her immediate plan was to share an apartment with Robyn. So, as the semester ended, Jan and I drove a small pickup pulling a utility trailer filled with construction tools to Dallas, where we met Karen who drove her car with us to Denver. As we labored in heavy head winds across New Mexico west of Amarillo, radio news blurted that Pope John Paul II had been shot and wounded in St. Peter's Square.

When Karen first arrived in Colorado, she moved into the apartment in Northglenn already occupied by Robyn. After a brief stay in the apartment, when Robyn moved in with a boyfriend, Karen joined us in our temporary Arvada house. By then a teller at Capital Federal Savings Bank, Karen went on a cruise with Robyn, during which she met a fellow from the Denver area whom she later dated.

Though all this became the end of her formal education, Karen has an uncanny knack with numbers and works well in corporate settings. Her career path has included banking and major corporate inventory management.

Son Becomes a Texan

After graduating from Southern Methodist University in 1980, Stuart made a key decision. That Fall, having considered law schools in Colorado and elsewhere in the country, he matriculated in the Bates School of Law at the University of Houston. While we had thought he, too, might move back to Colorado, this decision was the prologue to his becoming a life-long Texan. But we were delighted that he was continuing in his commitment to becoming a lawyer. He was hoping to help clients deal with their personal and professional challenges.

Stuart seemed to have found a home. He liked the local culture, the warm climate, and the topography with its lakes and natural surroundings. We should have known he had become a Texan as early as when he got off the plane after having looked at a college in cold Ohio.

Reflection

I had been at the Woodlands for 8 years, from 1973 to 1981, and after my sixth year, I began to have an emerging new sense of myself. During this window of my life, I subtly shifted from one whose identity was most clearly described by his employment role to one whose identity transcended the particulars of that job. I was coming to know myself as an independent, unconventional, societal transformer. This was the Holy at work in my life. The Jesus who expressed his faith outside the Temple in the street filled my soul.

As I closed my eighth and last year in The Woodlands it was becoming obvious that my continuing ministry would be in secular settings outside the structure of the church, but that my societal value framework would be deeply rooted in the Holy's Biblical vision of a just and embracing community of human beings of all sorts.

So far, my Mitchell days were the most fulfilling chapter in my life. I was good at what I did. I learned that I could be a functional part of a corporate management team as a Christian infiltrator. I liked the work. I was pleased to be in "The West," albeit in its very southeastern corner. We were creating a significant and functional structure within which major cross sections of the larger culture could live together. I had better personal outcomes than I had experienced at the Fair Housing Center or in Gananda. Our family functioned well. Jan's life had taken a turn into a new career. The children, though typical teenagers with typical teenaged challenges, communicated well with us, even though we did not always fully appreciate their thoughts or behavior.

For me, helping create The Woodlands is a testimony to the holy power that creates hope for the future of human existence, and an invitation to stay the course of trying to make life work for everybody.

But returning to Colorado, which had become Jan's and my adopted home state, was a fulfilling return from a ten-year exile precipitated when I had responded to the Holy's call to help create equal opportunity in open housing for people of all races, particularly African Americans.

SECTION VI
1981 – 1990

BACK HOME IN COLORADO

Chapter 29

～～～

TIME OUT TO BUILD A HOUSE

BEFORE OUR MOVE back to Colorado, we hired Denver's foremost passive solar home architect to design our mountain home, which I planned to build myself. Jan and I made a special trip to Denver to meet with our architect to lay out the parameters of a design and site plan. Shortly after he completed the preliminary sketch design, he was in an auto accident that severely injured his head and brain. He died a few months later. This was a shock for us and a true loss for the region's passive solar movement.

But this talented architect had already influenced the ultimate design of our new home. He had selected its specific location and solar orientation in an area just north of the western exit of the D&RG Railroad Tunnel 19. And he had sketched a very contemporary structure, much to my surprise, as I had pictured a more rustic, traditional structure. The tall side of the house, filled with windows, was to face about ten degrees east of due south. There were few windows on the north side, as both the architect and I assumed the prevailing wind would come from the northwest. As it turned out, the major winds hit a long ridge southwest of the house then glanced back north to blast the southwest corner of the house. But that is another story.

Because of recent eye cataract surgery in Houston at the time we moved, I could not do any physical labor, particularly at an altitude of 8,000 feet. So, using the architect's preliminary design, I sat at our dining room table substantially modifying the house plan, making it a bit larger and redesigning the interior. But I stuck with his contemporary concept.

Jan played a significant role in the design revision process. She recommended putting the laundry on the level where clothing was donned and shed, rather than on the main floor where it had initially been placed. She suggested we move the kitchen from the interior to an outside wall where we could have a view of the nearby wooded hillside and the passing trains. She opted for having a large pantry, and a freezer, as well as a refrigerator, in the kitchen. The dining room was expanded to accommodate a twelve-seat table for intergenerational family gatherings, as well as a china cabinet she hoped to get someday.

The lower level included a two-car garage, a bath with shower, a bedroom, a workshop, and a water well pump room. Since the house was dug into a hillside, the entry to the garage was the only part of the lower level that was visible from the outside.

Drawing on large velum sheets spread out over the dining room table, I completed the floor and exterior plans, hired an engineer to add structural detail and stamp the plans, then took the sheets to a blueprint shop. From there I went to the Boulder County Building Department and was issued a building permit after making several recommended changes. Our getting a building permit with home-drawn plans was a real coup, as the Boulder County Building Department was widely known as being extremely particular about its approvals.

But I did not have any trouble. I found the staff both very helpful and accommodating.

Initial Site Work

Our first construction-related purchase was a chain saw. Wearing new un-tattered blue jeans and a fresh straw cowboy hat, I cleared trees where the house would be located, carefully saving a gallant Spruce tree that would stand just east of the tallest part of the house.

Next came the task of digging a foundation and cutting a driveway along the edge of a small hill. Jan and I had been exploring the mountain areas west of our site when I spotted excavating equipment stored in a yard along the road in the mountain town of Nederland. The sign said, "Len's Excavating," and gave a number. I called, and the next day Len showed up with a large loader and a tandem dump truck. We cut a road from the north end of a county gravel road to the house site, then did a cut-and-fill to make way for the basement. When Len was finished, I spent several days with a pick and shovel completing deep trenches for the footers.

Before we went any further, I wanted to be certain we would find water. To drill the well, I hired a company whose rig I had seen days earlier in the canyon. The rig was so large it could hardly negotiate the newly cut drive. But when it was in place over the well site, Jan and I stood by, watching the auger turn, knowing that each descending foot was costing $11.00. At $3,630 our driller found good water. The well tested at 5 gallons per minute. A few years later, during a drought season, we added a 500-gallon cistern in the house basement to assure adequate supply and pressure.

Still in the first fall, I hired a two-guy contractor to bring concrete forms which I helped set for pouring the foundation. Next, a huge pumper truck unloaded 75 yards of concrete into the foundation wall forms. On another day, when the exterior foundation walls had set, I had to lift, a shovel-full at a time, five yards of heavy wet concrete over the exterior wall into forms framing an interior foundation wall. I was ecstatic when the foundation was finished!

We called and asked Len to return with his loader and truck to transfer many tons of decomposed granite from a nearby location for fill around the newly completed foundation. Len also installed a 1,000-gallon septic tank adjacent to the foundation and built a large leach field to the north of the future house.

In one of my early visits to the Boulder County Building Department I overheard two men talking. One asked the other, "How are you coming with placement of that rain gauge the Sheriff wants south of Gross Reservoir?" The fellow responded, "I've been waiting for months to hear from the D&RG Railroad. I submitted a request to place the southern county gage on the railway easement over Tunnel 19."

Finishing my business at the counter, I walked up to the men and said, "If you're willing to move your rain gage site 20 feet north, I will give you the 10' by 10' patch you're discussing." One of them responded, "Oh, then we could lease it from you."

He was the Boulder County Engineer. As we talked, I had an idea. Instead of a County lease payment, I asked, "Will you sign an agreement to provide year-round maintenance of the gravel road leading down the hill from the Gross Dam Road to your rain gage?" "Yes," he said, "the County will." When drafting the agreement, the County needed a road name. "Tunnel 19 Road," I offered. Boulder County thereafter maintained Tunnel 19 Road, providing critically needed snow plowing and spring grading.

100 Tons of Concrete Blocks

Each day, I checked the "Building Materials for Sale" columns of the *Denver Post* classifieds. While doing the foundation walls in later 1981, I spotted a liquidation sale of a cement block manufacturing facility in northwest Denver that had been purchased by the Denver & Rio Grande Railroad for expansion of its freight yard. A fellow from Oklahoma had purchased the entire inventory of blocks, but had to quickly move or sell them.

He had many tons of solid 6x8x16 inch blocks, each one of which weighed 40 pounds. He also had a supply of smaller and larger hollow core blocks. I bought 100 tons of these blocks for pennies on the dollar. It took 17 trips on a large flatbed rental truck to carry the blocks from central Denver to our mountain site.

Jan helped unload them, which we did by hand, block by block, day after day. Then the winter snows came, and we had to wait until Spring before starting to use them in our innovative design for capturing the passive solar heat.

So much for construction until Spring of 1982! For most of that Winter I could not get to the site because of deep snow.

Winter Ends

Beginning the next Spring, I lifted and hand-carried each block three more times, once to load them into our Toyota pickup, once to unload them by the house foundation, and, finally, to lift them into place in a wall.

It was emotionally very fulfilling to move these blocks. Carrying them one by one, each block symbolized the transformation of a dream into a concrete reality, not to make a pun. Contrary to being drudge work, my days were exhilarating. I was recovering from the intensity of the Texas new community development ministry. The Holy had whispered, "Take a break!"

Framing started with floor joists, then two layers of plywood sheets for the subfloor. As I framed the main floor, generally using heavier members than was required by code, and two-by-sixes in the exterior walls instead of two-by-fours, I quickly came to the time for laying up concrete block interior walls for the solar mass. I decided I needed a little help, so I hired a part-time CU student who at least allegedly had some masonry experience. As it turned out, hiring him was a good idea. After a few weeks he asked if I would also hire a friend. The friend turned out to be the more competent and harder worker, but they both were very helpful.

As we completed the second story framing, I was growing frustrated with my slow progress. One day, while at the lumber yard in Arvada arranging for delivery of another load of framing lumber, I commented to a fellow customer about the slow pace of my framing work. He asked if I'd be interested in hiring him and his friend, both carpenters, to help with the attic and roof framing.

"Yes!" I exclaimed.

Somewhere I had read about "cold roofs." Cold roofs consist of two layers of plywood separated by rows of 2x2 spacers, thus making an air space that would help insulate the roof. When our cold roof was completed, my hired carpenters had contributed significantly to the overall project.

There is an additional tale about the second carpenter. He wanted to marry the woman with whom he was living in northwest Arvada. The wedding was to be at the new Denver West Ramada Inn. Would I officiate? Sure. I often was asked to "do" weddings that involved people who had no formal church affiliation but who wanted a minister, just to be on the safe side. I did the appropriate premarital counseling. When we got to the service itself, it was in a Ramada Inn in a room very near the bar. There already had been several trips to the fount. The Best Man could not stand up. I took the Groom aside and said to him, "There will be no ceremony if anyone in your wedding party has any more to drink." He agreed. Then, since he and his bride were in pretty good shape, we proceeded without any standing attendants. Pastoral Ministry unfolds in unexpected, and sometimes amusing, ways.

Mother came for a Colorado visit in the summer of 1982 when she was 75. On each of several days she visited the new house site, and, with Jan, carried board after board from a delivery pile and stacked them closer to where they would be used. Tough woman!

After the skeleton of our wonderful house was complete, I turned to roofing, exterior insulation and windows. Each of these steps, as with the concrete blocks, involved my watching the *Denver Post* ads for building materials. I found surplus concrete roof tiles in Littleton, closeout rigid insulation sheets in Lower Downtown Denver, and German-designed triple glazed windows in Fort Collins. Pine siding came from a mill in Saguache, and I found beautiful moss rock at a yard near Lyons, north of Boulder.

Falling Off the Roof

On a cold day in the Fall of 1982, after a night of light snow, I climbed up to the living room roof, which, at that point, was still just a smooth plywood surface. I had a shovel that I wanted to use to clear the roof before starting on roof tiles. As I took my first step on the sloped roof,

I skidded down the roof, over the edge, and twenty feet down to the ground. That day both my Boulder helpers were there. They watched me disappear and ran around the house to see what had happened.

I was doubled over on the ground, having been able to throw myself out over the open joists of a deck on which, if I had landed there, would surely have killed me. I had landed in snow not more than a foot deep, but which packed enough to cushion my fall. My upper right leg hurt. One yelled, "Robb, are you all right?"

Struggling to get up, I shook myself, and said, "I think so. I can move."

The other kid added, "We were watching you, and you suddenly disappeared." Helpfully, he added, "You shouldn't have stepped out on that snowy plywood!"

I kept my mouth shut and suffered through the rest of a day's work, keeping quiet about the pain. When I got home later that afternoon, I confessed to Jan, who worried lots about me anyway, that I had fallen off the roof, and that my leg was sore. Just as she has said solicitously on many occasions, she exclaimed "Oh, honey!"

I must only have pulled a few muscles, as I was walking evenly within a few days

When the roofing was in place, and rain or snow could no longer penetrate the interior, I turned to the insulation, siding, and windows.

Early in 1983, partly because of the national economic downturn, Jan and I discovered that we needed the funds invested in our Simms Street home for construction and daily living. We quickly sold the house and, on my 50th birthday, moved into an apartment in Arvada very near the mainline Denver & Rio Grande tracks that continued west through

Tunnel 19 under our new house driveway on their way to Winter Park, Grand Junction and San Francisco. One evening we ran over to the tracks to watch the final eastbound run of the classic California Zephyr. Next evening, we watched the first less fancy Amtrac passenger train go by.

Later in 1983 we again moved, this time to a rental house on Tunnel 19 Road, where we stayed until moving into our very incomplete new passive solar house in mid-1984.

Once the framing and exterior of the house was completed, the plumbing and electrical rough-in work had to be done. I hired a plumber for the initial fresh and wastewater piping, but did the rest when I discerned that he was dragging his feet to run up his hours. I installed all the electrical wiring myself. Wanting to have plenty of outlets and multiple switches for almost everything, I used over a mile of heavier-than-code 12-gauge, plastic covered flexible wire. I even managed installation of the main electrical panel without shocking myself or burning down the house. It all passed final inspection.

Jan decided we should have a telephone at the construction site in case of an emergency. I called the phone company. The clerk said, "Oh, yes. We can install a phone line for $35.00." When the crew came and saw where we were in relation to a connection pedestal on an existing line, the foreman said, "Mr. Lapp, for the work we'll have to do, the installation will be $3,500." I fussed, repeating the $35.00 quote.

Then I remembered that down the hill on our property in the telephone company easement, there was a 10x10 fiberglass building housing a 1,600 pair phone-repeater station. I said to the foreman, "You know that repeater station down the lower road? I have seen kids roaming through the woods with guns. I could watch out for mischief."

The foreman went to his truck, took down a long roll of cable, dropped it near me, and said, "If you can figure out how to bury this from that pedestal down there near the repeater station up here to your house, your fee will be $35.00. "Done! A $150 trenching machine rental and a day's work was all it took.

After all the rough-in work was done, it was time for moss rock and drywall. Early on, I had concluded I was not going to hang or finish the drywall, nor was I going to do the tedious work of laying up the moss rock interior and exterior walls. So, I hired out both jobs. The stone masons were a couple of Denver firefighters who did rock work on their days off. They did a beautiful job. The sheetrock guys were able to trowel drywall mud across all the block walls, so they looked just like the sheetrock walls, even and slightly textured. When we moved out of the house 25 years later, there were absolutely no cracks in any of the walls or moss rock work.

In planning the house, we imagined that winter heat would come from sun rays being absorbed into the block walls and from two wood stoves. We bought two Vermont Casting wood stoves. One was mounted in the corner of the living room where it would heat the massive moss rock walls. The other was in the breakfast room, so that it would heat the kitchen as well as the upstairs bedrooms and baths that opened out onto the large open space above the breakfast room. To be on the safe side, I installed 17 zones of electric radiant heat panels in ceilings throughout the house. It turned out that sun light and the breakfast room wood stove were all that was needed for warmth. We never used those radiant heat panels.

To supplement the passive solar heating, each winter we consumed about five cords of split pine I cut on our property during the prior summer. Each morning Jan enjoyed removing the prior day's ashes and starting a new fire.

It all worked. We spent very little money for electricity.

Because the landlord of our Tunnel 19 Road temporary house wanted to rent it to another tenant, we had to move into our new home way before it was completed. We had a stovetop but had not yet installed kitchen counters. There being no sinks anywhere in the house, we had to wash dishes in the upstairs bathtub. There were no floor tiles in the kitchen or breakfast room, and no floor covering anywhere else in the house. Most light fixtures were not yet installed. For light at night, we strung droplights. Only one toilet was hooked up. We had a freezer but no refrigerator. The dishwasher sat among the unfinished cabinets but was not hooked up. Nevertheless, we were thrilled. We were in the "House that Robb Built."

How did Jan feel about the project? She was excited from beginning to end. The promise of a home in the state from which we had been driven ten years earlier buoyed her through all the construction sacrifices. She participated in each major decision from site acquisition, building design, and interior finishes to appliance selection, kitchen cabinet design and the solving of financial issues. Because she was employed full time, many days she did not get to the site. When she could come, she repeatedly exclaimed about newly completed installations.

Problem Windows

Very early in the planning process, Jan and I went to a Parade of Homes open house in Westminster. One of the show homes featured some sturdy looking, well insulated windows that were triple glazed. The builder swore by them. We liked them. Their dark brown heavy plastic frames would look good against the medium tan-stained exterior wood siding we planned.

Alas! The windows had been in the house less than six months when the sun's ultraviolet rays began destroying the dark plastic frames. Some shrank so much the glass panes broke. I could not do the interior wood trim until we got the problem resolved. I also didn't want to finish the floors or install carpet while this was an open issue. The manufacturer would not do anything to fix the problem. I found a lawyer, won a lawsuit, and received enough in damages to pay for replacing them all with some well-designed Andersen Windows.

The contractor who showed up with the Andersen Windows installed them very nicely. Then I finished the remaining interior work. Window trim, paint, tile, and carpet made the house exquisite.

While we were facing the window fiasco, Jan's nephew, Bill Wallace III, was married in Denver. The whole Wallace gang stayed with us, and we hosted the rehearsal dinner in our unfinished house. No floor covering. Splintery plywood subfloors. Incomplete walls and window trim. Yet, the high emotions of a family wedding forgave it all!

After spending two and a half years trying to succeed in most of the building trades, I had discovered doing the electrical wiring and fixture installation was the most enjoyable. Cement flatwork and drywall floating were the jobs I disliked most.

"Dad, if you could see me now!"

One bright, sunny afternoon, when the project was finished, I stood on the highest level of the roof, and slowly gazed around. On the west I could see the Continental Divide and the snow-covered Never Summer Range. To the north was an expansive view of Gross Reservoir and miles of foothills. To the northeast were the backsides of Boulder's famous Flatirons. Directly east were the vast plains where Denver International

Airport would one day be built. And to the south was the ridge that separated us from more populated sections of Coal Creek Canyon. As I stood there, I could see forever. I was atop my accomplishment. I said aloud, tears in my eyes, "Dad, if you could see me now!" I had built a house. I was now a peer of a man who had had the ingenuity to build rocket planes, though he had no formal training for doing so.

HOUSE THAT ROBB BUILT

I have done many things over the years, most of them cerebral, technical and/or humanitarian, but building our house stands out uniquely as a restorative life experience. The break I needed resulted in re-energizing me for social change ministry.

Chapter 30

<div align="center">~~~</div>

ROCKY MOUNTAIN
CONFERENCE VOLUNTEER

WHEN JAN AND I first returned to Colorado in 1981, I was elected to serve on the Board of the Rocky Mountain Conference of the United Church of Christ (RMC-UCC), successor to the Colorado Conference of the UCC. Close friend and seminary classmate, Dr. Clyde Horace Miller, Jr. was the new Conference Minister. I was very impressed that in the mostly white rural west, the Rocky Mountain Conference had called a black man to its top leadership position.

The Conference was struggling financially. Though it was valiantly trying to continue in its role of supporting local church growth, mission giving was not covering its work. Not yet focused on ministry as community service and social change, in those days the church model was still one of helping people feel comfortable with their lives. Good pastors were the ones who could do this best. Money was being invested in new churches that would follow old models. Local churches were beginning to decline in membership numbers; some even closed. As a corollary, Conference revenue was also diminishing. Even its premier camp, La Foret, was experiencing financial difficulties.

Creating an Ecumenical Office Center

One of the Conference financial challenges was office space. RMC-UCC was renting a house immediately adjacent to Cherry Creek Shopping Center in southeast Denver. Our high rent reflected this proximity to the shopping center. Further, the office space was not very efficiently laid out.

The RMC-UCC was committed to increasing cooperation among mainline denominations in our region. One day I said to Clyde, "Why don't we see if several denominations would be willing to share leased space? We would need only one conference room, and a single office machine and storage area. A single receptionist could cover all the groups." He thought it might be a good idea.

The judicatory boards of the Presbyterians (PUSA), Disciples, Lutherans (ULCA) and the UCC all thought this would be a good idea if I could find an appropriate location with facilities that would work for everyone. But it soon became clear that the creating of four separate leases was more than an office building owner was willing to do. An over-the-top idea soon evolved. Why not create a separate nonprofit entity that could be the single tenant, with the church groups being lessees of the nonprofit? This led to my organizing Rocky Mountain Ecumenical Center, Inc. to lease a large office space, then sublease it to participating denominations. Representatives of each group made up the board of this shell nonprofit. I was its sole officer and registered agent.

I found a vacancy in a building that had at one time been a Catholic

Convent. It was located at 14ᵗʰ and Pennsylvania, just five blocks from the Colorado State Capital complex in downtown Denver. Perfect! Windowed offices surrounded a large central conference space, enabling the staff persons of all the participants to encounter and work with one another through the working day.

It worked very well, bringing these four denominations into a much closer working relationship. It also helped all the groups with reducing their office rental expenses.

Jan Becomes Client Advocate

After we returned to Colorado in 1981, Jan discovered that getting into a social services role in Colorado was more difficult than it had been in Texas, as State and County Social Workers were expected to have an MSW degree. Shortly after we started construction of our mountain house in 1981, the economy took a serious nosedive. Jan felt she needed to find almost any kind of employment just to keep us afloat. Her first job was as a temporary Christmas season clerk for the Denver Dry, a large department store.

Simultaneously, she landed another temporary post as Director of the Santa Claus workshop, run by the Adams County Department of Social Services. It was her task to raise funds, buy toys, and collect gifts for needy kids in south Adams County. One evening I accompanied her to the local Target to purchase $1,100 worth of toys. We went around the store filling six carts. Many onlookers laughingly asked us how many grandchildren we had. It was an unabashed hoot to assist her with this shopping!

In early 1982, Jan's job became more permanent at the Denver Dry after the holiday season. This was not particularly inspiring work, but she enjoyed interfacing with customers. Then a very interesting job materialized. The Episcopal Pastoral Center had a welfare client-advocacy program. Jan became a Client Advocate. She and a co-worker took turns working a desk in the lobby of the Denver Welfare Department office. Their job was to assist people who were having trouble negotiating their way through the system in their application or appeals for aid and assistance. This advocacy role was at first viewed by Welfare Department case workers with alarm. But, over time, Jan and her partner gained their confidence, being seen to be helping the system work better. In working for the Episcopal Pastoral Center, Jan also helped clients of the St. Francis Center, another Episcopal mission program that served low income and homeless people.

Mountain United Church Housing

During my New York and Texas exile from Colorado, a member of Lakewood United Church of Christ, Peg Stokes, literally "a little old lady in tennis shoes" started a nonprofit to assist lower income families and, eventually, seniors, with affordable housing. It was called Mountain United Church Housing ("MUCH"). Its first project was to purchase sixteen cottage schools in Arvada from the Jefferson County School District. These were overflow school buildings that looked like houses located in residential neighborhoods. MUCH converted each one into a four-bedroom rental home.

MUCH also had initiated two projects in Denver, neither of which it ultimately owned or managed. The Olin Hotel, an old 107-unit facility at 1420 Logan, was made into a senior home. It was owned and managed by the Ecumenical Housing Corporation, an interfaith nonprofit formed by MUCH. Next, MUCH, still under the tireless leadership of Peg Stokes, converted the Barth Hotel at 17th and Blake into another senior project, also ultimately owned by Ecumenical Housing Corporation.

As its last effort to improve housing opportunities for seniors in Denver, in 1981 MUCH developed a 50-unit expansion of the Ladies Relief Society home on West 38th Avenue. By this time, I was back in Denver and was a member of the MUCH Board. I helped oversee the design and construction of these 50 units.

At this point, the Minister of First United Church of Arvada and President of the MUCH Board knew that I had directed the building of low-income housing as part of my work at the Metro Denver Fair Housing Center and in The Woodlands in Texas. Late in 1981, he asked if I would become part time Executive Director of MUCH. I did, mostly as a volunteer. My role was to manage the sixteen single family homes in Arvada, and to create a housing development fund so that MUCH could build additional affordable housing.

While managing the operation of the sixteen Arvada Cottage School homes, I soon learned that some of the immediate neighbors were particularly sour about having "those people" living nearby.

This negative attitude was so strong that when a fire broke out in one of the MUCH homes occupied by a Russian immigrant family, a holier-than-thou neighbor called me to report the fire. My first question was, "Have you called the fire department?" "No," she responded, "why would I?" After hanging up and calling the fire department, I raced to the scene. This callous woman was sitting on her front porch, watching, and hoping the house would burn to the ground. It did not. When I stopped to encourage her to become acquainted with a neighbor who obviously needed help, she would not talk to me.

I soon was asked by the Minister of the UCC church in Silt, Colorado, a small town just west of Glenwood Springs, to help with a low-income housing project there.

The Minister of the Silt Congregational Church, who was also Mayor of Silt, was a visionary who imagined seniors in the community could have affordable, decent housing. So, I began working on the formation of a Housing Authority in greater downtown Silt, a small community of 2,200 people. Though MUCH had previously developed low-income housing only in the Denver area, he saw no reason why this UCC mission program could not do something in Silt. He became the community activist that made the development possible. I did all the project development work, including the formation of the Silt Housing Authority. Then, with a design done by an architect who was a very committed member of our UCC church in Grand Junction, we built a 26-unit senior facility in Silt, using Garfield County oil extraction fees for construction. Volunteer members of the Silt Housing Authority Board operated the facility. There was no permanent loan or real estate taxes, so resident rents had to cover only utilities and long-term building maintenance. They were very affordable.

One afternoon, the Silt Minister and I had to go to Montrose, the Garfield County seat, for a meeting with county commissioners. We drove there in the City Manager's vehicle. After we had completed our mission, the Minister elected to take a "short cut" over Grand Mesa, a huge high plateau southeast of Grand Junction. As we traversed the top in the dark, a heavy spring snow was falling. Just as I started to say to him, "Don't you think we're going a little too fast?" he lost control of the car. We skidded off into space and landed with a lurching crunch on the rocks below the road. The Minister-Mayor's leg was injured. Even though it might have been broken below the knee, he insisted I help him up the slope to the road. A passing motorist stopped and agreed to take him to the next community where they could call for help.

I stayed with the wrecked car and waited until a tow truck crew showed up. We spent the rest of the night hoisting the car off the rocks and back onto the road. I rode in the tow truck as we dragged the obviously totaled city-owned car to the town of De Beque on I-70. The Silt City Manager met me there for the drive back to Silt. He had taken the Mayor to a hospital. We arrived in Silt at 9:00 a.m., and I immediately drove the several hours over the Continental Divide for a church meeting. My conviction that most things worth doing are never easy was reinforced that day.

During the height of the oil shale extraction boom in western Colorado, the town of Parachute was expanded to house workers who never arrived because the project was not economically feasible. So, the new housing became home for underserved Western Slope families and seniors. There was an abandoned schoolhouse in the center of the community. Residents asked me to help them convert the school into a community center. With the same architect who had designed the Silt senior housing, we redesigned the school, raising necessary funding, and created a very functional community center.

Though I continued to make MUCH a viable low-income housing non-profit, my effort to create a housing development fund, eventually led to my separation from the nonprofit as an employee/consultant. The futility arose from the negativity of a board member lawyer who did everything he could to be an obstructionist.

I also was part of a small team of RMC Board members that monitored the activities and on-site management of La Foret. In a way it was a very sad time. All the buildings were deteriorating through lack of funds for maintenance. RMC-UCC use of the camp was slowly diminishing. Rentals to groups outside the RMC-UCC were difficult. And it was becoming harder to recruit counselors and deans. My dream was to make this special camp a place where people of all faiths or no-faith would be inspired to reflect on their relationship to God's claim on their lives.

A Second Ecumenical Office and a Retirement

In 1982, the ecumenical office space had become increasingly expensive because of its prime downtown location. We also needed a bit more room and staff parking flexibility. I found an office building on the north edge of the city, which was more convenient for members of our four partner denominations. This new ecumenical rental agreement lasted for the better part of the decade. Then, for various reasons, each group went its own way. During this lease period, however, RMC-UCC saved significant sums, aiding its budget.

After thirteen years of spiritually energetic leadership of the Rocky Mountain Conference, Dr. Clyde Miller retired in 1993. Because of his dramatic and faithful commitment, Board members pondered how to do a meaningful thank you. I recalled that the Conference had, years earlier, finished paying off the mortgage of the house in which Robert and Lucille Inglis lived when Robert retired as Conference Minister. I suggested we do the same for Clyde and Eva who, among other things, were having financial stresses associated with the raising of two grandchildren. I identified funds that could be used for this. By majority vote of the Board, the gift was accomplished. This did not turn out to be a popular move because Clyde was not totally embraced by all fellow Conference clergy. I have never been clear what role subliminal or even overt racism played in this dynamic.

Chapter 31

∼∼

To A Wild Rose

Should There Be a UCC Church in Evergreen, CO?

CLYDE MILLER CALLED me one day early in 1984 while I was still managing MUCH and serving on the RMC Board. He told me that a group of spiritual seekers was holding Sunday worship services in the Wild Rose Grange Hall in the mountainous woods south of Evergreen, CO. Describing them as folks with various religious backgrounds, as well as some who had not ever been part of a worshipping community as adults, Clyde said they had shown interest in exploring a relationship with the Rocky Mountain Conference.

He then got to the point, "Robb, is there any chance you could meet with these folks some evening soon to help them explore future possibilities? As a Conference, we are supporting a new church start in Castle Rock. But these people in Evergreen insist they are really interested in a church that wrestles with the emerging changes in the American culture. You are the only one I can think of who could give them appropriate guidance and help them with new ways of thinking and talking about God. Maybe you can give them some contemporary spiritual guidance and help them decide if they'd like to try to become a church."

"Why not? I'll try." I drove the 50 miles to Evergreen one evening and heard a tale of hope. These people thought they could start a new UCC congregation despite having been told the Conference's new church start leadership funds would go to the Castle Rock project.

Conference staff and board members had persuaded themselves that a new church start in Castle Rock in burgeoning Douglas County south of Denver, was pretty much an assured success. Located in the remote foothills west of Denver, a new church in Evergreen was far more questionable. But this gathering of theologically progressive folks persisted.

I met with these quiet determined Evergreen people in one of their homes. They wanted to know how to find a minister. The Rev. Dr. Charles Milligan, an Iliff Seminary Professor, was occasionally leading worship in the dilapidated Wild Rose Grange Hall, a small single room wooden structure whose bathroom was an outhouse, on North Turkey Creek Road, south of Evergreen. The gathering group's priority was to find a minister who would lead worship on a regular basis. I suggested they form a steering committee to figure out what was needed to make a new church work. A church school that met every Sunday both to teach their children and to attract new families was high on their list. They also wanted to find ways to explore and express their spirituality. They determined that to start they should have guest ministers when Dr. Milligan could not lead worship. They developed a newsletter and began publicizing their activities in the local community weekly. Essentially, they were a refreshing alternative voice in a mountain community where "life is about me."

They soon began gathering for worship in the Wild Rose Grange Hall each Sunday. Through the spring and early summer, I occasionally was the morning worship leader. After an hour-long morning drive, the outhouse behind the Grange Hall was a welcome sight before I entered to lead worship.

I also told them, "For an emerging identity, you need not be shy about your vision of what society should be like, and what people who listen to God's still small voice should do when societal relevance is at stake." They were excited.

In August of 1984, I began serving as their minister on a part time basis. That is probably what Miller had in mind all along.

Before long, it was obvious that we needed to find a more welcoming place in which to meet and hold services. We soon contracted for Sunday morning use of the cafeteria in the Jeffco Marshdale Elementary School on North Turkey Creek Road. On August 5th, we held our first worship service there, having moved tables, set up chairs, dragged in a piano, and even formed a rag-tag choir.

This was crazy. I had other obligations, primarily my work as a Board member of the Rocky Mountain Conference and my management of Mountain United Church Housing, including development of the Senior Housing project in Silt. This new church stuff could not last. But it did. Jan and I drove 100 miles every Sunday for over two years. And I went to Evergreen several times a week for committee meetings and to do pastoral calling and counseling.

One of these Sunday morning trips nearly became the last. Following the church service Jan was driving us north toward home on a highway that parallels the foothills which tower skyward just west of the city. As it often does in winter, the wind was blowing fiercely from the west. Strips of blowing snow crossed the highway, leaving extremely icy swaths. Just as we came to a stretch of road where there was a deep drop-off to the right, Jan lost control of the car. We skidded sideways toward the precipice, with Jan screaming at the top of her lungs. I reached over and shifted the automatic transmission into neutral and told her to jamb on the brakes. It was a good move because two wheels caught the roadside gravel and stopped our certain flip down the hillside. After we restarted, Jan drove a quarter of a mile, and then pulled over. "Here, you drive this thing," she whispered.

In our two years of leading Wild Rose, it grew from a handful to well over 150 adults. Kids were everywhere. Worship services moved from the Marshdale cafeteria to the gym. One little boy told his mother, "I like the Father because he sits on the floor with us for children's time." As is typically the case, volunteer leadership quickly emerged. Three women stand out. One, along with her husband, an oil patch guy, was a great organizer. They had a UCC background which was the impetus for her having contacted the Rocky Mountain Conference in the first place. Another, who came from a Roman Catholic upbringing, was wonderfully engaged in organizing a church school program. The third, a member of First Plymouth Congregational Church in Denver who, with her husband, had created a mountain horse facility, was the one who majored in "community building" among the participants.

There were many more deeply engaged people. After his first Sunday, a fellow assembled and directed a respectable choir accompanied by a delightful pianist who played each Sunday. Church school classes were held in the cafeteria, as well as in school classrooms.

A Church Tries to Make Life Work Better

My sermons began to be substantially different than they had been in Arvada eighteen years earlier. I had moved beyond helping people focus on their personal beliefs about God and implementing these convictions in their interpersonal relationships. I was coming to see Christian faithfulness as engaging in the transformation of the evils of our society and culture. My language of faith was becoming much more contemporary, helping people understand the stories of the Bible as metaphors for positive human existence. We jointly searched for what God was claiming from our lives and promising for the future. We saw God as integral to the work of bringing about justice and mercy for the whole people of God. Religion is counter-cultural, and all people go on spiritual quests whether church participants or not. The church moved from being a traditional comfort station to a dynamic mission center.

At Wild Rose, creative survival in the chaos of contemporary living set the agenda for my ministry, my preaching, and my counseling. My message was that it is possible to make other people's lives more functional by caring sacrificially for them, as Jesus cared for those around him.

From virtually the get-go, we talked and thought a lot about what is wrong with our society and societies of others around the world. What about the use of power to create harsh injustices? What is wrong with war as an international problem solver? What about economic inequality? What about an emerging oligarchy in American social and economic structures?

We had a very active world-peace committee. Its members invited a Denver lawyer, an anti-nuclear advocate, for a workshop. It was held in a barn belonging to our horse lady. I can still hear the haunting sound of a pail full of buckshot being dropped into a large metal garbage can. Before our guest started pouring the buckshot into the echoing container, she said, "Each pellet is an atom bomb. Listen for the number of atom bombs that are stockpiled by various nations around the world."

It was a phenomenal image, with thousands of pellets dropping for more than two minutes!

A few weeks later a group of cross-country peace marchers headed from San Francisco to Washington were going to pass by Evergreen on Interstate 70. The Wild Rose people wanted to know how they could help. I learned the marchers needed peanut butter for sandwiches they made each day as they marched. So, we had a peanut butter drive. We collected so many jars that I had to use my pickup truck to haul our contribution to a stop in Denver. I am sure they ate our peanut butter all the way to Washington!

The growing congregation was made up mostly of young families and still-employed empty nesters. Most were overcommitted. All were serious about accountable living. Many had come from other faith communions or no religion at all. Regardless of background, virtually all of them sought new insights about God, the Bible, praying, and discipleship. This was an exciting place for a minister. In sermons, I used contemporary metaphors to elicit visions of the Holy. In addition to seeing ministry as pastoral care, I was coming to see ministry as challenging people to express their faith by making life work fairly for others. After all, living in community is the call set out by God in the whole act of creation. My leadership style became that of mentor. It was their ministry, not mine.

My entire time with them turned out to be coaching them on how to "be church" in the world.

Being a part-time minister had very spongy time boundaries. When a parishioner was confronted with crisis, I could not say, "Oops. Sorry. I've already worked my fifteen hours this week." Or, when I already had driven four 100-mile round trips that week, I could not stand up on a Sunday morning and say, "Woops! There was no time left for sermon preparation this week."

One Sunday, a visitor stood out as one who wanted to engage with all comers. A very proper 86-year-old widow from Kansas City, she said to me after attending for two Sundays, "Rev. Lapp, I don't think I can help set up chairs, but you need someone to greet people at the cafeteria door and give them proper welcomes no matter what they look like." With a wry sense of humor and twinkly eyes, she was an immediate hit. All comers loved her, and she loved them. She was at the door every Sunday for the remainder of my time there.

After I was no longer Minister of Wild Rose, Jan and I called on this woman in a nursing home north of Denver. As we sat by her bedside, she said, "Robb, I'd like you to have my funeral, that is, if you live long enough." Well, I did. A few months later I conducted a proper remembrance in a church filled to the doors with folks who loved this delightful, caring senior.

After my second year at Wild Rose, with the idea that the church would soon be ready to construct its own facility, the Church Council arranged for a loan from the UCC Church Building and Loan Fund. Wild Rose bought an undeveloped site on Highway 73, south of the main town center of Evergreen. It was 26 acres in size and most of it had been zoned by Jefferson County as open space. The location for a church building was on a slight hill on the back of the property but visible from the highway with a large mountain meadow in the foreground. The goal was to have the church center itself clearly seen by any passing Evergreen resident. It was becoming obvious that the people of Wild Rose UCC were serious about their mission as Progressive Christians.

Meanwhile, the UCC establishment "new church" in Castle Rock stumbled and failed.

While Jan and I were busy with our church, community, and work lives, our kids were experiencing life changes.

Robyn Becomes a Mom

In December of 1982 while working for Continental Airlines in Denver, Robyn met and became engaged to Keith Gregg who also worked for Continental. Earlier, Keith, a native Coloradan, had been in the U.S. Navy.

Robyn and Keith were married in 1983. Keith worked as an aircraft mechanic. Robyn was still a freight-counter attendant. Shortly after their marriage, they were both laid off and Keith decided that he should return to career military service in the Navy, having already served his full enlistment term. This led to their moving to San Jose, CA in 1984. Shortly, Keith was deployed to Misawa, Japan, for seven months. Our first grandchild, Brittany, was born on September 30 that year. As a flight engineer on a P-3 Orion patrol plane, Keith was assigned to Diego Garcia for offshore patrol. After Keith returned to San Jose, Jan and I visited them and enjoyed spoiling Brittany, but we noticed that their marriage seemed tense.

Keith and Robyn were transferred from California to the naval base in Milton, FL, where Keith had shore duty. Several times, Jan and I found our way to the western tip of Florida's panhandle to visit them. We thought our first grandchild, Brittany, was wonderful.

In November of 1987 Jan went to Milton for a couple of weeks to help care for Brittany while Robyn was in the final stage of her second pregnancy. Our second grandchild, Chelsea, was born in Pensacola on the Tuesday evening before Thanksgiving. I flew to Milton for the holiday and absolutely loved holding a tiny infant way more than a turkey dinner.

Brittany, then Chelsea, were the biggest draws in Florida and were the beginning of Jan's serious grand-mothering.

Before long, in 1988, Keith was deployed for sea duty, this time to Rota, Spain. Before Keith left Milton, Robyn persuaded him that she and the kids should move to Arvada, CO, to be near the support of her family. I was guarantor for Robyn's purchase of a house in the neighborhood where we had started First United Church of Arvada. Wanting to get on with her life, while Keith was in Spain, in 1989, Robyn enrolled in the University of Colorado – Denver to complete her undergraduate degree.

Stuart Becomes a Lawyer

Stuart graduated from the University of Houston Bates School of Law in 1983 in a ceremony that Jan, Karen, and I attended. He had majored in business and contract law. He then passed the Texas Bar Exam in his second attempt, was admitted to the Bar, and worked briefly in private practice for a lawyer with whom I had worked earlier at The Woodlands Development Corporation.

Stuart became an Associate at the law firm of Dunn, Kacal, Adams, Pappas & Law, a commercial practice in Houston, and was an Associate from August 1985 to April 1991. Over time we got the impression that he was uncomfortable with what he was doing, both in his personal life and in his practice of law. But he persisted in his pilgrimage to figure out how to be the person he was meant to be.

Karen Works in Finance

While working as a teller at Capital Federal Savings in Arvada, Karen rented a house in old town Arvada from a bank customer who needed a tenant while temporarily gone from the community. Later, Karen left Capital Federal and went to work for First National Bank of Lakewood. She then registered with a temporary employment agency through which she worked for several outfits including Safeco Insurance, and, finally, AT&T.

Karen's job at AT&T became permanent in May 1985. Next thing we knew, Karen had moved in with the fellow she had met on the Gulf cruise with Robyn a few years earlier. They started out living in the mountains up Coal Creek Canyon, west of Arvada. Although Karen was smitten with the mountain living bug, she and her guy eventually moved into a rental in Arvada. That relationship did not last.

In 1991, Karen bought a house in Arvada, where she lived on her own.

Mother and Kathy in Tonawanda

In 1984, at age 77, Mother was still living in the little house into which the Lapps had moved just before the outbreak of World War II. One afternoon she lost her balance and fell the entire way down the cellar stairs. She broke her pelvis, her arm, and had a double compound fracture in her lower leg. After lying a while on the cold concrete floor, she crawled to a rack of winter jackets, pulled several down for warmth, and wrapped her bleeding leg. She laid there for nearly 24 hours before Kathy came for a visit and found her.

Jan, Stuart, Karen, and I soon located a modest one floor apartment on Chatsworth Road in Kenmore, NY. Moving her and disposing of 53 years of precious belongings took a while. After that move I flew several times to Buffalo to visit her. Stuart joined me for a couple of these visits.

Once, while we sat in her apartment living room, she handed me a thin book whose blue cover revealed it was the 1924 Proviso Township (west of Chicago) High School Yearbook. I had seen it years earlier, as it had a prominent place in a glass-door bookcase in her house, but I had only glanced through it. Mother graduated from this school in Maywood, Illinois, in the spring of '24. Her father was the minister of First Baptist Church in Maywood. They had moved to Maywood from Des Moines, IA, where he held a similar position.

Without a word, Mother opened the book to the frontispiece and, with a bony forefinger, traced an elaborate frame drawn around the contents of the page. It was a black pen and ink drawing of leaves, vines, and fruit. She turned pages and pointed to similar etchings decorating all the sections of the book. I had noticed but had never known anything about these tracings. This was her work, drawn at seventeen! Finally, she spoke. "I always wanted to be an artist." That short sentence spoke volumes about her life. It was full of unfulfilled dreams. Hers had been a lifetime of interruptive assignments.

While living in the Chatsworth apartment, she continued to manage the Ken-Ton Meals on Wheels program for another five years

Chapter 32

~~

RESCUING THE TIMBERS

WHILE SERVING BOTH as part-time Minister of Wild Rose United Church and as part-time Director of Mountain United Church Housing, I found myself also being drawn into helping a young church member solve a business challenge. In a pastoral call, I had learned that Phil was General Manager of a high-end gated residential housing community called The Timbers, right next to Marshdale Elementary School where Wild Rose was holding its Sunday services.

A few weeks after a pastoral call on this young man, he asked if he could show me The Timbers. It was an up-scale 26-lot mountainous subdivision. A pretentious gatehouse and stone wall had been constructed at the main entrance to protect residents from intruders. There being no municipal utilities, each lot required a water well and a septic system.

In the center of this beautiful wooded one hundred plus acre tract, there already stood a luxurious stone mansion. It had been built by Robert and Janice Smith, owners of a large a large homebuilding company in Pinellas and Pascoe Counties on the west coast of central Florida. They had hired Phil to divide the property into 25 additional estate lots and to sell them for private homes. Phil told me that this Evergreen mansion was the Smith's primary family home. He explained that they maintained their legal residence near Clearwater, FL, because, unlike Colorado, Florida did not have a state income tax.

During the tour, Phil wanted to know if I would help him with the closing and transfer of two lots to a couple of guys who, it turned out, had never built anything. Phil offered to pay me modestly for my supervisory assistance. Because this would supplement my part-time income as Minister of Wild Rose, I agreed. We got the two lots transferred to the inexperienced builders.

This led to my understanding the financing of the Timbers road building and lot development. Phil had formed the Timbers Estate Metropolitan District to sell municipal bonds, which had netted well over $5,000,000, enough to build the gatehouse as well as steep roads to the additional 25 lots. The bonds were to be paid off by special real estate taxes on the lots, tens of thousands of dollars more per year in taxes than on competitive homes in the immediate area. This was a good deal for the Smiths as they paid little to get a gatehouse, significant protective walls along the main highway, and a beautiful, paved road to their retreat home.

After several weeks of work, just before Easter of 1985, when Robert and Janice were in town, Phil took me to the mansion to meet Robert. It turned out that Phil had not previously told Robert about my involvement in the Timbers project. Nor had I been paid.

Sitting on a couch with Phil in Robert's Evergreen mansion study, watching this hulk of a man stride around his desk, I heard Phil introduce the subject of retaining me. It was very clear Robert did not know who I was or what I was doing in his house. After Phil introduced me,

Robert asked what I thought of the project. Prior to the meeting, I had figured out that the special district bonds for the subdivision development would result in property taxes of more than $35,000 per year for each lot, an amount that would severely impede sales. So, I answered, "Robert, I am interested that you think it'll work for the Timbers Estate Metropolitan District to bill each property $35,000 in taxes, over and above County, School, Fire District and other assessments."

The look on his face told me he had paid scant attention to the impact of creating a bond issue of over $5,000,000 for 26 lots. Showing little emotion, which I soon learned was his style, Robert turned to Phil and said, "When you did this bond issue, you should have told me how it would undermine our selling of the lots! I do not think you are qualified to run the Timbers project. I will see that you get your final paycheck. I'll pay you through today." That was it. Phil, without a word, got up and left the room. After visiting a bit to learn of my background, particularly at The Woodlands, Robert asked, "Robb, could you watch operations here while Joan and I are on vacation in the Pacific? We will be gone for two weeks. We'll stop here on our way back to Florida."

I said, "I can certainly give it a try." After I was given the key to the gatehouse, the meeting was over. I wondered what really made Robert tick.

This encounter was my first hint that there was mismanagement in Robert Smith's corporate world.

This preemptive firing of a parishioner led to some interesting pastoral care. Within days Phil checked himself into a local hospital, had no serious problems, then left without being discharged or paying his bill. I soon found myself in a marriage counseling series with Phil and his wife, who eventually divorced him.

When he returned two weeks later, Robert asked if I would manage the Timbers project. By the time I took over project management, the young fellows who purchased the two lots had partially framed both houses which they had not yet sold to any buyers. Very shortly, they defaulted on both their construction loans and lot payments. I negotiated deeds in lieu of foreclosure for the lots, assumed the construction loans, and took over the building of the homes. They had been so poorly designed that I had to make major exterior and interior modifications before continuing. Just what a minister goes to seminary to learn!

Next, I persuaded Robert's home building company to pay off the $5,000,000 in special district bonds, thus reducing the property taxes to reasonable amounts. Between the summer of '85 and Thanksgiving of '86, I had completed the internal road and community amenity construction and had finished and sold the two houses on which I had foreclosed. I also sold three more lots in the Timbers, on which their new owners were building homes.

My ministry during this period was primarily the new church start at Wild Rose and my building of the affordable senior housing project in Silt. I did not see my functions at the Timbers as a holy commission for social change. But at least I was making a corporation function honestly. Little did I know what was coming.

Leaving Wild Rose

By the summer of 1986, it was clear the Wild Rose church in Evergreen could support, and indeed needed, a full-time minister. Wild Rose people very graciously wanted me to continue, and to move into the Evergreen community. Jan and I thought carefully about the challenge. But it was not what God was calling me to do.

My secular ministries in fair housing and new community development were but a prologue of undefined social transformational work that lay ahead. We also wanted our home base to continue to be our house in Coal Creek Canyon. So, we urged the congregation to form a search committee.

Eventually, they called a UCC Minister who was serving the United Church in Douglas, WY. He and I joined in leading a transitional worship service on the Sunday after Thanksgiving, my last day at Wild Rose.

Sadly, the new minister's wife became terminally ill within a year of their arrival. Focusing on her illness and death, his ministry lost energy. With the church membership in steep decline, he resigned. The church survived but did not thrive. With grief of my own, I later helped the UCC Church Building and Loan Fund sell the church site to another denomination.

If my "take-away" from the Arvada parish experience was that ministry requires pleasing most of the people most of the time, my experience in Evergreen was that, given encouragement, people can respond positively to God's claim for loving others more than themselves. Certainly, my age and life experience had much to do with this transformation. I was able to help people concentrate on God's claim on their everyday lives in a much more straightforward way than in Arvada. In Arvada, my subliminal message was, "You ought to...." In Evergreen, it was, "You can ...."

Being the minister of Wild Rose was a very important interlude in my non-traditional ministry pilgrimage. When I agreed to help the local organizing committee do some early planning, I had neither the intention nor the desire to be back in a church pastorate. But as weeks of pulpit supply become months of full-blown church leadership, I was increasingly engaged in helping people hear their own calls to an authentic life. However, I was more than a little uncomfortable that I was not back in the thick of making secular community and financial institutions just and fair. The Holy would not leave me alone.

Chapter 33

~~

AFFORDABLE HOMES FOR
RETIREES IN FLORIDA

Can You Meet Me in Tampa?

ON THANKSGIVING MORNING of 1986, my home phone rang early.
It was Robert Smith. I knew he was not calling to wish me Happy
Thanksgiving. He said he was at his Colorado house. Could I fly
with him on Sunday to Tampa? He had just fired his company's Vice
President for Commercial Development before flying to Denver the
night before. He wanted me to pick up the pieces and recommend
next steps in managing the construction of a 51,000 square foot office
building in Clearwater, Florida. I told him I couldn't go on Sunday as
it was my last Sunday at Wild Rose, but would meet him in his office
first thing Tuesday morning. It was not at all clear where this would
lead. I simply saw it as an extension of the work I was doing for Robert
in Evergreen. However, it soon became another unexpected chapter in
ministry.

I flew to Tampa on Monday afternoon, and met Robert on Tuesday morning as promised. Within a day or two I understood the commercial development challenge and agreed to help. I made three round trips from Denver to Tampa in the next two weeks, giving temporary leadership to the commercial development staff, and analyzing what should happen next.

Prior to the Christmas break, believing I was going home for good I shared my perceptions with Robert. With no forewarning, he asked if I could continue my consultative management work into the new year as the leader of the Commercial Division in a corporate structure whose major focus was home-building. This was a sudden challenge. Why would I want to commute to Florida, more than two thousand miles away? How would this assignment manifest my commitment to street ministry in Jesus' name? What human or social injustice was to be addressed?

Back in Colorado for Christmas, I searched my soul. What to do? Though the main corporate driver was greed for high profits, its business was the building of modest homes for lower-end out-of-state retirees and local vacation facility workers. This human need could make my ministry valid. Additionally, the company was being managed poorly. It was a conglomerate of self-serving individuals who were each competing for the attention and blessing of the owner. Getting them to care more about one another would be another valid element of this ministry.

I called Robert and agreed to proceed. I was still to be a consultant in a temporary position. I was back on a plane to Tampa four days after Christmas. For three or four months, flying to Denver and back most weekends, I concentrated on straightening out the financing and supervision of the large office building construction.

I also worked closely with Paul Herskowitz, a very able and key manager in the Commercial Division who was working on building four tax-exempt bond-funded low-income apartment projects spread across the state.

Whenever I was in the corporate office, I observed that the company's Residential Division was severely overstaffed and bureaucratized for the number of homes being built, even though many. The corporate president, who managed the Residential Division, was far too controlling, removing authority from staff by seeking to approve every detail of their decisions. He also was meddling in what I had been retained to do in the Commercial Division. Among other things, his interventions were inhibiting the company's completion of Paul's four large low-income apartment projects around the state.

Before the dust had had a chance to settle, following my observations to Robert, this corporate president had been "retired." Robert converted my consultancy to employment and named me COO of the parent corporation. The first thing I did was to liberate managers from the need to get prior approval for every routine step they were to take. I was a hit, and we quickly began moving toward becoming a team. But life with Robert on matters relating to projects in both Florida and Colorado was always an ordeal.

Living Temporarily in Florida

I rented an apartment in a high-rise overlooking Clearwater Beach, but frequently flew home on Fridays and back on Sundays until August of 1987. Jan loved her occasional visits to Florida, as we got to walk long distances along the beach watching the spectacular dolphins and water birds. In July, Jan chose to leave her employment with the Episcopal Pastoral Center in Denver because she wanted to join me in Florida.

Not knowing how long this corporate restructuring effort would go, we bought a house in Clearwater. It had an outdoor pool with a screened-in cover which locals called a "Geezer Cage." Less than a year later we sold this house and moved into an apartment in Pasco County to be nearer to the company's housing developments.

Jan immediately landed a job as a case manager for the Pascoe County Department of Human Services. Her work consisted of providing support services to elderly clients.

During this window when we both were in Florida, we occasionally flew home to check on our mountain house. On one trip we discovered that extremely cold weather had frozen and ruptured copper pipes that were in the ceiling over the kitchen. Destroyed drywall drooped down over the kitchen sink. I cleaned up the mess but did not have time to do many repairs.

Vic - Dead

When Jan and I were still working in Florida, Mother called and matter-of-factly reported that Vic had died. We did not go to the funeral, but Kathy sent us a photo of Vic's body lying in a casket. She had carefully scrawled under the picture, "Vic – Dead." Vic was buried in one of the lots in the Lapp family's Tonawanda Elmlawn Cemetery six-pack.

A short time after Vic's funeral, Mother called again and said, "Robb, I think Kathy could handle a small car. It would keep me from having to drive her to the store and to church. She's had a driver's license since before Vic died."

I thought the better of it, but said, "I'll see what I can do." I found a small used Dodge in Florida, and after having new tires mounted, drove it to Tonawanda on a long weekend. After a quick visit with Mother, I flew back to Florida.

In less than two weeks, Mother called again, "Oh Robb! Kathy has had an accident."

"Is Kathy okay?"

"A little shaken, but otherwise not hurt. She was trying to squeeze next to a bus, to make a right turn, but the bus turned too, and knocked her car into a ditch. Kathy's fine, but her car can't be fixed." "Good," I thought to myself, "no more danger for other motorists!"

Corporate Financial Crisis

In my first year in Clearwater, we completed the 51,000 square foot office structure, which was sold as a medical office building. That done, I was able to concentrate on residential land development and the construction and sale of modest homes, mostly to lower-income retirees from northeastern states. We also completed all four of the rent-assisted apartment complexes. I had come to see quality housing and fair contracts for buyers and tenants as the focus of my Florida mission. In the big picture, we facilitated the retirement of many modest-income folks in providing well-built lower end housing at fair prices.

To conserve operating funds, I moved the office to Pasco County. I had realized that the company would have to declare bankruptcy if I did not take drastic action.

We had way too much land and far too many finished lots in inventory for the pace at which we were building and selling homes. I discovered that with limited cash flow we were failing to pay taxes to the two counties in which we were working. First, in a very painful move, I reduced the staff by over half, retaining the most productive, who easily handled the workload. Next, I started selling lots to other low-end builders, then developed vacant land we owned into 1,200 more buildable lots. I sold most of the lots to a single, large merchant builder who then successfully built and sold homes to lower income retirees, mostly from New York and New Jersey. I also had to conduct extensive negotiations with the Pasco County Manager to make payments on delinquent real estate taxes.

Working with banks on refinancing sometimes has a weird ancillary effect. In straightening out our relationship with our bank, I was asked if I would supervise the homeowners' Community Association in a large nearby senior community for which they were the major lender. Each lot in the community had a vote in community meetings. Because of yet unsold lots, I held more votes than the assembled homeowners taken together. The monthly meetings must have been the major event of interest in the community, as I often had over 400 residents in attendance. Though I held the majority vote, I was able to work through issues with residents until a majority was satisfied with the outcome.

Long story short, the whole Florida corporate assignment turned into a bank work-out. The Smiths still had $5,000,000 when the work-out was completed.

I would have to say Robert was one of the most difficult persons of authority with whom I ever have worked. Somehow, he thought that he could impose virtually any idea on others simply by holding them in a room for hours, doing most of the talking. It did not make any difference how wrong he was. His perception was that his beliefs and economic stances were absolutely and inalterably correct. He simply kept talking until others exhaustedly agreed. My relationship with Robert was one of continuously challenging his self-serving ideas.

The framework for my efforts in Florida was that of trying to bring honesty, transparency, and fairness in all behavior of the business. I wanted the employees to have a real sense of fulfillment that would grow from their efforts. I thought our home buyers and the tenants of our affordable apartment projects should have quality housing at affordable prices. I sought to have the company owner learn how to inspire good work without intimidating his employees. I saw this as social justice work on behalf of "little people."

The restructured organization I left behind was not only more efficient and straightforward, but it had also become more fulfilling for employees.

A cheerless epilogue to this Florida chapter came when Robert was arrested in Colorado for duping homebuyers after taking back the reins of the homebuilding company I had rescued. Nevertheless, I was saddened when I learned of his death following a heart attack while jogging.

Chapter 34

~~~

MISSION ACCOMPLISHED

BY THE SUMMER of 1989 Jan decided that she preferred to be in Colorado, partly because she didn't like living in central Florida, and partly because Robyn had moved to Arvada, raising two daughters pretty much on her own, while her husband was overseas. So, Jan moved home.

Her experience working with seniors in Florida led to a new job in Colorado, working as a case manager for Adult Care Management, Inc., a private nonprofit human service agency. Her work involved arranging for housing and necessary social services for both indigent and private pay clients.

In addition to her work for Adult Care Management, Jan spent significant amounts of time supporting Robyn while she was in graduate school. Jan provided supplemental childcare for Brittany and Chelsea, mostly by taking them to, and picking them up from, daycare nurseries, and, later, public school.

After Jan returned to Denver, I continued working in Florida for several months, but it was clear that I would soon wrap things up and move back home to Colorado.

I flew back and forth several times, and finally suffered a heart attack early in 1991 from the stress of working with Robert. It occurred in Denver's soon to be closed Stapleton Airport before a flight to Tampa. As I was waiting for my flight, I felt pains in my chest and was faint. I was transported by Denver Paramedics to St. Joseph Hospital in Denver. The heart attack was neither severe nor disabling. I had no surgery but started a relationship with a Cardiologist that lasted more than two decades before he retired.

In my concluding months in Florida, I focused on completing the construction of for-sale lots and getting them transferred to my merchant builder buyer. I also continued to run the senior home community association. By mid-1990 I wrapped up my Florida contracts, said goodbye to Robert, and moved home.

Between Thanksgiving of 1986 and June of 1990, I made 65 round trips from Denver to Tampa on United Airlines. Any time there was an empty First-Class seat, the boarding agents I had come to know in Tampa would give it to me, courtesy of the airline, at no upgrade cost.

During all this, Mother started receiving public awards for her work. One was from Nelson Rockefeller, Governor of New York. But her most prized accolade came from Cornell University which, in 1988, named her a Distinguished Alumna on the 60th anniversary of her graduation. Among other citations at that grand event, she was recognized as one of Cornell's earliest female Bachelor of Science graduates.

Prior to my leaving Florida for good, Stuart and I had discussed his moving to Colorado to practice law. Since I had finished a difficult time in Florida and had just recently suffered a heart attack, I was feeling quite vulnerable. But I was contemplating doing further social change institutional and business consulting in Denver, even though I did not yet have a concrete plan. Stuart and I had had several conversations about his moving to Denver to collaborate with me in some kind of social change venture that would bring together his legal expertise and my business and institutional management experience.

I had come to believe that Stuart's plan to move to Denver in the Spring of 1990 was a "done deal." On my final trip home from Florida, I headed for Houston.

When I arrived at the end of a long day, we went to dinner. During that fateful meal Stuart told me that he was not thinking seriously of moving to Denver. I could not tell why. That evening, when I was back at my motel, I was dumbfounded. Next day, I headed for Denver in stunned silence.

Shortly afterward my fateful dinner with him, Stuart emotionally crashed and burned, was hospitalized, and ultimately became, very successfully, a recovering alcoholic. The courage this recovery required has characterized his approach to his personal and professional life every day since.

Instead of moving to Colorado, Stuart opened his own practice in 1991. He officed with a successful solo practice attorney near the Galleria in Houston. This fellow mentored him in the development of his business and practice.

Sharing an office with this fellow had another life-changing impact for Stuart. A legal clerk who worked there introduced Stuart to her cousin, Eve Micklea Nall. They immediately began dating. I soon flew to Houston to help Stuart move into an apartment in The Woodlands, where he would be nearer Eve.

SECTION VII
1991 – 2002

HELPING PEOPLE
FUNCTION TOGETHER

Chapter 35

∾

TRANSFORMATIVE
SECULAR MINISTRY

WHEN THE HUMAN species evolved, it was clear that people were not meant to live in isolation from one another. People had to learn how to create organizational and political structures that would make it possible for them to live and survive with one another. When my Florida institutional change ministry came to an end, I heard the Holy whisper, "See what you can do in Colorado to make it possible for people to live and work with one another, institutionally and culturally." I had very little clue as to what this would mean for my ministry.

Transformative secular ministry has no blueprint. Just as Jesus never knew what challenges a new day would bring, my journey had been almost totally unpredictable. In 1990, there were two elements of consistency in my work that had fulfilled the covenants of my ordination. One was that mostly as a volunteer I had been an innovator in the mission life of the church since before my 1957 graduation from Chicago Theological Seminary. This work was characterized by pulling or pushing local churches and organizational instrumentalities of my denomination, the United Church of Christ, toward equipping lay and ordained participants for transformative rescue work beyond the walls of the church.

The second element of my ministry, though characterized by my not ever knowing what I would be commissioned by God to do next, was consistently focused on creating circumstances in which people could know justice, mercy, and soul-saving recovery from poor personal decisions. This had involved leading an interracial, interfaith fraternity at Ohio Wesleyan, fighting racial discrimination in Denver, CO, facing down the malfeasance of an owner board member in Rochester, NY, inventing all the community service and governance structures for an eventually huge racially and economically integrated community near Houston, TX, and rescuing a large housing development for lower income senior retirees north of Clearwater, FL.

From the time I left First United Church of Arvada until I finished the project in Clearwater, I had been earning a salary from the very outfits in which I had been a Christian infiltrator. After weeks of quietly looking out our mountain house window at the beautiful Continental Divide, I decided I should continue my community development work, but this time as a social change entrepreneur. This meant I would have to go to work every day with neither an employer nor a paycheck. Jan was earning barely enough as a social worker with disabled seniors to cover our basic family expenses. So, whatever I did had to pay for itself and cover my expenses. I had to create a social change ministry from scratch!

Societal Economic Injustice is Not Fair

The Holy kept reminding me of the economic struggles countless thousands of folks were facing in the Colorado Front Range area. People could not afford decent housing, nourishing food for their children, bus fares, or medical care. Some had jobs; others were on welfare. Their kids were suffering in underperforming schools. Women were receiving lower incomes than men for identical work.

A new ministry vision began to sneak into my mind. There must be some way to recruit or assist owners of small businesses that could provide employment or better incomes for people who simply were not making it. Jan and I had life savings of just over $100,000 which we agreed I could use in trying to create job opportunities for the little people. Our motive was that of assisting the poor rather than creating one or more business enterprises that would yield personal gain for us. Additionally, I dreamed that each venture would contribute in some way to the good of the larger community.

I spent weeks perusing the "Business Opportunities" section of the *Denver Post*, and finally focused on a shoestring operation that was for sale.

It appeared that its revenues were marginal and that it was not growing. It was a company owned by a husband and wife. It delivered lost luggage and parcels to airline passengers at the time DIA was replacing Stapleton as Denver's airport. Upon investigation I discovered that this outfit had no employees, just three dozen or so independent contractor workers, a strategy that would allow the owners to avoid providing health insurance or paying an employer's portion of employee state and federal income taxes. Company drivers all were living on the margins. The owners were squeezing their drivers. The contract drivers would go regularly, night and day, in a company truck to the several airline terminals to pick up suitcases and small freight items that were "lost luggage" for delivery to homes and businesses. They would take those items to a central sorting warehouse to create loads to be carried by the workers in their private vehicles to different geographical areas of the Front Range.

Drivers were paid on a fixed fee basis for each-item delivered. With few tips, the costs of income taxes (as self-employed persons), and car maintenance and insurance, these contract workers were barely making it. I thought surely, through operational efficiencies and increased fees from the airlines, I could improve the lot of delivery drivers, making them employees and hopefully earn back any funds I invested for the company purchase. I might even be able to get a little desperately needed income.

My best description for the sellers is that they were squirrelly. Before we closed the deal, they wanted me to be around the operation so the drivers would think I was coming in as an assistant manager. They did not want anyone to know I was about to become the new owner. To play along with the sellers, I even started going to the various airline terminals at Stapleton with the company van to pick up lost bags. Then, for a reason I never understood, the sellers decided not to close their sale to me. Somehow, they grew suspicious of the changes I talked about making, particularly the compensation arrangement with the drivers. We even met in court over their breach of contract, but the judge decided they had the right to change their minds. Six months of lost effort, to say nothing of about a quarter of our savings!

What an auspicious start for my new ministry!

After this rather disastrous start as a social change entrepreneur, I was still feeling called to help people deal with the economic injustices of life in America. I continued to explore other options for helping people with their employment and social survival. I landed on the idea of helping people start businesses that would make life work better for their employees.

I formed a corporation, Lappland, Inc., as a vehicle that could enter partnerships with people whom I hoped to coach.

Special District Management Services

Back when I had been rescuing the Timbers, the mismanaged upscale housing development in Evergreen, Colorado, I had met the owner of a small municipal special district management company, a woman named Debbie McCoy. She provided management services for subdivision Homeowners' Associations. Her work was intended to benefit residents in unincorporated enclaves west of Denver. She hadn't been in business for long, so I thought she might be a candidate for mentoring in corporate growth. In working with her initial clients, she did not need much technical help with Colorado Special District law, but she needed to learn more about running and promoting a business. She turned out to be interested in my mentoring.

Because my new ministry would involve dealing with more than one potential small businessperson at a time, I decided I should have an office space from which several underemployed persons with entrepreneurial vision could work.

As did I, Debbie felt she could function better in a real office. This fit with my thought of working from a city office rather than from a space in a mountain house 30 miles from downtown Denver. I found and leased a small suite in a dramatic all-glass exterior building in Lakewood with a wonderful view of downtown Denver to the east. Debbie and I shared the space.

Before long, Debbie and I decided she needed and could afford a bookkeeper/general office person. I helped her hire a young woman, recommended by my accounting firm, who was the wife of one of the partners. After about three months, I noticed this clerical person's handwriting had suddenly become illegible. It did not take us long to uncover this young woman's drug use. The CPA accountants, without reference to this drug habit, had apparently thought a team like Debbie and me could help her recover. This did not work, and we had to let her go. But Debbie graciously spent significant amounts on therapy for her ex-bookkeeper.

While Debbie worked on serving client districts and growing her business, I rounded up a half-dozen men or women who were solo operators interested in starting or growing their tiny businesses.

Peter Burch

Not long after that secretarial difficulty, Debbie and I advertised for a bookkeeper/office manager to support both of our enterprises. The ad directed people to submit their resumes. One morning I called a young man named Peter Burch who had responded by dropping off his resume at our front desk. After a brief phone interview, I asked him to come in. He startled me by asking where I was. I said, "I'm in the office where you left your resume."

He responded, "Oh, I was going up and down Union Blvd. dropping off resumes at dozens of offices."

Inspired by both his resume and his initiative, I was ready to hire him on the spot. After an interview with Debbie and me, we hired Peter. He turned out to be an excellent accountant and operations manager. He helped both with special district management, and with supporting the sprouting businesses. As the little companies I was coaching grew in number and size, Peter became an employee of Lappland, Inc. Debbie then hired another bookkeeper who worked for Special District Management for years.

Peter, who was about the age of my son Stuart, worked with me for several years. Our closeness led to my officiating at his marriage to his second wife, one of the many ceremonies I have performed for couples living outside the confines of the organized church.

As word of my work with would-be entrepreneurs got around, I soon began being approached by young men and women who wanted help in starting small enterprises. I quickly discovered what they needed most was small amounts of money along with management support. For one of the early candidates, we went to a bank for a loan. The banker said he would be happy to make a loan if I put up an equal amount as collateral. I decided I did not need a middleman. I made the loan myself.

Making this loan brought an unexpected positive twist into the way this ministry would unfold. I found that I had to become a partner in each of the businesses, and to become a minor shareholder and director in each. Sometimes this led to my receiving a few dollars for living expenses. Sometimes it did not. Meanwhile, Peter was evolving into an informal partner in my secular street ministry.

I aided small businesses with an amazingly wide range. There was an American fellow in China who was assisting entrepreneurs with their advertising. Another young fellow, who had horrible difficulty with his teeth to the extent that one could hardly understand him, wanted my help in opening an office cleaning franchise. This venture became Rent-A-Cleaner ("RAC"). It crashed when the owner was photographed by a security camera stealing cases of Coca Cola from an Aurora gas station using our RAC truck. For a few nights, Peter and I did all the cleaning jobs, mostly child-care centers, after being in the office all day. When the RAC fellow went to jail we closed the business.

With a franchise offer from a small outfit in Boston, I helped a long-time friend start a company that was a facilitator for IRS Code Section

1031 Exchanges. Our hired employee, who was a great guy, never closed a single deal. That effort also disintegrated.

Laser Cartridge Remanufacturing

Right after Peter joined us, Debbie wanted to introduce me to her brother Scott Hewitt. She explained that he was trying to remanufacture Hewlett Packard laser printer cartridges. He came to our office carrying a cartridge and told me how one could take the thing apart, replace worn or broken parts, and then refill it with something called toner. This was in the days before Inkjets, when almost all computer printers used toner cartridges, which were very expensive when they were new. Scott had a partner, Tim, who was trying to manage sales and delivery of these strange objects to offices across Denver. Scott struck me as someone who understood the mechanics of remanufacturing, and who was good with his hands. Tim was stiff and distant as a salesman. At the time I met Scott, they had no employees, and Scott was doing the remanufacturing in his garage.

I helped Scott and Tim form LCR, Inc., (Laser Cartridge Remanufacturing), and became a one-third owner, contributing my management and organizational skills without compensation. We hired Peter who, with his great business and bookkeeping skills, was very helpful. Scott knew another fellow who had formed Source Management, Inc., an office supply sales company. Scott thought there was a deal to be made for the marketing of these remanufactured cartridges. Source Management quickly became a very effective sales operation for our cartridges. Early on, LCR, Inc. rented warehouse space north of the Denver Stockyards and, quite soon, began seeking and hiring mostly minority women to be trained to do the remanufacturing. Almost immediately, it was clear that we needed working capital to purchase the large supplies of toner that were needed to refill the cartridges. I took a huge risk and loaned the company Jan's and my entire life savings that had regrown to approximately $100K after the lost baggage debacle.

The employment of minority women became one of LCR's hallmarks. We paid living wages equal to male compensation, provided health insurance, and really tried to care for them as they wrestled with myriad domestic and parenting issues. LCR eventually employed fifty young women in our manufacturing facility. It grew to the point where we were receiving truckloads of spent cartridges from around the country, remanufacturing them, and reshipping them to office supply vendors.

At first, Peter and I ran the operation from our office in Lakewood. Before long, the production facility needed more space, so we leased the vacant and generally unfinished first floor of one of the four multistory office buildings at Diamond Hill, just across I-25 from downtown Denver. We moved operations over the 1991 Christmas/New Year break. Simultaneously, we persuaded Source Management, Inc., which now, because of the demand for our remanufactured printer cartridges, had hired many salespeople, to move into one of the adjoining Diamond Hill office buildings.

One day our manager of customer printer repairs came somewhat hesitatingly into my office. I invited him to sit down and tell me how things were going for him. After a couple of sentences of small talk, he took a deep breath and said, "I need you to know I am gay." He said he had never told this to anyone, even in his family. Then he paused and watched me carefully. I perceived he was frightened about losing his job. I said to him, "I am pleased that you trusted me enough to share this reality. You can be sure that the company will continue to support you in your position. Do you want me to share your story with Scott or Peter? If so, it would get around. If anyone ever gives you any trouble I will want to know." He said he would rather wait a few weeks to see how it felt that someone knew. I then asked him how he felt about himself and his life. "Pretty good," he said, "I am comfortable with who I am." In a few weeks he told me it would be fine if I shared his "secret." Over time I was amazed that he was able to develop a sense of humor and an openness about being the gay printer fixer. It soon became apparent that LCR, Inc. played the role of a church family for him.

A very disruptive event in an otherwise successful operation happened in September 1993, when Tim departed as an LCR, Inc. partner. He had refused to adjust to, or work with, the growing sales team developed by Source Management. Scott and I offered to buy his share of LCR, but Tim hired a lawyer and leveraged a settlement amount substantially higher than one third of the corporation's then current value. Scott and I paid it and moved on. I was learning that helping disadvantaged people find sustainable employment was no easy picnic.

Following Tim's contested departure as a partner, Scott and I were the sole owners of LCR, Inc. Our production of remanufactured cartridges grew. Our female employee model continued to provide good salaries and health insurance for women, often single moms. Scott supervised production and I was COO. Peter Burch was our Chief Financial Officer. Peter and I also assisted the owner of Source Management, Inc., our sales arm, with the operation of his company. In August 1997, both corporations started working on a plan that would lead to Source Management's purchasing the stock of LCR, Inc. This was consummated by mid-1998, at which time I was able to leave. Peter Burch then became the CFO for Source Management. This sale of my LCR stock to Source Management led to the recovery of Jan's and my life savings. The development of ink jet printers by major printer manufacturers would soon lead to a gradual decline in use of laser printer cartridges. Later, Scott also accepted a buy-out, and became a franchised driver-owner for Federal Express.

With the decline in cartridge sales, Source Management changed its focus toward becoming a major distributor of office products of all sorts. Its name was changed to Source Office Products, Inc. Peter and the owner of Source Management personally bought a large warehouse-office facility in Golden near the intersection of I-70 and Colorado SH 58, and moved all operations to that location. The company has continued to grow and thrive. Eventually Peter left Source as COO, and went into business consulting, with Source as a major client.

Developing and running this business in a manner that served the best interests of otherwise marginalized people was a fulfillment of my vision of working for economic justice when I returned from Florida eight years earlier.

As for what kind of ministry it was, I think that getting people to take responsibility for their everyday decisions is a way of making explicit God's claim for accountability in the human enterprise. This enables one to accept and claim God's love and grace.

Even if some church leaders did not view it as ordained ministry, it was consistent with the Creator's intent.

Other Start-Ups

As it happened, Peter's and my work with other little companies did not stop when we were swamped with LCR, Inc. In the days before computers had built-in operating systems, instead using installable Microsoft DOS disk drives, a young man came along with an idea about starting a business that would help users understand their computers. We called his business "The Wizard of DOS." He consulted with small business owners who were having computer and system problems. I took him into my office suite, and we employed several computer techs, mostly young women. This business was very successful and provided employment for several would-be computer gurus. It all collapsed when the "Wizard" ran for a seat in the State Senate and failed, and then gambled away all the company funds in casinos in Central City, one of Colorado's three newly legalized gambling centers. He also wound up with severe domestic stress which my counseling never helped resolve.

Another start-up was possible because of the emergence of HP handheld minicomputers. A long-time Postal Service employee and home-taught programmer who was interested in how lawyers recorded and billed their time, somehow found me. We came up with an application that allowed attorneys to enter pre-described categories of activities performed for clients. The little computers automatically recorded the time spent on each activity for each client. We called the company CompuTime, Inc. and patented the software and obtained a copyright for the name. Each month we downloaded the data from each attorney's handheld HP, and then printed their bills on their letterheads. I did most of the marketing and the monthly interfacing with attorneys. My partner in this activity did all the computer work. This company began to fade as commercial legal billing software began hitting the market. However, it lasted long enough for this fellow to put his son through college with his earnings from this project.

Even though I was doing many outreach and administrative projects for the Rocky Mountain Conference of the UCC as a volunteer, several of my ministerial colleagues as well as the Association Committee on Church and Ministry felt that I should not have ordinational standing while doing this street ministry. But being an ordained minister was part of my Christian identity. It kept me focused on the meaning of my life. I did not give in.

Chapter 36

~~

UNITED CHURCH BOARD FOR HOMELAND MINISTRIES

Seeking a New Executive Vice President

EVEN THOUGH MY street ministries were outside of contemporary church structures, Clyde Miller, retired Rocky Mountain Conference Minister, began pressing me to consider becoming a candidate for the vacant position of Executive Vice President of the Board for Homeland Ministries ("BHM") of the United Church of Christ The BHM is the United Church of Christ instrumentality responsible for the work and witness of the UCC in the "homeland."

No matter how "outside the box" my ministry had been, I felt a strong commitment to making the UCC a relevant agent of community transformation. Having pursued secular ministries in affordable housing, community development, and fair employment from the time I left my Arvada parish to initiate the Fair Housing Center as a civil rights venture, I thought I was ready to make a contribution to transforming the future of my liberal denomination. God seemed to have commissioned me to the vocation of making life better and more manageable for all, whether it was inside or outside the structured church. I felt a surge of excitement at the prospect of having an opportunity to help the church be the church in the world.

As a Corporate Member of the national UCC Board for Homeland Ministries, I had had many opportunities to visit with BHM staff as well as participate in national gatherings. But in a few short months, it had become clear to me that there was serious internal dysfunction in BHM's structure and operation. There was plenty of "We've always done it this way before." And there was substantial infighting and insecurity in the face of the pending restructuring of the UCC's national instrumentalities.

The Holy Says, "Go for It"

I came to see that what the outfit needed was someone whose skill set included organizational management and a willingness to lead an historic organization through the uncharted waters of denominational restructuring. As a candidate for the EVP position, over a period of several months I shared with national UCC groups and individuals my visions of the future of the Board for Homeland Ministries and made known my professional history. I even went to the June 1991 General Synod in Norfolk to "press the flesh." Partly because of Clyde, and partly because of my own commitments, I was well regarded and supported by minority constituencies across the church. Though I was less known by establishment white leaders, as I shared my visions for the future of a denomination in need of transformation, I began to believe I had a chance at being selected.

I thought I could help the Board for Homeland Ministries face the future, learning to do ministry outside the door, something it needed to do to thrive and survive, and be relevant in the emerging 21st Century. Listening for the Holy had brought me to this moment.

My interview was in the Red Lion Hotel in Denver on August 17, 1991. As I walked down a conference area hallway with the Secretary of the UCC Board for Homeland Ministries, she said, "You are one of five finalists being considered for Executive Vice President. Some are already here in this hotel, and all are being interviewed today. So that you do not see any of them, you and I have to pause momentarily." Then she steered me into a bleak small room.

While sitting there I recalled that a member of the Search Committee had called me with a long list of questions. His task was to become familiar with my history and qualifications, and to answer any questions I had. Apparently other Search Committee members were assigned to other candidates. I should have suspected something when the young man who was assigned to me didn't seem to know much about the work of the Search Committee, nor could he give much detail when I asked about both the position and the search process.

Momentarily, a woman who I did not recognize stuck her head in the door, and said stiffly, "Okay."

I was ushered into a room with a large conference table where fifteen formally dressed men and women were seated. A young African American woman from New Orleans and Chair of the Search Committee, said officiously, "Rev. Lapp, would you please be seated in that empty chair."

In the process of sitting down, I smiled at each committee person. I knew about half of them. The Search Chair, surprisingly, did not ask them to introduce themselves. Right off the bat she said, "Rev. Lapp, thank you for being here. We have about 45 minutes for this interview, so let's get started. Would you begin by telling us about yourself and your ministry?"

In an attempt to be imaginative and non-traditional about the interview, I had a cloth grocery bag containing four items: the newly published UCC Book of Worship, my very well-worn leather Revised Standard Version of the Bible, a current issue of *Time* magazine, and a hammer.

As I sat in my chair, I noted that it was still warm from its last occupant. Suddenly, a silent voice from outer space whispered, "Tom Dipko." I had the emerging sense that he had just vacated the chair in which I was sitting. I had heard his name at several Board for Homeland Ministries meetings. He was Conference Minister of the Northeast Ohio Conference, and an important player in the national United Church of Christ structure. The national UCC offices were in Cleveland, in Tom's Ohio Conference. I thought, "At least one of my competitors stands out on the national scene."

Taking the worn Bible from my bag, I said tenderly, "This Bible was given to me by Bishop W. Earle Ledden in June 1957 when he ordained me a Methodist Traveling Elder in my home church in Kenmore, NY. It quickly became obvious that having been ordained in another denomination was not one of the stars in my crown. In the context of this interview, the reason I was no longer a Methodist drew favor from several of the more liberal search committee members, while my not having been loyal to the very institution of my ministerial authorization may have raised questions of my denominational allegiance.

Nevertheless, despite my having begun Jesus' ministry as a Methodist, by the time of this Executive Vice President interview, I had been a member of both the Michigan and Colorado UCC Conference

Boards each of which supported the restructuring that led to the United Church of Christ. I had been the new church start minister of two UCC churches near Denver. I had been a leader on the Board of the nationally known La Foret Conference and Retreat Center in Colorado Springs. I had served on the Board of Settegast Heights, a 300-unit transitional housing project sponsored by the Houston Association of the South-Central Conference of the UCC. I was currently serving as a corporate member of the UCC Board for Homeland Ministries, and as a member of the Board of the National UCC Office of Communications. And I was serving as Treasurer of the Rocky Mountain Conference. However, I had not participated much in the denomination's national politics.

As I held up my well-worn Bible I said, "My sermons are almost always about the call of the Holy to love neighbor more than self, and to structure ways in which all of God's children would know justice and love." I made it clear that I was inspired more by the Historical Jesus than by the Living Christ.

Next, I retrieved the *Time* magazine, and asserted, "I always try to preach sermons with a Bible in one hand and current commentary on the human scene in the other. I cannot lead worship without focusing on the real world in which God calls us to listen to her voice and to serve her people. Christians need to be aware of ways in which to navigate life's rough places." Again, I was at the left of then-current UCC articulation of proper Christian worship and belief.

Then I took out my hammer. People looked really puzzled. I said, "One of the things I have learned is that it's important if you're going to build or fix something you must locate the precise issue and hit it on the head. A leader has to know what specific issues people are facing in their attempts to create holy community." A few smiles.

Finally, out came the new UCC Book of Worship. I said, "I'm not quite what sure to do with this. It is way too stuffy. I don't think the average lay worshipper will be turned on by the formal turns of phrase it expresses. I am not sure how this heavy focus on traditional ritual language will help people deal with the challenges of avoiding self-service in their daily living." A couple of interviewers shifted uncomfortably.

Someone said condescendingly, "You know, don't you, that Dr. Dipko led the group that developed the new Book of Worship." I knew this, but very little else about him. Now I was seeing how wide a swath he cut in upper UCC circles.

Wanting to be more specific, I recited the story of my ministry, both within and beyond the organized church. I concluded, "I think I could help the United Church of Christ move meaningfully into an unknown future where 'being church' will require dramatic new models."

Without giving members of the Search Committee further opportunity to ask questions, Cheryl next said, "Of course you've seen our job description, and know what we're looking for in an Executive Vice President."

I responded, "No, no one has even mentioned it to me. May I see a copy of it?"

"No," said the Chair, "we don't have time for that." I looked over at the young man, the Search Committee member who had been assigned to me earlier in the summer. He simply sat there, head down, looking embarrassed. He said nothing.

By this time, I was beginning to realize the whole process might be a setup. At best, the committee had privately prioritized their list of candidates. At worst, they had already informally decided whom they would select, and these interviews were simply to show the committee's careful open-mindedness.

The Chair then said, "And, we assume you have experience in organizational management, institutional development, and human relations." "Yes," was the only word they gave me time for, and my strongest suit went down the drain. The interview was over. Coming into the interview I had thought that significant personnel problems within the Homeland Ministries staff, and mounting financial problems were good reasons for my involvement. Now, I felt almost totally out of place.

The Chair concluded with, "You'll hear from us. Thank you for coming."

The Board Secretary who had met me at the front door appeared, and, with the demeanor of an undertaker, ushered me out of the room. In the hallway, as if reading from a script in a monotone, she said, "The committee will be in touch with you soon. Be sure to leave the hotel immediately so none of the other candidates see you."

"Thank you, and best wishes in your work," I responded as I turned away.

Getting into my car, I entertained no fantasies that I would be selected for the BHM job. "What a drag!"

After the selection process was over, I realized that unlike the others, I was a church institutional subversive trying to get back into the established church structure to bring about the transformation necessary for building a new community in Christ. My theme was: "Let's get into the trenches with the society's culture makers and see what God's love as creator and redeemer can do to reshape society for the future, especially when the culture's self-image is becoming more secular." But the denomination's search committee was more interested in restoring the church as an institution that stood piously and theologically over and against the emerging new society.

Sucking My Thumb in Vermont

While I had stayed in Denver for the BHM interview, Jan flew two days earlier to New England for a Wallace family reunion at their Waterbury, VT dairy farm. Driving home I was quietly disappointed. All my fantasies for transformative ministry within the church were dashed. I felt terribly inadequate. I felt I had been treated very shabbily. I went home to an empty house and felt as empty myself. I called Jan with my perception of the outcome, but had little to say.

The next morning, I stood in the boarding area at Stapleton Airport for a flight to Burlington, VT, and spotted the Vermont Conference . Minister. He was a member of the BHM search committee. Seeing me, he smiled and said, "Let's see if we can get seats together."

We succeeded. But as we were seated, I did not know what to say. I blurted, "I don't feel like I handled the interview very well. Particularly, when it turned out that I hadn't been provided the job description, I was at a loss for words."

My seat mate responded, "No, you didn't get much chance to tell of your unique ministry. But you shouldn't worry. You were in a very elite group. The other four are much more well known in national UCC leadership circles. You just haven't had enough real church work." He continued, "It's amazing that the committee even seriously considered someone whose ministry was mainly outside institutional boundaries."

He then told me the names of the other candidates. They each held prestigious denominational roles. Three were Conference Ministers and the fourth was a seminary professor. They had paid their dues as leaders within the structural church. I, obviously, had not.

I personally knew all of them but Tom Dipko. As I sat in my plane seat on a clear skyed August Sunday morning, it was clear I had not been selected. I thought to myself, "Likely I was the fifth choice." I knew that I was much more an institutional management "fixer," seeking to shape the church for more relevant social change. The others seemed to be more traditional preachers and teachers.

Cutting short my private reverie, the Vermonter continued, "Robb, you've had a very interesting ministry. Tell me more about the community development work you did in that New Town in Texas."

I did.

Then I asked him about his history and current work in Vermont. He graciously shared his personal story, which made it clear that he was among the more progressive Conference Ministers.

A light finally flashed. The committee had been looking for a candidate who was institutionally well equipped to take the denomination backward into the future. As the Post-Modern era of American culture was beginning to emerge, the committee's vision was that a sharpening of the theological orthodoxy and doctrinal worship of the past would restore the church to its historic vitality. As an ordained secular pioneer, I had spent over twenty years committed to the notion that being a Christian is much more the imitating of Jesus in secular settings than it is a proper search for personal salvation or wish for a heavenly eternal life. Though I had been asked very little about my "constructive theology," it was clear to me that my years of not having preached classic Christian beliefs was a strike against my being selected to lead the Board for Homeland Ministries even one step into the future.

That flight with a caring listener on the day after the interview was the beginning of my recovery.

Our son Stuart was in Vermont from Texas for the family reunion and met me at the Burlington airport late that Sunday afternoon. Most of the Wallace clan already had left the farm in Waterbury. None of those still there were particularly interested in my involvement in a foreign world of denominational intrigue.

The next day Jan and I drove to Bill and Barbara Hobbs' beach cottage in Old Lyme, CT. In frustration, as we sat overlooking the waves on Long Island Sound, I vented at length while Bill and Barbara quietly listened. Earlier, Bill, the closest male friend of my life, had been President of the Board for Homeland Ministries. He knew the territory. I shared and explored my feelings of having been hung out to dry by key people on the search committee. By the time we left Barbara and Bill, I knew I would survive.

Several days after the interview I learned in a phone call that Tom Dipko had been selected. "But, Rev. Lapp, we really appreciated your being a candidate," the caller intoned.

Nevertheless, I still had high hopes about the future of the national structure and witness of the United Church of Christ in the emerging world.

After Dr. Dipko was selected, I had several opportunities to meet and work with him. He was competent, intelligent, and a very good Biblical scholar and theologian. Over time, as I learned how stressful his life had become, primarily with intense travel and significant conflict in staff ranks in a time of change, I became more comfortable that I had not been chosen. I also had occasion to chat with the other three finalists, each of whom thought it had been an honor to get to the Denver interviews. All of us had experienced personal chagrin in not being selected, but we respected one another as visionaries within a vital denomination.

It happens that as the United Church of Christ moved into the Twenty-First Century, emerging new leaders are helping it engage very productively in the positive transformation of the world in which it lives. People like The Rev. Dr. John Dorhauer, President of the United Church of Christ, and The Rev. Traci Blackman, Associate General Minister – Justice and Local Church Ministries, are making the UCC a relevant and effective witness for the Holy's vision of a functional humanity.

Nevertheless, this candidating experience, along with my being fired from the Metro Denver Fair Housing Center and from the Gananda Development Corporation, made me know disappointment as a significant experience of an authentic life. God teaches us in curious ways.

I keep hearing a whispering voice say, "Stay the Course!"

Chapter 37

~~~

COAL CREEK CANYON
FIRE DEPARTMENT

BECAUSE I DID not get the Vice President position, I was able to again focus all my energy on transformative secular ministry. While I was helping young people with their attempts to find or create jobs I simultaneously became involved in several community volunteer activities. One of the most unusual began very innocently at a lawyer's conference in Vail, CO. I was there in the summer of 1992 seeking new clients for CompuTime, the legal billing company in which I was involved with one of the entrepreneurs I was mentoring. Mary Frederickson, an older attorney with an office in Boulder, started a conversation with me. An interesting backstory of her history is that Mary was the attorney who negotiated the sale of a portion of the Church Ranch situated east of Hwy 93 and north of Hwy 72 to the U.S. Government for development of the Rocky Flats nuclear plutonium enrichment plant, the largest and most controversial facility of its kind in all of America.

I learned that she lived in Coal Creek Canyon, where I lived, and that she was President of the Coal Creek Canyon Fire Protection District. As we became acquainted, Mary asked if I would be willing to serve as a Board member. She said she wanted to leave both the Presidency and the Board sometime soon. I told her that having organized and run the Fire Department in The Woodlands, I would like to serve. She was interested.

I had first encountered the CCC Fire Department in 1965, when I was Minister of First United Church of Arvada. One afternoon, Gene, our next-door neighbor, frantically knocked on the parsonage door. "Dorothy is up at Gross Reservoir trying to commit suicide! Can you help me?" he yelled. We raced up the Canyon highway in his pickup, passed Station 1 of the CCC Fire Department, tore over gravel roads to the west side of the dam, and found Dorothy lying on the ground. The reservoir superintendent was kneeling by her side. He had called the fire department. Dorothy was barely conscious but was breathing. The superintendent said, "I think she has taken an overdose." On the way up the Canyon, I had learned from Gene that they were struggling with domestic stress. When the ambulance arrived, to keep them temporarily apart, I volunteered to accompany her to the hospital. I squeezed onto the far back floor of a Mercury station wagon that had been outfitted as an ambulance and held on as we raced down the canyon to Lutheran Hospital in Wheat Ridge. I spoke softly to Dorothy as we went. She seemed to revive a bit. Two days later she was released from the hospital. I perceived that the overdose was an attempt to get Gene's attention. I urged them to seek counseling, which they did. They successfully worked out their issues.

Prior to being elected to the District's Board I attended two meetings to see how it functioned. Mary announced her retirement at the December 1992 meeting. Because of my fire department leadership at The Woodlands, Mary recommended that I be appointed both a Board member and its President. Amazingly, there was no resistance to this.

SECTION VII: 1991 - 2002

I was suddenly a public official in a visible leadership role. So, the fact that I was an ordained UCC minister seemed to be a plus as the Board and community members were looking for someone whom they imagined would be fair in his relationships and management.

One of the special things about this mountain fire district was that its vehicles were painted bright yellow. Years earlier, the Chief and others wanted their equipment to be particularly visible on the curvy mountain roads, so they decided yellow was the best color. Their equipment stood out at in gatherings with trucks from other districts, most of which had red vehicles. A couple of districts had white equipment, which made them nearly invisible in heavy snowstorms. But our trucks were yellow. I loved it.

Making the Department More Efficient

Board meetings were held in Station One, located about ten miles up the Canyon from Hwy. 93 in the heart of the initially populated area of the Canyon. I gained the confidence of other Board members because I accepted the assignment of retiring the antiquated Mercury station wagon ambulance in which I had ridden down the canyon with my neighbor in 1965. I led the Board members and paramedics in setting the design parameters for a new ambulance and advertised for a purchase and selected the winning bid. It was a fine yellow four-wheel drive vehicle with all the latest medical equipment.

During my incumbency, I arranged for the purchase of five other fire and rescue vehicles, for several of which I was able to obtain state grants. Two of them were an innovative departure from local tradition. In each of the four stations, which were located in strategic areas of our 50 square mile district, we had a large 4-wheel drive fire engine. But most of our calls were for rescues, not fires. These large engines would carry first responders and paramedics and be driven slowly up or down curvy mountain roads to medical emergencies or vehicle crashes. I thought this was crazy, so I bought two crew-cab 1-ton trucks and outfitted them with standard utility bodies equipped with rescue paraphernalia and small fire-fighting pumps. They were much easier and more economical to maneuver through our mountains. They, and other vehicles I procured, were well received by the fire fighters and the community alike.

Also, when I became President, the construction work on Station 4, a new facility in a remote area, had ground to a halt. Spending very few dollars, but hiring a hauling contractor who had large equipment, I blitzed the site, removed trashed building materials that prevented access, and built an entry drive. A couple of small construction contractors were then able to complete the structure, to the delight of the residents in that quadrant of the District.

One of the department's challenges was locating an incident scene during an emergency. There was no clear procedure for identifying properties on the District's often unpaved roads. The Fire Chief and I devised a plan for providing highly visible green numerical signs for owners to post at property entrances. These signs became very useful in emergency response situations.

As an additional way of assisting the volunteers, though I was not a certified firefighter or EMT, I frequently responded with them on calls. A memorable one was a forest fire in the northern part of the District that lasted just over three days. The Chief asked that I manage the office in the main station, especially our radio communications with other departments and the Sheriff Dispatcher's office. The funny part was that I could not see the fire from the main station, but it could be seen from our home, which was on a ridge closer to the flames. The Chief, who made all the command decisions, went to my house, and joined Jan on our large deck as a vantage point for supervising the fire fighters. I frequently called Jan to get late news on the fire's movement. Gratefully, the fire was extinguished without the loss of a structure or injury to any of the several dozens of firefighters from our and adjoining Districts.

Another time, I got up in the middle of the night to use the facilities. I realized that I was seeing a bright glow to the southwest. However, it took me a few moments to realize that it was not the sun rising. I threw on some clothes and raced up our hill to the main highway and turned west. Upon arrival at the scene, I saw that a large house was burning vigorously and that there were three cars in the drive. But there was not a fire truck in sight. I tried radioing the County Dispatch Office in Boulder, but a mountain blocked our short-wave communication. There was no way that I could determine if anyone was in the house, so I jumped back into my car and raced the mile to our main station, where I phoned the dispatcher to notify our firefighters. Then I called and woke the Chief. Our firefighters battled the fire for the rest of the night. It was a great relief to learn that the occupants had driven a fourth car to the airport for a flight to California. The house burned to the ground, as homes sometimes did in a district without water lines or fire hydrants. We referred to calls like these as "saving the woods."

Movie Train Starts String of Fires

I always carried a short-wave pager, even in the city. One afternoon in August 1994, when I was in my office in Denver, my pager beeped. The Department was being toned out for a series of fires along the Denver and Rio Grande Railroad right of way. I jumped in my car and raced to an area northwest of Arvada, just east of our District boundary. Sure enough, there were patchy areas of smoke and flame across the Flats and into the foothills. I went on to our station at the mouth of the Canyon and learned that a movie train with old diesel engines was scattering burning residual oil soot along the right of way. The Chief was focused on extinguishing the fires.

I grabbed a phone and called the railroad office in Denver and, citing my authority as a public safety official, demanded that the train be stopped immediately. It was. Then I called again and asked that two regular freight engines be sent to the scene to tow the movie train backward out of the Canyon. Turned out the errant train was the key prop for *Under Siege 2: Dark Territory,* a 1995 action film starring Steven Seagal. The movie was set on board a train traveling through the Rocky Mountains from Denver to Los Angeles. As the train was towed backward past our command post, we all laughed. The movie stars and supporting cast looked out woefully from open windows. My stock among peers went up when I was able to arrange for a $60,000 insurance settlement for 13 fire districts whose trucks had been damaged by driving on the railroad tracks to fight all the fires.

Lots of Politics

During my tenure I was able to guide the District through annexation of several tracts that added to our tax base. Because the President of the State Land Board was a church friend, I was able to annex a square mile tract owned by the Land Board, a move that clarified our jurisdiction over the intersection of Colorado State Highways 72 & 93.

In improving our operations and equipment, our need for stable tax revenue became very clear. Colorado has a constitutional provision called the TABOR (Taxpayer Bill of Rights) amendment, championed by a Senator named Douglas Bruce. It required that a taxing jurisdiction submit any mill levy increases to its constituency, which was a pain. We were able to get voters of our District to "de-Bruce" our annual finances so that we could adopt budgets and mill levies without public controversy. This led to a financially healthy operation.

However, my life as an elected public official ended humiliatingly, partly because I got too far ahead of my constituency. With eyes always on the goal of making the District financially viable into the long-term future, I was continually looking for ways to increase our revenue. I spent a great deal of time and energy working to expand the District's boundaries to gain tax-base.

There were three areas on "The Flats" east of our mountainous district that were potentials for annexation. There was a huge area of land just east of the mouth of the Canyon that was soon to be developed for residential, commercial, and industrial uses.

Second, there were several businesses along the Denver & Rio-Grand Railroad right of way: a dynamite and blasting company, a very large motor oil recycling operation, a seismic company that worked in the mineral exploration field, and an abandoned oil shale cracking tower, a remnant of Exxon's effort to develop huge shale deposits in northwest Colorado. None of these properties were in a fire district.

Third, the Rocky Flats nuclear emporium, also just east of our District, was in the process of shutting down. I had served for two years on a commission that was charged with advising the Feds on the transition of the property to peaceful use. I learned that officials at Rocky Flats were interested in contracting with a nearby fire department for the management of their operations during a several year-long shut down period, at the end of which all their trucks and equipment would become the property of the contract operator, a huge windfall.

As I began to share these three opportunities with my Board members, a small group, led by one of our firefighters, became vociferously opposed to development of any kind, particularly west of Hwy 93. "Protect the Mountain Backdrop," was their cry.

Run Out of Office

A "Get Robb" campaign evolved as we moved toward the 1998 fall District Board election. In the entire history of the District not more than 30 people had ever voted in the biennial election for Board Members. When I came up for re-election in November 1998, I lost by three votes out of over 400 cast. Oh well. I tried.

As for being an ordained minister holding public office, I discovered that the opportunities for making a difference in the way community people were treated and in the way the organization operated were no different than infiltrating a secular non-profit or for-profit enterprise. If anything, I had to deal with more highly charged emotional situations, both because fire department volunteers tended to be "high strung," and because many of the emergencies to which we responded called forth substantial empathetic pain and panic. But on virtually every call I could feel the invisible transcendent energy which generates hope that things will work out as well as they could. Hope permeated every call. My ministerial counseling training and instincts helped me support the rescuers and the injured.

Being an elected public official turned out to be very meaningful but humbling for this ordainee.

Chapter 38

Chapter 38

~~

TREASURER - ROCKY MOUNTAIN CONFERENCE

A Time of Uncertainty

AS IF MANAGING a secular ministry that sought employment economic justice for "God's little people" and running a fire department were not enough, I also agreed to serve on the Board as Treasurer of the Rocky Mountain Conference. The most immediate challenge facing the Board was that of finding a new permanent Conference Minister to follow Clyde Miller after his thirteen-year incumbency. In the United Church of Christ, an Interim Minister is hired to lead a Conference during a window in which it contemplates its future priorities and selects a permanent leader. Upon Clyde's retirement, the Rev. Lynne Simcox became our Interim Conference Minister. Her most stellar accomplishments included the restructuring of office staff and clarifying Conference relationships with local churches.

During Lynne's Interim, the Rev. Bill Dalke, a "down-easter" from Maine, became the next Conference Minister, and served until the beginning of the new Century. Bill and his wife ended up buying a house near us in Coal Creek Canyon, so he and I often rode together to Conference Board and committee meetings.

In addition to my Treasurer role of helping the Board focus creatively on the Conference's somewhat precarious financial status, I served on the Conference Board's La Foret Facilities Committee. This was personally meaningful because La Foret gave direction to so many young peoples' lives.

La Foret, a Gem in a Ponderosa Pine Forest

La Foret was originally the summer estate of Mrs. Alice Bemis Taylor. During the 1920s, Mrs. Taylor began construction of a summer estate, which she called La Foret, on a 500-acre tract in the Black Forest. Ponderosa Lodge, the main residence, is a magnificent log and stone structure, constructed in 1928.

The other key building on the La Foret property is the Taylor Memorial Chapel, located at the west end of a large meadow, on the east end of which sits Ponderosa. The Chapel is an intriguing Spanish style stucco building with design roots in Santa Fe, NM. From its entrance one can see a stunning view of Pikes Peak. The Taylor Memorial Chapel was built in 1929 as Alice's memorial to her husband, who unfortunately left the world before ever visiting the property.

The chapel is an outstanding work of architecture inspired by Mrs. Taylor's interest in the old Spanish Missions of the Southwest and by her appreciation of early Spanish Indian Art. The bell is from an old mission in Santa Fe, and the chancel woodwork was hand carved and painted by a Santa Fe artist.

Additional original buildings on Mrs. Taylor's estate included Juniper, a log cabin in which her staff members lived. There was a carriage house nearby, and a horse stable complete with stalls just over a hill to the east. In a lower creek-side gorge to the west is a large log cabin, Blue Spruce, which housed Mrs. Taylor's frequent guests. On the north end of La Foret by the access road sits a gate house, another log cabin originally called Way Inn by Mrs. Taylor, in which the property manager and his family lived. It is difficult to imagine a more elaborate estate in a Ponderosa forest!

La Foret became the property of the Colorado Congregational Conference, predecessor of the Colorado Conference of the United Church of Christ in 1944. The title to the land was free and clear with no conditions or restrictions.

Very early in its use as a summer camp for kids from Conference churches, there was not room for all the campers in the existing buildings. An ingenious scheme was devised by the Conference Board. A small fleet of covered wagons was acquired. The wagons, each one sleeping four, were parked around the large meadow in the center of the La Foret property. Simultaneously, between 1944 and 1948 four cabins and a large Dining Hall were constructed. By 1954 there were nine cabins.

Tragedy struck in April of 1954 when the dining hall burned to the ground. This was a heartbreaker for all, but with limited insurance and generous supplemental gifts, the building was replaced in time for the 1955 camping season. It was built on the existing dining hall site, using the original foundation. Both the new exterior and interior were very similar to the original. Much of the labor was provided by volunteers from Colorado Conference churches. Tens of thousands of great meals have subsequently been served and enjoyed there, highlighting the joy of camping at La Foret.

In my time on the Conference La Foret Facilities Committee, we were able to upgrade the Ponderosa bathrooms and make Mrs. Taylor's original kitchen more functional. We updated the Juniper office building, adding three private offices for staff. We also converted what had been the estate's horse carriage house into an attractive meeting space with a large room, a small food service room and two restrooms.

However, mounting financial issues in both the Conference and at La Foret led Rev. Bill Dalke and Conference Board members to begin worrying about whether the Conference could continue ownership of La Foret.

Sale of Unused Conference Assets

One day, I stumbled onto the fact that RMC-UCC owned an abandoned church building in Cripple Creek, CO, a mining ghost town west of Colorado Springs. I drove to Cripple Creek and discovered that the building was still standing but had been vandalized. At about the same time the Colorado State Legislature passed a bill allowing limited stakes gambling in Central City, Blackhawk, and Cripple Creek. I soon learned that there was interest in our vacant church building. We sold it three times. Once was to a non-profit that planned to use it for community youth activities but defaulted. Second was to a conservative church group that wanted it for worship, but also defaulted. In both cases, the buyers forfeited healthy earnest money deposits. Then, I sold it a third time to group that wanted to convert it to office space, for a price more than double the earlier two contracts. The Conference treasury got a little breathing room!

When the Intermountain Conference of the UCC joined the Colorado Conference to form the Rocky Mountain Conference, we inherited an interest in the Pinecliff Church Camp in Coalville, Utah co-owned by the Methodist Conference. The Methodists were pleased to buy our interest. More solvency!

Funding for African American New Church Start

Later, the minister at the Lyons Congregational Church wanted his congregation to leave the denomination and take their building with them. RMC-UCC had a lien on this church property that dated back to a loan the Conference had made to the church many years earlier. I was able to negotiate a release of the building lien in return for funds that would create a youth program at Heritage UCC, an African American new church start congregation in Aurora.

Closing Dillon High Country Camp

A not so pleasant role as Treasurer was my disposition of the RMC-UCC High Country Camp in Dillon. In the early '60's the Conference had leased land at a very favorable rate from the U.S. Forest Service and had built a facility called High-Country Camp, which provided a rustic mountain setting for youth retreats and adult contemplative camps handling about 60 campers.

In 1995 the Forest Service abruptly changed its policy and upped the land lease rate from peanuts to something around $25,000 a year, an amount about equal to the Camp's entire revenue. Terms of the original lease required the Conference, when opting out of the lease, to raze the buildings and return the land to its natural, forested state.

After five years of negotiation which occurred during a period of declining church interest in the facility, along with a new local government requirement that we hook up the camp to a municipal sewer line, we threw in the towel. Along the way I learned that the camp manager had crossed swords with a County Commissioner, and that the Commissioner had been the one to push the Forest Service to raise our lease rate to current market level. The only thing to do was to abandon the High-Country Camp.

I tried a variety of solutions including our proposed purchase of another site for a land-swap with the Forest Service, even meeting with a Colorado US Congressman in an attempt to make it work. In the end, the Forest Service cancelled our lease and required us to return the land to "its original forested condition." The local fire department agreed to hold a training session at our camp for the purpose of burning the buildings. This worked for only one structure, as the fire spread into the surrounding woods. We next hired a contractor to remove the remaining buildings and to reforest the area. The same County Commissioner who had pushed the Forest Service to defeat us refused to allow us to deposit building debris into the County dump until we paid a large fee.

Such was the ignominious end of a beloved facility! When I was finished, the Forest Service was satisfied with its restored acreage. However, in the RMC-UCC, I ended up as the guy with the reputation of having closed and burned Dillon.

Oh well!

Through these fortuitous steps, the Conference was able to get back on a sound financial footing, replenishing the accounts that had become unfunded during the '80s. In my entire formal education, I had never taken Finance 101, but I had learned that effective ministries require financial models that work.

Restructuring Metro Denver Association

Somehow, I also allowed myself to be elected Moderator of the Metropolitan Denver Association for a term in the late '90s. My main activity was a restructuring of Association Committees and the creation of a new set of By-Laws. These By-Laws clarified the process of walking people toward ordination in the United Church of Christ, a role of UCC Associations.

Reflecting, I find it interesting that my social-change ministry was in secular settings but that, as a volunteer, I spent so much time making the church work more effectively.

The Holy has visions for the Church as well as for the world!

Chapter 39

～～～

HOMELESS FOLKS NEED
SAFE PLACES TO LIVE

IN 1994, TWENTY years after Mountain United Church Housing ("MUCH") had started its work as a Rocky Mountain Conference low-income housing mission, a friend called me out of the blue one afternoon. Though we never belonged to the same UCC church, I had known David Nestor, a wonderfully selfless fellow, ever since he was a youth camper, and I was a counselor at La Foret. He now owned a successful lighting fixture sales business in Denver. We had had many occasions to work together on incarnations of the Rocky Mountain Conference – UCC. At one point while I was Treasurer, he was Moderator of the Conference.

The first words out of his mouth were, "Robb, what do you know about housing the homeless?" For a moment I was struck by the anomaly of this question coming from him. He was active in the Victim Offender Reconciliation Program of Colorado. Why had the homeless issue become hot for him? Perhaps many of the offenders with whom he was dealing were homeless. He knew very little about low-income housing and all the government hoops that then went with developing safe places for a community's marginalized people. But it turned out he was asking a serious question. He wanted to do something, he did not know quite what, to serve area homeless folk. He knew that I had lobbied many years earlier for the creation of the Colorado Housing Finance Authority, and that I had been involved with housing and community development in several parts of the country. He had forgotten about my Mountain United Church Housing work.

David's phone call was a trigger for our UCC Conference engaging in a new effort to provide affordable housing for struggling folk.

A safe and clean place to live is often the first amenity of life to go out of reach for the marginalized, particularly in metropolitan areas. For the most part, even when people are making good decisions about their lives, their inability to have adequate housing is often not their own fault. A community's lack of jobs that pay a living wage, along with an inadequate supply of affordable housing, are the largest drivers of falling victim to insufficient housing. Then, on top of this, especially in America, there is both social and employment discrimination against ESL immigrants, African Americans, Muslims, and Hispanics. And, illness, primarily mental, disables many.

Knowing the Federal housing loan programs from previous incarnations, I was certain that our first effort, without substantial grants and gifts, would not serve totally homeless street people, which had been David's admirable initial concept. However, there were options for building apartments that would serve people in the 30% to 60% range of "Area Median Income," a Federal calculation, in the Denver metro area. Tenants would pay less than half, to just more than half, of the rents that were being charged for similar market-rate apartments.

Following his call, David and I had a fruitful luncheon with another member of First Plymouth UCC in Englewood, the president of an affordable housing consulting firm. He was supportive of our trying to form a church-based non-profit that would execute our dream.

With the retirement of most of its volunteer board members, Mountain United Church Housing had not created any new low-income housing in over a decade, but it continued to own and manage its 16 family homes in Arvada. David and I decided to form a fully governmentally qualified low-income non-profit housing developer corporation rather than try to restructure MUCH for new projects.

We recruited two original MUCH Board members to help. They, and I, were the remaining legal members of the still functioning MUCH Board. The new team thought it could finance and build about 75 apartments in our first project.

We formed Rocky Mountain HDC, Inc., ("RMHDC") as a non-profit affiliate of the Rocky Mountain Conference of the UCC, whose board agreed to the new ministry, but which had no money for supporting the effort. RMHDC needed a Federal 501(c)(3) standing to qualify for a Federal Tax Credit low-income housing development loan. I succeeded in creating the corporation and arranging for a church-related non-profit certification.

First 72 Unit Project Built!

Before long, with land at Eighth and Union in Lakewood, and the commitment of a major predevelopment loan from Nestor, we saw a project in the making. David also made a financial gift and guaranteed an additional bank loan to RMHDC for predevelopment. The major financing came from HUD's "Low Income Housing Tax Credit" funds administered by the Colorado Housing Finance Authority ("CHFA"), whose Executive Director was none other than David Herlinger, who had worked with me years earlier at the Fair Housing Center, and who had helped spearhead the Legislature's creation of CHFA.

David's low-income housing expert from First Plymouth UCC became our development consultant. One of the prior MUCH Board members agreed to keep the project books. The other prior MUCH Board member, a real estate land broker, negotiated the land purchase contract. I refereed, which is to say I was chair of the team, with the next kazillion meetings held in my job-creating consulting office near downtown Denver. I arranged for the national UCC Council for Health and Human Services to give RMHDC standing under its 501(c)(3) nonprofit status umbrella. RMHDC became the legal entity that developed Foothills Green, a 72-unit townhouse property for low-income families. Meanwhile, MUCH continued its ownership and management of the 16 homes in Arvada.

We volunteers bought the land, hired, and coordinated the work of an architect and a contractor, and supervised construction before we were ready for our first tenant. I represented the RMHDC Board in frequent meetings with our architect and contractor. Along the way, we encountered every negative bureaucratic trick in the book, and even were greeted by a NIMBY (Not in my back yard!) neighbor who released some parrots into a tree on site then cried, "Endangered species!" But 72 families moved into Foothills Green before the end of 1997, with rents mostly under half of the then current market. Not bad for church volunteers!

An interesting windfall twist arose at the time our board member broker negotiated the purchase of the land. Instead of buying just what we needed of a tract that was too large for the number of apartment units we could finance, he suggested, "We could sell lots around the edges of the property to a builder who might buy them for duplexes." I wondered aloud, "Do you think we could we find a land development contractor who would prepare our apartment land, build the needed roads, and create the duplex lots?" We, indeed, found such a contractor and sold the adjoining finished lots to a single home builder at a profit for RMHDC, gaining some funds for our mission. As a person who also felt God's call to care for others, our broker Board member also contributed his substantial broker's commission to RMHDC. This sequence left us with enough money to immediately start dreaming of a second project.

With the one-project self-confidence the RMHDC now had as developer and manager of the 72 Foothills Green units, and with operating funds we were beginning to accumulate, David Nestor said at a Board meeting, "Now that we know how to find land, arrange HUD Tax Credit financing, get local government approvals, hire architects and supervise building contractors, let's do it again." The Board agreed, and so began a search for another property.

We found a property at the corner of Xenia Street and Mississippi Avenue in unincorporated Arapahoe County, on the far opposite side of the metro area from our first project. Using "Green" in the name again, this one was to be called Arapahoe Green. As the design phase evolved, we determined that there would be 60 units.

RMHDC closed on the Arapahoe Green site purchase and started construction in the summer of 2001.

As we started our second project as volunteer developers, we determined that we really needed to create a paid development and property management team. RMHDC hired Joyce Alms-Ransford whose qualifications included her years with the Denver Housing Authority and the Denver Coalition for the Homeless. Joyce became the senior employee and executive manager of RMHDC.

Turns out, this was only the beginning for our faith-based non-profit.

Chapter 40

∼∼

CTS TRUSTEE

Lots of Flights to Chicago

AFTER MANY YEARS of parish and street ministry, I was able to give CTS a modest endowment gift in the early '90s. In arranging for this gift, I had had several conversations with the seminary's Development Director. In 1996 he recommended to then President Dr. Ken Smith that I become a Trustee. Dr. Smith was resistant, saying he thought it was inappropriate for one to be a Trustee just because he had given money to the seminary. I think the real reason for his hesitation was that he did not know me and had not been the one to come up with the idea of asking me to serve. Nevertheless, Ken agreed to invite me to join the Board. My first Board meeting was on November 21, 1996.

I quickly learned that the immediate issue was more the need for financial survival than it was for imagining how a seminary should give leadership to a religion and church in transition. With Dr. Smith's immanent retirement, CTS was in a window between presidents, making uncertain the question of future institutional priorities and leadership.

CTS owned a substantial amount of real estate located on the University of Chicago campus. This was the second location for CTS, the first having been near downtown Chicago, south of the river on Roosevelt Road where it had been since the time of the Civil War. This first physical incarnation of CTS just barely survived the disastrous Chicago Fire of 1871. In the later 1920's, CTS began a functional working relationship with the University of Chicago and began erecting buildings in Hyde Park, while selling its Roosevelt Road property.

Thus, all but one of CTS's buildings were nearly eighty years old at the time I became a Trustee. Though they were beautiful brick and stone buildings, dramatic in architectural design, they had become very expensive to maintain. Further, as the student profile was evolving away from those who needed on-campus dorm rooms or apartments there was a good deal of vacant seminary real estate that no longer produced operating revenue. The bottom line is that for Trustees there was a great deal of preoccupation with the financial future of CTS, to the neglect of focusing on curricula relevant to emerging models of ordainable ministry.

Working With a New President

A few months after I became a Trustee, in a move consistent with characteristics of my non-traditional ministry, I agreed to serve on the Business Affairs Committee. Before that role started, however, my first significant contribution was to serve on the Search Committee to replace the retiring Ken Smith. The committee quickly assembled a list of impressive candidates, both men and women, both black and white, flying some of them in for interviews. There were some very well-known church leaders on the short list. The committee had already started its face-to-face interviewing when it occurred to me to sit down privately with the Academic Dean, Dr. Bill Myers, to hear of faculty interests in the selection of a president. He and I slipped away from campus for a dinner at a lakeshore restaurant. Listening at first to Bill's reflections on his role as Dean, I eventually asked, "What are members of the faculty saying about our search for a President?"

Bill was forthcoming, responding without hesitation, "Have you given any consideration to Dr. Susan Thistlethwaite?" At the time she was Professor of Theology and Public Policy at CTS. How fortuitous! The committee had not given any "insider" much thought. Before leaving for Denver, I shared Dr. Myers' thought with Tom Fulton, Trustee Chair, and fellow member of the Search Committee. The rest is history. Susan became one of the most influential leaders in the seminary's modern history, serving for ten years as President before returning to teaching and writing.

As it turned out, Susan and I worked very closely throughout her entire incumbency. When she assumed her duties, she got the Board to appoint me as Chair of the Business Affairs Committee. We were in roles that were taking top priority at most seminaries – financial survival. Susan and I worked aggressively on the issue of making operating budget revenues meet expenses. We sold a farm in Indiana that had been purchased by an earlier business manager. We sold townhouses the seminary owned in a nearby Hyde Park compound, some to faculty members and others to unrelated parties. We fixed up the "Six Flat," an apartment occupied by young faculty and staff, and began insisting on receipt of monthly rents which previously often had been forgiven.

We also tackled the structure and population of her support staff, primarily in the Business and Development Offices. Not only did we sharpen assignments, but we also replaced several people. We even moved offices around so that the Business Office was immediately adjacent to her office, signaling the importance of clear and accurate financial management and reporting. The need for qualified Development Office leadership and staff led to larger quarters for that team.

Running CTS Construction Projects from Denver

Another contribution was, at first, inadvertent. Susan and her husband, Dr. Richard Thistlethwaite, a highly respected surgeon and Professor at the University of Chicago Medical School, and their three sons lived a long commute to the southwest of Hyde Park, home of the University of Chicago and CTS.

CTS had long owned a single-family house that had been home to previous seminary presidents. It was adjacent to Roby House and McGiffert Hall. With a vacant president's house and a new president who was spending two hours a day commuting, it seemed a no-brainer that the Thistlethwaites should move to campus. However, there was a problem. The house could not really accommodate a university couple and their three grown or nearly grown sons. The kitchen was dysfunctional. There was no dining room. And there was no space appropriate for entertaining faculty, students, or board members. The classic shingle roof leaked. Besides, the garage off a side alley held only one car.

It quickly became obvious that the President's House would have to undergo a major renovation and addition. Though I lived 1,000 miles away, I became the project manager for the architectural and construction work that was to follow. This activity updated the entire house, repaired a failing roof, added several main floor living spaces, along with a new attached three car garage along the alley which separated the residence from McGiffert Hall, the newest building of the CTS campus.

After they had moved into a not quite complete house, Sue called me at our mountain home early on New Year's morning. The call was not to wish me a Happy New Year. I could hear shouting in the background. She frantically said, "We're having a big snowstorm and the garage roof just fell down on our cars and freezer! Dick is out there now trying to rescue things!" I replied, "Yell out and tell him his first job is to get out of the garage." She did, and he did. It turned out that the ledger board all the way around the top to hold the roof joists had not been bolted properly into the concrete block walls. I caught an early flight to Midway, assessed the damage, and ended up terminating the contractor and finding another to finish the job. When we were done, the house appraised for well over $1,000,000. Befitting Susan's extroverted leadership style, it became one of the seminary's most used entertainment and social activity centers. At Board receptions, many good ideas were hatched, and Board member relationships strengthened.

Converting Dorm Rooms to Medical School Offices and Apartments to Business School Offices

Concurrent with working on the President's House, other fun began. Susan and I faced the reality that many of the dorm rooms in Davis Hall that had for decades been used to house single students were now either vacant or were being rented to University of Chicago students. We began a two-pronged effort that eventually led to the seminary's moving to yet a third Chicago location. First, we turned the Davis Hall dorm rooms into small offices, and made other changes including installation of an elevator and the creation of a separate entrance. We then rented Davis Hall to the University Medical School for use by its administrative support staff.

Next, we turned to the increasing loss of useability of McGiffert Hall, the newest building owned by the seminary, and named after Dr. Cushman McGiffert, the seminary President who had persuaded me to attend CTS rather than the Boston University School of Theology. Its kitchen and large dining room had long since ceased to be used for their intended purposes. The upstairs apartments were not functional for current students. In fact, most students, by then, were living off campus, and McGiffert Hall apartments were standing empty. We needed a few dorm rooms for the single students who had been displaced by the office construction in the main building. So, we rearranged a few of the apartments to accommodate multiple students. We then converted the remaining apartments into offices which we rented to the University School of Business, which had just completed a large facility just south of McGiffert Hall.

All these physical changes to seminary property, as well as the streamlining of administrative staff, led to CTS's return to operating in the black. This so liberated the Board, the faculty, and President Thistlethwaite's team, that the real work of shaping CTS for the 21st Century could begin.

Throughout my life I kept hearing the Holy ask, "Can you make things work financially, and can you design buildings and community institutions that work?" This was a skill set for which I had been wired at birth.

Preaching in a Seminary!

Odd as it may sound, one of the most personally poignant moments of my entire trusteeship was my delivery of the sermon at a Wednesday Chapel Service in 2000. With all the students, faculty and staff who typically attended this community event, I was scared to death. Just before worship was to start, I was standing in a hallway near the chapel, where I must have looked like a frightened kid. I was! Dr. JoAnne Terrell, Professor of Christian Ethics, came along, put her arm around my shoulder and said, "Robb, it will be fine. Your life is your sermon." Once I got going, I was comfortable. A listening community is very supportive. My sermon entitled, "'Getting it' in the <u>Real</u> World," concluded with these words:

> "As a kid at a Methodist church camp in Western New York, I was nearly overcome when we sang *Are Ye Able.* "Are ye able," asked the Master, "To be crucified with me?" "Yea," the sturdy dreamers answered, "To the death we follow thee." Even at 16, this call seemed to me to be central to a saving relationship with Jesus – far more on target than the comforting words of "*Jesus Loves Me, this I know.*"

> "The Christian Faith's greatest paradox is this: If you live or witness or preach beyond your own self-interest, you're apt to be crucified, but will find your life. If you go with the real world's picture of the successful achiever, you will not be crucified, but you will lose your life.

> "When James and John, after three years of voluntary service, felt they deserved an honorary degree, Jesus was forced to ask the defining question. "Are you able to drink the cup that I drink, or be baptized with the baptism that I am baptized with? As it turned out, 11 of them were, at least some of the time.

> "Are YE able, at least some of the time, to give up your own glory in responding to God's call to do justice and to love mercy? AMEN."

I received many embraces at the close of the service. How reassuring!

As was the CTS community custom, following a Wednesday Chapel, staff, faculty, and students convened in a large room in McGiffert Hall for a catered lunch. I saw that Jesse Jackson, who I had previously helped at CTS, was at one of the tables. As I approached, he called out, "How's that Clyde Miller?"

Responding, I said, "Perhaps you haven't heard. His kidneys have failed, and he undergoes dialysis four days a week." Jackson was genuinely saddened.

Chapter 41

~~~

A RADICAL MOVE FOR LA FORET

Conference Minister Wants to Sell the Camp

WHILE IT WAS a lot to manage my trips back and forth to Chicago, I was most dumbfounded at an RMC Board meeting in 1997 at Lakewood UCC when Rev. Bill Dalke recommended that the Conference sell La Foret. He announced this without any prior conversation with me or other Board members. There was total silence around the Board table. La Foret, in many minds, was the key ministry of the Conference's reaching out meaningfully to its people and churches. Though I was stupefied, deep inside something said, "This cannot happen. There's got to be a way!"

Next morning at breakfast when I told Jan about Bill's recommendation to the Board, she jumped up at the kitchen table hands on hips, and said piercingly, "Well, Robb, what are YOU going to do about this? La Foret is a place that holds special meanings for many, many United Church people whose lives have been indelibly transformed. We can't just let it go!"

Well, I had my marching orders! Jan was clearly the voice of the Holy.

A plan began to evolve as I wrestled with this deep dilemma. I thought that the Conference Board could separate La Foret from Conference operations and place it under its own Board of Directors. Having already formed the Rocky Mountain Ecumenical Center, Inc., and Rocky Mountain HDC, Inc., I knew we could create another independent 501(c)(3) nonprofit with a separate Board. I figured that an independent board committed solely to the unique outdoor ministry of La Foret was the way to go.

Before sharing this idea with Bill Dalke, I called David Nestor, Moderator of the Conference Board, with whom I had recently formed Rocky Mountain HDC, Inc. I said, "David, we've been working on the homeless project. Here is another opportunity. We need to rescue La Foret."

We devised a plan under which La Foret Conference and Retreat Center, Inc. would be formed as a separate non-profit 501(c)(3), and that the Conference would deed La Foret to the new entity, with a reversionary clause that would return ownership to the Conference if the new ownership Board ever determined that La Foret's role as a camp benefitting UCC members had ended.

With Bill Dalke's support, the RMC-UCC Board agreed. I submitted all the necessary paperwork to the Secretary of State and to the IRS. "La Foret Conference and Retreat Center, Inc." was a new reality! Finally, I had to prepare the deed that that transferred the camp property to the new ministry.

Our next task was to round up a cohort of qualified Board members. David and I did this, and I was elected Chair of the Board. The Board soon hired an Executive Director who supervised the staff and was responsible for all facility operations and guest services. With a quickly emerging list of needed facility improvements, Board members managed all the construction and related fund-raising and financing. I spent many days over the coming years at La Foret supervising contractors and securing County approvals.

Staff Leadership

Our first Executive Director did not last long. In November 1998, a fellow Board member, Carole Westphal, both an Iliff Seminary graduate and a retired telephone company executive, became the La Foret Executive Director. When she left the post in the spring of 2002, having done a great job, I had to step in as Acting Executive Director for a seven-month period through November. Jan frequently joined me at camp. Because of the variety of client sleeping facility needs, Jan and I slept in every building except Taylor Chapel. We even stayed in two different basement rooms in the Dining Hall. During my interim, an ED search committee selected Susan Lander, a person from California with extensive conference center management experience. I lived and worked at La Foret for another month after Susan's arrival to introduce her to the Center's operations.

Major Upgrading of the Retreat Center

In the early days of the independent camp entity, we spent almost two million dollars upgrading buildings and grounds. To pay for this we sold a small, isolated tract on the west edge of the facility. Hocking unused portions of the retained acreage, we also took out a construction loan. David Nestor loaned funds to be used for updating the swimming pool and the tennis and volleyball courts. Early on, we invited a prominent land planner and member of the Wheat Ridge UCC, to create a land use plan for the camp. We did this so we would have an idea what the camp should look like as we did future development.

Under the new ownership, we refurbished all nine cabins, upgrading the bathrooms, plumbing, and heating. We also repaired and re-stained the exteriors of the cabins, making them much more inviting. In the Dining Hall we restructured the kitchen into a much more efficient facility. We bought and installed six twelve-bed Yurts near the old horse stables to house younger campers during the summer so that we could hold more than one camp at a time. We designed and built a bathroom & shower facility near the Yurts. With a major charitable contribution honoring a UCC church member, Ben Smith, we converted the old stables into an activity center for the Yurt camps. Finally, we added a kitchen and extra bedrooms to Kinninnick cabin so that another of our staff members could live on site.

Next, I designed and supervised the construction of a large multipurpose activity building to take the pressure off Ponderosa Lodge, Mrs. Taylor's original summer retreat house. The new building, Inglis Hall, was named after Robert and Lucille Inglis, the Conference Minister couple who had mentored my coming to Colorado in 1962 to start First United Church of Arvada. Inglis Hall has become the activity center for all manner of youth, adult, and family activities at La Foret. It has a large fireplace which I sketched at my breakfast table one morning when the contractor called and asked what I wanted it to look like.

With all the upgrades and additional facilities, La Foret became a popular place for public and private schools, churches of other denominations, and non-profits. In fact, things went so well, we had to hire a full-time scheduler.

INGLIS HALL – LA FORET

Driving Van Loads of Kids to Summer Camps

Meanwhile, in the mid-1990s I started driving youth campers back and forth from La Foret to Green River, WY. This allowed kids from Utah and western Wyoming to attend Conference-sponsored camps. Eventually, Dave Nestor and I bought a used 15 passenger Ford van because more and more kids wanted to attend the camps. After several similar vans had rolled over on highways across the U.S., the RMC-UCC Board terminated use of that van. I asked the Board to transfer it to our low-income housing corporation, with the understanding that it would be used in the Denver metro area, and not on the open highway. The Conference then purchased a larger used airport passenger van to pick up the UCC campers from Wyoming and Utah. Sometimes there were so many kids that my daughter Karen would drive my minivan with six additional campers while I drove the larger van. I came to know a whole generation of kids who were growing in their faith at La Foret.

The Transformation Worked

By the turn of the Twenty First Century, La Foret Conference and Retreat Center had become a haven that cultivated the spiritual and program needs of all groups that come to La Foret. It was now open to all children, youth, individuals, and families of any denomination, and any educational or non-profit group which needed a setting for personal transformation and self-discovery. The beautiful quiet wooded environment of La Foret encourages spiritual renewal and outreach opportunities. It truly has become a sanctuary and place of reflection, which repairs souls for re-entry into a world of critical human need. It is the scene of many life journeys through the unknown.

Chapter 42

∽

THE FAMILY MATTERS

Mother and Kathy Move to Colorado

MOTHER'S TIME IN Kenmore ground to an end when she fell in her apartment building parking lot and broke her right wrist. Once casted, she could not shift her car's automatic transmission lever, so she had to quit driving. She tried to live in the scruffy trailer where Kathy was living after Vic died, but that did not work. She did not want to move to Denver yet, so Stuart and I flew to Buffalo and moved her to Tonawanda Manor, an assisted living facility. We packed most of her belongings into a monthly rental storage unit. That arrangement lasted eight weeks.

With Mother in an assisted living facility, Kathy could no longer manage living in her trailer. The only way Jan and I could manage their care was to move them to Arvada, the city closest to our mountain home.

Mother agreed. Before she moved, she wanted to have her picture taken for a local article that was to feature her being awarded a significant community gift for Ken-Ton Meals on Wheels. Because she had just broken her glasses, we borrowed a frame without lenses from the family oculist which she wore for the portrait photograph.

When it came time to clean out the trailer and move Mother, Kathy, and their lifetime belongings to Colorado, our daughter Karen flew to Tonawanda with me to help. Next morning, we took Mother and Kathy to the Buffalo airport. When they were at the boarding gate, we pinned name tags and destination notes on their coats. They had to change planes in Pittsburg but made it to Denver. Late that afternoon, Jan met them at the Denver terminal and took them to stay in our mountain house until Karen and I returned.

As soon as they were safely on a plane, Karen and I tackled Kathy's trailer. Using snow shovels, we literally pushed detritus from the back of the trailer to the front door, filling seventeen 60-gallon bags that we then stashed out front for the next trash pickup. I had no idea what we would do with the trailer.

Just then a woman came walking up from a nearby trailer. "What are you going to do with that trailer?" she asked. "I am living in a trailer with my sister, and I'd like to have my own place." $1,800 in small bills, and ten minutes later, we had gotten rid of Kathy's trailer. We used the money, as well as another $1,800 we were paid by a Tonawanda Manor patient attendant for Mother's old sedan, for gasoline, meals, and motels for our drive to Arvada.

We rented the largest yellow Hertz/Penske moving van we could find and took off for Denver. On the third day of driving, I told Karen we would not make it home that day if she did not take the wheel for a while. No problem. She hopped into the driver's seat and we took off once more. After an hour I noticed that we needed fuel, so I told her to stop at the next exit. As we neared the exit ramp in the 28-foot van, she pulled over along the freeway.

"What're we doing?" I asked.

"I don't do gas stations in this thing!" she quipped.

The moving van was a challenge to her, but we made it home that night. I slept on a bed in her basement, as I could not keep my eyes open for another 30-minute drive to our foothills home.

Mother's Life Ends

Mother lived at first in an independent wing, then an assisted living section at Springwood, a senior facility in Arvada, but another fall and her osteoporosis-weakened broken bones led to her placement in the Life Care Center in Evergreen.

At the end, I happened to be nearby when I received a phone message from the Life Care Center. Mother was fading. I quickly arrived at her bedside. She was essentially unconscious. I took her hand. I told her she had given about all she could give, and that the world was a better place for her having walked in it. Then I prayed, "It is okay, Mother, you can let go now. It will be all right. God will understand." She opened her eyes. With an almost imperceptible movement of her lips, she mouthed, "I love you." Within 30 minutes it was clear she had finished all that life had assigned to her.

When Mother died, several of my cousins came from California to honor her. I took a fiftyish female cousin to Kathy's nursing home for a brief visit. I asked Kathy, "Do you have any idea why Sharon might be here all the way from California? Kathy grinned slyly, and offered, "Sharon is pregnant!"

"No," I said. "Mother has died, and Sharon came to remember her." Blank look. I do not think Kathy ever understood that Mother was gone. Because she was physically and emotionally unstable, Kathy could not attend the memorial service for Mother we had in Denver before we took her body back to Tonawanda for another service and burial.

I conducted Mother's final service in Kenmore United Methodist Church. Even though she had not lived in Kenmore for more than four years, the church, a large Gothic structure, was packed. Later that day, I prayed a prayer of committal as she was interred in the fifth of the six slots in the Elmlawn Cemetery plot in Tonawanda, purchased by my father the day my brother was killed. Of course, I cried.

As I stood at her grave side, my emotion was more than one of sadness. Mother had lived 91 years, longer than anyone in her family. She had lived bravely and honorably. She had loved people in profoundly caring and selfless ways. She had conquered every obstacle and heartbreak life had handed her. My heart was overcome with a deep, peaceful gratitude that she had made it from the beginning of her life to its conclusion without breaking. She was a true victor. Her faith was her abiding conviction that life is filled with zest, irony, and responsibility. I felt a deep honor to be her son and soulmate.

Kathy's Life Ends

Under very careful supervision from Jan, who, by now, was an Elder-Care Case Manager, Kathy lived independently for a while in an apartment in Arvada. At first, Kathy was able to ride a city bus to Evergreen to visit Mother. Gradually, though, Kathy became more confused and missed buses often enough that she could no longer visit Mother on her own.

She eventually had to be moved into Allison Nursing Home in Lakewood. This facility happened to be located right down the street from a United Church whose members were very charitable to Kathy when she went there for Sunday Worship. One Sunday when I was present, Kathy stood up during the sermon and announced, "Well, I have to go to the bathroom." Then she lumbered out, interrupting again upon her return. On another Sunday when I was guest worship leader, she stood up during a pastoral prayer and said loudly, "That's my brother. He's a minister."

I smiled. God embraced us all.

While she was a resident of Allison Nursing Home, Kathy participated in a day-care program at a wonderful place named Summit Center. She went there daily for months and was well regarded by her peers.

Before she turned sixty, Kathy was remanded to Fort Logan Mental Hospital for another round of psychotic behavior. Not long after she was back in Allison Nursing Home, she died in 2001. Intriguingly, her death certificate read "Cause of Death: Global Decline."

I asked the minister of Kathy's United Church whether I could lead a service in her memory. He said, "Sure. You know her better than I do." As people gathered for the service, held on a Saturday afternoon, I was astonished. More than half of the church members appeared. But the beautiful part was the arrival and participation of two large van loads of developmentally disabled and chronically mentally ill men and women from Summit Center. Supervisors had come in on their Saturday day-off to drive them to the church in the center's vans.

I did a very simple service, lifting a woman who had struggled all her life to love and to be kind to the people who came her way. I closed, saying, "We'll be taking Kathy's body to Tonawanda, New York, where she will be last to be buried in a six-unit plot with her brother Stuart, her father, her grandmother Lapp, her husband Vic, and her mother. May God rest her soul in peace."

At the end of the service, none of the people from Summit Center exited. At first, they just stood there looking at me. Then, one by one, they started crowding around me at the front of the sanctuary. It was not over until each one had told me his or her personal story of how Kathy had loved them, been nice to them, or helped them with their problems. In over 60 years of ministry, I have never had such a genuine outpouring of simple gratitude for a life well lived.

In the end, Kathy had done the best she could with what she had, and had loved more purely, more unequivocally, more unconditionally, than most ever achieve! You see, all people have equal opportunity in the eyes of God.

Immediately taking her body to Tonawanda for the burial service, my longtime church friend, Jeanne Grace, drove from Rochester to Tonawanda and was the only non-family member to attend the memorial rites I conducted for Kathy at the Bury Funeral Home in Kenmore.

When Jan and I stood at her grave, the sixth and final slot in the Tonawanda, NY six pack, and watched the dirt being thrown over her simple casket, I felt eerily alone and diminished. The last one of my ancestors and siblings was in the ground. My assignment was to carry on for them all, an emotion I first felt the day we buried my eight-year-old brother.

Parkinson's Does not Take Dr. Bill - Yet

Totally unexpectedly, on September 10th, 2001, Jan received a somber phone call from her sister-in-law, Marilyn Wallace. Jan's brother, Dr.

Bill Wallace, was in the hospital – again. Only this might be his last hurrah. Marilyn said to Jan, "I think you should come right away."

Dr. Bill, who had been fighting Parkinson's for years, was in the Concord hospital. Obviously, Jan wanted to go. We made a reservation for the next morning, 9/11/2001, for Jan to fly through Chicago to Manchester, NH.

I took her to DIA, and as we approached the United check-in counter the usual terminal hubbub seemed strangely hushed. I then saw that the counter clerk was crying. She said without prompting, "A plane just hit one of the towers of the World Trade Center in New York. The pilot, crew and passengers all are dead." Just then, a manager came running up and shouted for all to hear, "We have to close the airport! Everyone should leave immediately. That's all I know."

I raced out to our car, which was parked in a short-term slot, and flipped on NPR. Bob Edwards was announcing that a second plane had just struck the other Trade Center tower. There was not yet any indication of what was going on, but Edwards reported that the White House was suspecting a terrorist attack. I went back into the terminal to retrieve Jan and her luggage. Driving away from DIA we received a call from Karen who had just been sent home from work. We met her west of DIA and drove home.

9/11 was a Tuesday. Jan called United on Wednesday. All flights were cancelled. Jan called on Thursday. All flights were cancelled. Friday. Saturday. Sunday. All flights were still cancelled. No reservations accepted. On Monday she was offered a flight to Chicago but was told the leg from Chicago to Manchester was not likely to operate for another day or two.

I was in my home office working on a management consulting report for the Sable-Altura Volunteer Fire Department located east of Denver. When Jan told me the latest flight news, I said, "Give me a couple of hours to finish up. You go pack. We'll start driving to Concord right after noon." She called Marilyn with our plan. Bill still was alive!

The drive to New Hampshire typically took four full days. We left our mountain home in the early afternoon on Monday. On Tuesday we drove over 900 miles. We arrived in Concord on Thursday morning, and were at Bill's bedside before noon. He seemed more alive than dead. In fact, despite his very debilitating Parkinson's, his eyes twinkled mirthfully as Jan entered the room.

We should have known!

The immediate crisis soon passed, and we helped Marilyn think through the need of eventually moving Bill to a nursing home. This did not happen right away. When Bill was discharged from the hospital, Marilyn took him home again, where she had round-the-clock caregivers.

A week after this rushed trip east, Jan and I drove back to Denver, stopping for a few hours at the Ohio Wesleyan campus in Delaware, Ohio, where we had first met. An indelible memory of that return trip was the incredible number of cars and pickups all across the country that were flying two miniature American flags, one on each side.

The next spring, Marilyn moved Bill to a Concord nursing home. For the remainder of his life, which turned out to be eleven years, Jan arranged for us to visit as often as we could, sometimes driving, sometimes flying. We travelled to Concord at least eight more times "to see him for the last time."

Though Bill gradually grew very unresponsive, Jan was dedicated to visiting. Bill could always summon a flicker of recognition, right up to the final visit. Jan spent many hours on the phone supporting Marilyn during those long years.

Jan – Adult Care Manager

In 1990, after her return from Florida, Jan started working with Adult Care Management, a non-profit social service agency, and worked out of three different offices in Denver, then one in Boulder. In this role, Jan made home visits in private residences and care facilities. Her work involved arranging for housing and other necessary services for both indigent and private pay clients. It finally became more efficient for her to work out of our home in Coal Creek Canyon, as her territory primarily included the mountainous portions of three counties, Clear Creek, Gilpin, and Boulder.

Sometime in April of 1995 we decided to host a big open house on June 11th, a Sunday that year, for our Fortieth Anniversary. We determined that 40 years would be a good time to celebrate because many people did not make their 50th. In addition to family, we invited four groups, Jan's fellow workers, my work colleagues, people from the Coal Creek Canyon Volunteer Fire Department, and church and denominational friends. Each group had differently crafted name tags so guests could tell how others happened to know us. At least 200 people came to our mountain home. It was a joyful day.

Our premonition that we might not make fifty years of marriage almost came to pass four weeks later when Jan was in a car accident.

One quiet Monday afternoon very shortly after our Anniversary open house, I was in my office in Denver when the phone rang. "Robb Lapp," I answered as I always did. A woman's voice asked curtly, "Is Janet Lapp your wife?"

"Yes," I responded, cautiously taking a deep breath.

The voice continued. "This is Clear Creek County Sheriff's Dispatch. It is a courtesy call. We just wanted to notify you that Janet has been in an auto accident. Her injuries are not serious. As a precaution, she is being transported to St. Anthony Hospital in Denver."

"Wait a minute," I said, "I am President of the Coal Creek Canyon Fire Protection District. Dispatch doesn't make notification calls like this unless it's a real emergency!"

Softening, the dispatcher said, "If I were you, I'd meet the ambulance at the St. Anthony Hospital emergency entrance."

As I rushed out to my car, the thought that we had just celebrated our 40th because we might not live to see our 50th flashed through my mind.

Jan had been driving south on State Highway 119 on her way to the Gilpin County Commissioners' Office in Blackhawk. She was just behind another car, struggling with sleepiness right after lunch. On a curve to the right, having nodded off, she went straight, crossed the oncoming traffic lane, and flew off into space. She awoke in midair over a steep drop-off and had the presence of mind to be sure while still flying that the doors were unlocked. The car instantly went from 55 mph to zero as it crashed against a huge granite boulder in a ravine out of sight of the roadway.

The woman in the car ahead thought the car following her might be her daughter. Suddenly, she did not see Jan's car. Gratefully, she turned around and came back. She discovered Jan's wrecked car in the ravine. Jan told her she had injured her back and thought it could be broken. The woman immediately went for help. A passing doctor, whose name

Jan recognized as the physician of one of her clients, climbed down the ravine and comforted Jan as they waited for the ambulance and rescue crew.

I arrived at the St. Anthony emergency room a few minutes ahead of the ambulance. An orthopedic surgeon happened to be there, having just seen another accident victim. He stood by with me to see what injuries Jan had sustained. In addition to her injuries, Jan had been motion sick all the way down the mountain and she was a mess. Hearing that she had injured her back, I was immensely relieved to see her move her feet.

In addition to two broken vertebrae, Jan had sustained trauma to her shoulder, chest, and abdomen from the seat belt that kept her from going through the windshield in the abrupt stop.

The accident occurred on a Monday. By Wednesday I was becoming concerned for her life. It seemed to me that the Morphine was causing a major deterioration. I asked her doctor to stop giving her this narcotic. He did. It turned out that she was allergic to Morphine! Jan's condition stabilized.

She did not eat anything all week, but on Friday someone brought in a cherry pie. Jan's eyes twinkled for the first time. She stuck her finger into the pie, speared a single cherry and tasted it. We were over the hump! She would make it.

Later, I was asked how this impacted me. Reflecting, I said, "In my adult years, when there has been a severe threat in the life of a loved one, even a death, I have tended to remain in control of my own emotions and make the necessary supportive decisions. I am not afraid of my own death, or that of anyone else." In the case of standing next to Jan's hospital bed, my major impulse was to try to analyze what needed to be done. I was not frantic or panicked. My major emotion was loving compassion. However, I cannot say that I did not shed tears when I was at home alone.

From the end of June until Labor Day, Jan lived in a huge plaster cast that encased her from neck to pelvis. After she came home from the hospital, I bathed her each day. I cut a hole in a large black plastic garbage bag and slipped it over her head to cover the cast so I could shampoo her hair and wash the remaining exposed parts of her body. This led to much laughter. I also used a wet towel under her cast each day to wash her covered areas. She often teasingly accused me of using water that was too cold!

One night when I arrived home after an evening meeting, she was in bed asleep with her slacks and shoes on. She had not been able to reach down to get her things off.

Shortly after her release from the hospital, Jan was back at her desk. She wasn't allowed to drive but was able to successfully manage most of her case work by phone.

In September she was well enough to have the cast removed, but she next had to have a Striker Frame metal brace that went all around her midsection and kept her spinal column thrust forward. She had to wear it all day but could be in bed without it. However, if she had to go to the bathroom during the night, my job was to get up, go around the bed, reinstall the brace, and then guide her.

Each day, she used a walking stick to climb up the steep hill of Tunnel Road 19 and back down. On one of her walks, she saw lots of coins scattered in the road near a neighboring mountain cabin. Because she was not able to bend over far enough to pick them up, she went back down to our house and got some chewing gum. When she got to the coins again, she put some chewed gum on the end of the walking stick and tediously picked up many of them, several dollars' worth. As the summer wore on, we found more coins in the dirt. We often wondered whether they had come from the cabin as part of a robbery.

By the next spring, Jan was fully recovered and didn't experience any residual effects. Throughout the ordeal I never heard her complain. That was Jan's style.

Jan worked with home-bound adults for another three years. After she retired in 1998, she continued working with a private pay patient who suffered serious dementia and was confined to a nursing home in Wheat Ridge. When this woman finally died, Jan and a volunteer were the only ones who attended her funeral, conducted by the Roman Catholic Priest with whom I had worked in my earlier days in Arvada.

Robyn – Single Parent

While Keith was deployed to Spain, Robyn contemplated seeking a divorce from him. After nine years, two children, and a husband who was away most of the time, Robyn had had enough. She pursued the divorce in 1992 when Keith returned home.

Living as a single parent in Arvada was very difficult for Robyn, both functionally and financially. But after she graduated in 1993 with two degrees from the University of Colorado Denver, she began a Masters-Degree in Biochemistry. She used Federally Assisted student loans not only for tuition but also for living expenses while she raised her two daughters, amassing a large student loan debt. She completed all the course work and a thesis, getting a foundation for medical work, but did not complete the board testing for her Biochemistry Degree, so she did not receive it.

Trying to be supportive, Jan spent many hours dropping off and picking up Brittany and Chelsea, first from preschool, then from a Montessori grade school. It seems like I was constantly doing house repairs and maintenance for Robyn, including a new roof, hot water heater, and new windows.

Of course, we always enjoyed time with our granddaughters.

In 1994, Robyn thought owning a motorcycle would reduce her daily transportation costs. She answered an ad and found a cycle she eventually could not handle. But she also met its seller, a very nice fellow named William Gorman. I officiated at their marriage in our mountain house on May 27, 1995. Unfortunately, he and Brittany could not manage a functional relationship. In addition, Robyn's trying to finish her coursework added to household tension.

Robyn finally divorced William primarily because she thought it would reduce the contentiousness between him and Brittany. William moved to western Idaho in 2001. Robyn felt ambivalent but decided to move with the girls to Idaho to be near William. Karen and I rented a U-Haul truck and helped move all her things to Idaho. When we returned, I had a house to sell.

In 2002, Robyn and the girls moved from Idaho to Grand Junction, where she loved it, partly because she found work in a hospital day-surgery center, and partly because she cherished the solitude of the nearby National Parks.

Stuart and Eve Marry

When Stuart and Eve met, she had been divorced from Tim Nall for several years. But, humorously, Tim was renting a room in Eve's house north of Houston where she was raising their two daughters, Neele and Nellaine. When Stuart moved in with her, Tim moved into the apartment where Stuart had been living. Stuart and Eve liked living with each other, and Stuart was comfortable with Neele and Nellaine. While he was still conducting his private legal practice in the office where he met Eve, they decided to get married. A lovely ceremony was held in St. Matthew Lutheran Church in Houston on March 18, 1995. Their reception was at the nearby Ritz-Carlton Hotel. As I walked in with six-year-old granddaughter Chelsea, she looked at the ornate shiny composite flooring in the entry and said, "Papa, I can see why they call this place the Rich Carlton!"

In July 1995 Stuart rented a small office on the southeast edge of The Woodlands and transferred his solo practice to Montgomery County. After they were married in 1995, Stuart and Eve wanted to move from Eve's house to an area north of The Woodlands. I flew to Houston several times to look at houses with them. They bought a beautiful wooded lot near Magnolia in what had been in a forested property owned by Mitchell Development Corporation of the Southwest, an affiliate of The Woodlands Development Corporation. We designed a house similar to one we had seen, and they hired a contractor to build it. I flew there several times to monitor construction. It became the Texas Lapp family headquarters.

Stuart's law practice went along very well. He was a solo practitioner for the whole decade. In 1998 a large fuel distributor and retailer in several southwestern states, Petroleum Wholesale, Inc., became a client.

Neele graduated from Klein Oak H.S. in May 2002. She started at Stephen F. Austin State University in Nacogdoches in August 2002. Nellaine attended Magnolia H.S. for her junior and senior years.

Karen Becomes a Ronzheimer

While Karen was working at AT&T in 1994, she met Joel Ronzheimer, also an AT&T employee. He was one of nine siblings who grew up in West Chicago, IL. One afternoon, as Jan and I were leaving our mountain house, we saw a green Jeep about to turn from the Gross Dam Road onto Tunnel 19 Road. The Jeep stopped and the driver smiled broadly at us. Karen hopped out of the passenger seat and introduced Joel to us. He turned out to have a big, thoughtful heart!

Eventually Joel moved into Karen's Arvada house. In early June of 1995 Karen went with Joel to Chicago to meet some of his siblings.

On the morning of June 11th, 1995, as Jan and I were doing final preparations for our Fortieth Anniversary open house, Karen and Joel appeared, having just returned from Chicago. Karen kept following us around. Finally, Jan saw her name tag. It said "Karen Ronzheimer." Jan gulped, "Oh my goodness (that's as close as Jan ever came to swearing), did you get married in Chicago?" Karen laughed, "No, but Joel has asked me to marry him. We're going to get a ring as soon as we can." It was a poignant moment for the four of us.

When Karen broke her news, I was reinstalling the locking hardware on our front door, after painting it the day before. This door handle could be unlocked from the outside with a key, and from the inside by turning a bolt in the handle. In the excitement, I mounted it with the keyhole inside the living room and the bolt on the exterior. Joel stared, wondering what I was doing, not daring to say anything to his father-in-law-to-be. But, laughing, Karen said, "Dad, look what you just did!"

We were pleased that Joel and Karen had decided to marry, which they did in the very living room in which they shared their news. The wedding was on April 20, 1996. Of course, I officiated. Joel's six brothers and two sisters were present for a rehearsal dinner the night before, and for the ceremony on a beautiful mountain Saturday. We had to delay the service an hour while we waited for Joel's adult daughter, Melanie, to arrive after a late flight. It was the first time all nine Ronzheimers had been together since their mother's funeral, and the last time, too.

Saving Karen's Life

On Christmas Day 1996, Karen and Joel were staying with us overnight on Christmas Eve in anticipation of holiday festivities that were to include them as well as Robyn and her husband, William. As I was putting the holiday turkey in the oven, Joel and Karen came into the kitchen from the bedroom below. Karen immediately collapsed on a couch in the adjacent study. Joel confirmed that she didn't feel good. As President of the Fire District, I had been certified as a First Responder and had relatively good experience in first aid. It was her abdomen. I felt around and thought that she could be bleeding internally. I decided we could not wait for the rescue volunteers to respond to the station to get our new ambulance. Joel and I carefully placed Karen into the back seat of my Outback. We grabbed William, who was just driving up with Robyn, and took off for Lutheran Hospital.

Since it was early on Christmas day, traffic was minimal and I made to the emergency room in record time, probably twenty minutes sooner than if I had waited for my department's ambulance. Joel and William commandeered a wheelchair and, as I dealt with a red-tape-encrusted reception clerk, they wheeled Karen straight into the main emergency room. As they approached the nurses' station, Karen passed out. She was suffering from a ruptured ectopic pregnancy and was, indeed, bleeding internally.

Before noon she was in a regular room after having had successful surgery. There wasn't any kind of chair in Karen's room, so I lied down on the floor of her room and, mission accomplished, promptly fell asleep. Shortly, a nurse came along and kicked me, determined I was not dead, and then told me I could not sleep there.

Meanwhile, Jan collected my sister Kathy from her nursing home in Lakewood and took her to my mother's nursing home in Evergreen, where they then "celebrated" Christmas.

Karen bounced back quickly, one of the best Christmas presents ever!

After Joel retired from AT&T, by then called Lucent Technologies, he began working as a grounds-maintenance employee at Green Gables, a Denver golf course. Later he was hired by the City of Arvada to work at West Woods Golf Course and loved working outside.

Karen continued her employment with the AT&T spin-off, Lucent Technologies. Her job was managing the inventory of used equipment and switchboards. She often flew around the country doing supply checks at warehouses.

Karen and Joel Become Mountain People

After they were married, Karen and Joel began talking about living in the foothills. In preliminary anticipation of building their own house, Karen, Joel, and I began clearing a wooded site on one of the 35-acre tracts Jan and I owned near our Tunnel Road 19 property. But that effort did not last long.

As I drove down the Tunnel 19 Road hill one afternoon in 1997, the neighbor to the south of our property was driving uphill. He owned a house on a 33-acre tract right across Tunnel 19 from our house. He stopped me to say that he and his wife were moving to town and that they would rent their mountain house. As he drove off, I yelled, "If you ever decide to sell, let me know." Within an hour, he called me, saying, "My wife and I have decided we'll sell." I immediately called Joel and Karen. Later that same day, after looking through the house, Karen and Joel had signed a contract to purchase thirty-three acres and a house in desperate need of significant repair and remodeling. After closing a couple of months later, and doing a few immediately needed repairs, they moved in.

The house had been built in stages beginning about the time of World War II. An already existing 10x20 structure with no foundation had been a cabin at a small lumber mill lower in the canyon before being moved to the site. To this cabin had been added a relatively sturdy extension containing living and sleeping spaces and a tiny bath. Then, three more disparate, tacked-on rooms had been added. I helped Joel and Karen with many repairs and small improvements over the next two years.

Adding Rooms to Our Mountain House

Meanwhile, I had been considering an addition to our house. Looking forward to the possibility that we might, one day, need to live on one floor as oldsters, I envisioned the addition of two north facing rooms and a full bath on the main level. The new main level rooms would be a study and a family room with the best mountain views in the house. The level below these rooms would contain a large bedroom with a private outside entry. The plan made the house much more livable and flexible.

The idea was that the main floor additions could become a bedroom and caregiver's room in case of the health deterioration of either one of us.

I wanted the exterior to look dramatic, so I consulted an architect who was known for his inventive exterior designs. He created a spectacular steel frame structure for several decks. The vertical posts which held up the decks extended many feet upward toward the sky, which he thought would be a good statement for a minister. He also vaulted the entryway and added an eye-catching triangulated window over the door.

I engaged the contractor who had installed the replacement windows to do the carpentry. I did the plumbing and electrical work. I hired Joel, who had left his Green Gables golf course job because of its distance, to do most of the interior painting and staining.

But the excitement came with the steel work. Looking around for a steel erection company I landed the outfit that had just completed the new Coors Field in downtown Denver. It was just before Christmas, so the heavy-duty crew had not yet begun its next project. In addition to large pieces of steel they brought a giant crane truck that worked in front of our house for the better part of a week.

Long before starting the house addition, we had discovered that very strong winds would careen off the ridge south of the house and blow the two-story south-facing living room wall back and forth. In one fierce storm I saw the wall move four inches in and out. I was concerned that the wall could cave in, allowing the roof to fall. So, when we did the house addition, I had the steel erectors install a long steel L-beam horizontally along the inside of the south living room wall, between the lower and upper windows. Then I created a box frame and covered it with drywall to hide the girder. Later, Jan suggested that we display pottery on top of this drywall enclosure. Not only did the girder reinforce the wall, which never flexed in the wind again, the resulting cover added a nice decorative touch to the living room.

An Almost Total Rebuild of Joel and Karen's House

In 2000, shortly after we completed the addition to our house, Joel and Karen Ronzheimer moved into our new basement bedroom, the one with the outside entrance, for several months while we tackled their house next door. We pictured tearing down about half the house, adding a foundation under the original rooms, then adding an expansive family room and adjoining bedroom with an additional bath.

I drew the plans, had an engineer add structural notes, and applied for a Boulder County building permit, which was issued with only one revision. Joel and Karen hired the contractor who had just done our house addition to do most of the work. To start, Joel and I used my sturdy tractor to tear down several portions of the structure we did not want to keep. Before the construction crews came, we bought several large steel I-beams and jacked them up under the original cowboy outpost cabin and adjoining living area to provide a stable foundation. The project included the installation of a septic tank and leach field, there having been none in prior incarnations.

Essentially, it became a totally new house. One of the fun things is that the kitchen is the original 10x20 cabin. Karen and Joel love their remodeled house. Its comfortable rustic style, along with Karen's and Joel's gracious hospitality, make it a great place for holiday gatherings and peaceful escapes.

Chapter 43

∿∿

"You Could Sue Your Surgeon"

Colon Quits

THOUGH I HAD a minor heart attack ten years earlier, I made it to age 68 without any life-threatening physical issues. However, a major medical drama began just after Easter in 2001. I woke up one night in bed at our mountain home in a large pool of blood. I was bleeding anally. I threw on a few clothes, and we drove immediately to St. Joseph Hospital in northeast Denver where I had been treated for the heart attack. In the Emergency Room I learned that I had several bleeding diverticula. Upon being admitted, the bleeding stopped overnight of its own accord. However, I lost copious amounts of blood. I wanted to avoid transfusions out of a concern for inheriting the genetic or organic problems of donors. Learning from the doctors that my blood would gradually replenish itself, I was discharged, even though I was so weak, I had to lie down every few minutes.

In my role as President of the La Foret Conference and Retreat

Center Board, that June I had to attend the Rocky Mountain UCC Annual Conference Meeting which was being held at First Plymouth Congregational Church in Englewood, CO. I spent most of the meeting on a cot in the minister's office, but I did the La Foret presentation! For the next few months, I went to a nearby lab for red blood cell counts every week. Each time my count inched back a little closer to normal.

Even with my disability, I spent almost all my daylight hours for the next many weeks monitoring the construction of Arapahoe Green, our church-related non-profit's 66-unit apartment project near Aurora, interviewing ED candidates at La Foret, and even attending a CTS Board meeting in Chicago.

Then, on the 28th of October, a Sunday morning, I awoke again with the same bleeding. Talk about being chagrinned! This time, before rushing off to St. Joseph Hospital, I made Jan her traditional Sunday morning cheese/egg omelet. I absolutely was not going to let a blood-leak take over my breakfast job! Jan drove me to St. Joseph as Karen and Joel followed in their car. I was immediately admitted, and though I continued to bleed, no one paid much attention until the next morning.

"Remove Your Colon or Die"

On Monday, there were exams and tests. I was still bleeding. By Tuesday, not having eaten anything since Saturday, I was feeling quite weak. Then a doctor in a white lab coat walked in and said with little prologue, "Mr. Lapp, you have two choices. We can take out your colon or you can die. The walls of your colon are weakened by diverticulitis, and you'll bleed to death if we don't remove your entire large intestine!"

He went on with details about how they would do it with laparoscopy, a new surgical technique that involved cutting small openings in the abdomen rather than cutting it all wide open. I took a deep breath, and said, "This seems like an easy choice. Try the surgery."

That settled, I related to him an experience I had had six months earlier when in St. Joseph the first time I was bleeding. I said, "I was lying in bed and a doctor came in and told me he might have to operate to remove my colon. He really scared me." The doctor said, "That was me." I gulped, and we laughed together.

When I regained consciousness late on Wednesday, I had a feeding tube imbedded in my left shoulder, a pain medication drip in my right arm, a totally wounded abdomen, a urinary catheter, and three tubes through my nose and down my throat. Barely conscious, I was told to squeeze the bulb in my right hand to release a liquid sedative when the pain was too severe. For the next 24 hours I was the object of a parade of inspectors, all wearing scrubs or uniforms. I could not have cared less.

My surgeon stopped coming in. Over the weekend I learned he had left town early Friday and would not return for several days.

Stuart showed up from Houston late that Friday, and, relieving Jan from a bedside vigil, stayed in the room with me for two days and nights, dozing on the vacant bed next to mine. He, too, was interested in the parade. He observed that it was mostly Medical Residents who came in groups of four and five, with increasing frequency. Stuart left on Monday for his return to Houston with the assumption that I would soon improve. But I did not. I got worse. Next thing I knew, the doctor, having returned, was peering down at me saying there was a blockage. It was mid-day Wednesday. He said he would re-operate first thing in the morning. I lost consciousness before the day ended.

The Surgery was Botched

The first surgery had been botched. Somehow, the connection between my surviving small intestine and my rectum was not complete. No wonder nothing made it all the way through! It was touch-and-go for days. For hours at a time, I would keep my eyes on the wall clock, saying to myself with each tick, "Breathe in. Breathe out. Breathe in. Breathe out."

Stuart came back from Houston that next weekend. Again, he stayed in my room. Each night, while hallucinating, I thought I had been taken to the hospital basement. I was certain I was in a different room. But it turned out that the way the lights from the adjacent parking garage shined on my ceiling it seemed like I was in a different room. But that is how "not with it" I was.

What were my emotions during this horrendous interlude? Interestingly, I did not experience fear. The Holy was whispering words of hope to my soul. Nevertheless, I was both diminished and frustrated by many things, the hoses down my throat, the feeding tube in my shoulder, the catheter in my urethra, the pain in my gut, as well as not being able to get out of bed. As I stared out of my hospital window at the Denver Museum of Nature and Science which was to the east, beyond our beautiful city park, I longed to be outside.

The next week, as I gradually gained strength, a Physical Therapist came in, looked at a walker along the wall, and asked as I laid somewhat helpless in the bed, "How long have you been using a walker?" I suddenly became very animated. "Lady," I said, "On the Saturday before I came into this awful place, I was in the mountains installing a new deck on the house my son-in-law and I are building!" "Oh," she said. "Then you might be able to walk out into the hall. You may need the walker the first time you try being out of bed." Two days later she got me to the foot of a staircase and asked if I could make it to the first landing. I did. Going home was on the horizon.

I was in St. Joseph for three weeks, for a surgery that should not have confined me for more than five days. As Jan drove me up Park Avenue on our way home, I was exhilarated to be alive.

It took almost two years for me to truly recover. Even so, my new shortened digestive tract has had a permanent negative effect on my diet.

This intestinal fiasco did not kill me. Why? Good question. Was God protecting me? I do not believe in that kind of God. Was it not yet "my time?" I do not believe in predestination. More than anything, it was the luck of the draw, as well as a good deal of persistence on my part. The Holy's call is to keep fighting, not give up. "Choose life, not death."

Even before I could get out of bed after the second surgery a bedside visitor, seeking to support and console me said, "You know you could sue your surgeon. He did not do an adequate follow-up exam following the first operation before he left town."

This idea seemed quite foreign to me. All my life, my response to negative events had been to cope and try to go on constructively. I could not think of a thing a spiteful lawsuit would fix. For months after I became functional again, I was grateful I could keep doing my United Church Rocky Mountain Conference, La Foret, and non-profit Rocky Mountain HDC work. I kept thinking about the Holy's call for forgiveness in a litigious culture.

Finally, one day I wrote an essay. It was later published in the national Quaker Journal, *What Canst Thou Say?* Because it so clearly expresses who I am, I include it here.

On a very cold, icy March morning during World War II, there occurred a terrible tragedy at a busy intersection near Buffalo, NY. A police-commissioned civilian crossing guard allowed three kids to start across the intersection in front of an out of control, skidding gasoline truck whose driver had been going too fast on ice when approaching a stale green light. Two of the children were critically injured. The third was squashed beyond recognition. The dead boy was my brother, with whom I had been talking seconds earlier.

Both the Town-paid crossing guard and the Richfield truck driver had been negligent. Even in those days, this was a lawsuit waiting to happen. But the gravity of what occurred next did not really sink into my soul for decades. A church member asked my father whether we would be suing the two parties and their employers. My father answered in such a low-key fashion that I really thought nothing of it. In fact, it made sense to an almost ten-year-old. My father said, "No, that truck driver has a family for which he is the breadwinner, and he already feels terrible. And, the crossing guard was an older man, actually deaf, who was the only one the Town could hire, given the War effort. No, we don't need to hurt them more than they already are. A lawsuit will not bring Stuart back."

Now fast forward to one Sunday morning in October, not long after 9/11, 2001, another day that would burn its way into my brain. I awoke bleeding anally for the second time in less than six months. I groaned in denial, stubbornly taking time to make Jan her traditional weekend omelet, and reluctantly headed for the hospital. Upon being admitted to St. Joseph I learned that my choices were to allow removal of my entire colon or to die. Easy choice. I thought. I chose the surgery, and almost died anyway. The surgery was not until Wednesday. It took several hours. On Friday, the surgeon left town for four days. But by the following Monday it was clear something was terribly wrong. There was a blockage in my G.I. tract. I was barely conscious by day's end. Medical Residents who had been attending during my surgeon's absence could not figure it out, so did nothing.

On Tuesday, the surgeon returned, poked around, and said he would re-operate the next morning. I don't even remember being taken to the Operating Room and was essentially unconscious for the next three days. But somehow the first surgery had been a major botch by either the surgeon or a Resident. There was an internal disconnect in the plumbing that resulted, among other things, in an abdominal infection. I nearly died. But when I finally regained consciousness, my first sensation was that I was alive! I could see light. I could see the tubes sticking out of my body in several places. I could see the large clock on the opposite wall. I would make it!

While I was still in that hospital bed a friend asked whether I would sue the surgeon. That seemed a very foreign thought. Making no connection at all to my father's response the day after my brother had been killed, I said, "All I want to do is live. If I do, the surgery will have been a success and I will be grateful for the skill of my surgeon. If I die, my family will have to figure out what they think is the right thing to do." The surgeon was in pain over the mishap, but his skill had given him the ability to correct the problem. I had no desire to seek to diminish him.

As an epilogue to this sequence, months later, I had a memorable conversation with this surgeon. I was having a small problem with the tail end of my plumbing and made an appointment to see him in his office. After he had given me a common-sense recommendation for my issue, I thanked him for his work on my behalf, paused, looked him in the eye, and asked him how he was doing. He seemed a bit startled, sat down and proceeded to tell me how he was having some heart difficulty, and was fearful that being a surgeon, something he loved, and was what he knew how to do, might soon come to an end. After twenty minutes he finished his sharing. I squeezed his shoulder, shook his hand, and have never seen him again. Not until after the appointment did I realize that he was more than a little nervous when he stepped into the examining room where I was waiting. But neither of us had mentioned the surgical debacle, I, on purpose, and he, perhaps out of apprehension.

The curious circumstantial similarity between my father's and my response to human failure has given rise to my pondering the important moral and theological question of right and wrong. Do we do what is culturally acceptable, or is there a divine imperative that transcends human perspective? Actually, I think the answer is "both." But why did my father buck the tide and do the merciful thing? Why did I?

I don't know why my father did what he did, but I think I know why I did what I did. I acted out of a sense of commitment that began with my call, at age 16, to ministry, and continued in my ordination. When I was 24, on a hot June Sunday in a crowded Methodist Church in Western New York, I knelt in front of a Bishop, and was ordained a Traveling Elder, the most sacred Methodist ministerial commission. Holding the RSV Bible I still have, my right hand gingerly touched Isaiah's words, "Whom shall I send, and who will go for us? Here I am! Send me." This verse still articulates my burning sense that I very deliberately and self-consciously made a walk with God my highest life priority no matter how it required me to fly in the face of custom and culture. I felt dedicated to seeking what is right, what God wants, no matter the cost.

And how does one know what God wants? While we have the sacrificial life of Jesus as a formidable indicator, there is a brief passage in Deuteronomy that may say it for all people of the earth. "...I have set before you life and death, blessing and curse; therefore, choose life, that you and your descendants may live, loving the Lord your God..." I was in my early 50s when I preached a sermon inspired by this snippet. It has ever since illuminated my sense of God's call for justice and mercy in all of one's decisions. What gives life is right. What takes life away is wrong. Parenthetically, the naturalness of physical death is the key to human finitude.

So, with an ordained sense that flying in the face of God is not an option, and a moral sense that we are called to embrace life for all of God's people, I did what I did.

I do not know why my father behaved as he did. But realizing that he did something unusual and brave has given me a fresh appreciation of the father who often seemed to live in a world that was foreign to me, and to whom, therefore, I did not often feel close. I was uncomfortable with his theology, which I thought to be simplistic and self-serving. I didn't enjoy his fishing or other recreational pursuits, in which he often insisted that I participate. I didn't choose the career path of which he dreamed for me. I was 26 when he died at age 51, meaning that we did not have much of each other's adulthoods in which to come to respectful terms.

But when I made the connection, only recently, between his very brave and loving stand in face of his second son's death, and my decision about the destiny of a surgeon's life, I was astounded. My father was, in his core, a good and admirable guy. This insight has led to an affirming review of the many decisions he had to make in a very difficult time in American history, a window punctuated by two World Wars and the Great Depression. He, too, was vigilant in his distinguishing between right and wrong. He was a counter-cultural model.

Must be he heard a still, small voice, far, far away.[4]

---

4   Robinson Lapp, "Why?" *What Canst Thou Say?* 88, no. 1 – Evil (November 2015): 1-2. (*What Canst Thou Say* is an independent publication by Quaker Friends in Rochester, MN)

~~~

SECTION VIII

2003 – 2012

~~~

NOT OFF THE HOOK
AT SEVENTY!

Chapter 45

~~

FACING THE
HOMELESSNESS CRISIS

As I ENTERED my eighth decade, I could not escape the reality that America is not really a democracy for all people. It works for the rich and powerful. It is systemically unjust for people of color. It discriminates against people whose gender identity does not fall in "straight" categories. It is patriarchal and does not support women's rights to control their bodies or to have wages equal to men's. It does not like voices that call for action to halt global warming. Its Constitution favors white supremacy. Its fundamental commitment to capitalism crushes the marginalized.

As I listened to the Holy, I could not get off the hook. No retirement. No cruises. No avoidance of criticism for loving marginalized others more than self. No basking in the comfort of being a privileged white man living under an umbrella of systemic racism.

A career of working to enable people of all ethnic backgrounds to function justly and productively with one another had brought me into my seventies still trying to create racially and economically integrated neighborhoods. A more recent commitment was that of working to guarantee that people who are marginalized by our cultural dysfunctions have safe and affordable places to live. So, my life was now one of trying to address both the symptoms and causes of America's failure to make life work for all its residents.

This manifested itself in the work I was doing to make Rocky Mountain HDC, Inc. ("RMHDC"), an effective provider of affordable housing for people of all backgrounds and national heritages.

2003 was a momentous year. For two years RMHDC had been successfully operating Foothills Green, its 72-unit townhouse property for low-income families.

Arapahoe Green

Then with our new Executive Director, Joyce Alms-Ransford, the construction and lease of Arapahoe Green was completed in early 2003. Some of the new residents were either Ethiopian or Somalian immigrant families. Most others were white or African Americans.

An interesting footnote to the construction of Arapahoe Green is that the contractor so appreciated the work that RMHDC was doing that he, at his own expense, added a large community activity room to the main building.

ARAPAHOE GREEN

This activity room became a great amenity as we had already hired Family Services social workers to run community programs at Foothills Green and Arapahoe Green.

In 2004 RMHDC sold its sixteen Mountain United Church Housing Arvada Cottages. The Jefferson County Housing Authority bought them for upwards of a million dollars. In addition to the money, a motivating factor for selling was that these dispersed-site homes were difficult to manage. RMHDC then used the proceeds from this sale as seed money for development of additional new properties.

Willow Green

Despite the fact that rules for "Tax Credit" financing were tightening, and competition was becoming greater, the Board decided to keep going. RMHDC was able to find property for a third project on property in an unincorporated portion of Jefferson County between Westminster and Arvada. The project, to be called Willow Green, would add another 60 critically needed affordable apartments. We closed on the land purchase in 2003.

One of my contributions to the site selection process was the concept that affordable housing communities should not be larger than 75 to 100 units and should not be located in deteriorating neighborhoods. The size issue was to avoid assembling larger groups of people with similar social problems in any one property. As for neighborhoods, my notion was that our residents should live in economically stable areas, with good schools. The fact that many of our residents were minority persons or legal immigrants also led to the integrating of mostly white neighborhoods and school classrooms.

We determined that for a series of strategic and financial reasons, we should seek the annexation of the Willow Green site into the City of Arvada. Meeting Arvada's annexation requirements took months. We also had a struggle with an adjoining Non-Denominational Evangelical church over their improperly constructed property drainage facilities. We were pleased that after the annexation, the City of Arvada loaned us development funds to supplement our Tax Credit investments and awarded us social service program grants for Willow Green!

RMHDC's construction began in October of 2004 and the Willow Green buildings were completed in December of 2005.

Many Willow Green residents were single parents with children. Forty percent of residents were Latinx, some of them Central and South American immigrants.

At first, Willow Green's neighbors were very unhospitable. Some kept calling Arvada police with complaints. Others made an issue about how Willow Green kids were overcrowding the neighborhood school and walking in the street to get there. But by our holding social events to which both residents and neighbors were invited, folks began engaging positively with one another. Interestingly, the adjacent Evangelical church soon became very supportive, and worked with our Family Services staff to provide after-school and summer activities for the kids.

Two snapshots of residents from Arapahoe Green and Willow Green are good examples of the manner in which the American economy and culture have driven a substantial percentage of our residents into living below the country's poverty line.

The first is "Resident A," in her late 30s, who lives in Willow Green and is a college graduate with a master's degree. She is a white single mom with three bi-racial young children. Her divorced husband is black. Resident A is a full-time elementary school teacher whose earnings barely cover her rent, food, and daily living expenses. In addition to being incensed that our government is totally controlled by people and corporations with money, she is even more angry that the school board in her district, controlled by people who treat education as a business, froze teachers' wages five years ago, leaving her $10,000 a year below where she should be on the wage scale that was in place when she was hired. However, she "gets by" each month, but with nothing to spare. She has no savings. She and her children are covered by her health insurance as a teacher. A new majority on the school board is even more conservative, and wants to cancel the teacher contract altogether, so Resident A joined the teachers' union and is ready to strike for both more compensation and more focus on academic achievement. When I asked her, "If a miracle were to occur in your life, what would it be? She responded, "For teachers to get paid enough to have college funds for their children."

The second resident is "Resident B," an African American woman who lives in Arapahoe Green. She was stricken with Multiple-Sclerosis when she was 23. She, too, is a college graduate with a degree in elementary education. She has not been able to work for the past ten years. She lives alone in her apartment, and, as a volunteer, has done many things to assist people in her complex, a significant number of whom are African immigrants. She lives on disability payments and has Medicaid with supplements. However, her ongoing MS treatments and recent major emergency surgery costs are exceeding her ability to pay. Her issue with the way our government and society function is that the health care system is woefully inadequate. She thinks taxes should cover health care for everyone, as good health is the foundation for life in America. Nevertheless, Resident B is remarkably upbeat and positive about life, insisting that she is not a victim. When I ask about her desired miracle, she says, "That I would be well and go back to work." If she knew of an effective one, she would join a group advocating for major change in America's health care delivery system.

Cornerstone

In a joint venture with the St. Francis Center (Episcopal), a home-less day-care facility, RMHDC next built a 50-unit midrise apartment at Park Avenue and Curtis near downtown Denver, in the heart of a concentrated area of depressing homelessness. Development took three years, with the building being occupied in 2010. RMHDC manages the rental and maintenance of Cornerstone while St. Francis provides Case Managers for each resident.

Cornerstone was both the toughest and most fulfilling project we had done to date, as we had to assemble all the parts with a partner, go through a downtown redevelopment process that included demolition of a vacant, run-down hotel, and get approval from the Denver Housing Authority for each new resident. We also experienced problems with our general contractor. I experience heartbreak every time I visit, which is often, as I see the pain of tenants struggling to survive physically and emotionally. Most of the residents, usually chronically homeless men, pay their rent with HUD Section 8 vouchers, which means they pay about $25 per month out of pocket. About a quarter of the residents are black and the rest are white.

The City of Denver continues to struggle with a growing homeless population. In many cases, being homeless was not the homeless person's fault. It is the result of a larger systemic capitalistic dysfunction that favors the rich and disables the poor. But all around the neighborhood of the Cornerstone apartment building, the sidewalks are crowded with the tents and scant possessions of hundreds of homeless folks.

From Foothills Green through Cornerstone, I was part of the RMHDC team that attended regular weekly construction management conferences. My presence let contractors know that the owner board knew something about construction. I also had the opportunity to suggest solutions to the design, material, and subcontractor problems that arose without warning.

Sheridan Ridge

Cornerstone was still being built when Joyce was asked by the Colorado Housing Finance Authority whether RMHDC would be interested in buying a financially distressed tax-credit property, Sheridan Ridge, just two blocks south of Willow Green on Sheridan Blvd. in Arvada. Though it took a while to get final approval from all the involved financial institutions, RMHDC eventually became the project majority owner and property manager in 2008. Sheridan Ridge has 65 units, occupied primarily by people who attain the status of 60% of "Area Median Income." At closing, most of these folks were two parent families with children. Half of the families were Latinx, and several were black.

One day, Jan and I met our friend Bill Haefele for lunch near the Sheridan Ridge facility. Another customer in the waiting line overheard me telling Bill about Sheridan Ridge. This fellow began a shouting tirade about how the project was destroying adjacent property values and how he disliked people who lived there. I got him to agree to let me introduce him to some of our residents. Before long, there was mutually positive communication among our residents and the community neighbors. Street Ministry involves lots of human relations work!

Greenleaf

Always on the lookout for distressed apartment and townhouse properties that could be affordably purchased and rehabilitated, Joyce came up with a project near old-town Aurora. Named Greenleaf, it contained 55 apartments and was in serious need of repair. Before the end of

2012, we arranged for conventional financing and government grants from Aurora and Adams County to pay for the purchase which occurred in 2013. At least a third of Greenleaf's residents were Nepalese immigrants.

As I turned 80, RMHDC had become a notable force in Colorado's low-income housing effort. We had 363 occupied units and a Family Services program that helped make life work for our residents.

Reflection

In America, our capitalistic economy is structured to favor the majority white rich and powerful. Even in good times, the economy fails to provide have-nots with adequate education, health care, welfare, social security, safe affordable housing, and mental health. This injustice is what makes RMHDC's work so relevant. Even though the larger societal challenge is that of transforming our nation's values and capitalist policies to serve all residents, majority and minority, rich and poor, healthy and ill, with life-saving equal justice, community service non-profits like RMHDC are invaluable interim lifesavers for the marginalized. Why do I spend so much time and energy on this? The Holy's vision of a just and loving community keeps me going. This is ministry!

Chapter 46

~~~

FAMILY LIFE IN A NEW CENTURY

Parents Should Be Mentors, Not Cops

WHEN JAN AND I were young adults, each of our dads, as well as Jan's stepmother, continued to treat us like children who had to be told how to do things. As an exception to the way many parents relate to their children, my mother saw us as emerging adults with our own values, identities, and challenges. Her style was to celebrate our victories and to be compassionate when days were tough.

We found our relationship with her to be much deeper and more meaningful than with the others. She reinforced our senses of being responsible for our own lives. Not a bad model.

As the new Century began, Robyn, Stuart and Karen were mature adults, each in their 40s. Robyn had become a hospital technician who helped patients navigate their way through medical service options. Stuart was an attorney with a practice in commercial law and a gift for mediating differences among contestants. Karen's financial and management skills served her well in her corporate administrative work. Each had a strong sense of their value commitments, and each was in control of their lives.

Three very different adults. Three very separate life trajectories. Three lives whose destinies Jan and I never could have imagined. Three people we love unconditionally, and about each of whom we worry in ways all caring parents are wont to do. But parenting one's adult children, at its healthiest, is essentially a walking with them for better or for worse. We have sought to be available for the giving of advice and support. We have tried to celebrate their human victories, and to show compassion when they share their trials.

Now, a bit about each one.

Robyn - Our Odyssey Daughter

In 2002, Robyn and Chelsea had left William, ex-husband No. 3, behind in Idaho and moved to Grand Junction where Robyn rented a house. Brittany joined them and quickly attracted a boyfriend named Curtis Gurkin. They were soon all living under the same roof.

After Robyn landed a good job with a day surgery center and seemed happy about being in Grand Junction, she and I purchased a house with me being the loan guarantor and provider of a portion of the mortgage payment each month. I viewed the house as her permanent residence where she might live out her years. I saw my supplemental investment as an early transfer of inheritance. Eventually Chelsea's boyfriend, seventeen-year-old Jonathan Cheney, a distant relative of Wyoming's Dick Cheney, moved in too.

Before long, seventeen-year-old Brittany was pregnant. Following the conception, but before a child was born, I supportively conducted a private family wedding ceremony for Brittany and Curtis Gurkin on the front steps of Ponderosa at La Foret, the family's beloved UCC camp.

Aubreyanna Gurkin was born on April 9, 2003. A short time later the Gurkins moved from Grand Junction to Loveland, Colorado. They moved in with Brittany's father Keith and stepmother Sandi Gregg. Keith was an independent trucking contractor. He found Curtis a job with a Loveland asphalt paving company.

Robyn was our first born and what a blast! By the time she was three months old, we should have known what she would be like through all her years: Ingenious in developing ruses, creative in doing things differently than most people, very bright, and liking to live outside the lines, wanting to do things on her own schedule, a little uncertain when challenged with big choices, a sense of humor that doesn't quit, fascination with the big picture of human existence, finding it hard to stick with her decisions on courses of action, an incredible disregard for accumulating stuff, and a blatant disinterest in money and other gems of our culture, not afraid to live well beyond the conventional, and concerned about others in their times of need, but not sure how to help.

Stuart and Eve in Magnolia, TX

Stuart and Eve settled into their Magnolia home and the Lapp family was very busy, each with their own activities. Neele and Nellaine were working their way through public school, and in 2003, Neele had become a Freshman at Stephen F. Austin State University while Nellaine was finishing at Magnolia High School. Neele decided to leave Stephen F. Austin after three semesters and eventually graduated from Texas

State University in 2010 with a B.A. in Advertising and Marketing. After high school, Nellaine worked multiple jobs and started taking classes at Lone Star Community College in Houston.

Eve worked for several years as a staff member at Jewish Community North Temple. In 2008, she started a costume jewelry making business, called Kitchen Table Jewelry, with her sister.

Stuart ran his solo legal practice in The Woodlands. A major client was Petroleum Wholesale, Inc. ("PWI"), a fuel distributor and retailer located in The Woodlands that did business in several southwestern states.

In 2003, Stuart closed his practice and became General Counsel of PWI as an employee. He had been de facto General Counsel since 1999.

In addition to being involved in intricate banking negotiations and real estate development, Stuart's legal work at PWI included defending the company against numerous capricious claims by the Texas Attorney General that were driven primarily by Texas' political intrigue. After several years managing the scuffle with the Attorney General, Stuart led the company to a successful negotiated settlement. Stuart emerged as a very competent and thoughtful professional.

Eve grew up in a multigenerational Romanian Orthodox family in southeast Michigan, while Stuart had virtually no church involvement following his graduation from high school. But in 2003, they started attending St. Anthony the Great Antiochian Orthodox Christian Church. Stuart was Chrismated in the Orthodox Church in February of 2005. He became a congregational leader and served as President of Parish Council, chairing the effort to acquire a site and construct a new worship and educational edifice.

Stuart first saw daylight 17 months after Robyn was born. Compared to Robyn, he was a very easy-going kid. He usually went with the flow. He was uncomfortable with change. He was not a picky eater and liked almost everything. He loved playing squad-team football and became a good swimmer. Sleeping was as good as eating. He tended to stay within boundaries and expectations far more often than did Robyn.

Stuart was, and still is, very thoughtful; calm and considerate in all his relationships; uncannily insightful into the dynamics of the human behavior of others; and one of the most nonjudgmental people I know. In a way that did not happen in the relationship with my own father, Stuart and I have developed a very productive and fulfilling adult-to-adult relationship.

Karen and Joel - Authentic Mountain People

Joel and Karen were living in their remodeled home. They managed well as mountain people, cutting, and gathering firewood for their wood stove and fireplace. Jan and I lived next door, and I enjoyed stopping each Saturday morning to visit with them over coffee on my way to pick up the *Denver Post*. As neighbors through 2005, we socialized and helped one another with the chores of daily living.

Joel continued to work for the City of Arvada at West Woods Golf Course. Karen worked full time for Avaya, successor to Lucent Technologies, and managed the storage of used phone equipment as it was collected and repaired for future use. She often flew to regional warehouses to do inventories.

Through her own efforts, Karen became a capable, responsible adult who worked hard for the well-being of others. She brooks little nonsense for the irresponsibility of others. While she is more reserved than either Robyn or Stuart, she, too, is a very caring person. She is exceedingly conscientious, quiet, and self-contained, a "tough chick" and competent mountain woman.

Robb Contracts Prostate Cancer

In November 2003, when the Colorado Division of Motor Vehicles required me to get a physical for a Commercial Driver's License so I could drive a large school bus to get kids to La Foret, I was told I had Prostate Cancer. I found a Urologist who confirmed the diagnosis and who proceeded to remove a lobe of my prostate. He ordered two months of daily radiation treatments at a clinic 35 miles each way from our mountain home, then surgically implanted 96 radiation seed implants. These implants subsequently set off the airport body scanner alarm each time I flew somewhere. But the good news is that my PSA score became favorable, and I have had no further trouble.

We Make 50 Years

In the summer of 2005, when Jan and I each were 72, our "big deal" 50th anniversary party was the simple sharing of sheet cakes with all the delegates at a church lunch during the Rocky Mountain Conference Annual Meeting we were attending at First Congregational Church in Grand Junction. One of our clergy friends took a snapshot of us standing in the church hallway. It was more like a staged portrait of a happy couple, all smiles. It captured a truth about our lives together. We were each other's closest friends. We were each other's strongest supporters. We had walked with one another through all kinds of positives and negatives, both professional and familial. We loved each other more than ever.

In our 50 years together, we had transitioned from being our birth family's kids to being a family's matriarch and patriarch. We had moved from having no children to having a great granddaughter. And, despite the dramas, we loved them all.

In terms of our life work, each of us had made a positive difference in the larger human family. This was despite the emotional and societal price we had had to pay for doing what seemed right. Throughout the victories and heartbreaks, the Holy call to make life work for all kept us both alive and in love.

Sharing anniversary cake at the Grand Junction church, I whispered to Jan, "See! We were able to sneak up to 50 years of marriage after all!"

But the Holy had so much left for us to do that we did not have time for a big self-celebrating spread. We just hugged and kissed and got back to work.

Chapter 47

~~

NEVER A DULL MOMENT!

A YEAR BEFORE our 50th Anniversary, on a Saturday night in August 2004 when Aubrey was 1½, we got a phone call from Brittany. She was crying hysterically. Between sobs Brittany was able to make it clear that she and Curtis and Aubrey had been kicked out of Keith and Sandi's house and had no place to go. They were homeless.

I told Brittany that she and Curtis should get in the car and drive straight to our house and that we would sit down the next morning and figure out what to do.

When they finally arrived at our house with baby Aubrey, Brittany and Curtis were demoralized and dispirited.

Can Brittany and Curtis Make It Work?

The next morning, we sat our kitchen table in the mountains making plans for the next step. Taking a sheet of note pad paper and a ballpoint,

I said, "Let's start by making a list of what we know." I paused and then said, "First, the good stuff."

Brittany gradually said. "We are safe." "Curtis has a job." "We have enough money to buy groceries."

Then I said, "What are the bad things?" Painfully, the list came out. "We don't have a place to live." "Our things are at my dad's house." "We don't know what to do next."

That afternoon we went to Loveland and retrieved necessities from Keith's house. The Gurkins stayed with us for a week, and either Jan or I drove Curtis the forty miles to Loveland before daylight each day for his job with a paving company, then picked him up. On the next Sunday, we helped Brittany and Curtis select and rent an apartment in south Loveland. They managed relatively well there for over a year. Curtis worked in the warm months for the asphalt paving company, the job Keith had helped him get prior to the blowup. During the winter, Curtis collected unemployment.

Jan and I often went to Loveland after the Gurkins had moved into their apartment.

One day, while I was driving Curtis on an errand, he appeared slightly agitated and confessed, "Papa, I did something the other day that I shouldn't have. I was driving with Aubrey and stopped at a video game store in Fort Collins. Since she was asleep, I left her in the locked car. When I came back, it was dark, and she was screaming. She had thrown up. I don't know why."

"How long were you gone?"

"Oh, not that long. Maybe a couple of hours."

"What did you do next?"

"I tried to clean her up and then took her home. But she would not stop screaming! I don't know…" I later realized that this had something to do with Aubrey's intense fear of being alone in the dark. But it was worse than that. She had felt totally abandoned.

After Curtis and I returned to the apartment, Jan and I headed for home. As soon as we were in the car, Jan said, "You won't believe what Brittany told me while you were gone." I asked, "Did it have something to do with Aubrey being locked in their car at a video game place in Fort Collins?"

Brittany and Curtis apparently trusted us enough to share this horrifying story. The question was, what was the Holy calling us to do about it? While we hoped Brittany and Curtis would grow into mature young parents, we were very concerned about Aubrey's safety.

"I Want Out!"

One day during that summer, Jan and I went to Loveland so that Jan could take Brittany to the local hospital for an afternoon outpatient procedure. I stayed with Aubrey and took her to a park area in the complex where we frequently played. When it was time to go back to the apartment, Aubrey cried and held back. She kept trying to hide and to go into other apartments.

When we finally got back into their apartment, Aubrey crawled on to my lap, stopped crying, and let me hold her close. Words failed her, but it was clear she was very afraid. to be in that apartment. She got off my lap and went to the entrance door of the apartment, pointing her little hand out into the hallway, her forefinger saying, "I want out!"

Just then, Jan and Brittany returned from the doctor visit. With Curtis still at work, we left Aubrey with Brittany and departed.

On our way home we talked about how we might go about helping Brittany and Curtis seek personal and marriage counseling.

However, before long, things further unraveled. Curtis lost his job. The Gurkins were evicted from their apartment. They once again moved in with Keith and Sandi, but that relationship quickly deteriorated a second time.

Just a few weeks later, to get away from Keith, Brittany and Curtis retreated with Aubrey to Grand Junction and moved in with Robyn.

It soon appeared the marriage between Brittany and Curtis was collapsing. They separated. Curtis moved in with his mother who also lived in Grand Junction, and left Brittany and Aubrey to live with Robyn, Chelsea, and Chelsea's boyfriend. But one night there was a physical fight between Brittany and Curtis at Robyn's house. Both police and child protective services were called. Curtis split. Robyn apparently convinced these officials that Aubrey was safe with her, so they left without Aubrey.

Chapter 48

∾

AUBREY HAD NO PLACE TO GO

Aubrey visits in Loveland for Christmas

NOT LONG AFTER, three days before Christmas 2005, Keith and Sandi made a round trip to Grand Junction to pick up Aubrey for a holiday visit in Loveland. The day before Christmas, Chelsea and Robyn came to Denver to see their family and to retrieve Aubrey. Brittany had stayed in Grand Junction.

On Christmas morning, Robyn called me from Keith's and asked hesitatingly, "Things are so screwed up between Curtis and Brittany, I don't want to take Aubrey back to Grand Junction. Could Aubrey come down from Loveland and stay with you guys for a few days?"

We agreed that Chelsea would bring Aubrey, and that they would join us for Christmas dinner at the Ronzheimer's house.

When they arrived, a 2 ¾ year old girl, slight for her age, with a big smile of recognition lighting her face, stood at Joel and Karen's door. Aubrey stepped in. After the holiday meal, Chelsea left without Aubrey. We did not yet know it, but a major die had been cast that Christmas afternoon.

After Robyn and Chelsea returned to Grand Junction, Robyn called to say she and Brittany wondered whether we could keep Aubrey for an indefinite period. Jan and I said, "We think we could handle that." While Aubrey was staying with us, Brittany, and Curtis each filed separately for divorce. In early January, I asked Robyn to get notarized statements from Curtis and Brittany showing that Jan and I had permission to have Aubrey, authorizing us to make medical decisions for her. No one thought at the time that she would be with us for more than a few weeks.

Move Down to Arvada Tomorrow

After we had put Aubrey to bed that Christmas night, Jan whispered, "Robb, do you suppose we should rethink the timing of our move down the mountain to Arvada?"

In anticipation of having to move to an elevation more hospitable for my emerging heart issues, we had listed our cherished mountain house for sale. It had not yet sold, but weeks earlier we had closed on the purchase of a patio home in western Arvada, 15 miles closer to the city, and nearly 3,000 feet closer to sea level. We had planned to move there sometime in the spring of 2006 once our mountain home had sold.

I whispered back, "Well, I suppose, with all our open balconies and multiple stairways here, it might be safer for Aubrey if we did. And we have coyotes and mountain lions here. How soon do you think we should we move?"

Jan playfully asked, "Don't you think we can wait until morning?" Thus, the decision to move immediately was settled as simply and quickly as our agreeing to take Aubrey for safekeeping had been earlier in the day.

The next day was filled with several trips to Arvada with carloads of clothing, dishes, bedding, and food. On one of my trips, I stopped to recruit a young couple who lived just up our mountain road. I told them, "Yesterday, we took on the responsibility of caring temporarily for our great granddaughter. We think we need to move down to Arvada right away. If I can borrow a van truck tomorrow, do you think you could help?"

"Sure," they graciously said.

On my next run to Arvada, I had a similar affirmative exchange with another neighbor, a British native who lived further up our road, whose 2¾ year old daughter I had baptized on their deck two years earlier. (One can see that the world, not a local church, is my parish.) When I got to Arvada with my next load, I called David Nestor, my long time UCC compatriot. "David," I said, "you're not going to believe this, but I'd like to borrow one of your delivery vans tomorrow. Aubrey has come to live with us temporarily and we are going to accelerate our move into the Arvada house. I'm at the new house now, unloading kitchen stuff and bedding." David said in his typically understated way, "Oh my, Robb, has it come to this?"

By the end of the second day after Christmas, the recruited team and I had moved enough stuff into the new house that we could begin staying there.

Little could anyone imagine what lay ahead!

Two days after Aubrey came for a short stay, we were living in our new house in Arvada. Aubrey liked her bedroom, although we discovered immediately that she was desperately frightened by being alone in a room that was even remotely dark. Also, we discovered that we could not put her in the back seat of our car and close the door without her trembling in fear. Nor could we leave her alone in her bedroom.

We moved a second bed into Aubrey's room so Jan could sleep with her at night. The tub in the adjacent bathroom became Aubrey's favorite after-dinner place to relax and play in the water before bedtime stories. And the toilet became a place for her to dangle her feet in the water while she sat on the back of the seat. We had to deal with traumatic experiences from early in her life.

But it must have been working, as Aubrey danced around happily many times a day.

Better Find a Lawyer

On the Wednesday after New Year's Day, I received a call from Brittany who was still living with Robyn while separated from Curtis. She said, "Curtis is trying to take Aubrey away from me. He and his mother are on their way to Arvada to kidnap Aubrey."

"When did they leave Grand Junction?" I asked. "About three hours ago," she said. Trying to ease Brittany's fears, I responded as calmly as I could, "Okay. Don't worry. We'll handle it."

With the domestic discord in Grand Junction, I thought we needed some form of authority for having Aubrey living with us. I searched for a domestic and family law attorney and found one in Golden who listened to my dilemma and said, "I think I can help you. Can you be here at 10:30 in the morning?"

The domestic relations attorney recommended that we seek temporary custody of Aubrey. A preliminary issue-defining hearing was held in the Jefferson County Court in February. Curtis appeared at this hearing without an attorney, saying that as her father, Aubrey should live with him.

Keith and Sandi also were present. It was apparent that they agreed with the notion that Aubrey should not be living with either parent. But it was quickly obvious that they disagreed with Robyn's and Brittany's request that Jan and I be the ones to care for Aubrey temporarily.

Though he had not planned to do so, our lawyer, seeing the perplexed look on the Magistrate's face, approached the bench and asked that we be granted immediate temporary custody for a period lasting until a formal temporary custody hearing was held. "Granted," responded the Magistrate. Trying to be accommodating, we offered to voluntarily give Keith and Sandi weekend visitation every other week. The Magistrate included this agreement in his temporary order. The formal hearing for Temporary Custody was set for April.

It was not Jan's and my intent to take Aubrey away from her parents. We simply thought we would be caring for her during an interim in which her parents would be getting their lives together.

An Uncomfortable Drama

After considering testimony and evidence at the April 2006 hearing, the Magistrate's Order stated that we would have temporary custody of Aubrey, that Curtis would have the right to visit Aubrey in our home, that Brittany would need to comply with certain Court imposed conditions before she was allowed visitation, and that Keith and Sandi would have Aubrey for various weekend overnights in Loveland.

Neither we nor the court had any long-range plan. We were an interim safe haven for Aubrey. During Easter weekend, Curtis and Brittany, by then back together, came to Arvada to visit with Aubrey. On Easter Sunday morning, we all went to our church. Jan, Curtis, and Aubrey went into the service. Brittany held back. I thought she might want to discuss what she and Curtis were doing to prepare for Aubrey's return. No such luck. Though she and her mother had requested that we care for Aubrey for some kind of interim, for the next hour Brittany told me how awful I was for taking Aubrey from her. Immediately after the service, she and Curtis went back to Grand Junction.

That summer, on one of our several trips to pick up Aubrey after a short visit with her parents in Grand Junction, we met them at a Burger King in a town east of Grand Junction. When we arrived, Aubrey ran expectantly over to our car and it was obvious she wanted to get right in. Aubrey's anxious exit from a weekend visit with her parents clearly upset Brittany but we left without incident.

Jan and I were still hoping for the best for Brittany and Curtis. We loved them and had no desire to have long term responsibility for Aubrey.

Chapter 49

~

TO MONTESSORI AT AGE THREE

AFTER AUBREY HAD been with us for a couple of months, Jan and I decided it would be very important for her to be enrolled in a teaching preschool so she could begin socializing with other kids. We learned she would not be accepted in a nearby Montessori school until June, so we found a daycare facility with a reputation for encouraging social development.

In June, she started at Cornerstone Montessori. For a long while her teachers and we struggled with her biting and hitting in moments of extreme provocation, but Aubrey learned to negotiate differences with classmates.

An extremely important life lesson that Aubrey learned early on, both at home and at school, is the distinction between being a bad person and being a person who makes bad decisions. So often a child is told, "You are a bad girl," or "You're so stupid!" Aubrey's teachers and we were able to embrace her following a negative incident, and say, "I love you, but don't you think you just made a bad choice?"

AUBREYANNA – Age 4

Aubrey learned so much! There were lessons on life in other cultures, on great musicians and artists, and on contemporary singing. Shortly after Aubrey turned four, Jan took her to a dentist. As she sat in the chair, she looked at a large-framed print on the opposite wall. Out of the blue she said, "Oh, that is Starry Night, by Vincent Van Gogh." The dentist could not believe what he had just heard!

In the car one day when I had the radio on, Aubrey correctly announced, "Papa, that music was written by Dvorak."

Seeing the passing world through a young child's eyes was refreshing. One morning I started to get Aubrey into the car to go to Cornerstone Montessori. She ran down the drive, stopped, took a deep, sniffing breath, and said with a big grin, "Papa, just smell the day! Isn't it wonderful!" On the way to school, upon seeing a frowning man at a nearby construction site, she asked, "Papa, why is that man sad? Maybe he's angry." I had seen him but wondered only why he was carrying a sledgehammer. Once, during a storm, "Papa, I love it when it rains. Isn't it beautiful?"

More Legal Challenges

The Court's April assignment of temporary parental custodial responsibility might have settled things for a continuing interim had the next set of legal maneuverings not taken place. After Aubrey had been with us a year and a half our lawyer called. "You're not going to believe this," he sighed. "The Greggs have hired an attorney and have filed a petition with the Court, seeking custody of Aubrey. On top of that Brittany and Curtis have filed a petition for reinstatement of their parental rights and recovery of Aubrey." Suddenly, the issue of permanent custody was on the table.

I asked our attorney how we should handle this. Since the Magistrate would need expert advice from an objective perspective, he suggested we request a Court appointment of a Child and Family Investigator ("CFI") to evaluate the fitness of all three homes for future care of Aubrey. "The parties would have to pay equally," he said. This seemed like a good way to resolve the question of long-term custody. The Magistrate appointed a reputable Clinical Psychologist he often used to serve as the Court's Child and Family Investigator.

In her thick formal written report, the Investigator recommended that Jan and I assume parenting responsibility on a permanent basis. Despite the fact that such parenting was a heavy responsibility for a couple in their seventies, we agreed to be available.

Following submission of this CFI report, at a hearing in October 2007, the Court assigned Aubrey to our care on a permanent basis.

After Aubrey completed two years in the Cornerstone Montessori, in 2008 we had to decide whether she would stay at Cornerstone for Kindergarten or go to West Woods Elementary. We chose Cornerstone which worked well. In the summers of her three years at Cornerstone we enrolled her for recreational activities at the Arvada YMCA.

One of the really important things Jan and I did with Aubrey was to take her to La Foret for a Grandparents and Me summer camp three successive years. We all loved it.

Jan and I comforted ourselves with the thought that the Holy's desire for a safe and just life for all humans often requires sacrificial giving.

Nine months after we were assigned permanent custody of Aubrey, she became a big sister. Trinity Gurkin was born in Grand Junction on June 9, 2008. While Trinity was still an infant, Jan, Aubrey, and I drove to Grand Junction several times to visit. I still thought there was a chance that the Gurkin family could reunite and become functional. The visits were at least borderline pleasant.

Chapter 50

∼∼∼

THE HOLY SAYS, "ADOPT AUBREY"

BEFORE AUBREY'S KINDERGARTEN year started in 2008, Jan and I decided enough was enough. It had been two and a half years since we had become Aubrey's custodial caregivers. She was thriving so we seemed to be doing the right things.

In spite of their having Aubrey for many visitation weekends, continuing friction with Keith and Sandi was wearing us down.

It was increasingly clear that Aubrey would not be returning to live with either of her parents, as we all had hoped. I called our attorney and asked, "Why don't we just adopt Aubrey?"

Our lawyer said, "Such adoptions go much more smoothly with a Voluntary Termination of Parental Rights. In Colorado, if parents have failed to pay ordered child support and have failed over an extended period to call or visit their child, they can involuntarily lose their parental rights through an assumed abandonment. Brittany and Curtis have failed on both counts. If you explained this to them, do you suppose they would agree to a Voluntary Termination of Parental Rights?"

I then drove to Grand Junction and told Brittany and Curtis that we felt we should end the family wrangling by adopting their daughter. They were not enthusiastic, but they agreed to a Voluntary Termination of Parental Rights.

The adoption hearing was on Monday, December 8, 2008. Aubrey went with us to court. To our attorney's surprise, the only substantive question the judge asked was why we did not petition for a surname change for Aubrey. I said, "I think it's very important for Aubrey to retain that part of her identity." After the adoption was approved, the judge invited Aubrey up to the bench. Aubrey chatted with the judge, who, it turned out, had had two of her own children in the same Montessori preschool Aubrey was then attending.

Immediately after the adoption, we arranged for our daughter Karen and her husband Joel to become her guardians, should we become unable to fulfill the responsibilities of parenting.

Our having become Aubrey's adoptive parents drove a permanent wedge between us and Brittany, a very painful experience as we loved her in spite of everything, and still wish a productive adulthood for her.

Following the adoption, life continued its positive trajectory for Aubrey.

Chapter 51

<a style="text-align:center">≈≈≈</a>

FAMILY LIFE GOES ON

Robyn Marries and Moves to Kapaa

HAVING FOUND A job at St. Mary's Hospital, Robyn continued to work in Grand Junction, but her home life was a mess. Not wanting to handle the stress of having her two daughters and their guys under her roof, she moved out of her own house right after Jan and I were first assigned temporary custody of Aubrey. She was "watching a friend's house and his dog."

Following a couple of competing courtships, on 06/06/06, selected for its repetitive numerical sequence, Robyn married Eric Witt, the guy whose house and dog she had been "watching." Eric was her fourth husband. She did not tell us about this wedding until later in the summer.

At the same time, Robyn was laid off from her hospital job. On the internet, she found a job at the Kapaa city hospital on the island of

Kauai, Hawaii, far away from the demonic family dynamics of life in Grand Junction. On 7/02/06 she flew to Kapaa. Eric followed.

Meanwhile, Curtis and Brittany had moved from Robyn's house to a nearby apartment, leaving Chelsea in charge of the house of which I had become the default owner. Chelsea, along with Jon Cheney and several additional friends, became responsible for renting the house from me. Before long, rental payments stopped. When I went to Grand Junction to assess the problem, I found an incredible mess. Just for openers, there was a stack of at least fifty empty pizza boxes next to the fridge in the kitchen. I evicted everybody, made repairs, and sold the house.

It had taken me twenty-five years of rescuing Robyn to learn that I was not really helping her by continually pouring in support funds. Even though I had learned I could not control the decisions of adult children, it took me longer to realize that continually subsidizing their daily living was very debilitating in their moving toward being in charge of their own lives.

Now in Kapaa, Robyn's relationship with Eric quickly disintegrated and she separated from him. But he did not move out until she paid for a one-way ticket for Eric to fly to Anchorage. He ended up on Alaska's north slope where he became a cook for roughnecks in the oil fields.

Brittany and Curtis were still living in Grand Junction and appeared to be managing with Trinity, although they were in the process of dissolving their marriage by divorce. When Trinity was two, Brittany took Trinity to Kauai to stay at least temporarily with Robyn.

While Brittany was in Kauai, a Grand Junction District Court granted Curtis a divorce from Brittany. Then, in a custody battle following their divorce, Trinity was placed with Curtis who took her from Kauai back to Grand Junction where they both lived with Curtis' mother, Granny

Annie Gurkin. Jan and I drove Aubrey to Grand Junction several times to visit Grannie Annie, Curtis, and Trinity. Brittany continued living with Robyn in Kauai.

Robyn lived in Kauai for seven years, where she grew to love the local culture and lifestyle. Over time, ex-husband William Gorman, Brittany, Chelsea, and Chelsea's next boyfriend, all went to Hawaii and lived in a series of abodes with Robyn.

After seven years in Hawaii, Robyn decided that she should leave Kauai and at least temporarily move to Arvada. Her thought was that it was time for her to be nearby us in Arvada to "help with the raising of Aubrey." Besides, she felt that she had been in Kauai long enough. Five days after arriving in Arvada she landed a job as scheduler in a pain clinic near St. Anthony Hospital, which had just relocated from Denver to Lakewood. For a brief interlude, it felt good to have Robyn openly sharing her life with us for the first time since she went off to college.

But, in addition to her not liking her job in the Lakewood pain clinic, wanderlust caught up with her again. After nine months, she moved to Anchorage, Alaska, not to be near Eric, but because that is where, through the wondrous recruitment utility of the internet, she landed another job, this one as a surgery scheduler for an orthopedic clinic.

Her odyssey continued.

And, in Texas

Before Stuart had met Eve, her girls had a neighbor friend named Ruth Mulkey whose family was dysfunctional. Gradually, since the three girls were teenage friends, Ruth grew close to Eve. Eventually, in 2006,

Ruth married a fellow named Aaron Stedman. Their daughter Erin was born in 2007, at which time Ruth and Aaron separated. At that point Ruth and Erin became Eve and Stuart's informal foster daughter and granddaughter and lived in their Magnolia home until Erin was 7 years old. Then Ruth and Erin moved to a rental closer to Ruth's place of employment. Eve and Stuart still love being called "Papa" and "Omma."

Neele stopped her studies at Stephen F. Austin State University after a year and a half, worked a variety of jobs, and then graduated with a B.A. in Marketing and Advertising in 2010. She lived at home while working early jobs in her chosen field. Nellaine graduated from High School in 2004, then worked several retail jobs and in a real estate broker's office while attending Lone Star College. Nellaine also continued to live at home.

In July 2007, Stuart was working as General Counsel for Petroleum Wholesale Inc. in an office in The Woodlands very near the hospital that was built there because of my community development work over thirty years earlier. One fine summer morning, Stuart realized he was having a heart attack. He got himself to the hospital, where a cardiac surgeon who was a member of Stuart's Orthodox Antiochan Christian Church happened to be in the emergency room. Stuart was quickly triaged and admitted. Jan and I alternated traveling to Houston to support Stuart and Eve during his hospitalization. Stuart survived the heart attack without complications.

The Coal Creek Ronzheimers

Karen and Joel enjoyed living in their mountain house on Tunnel 19 Road. Jan and I were right next door until we moved with Aubrey down the mountain to Arvada in late 2005. Joel continued working for the City of Arvada at the West Woods Golf Course. Karen drove each day all the way to the Avaya office in Northglenn, a suburb north of Denver. Jan and I often met Karen for lunch near her Avaya office in the city. We enjoyed many visits and holiday meals in the mountains. The Ronzheimer home became the Colorado "family headquarters" after we moved to town.

As Jan and I worked our way through our 70s and our parenting of Aubrey, Joel and Karen were the descendants most involved in supporting our pilgrimage. Being nearby, they could help with both our decision-making and our errands. Their home became Aubrey's favorite overnight retreat spot.

Three very different Lapp kids, each one seeking to be decent, loving human beings in ways that felt right to them.

Chapter 52

~~~

MINISTRY INSIDE THE CHURCH'S DOORS

Chairing the New La Foret Conference Center Board

IN SPITE OF everything I was doing to create affordable housing for low-income folks and the huge challenges of caring for our great-granddaughter life, I continued to serve as Board Chair of La Foret Conference and Retreat Center, Inc. through 2007.

After completing the construction of Inglis Hall, the La Foret Board applied for and received a State Historical Society grant early in 2003 for the restoration of Taylor Chapel, the classic Southwest adobe church and courtyard that had been built by Mrs. Taylor as a tribute to her late husband. A massive effort was required to repair all the inside and outside stucco walls and the large front courtyard stucco enclosure. I hired the contractor who had built Inglis Hall do the work. One of the board members and I rented a ditch-witch and laid electric cables from the center of the campus to the Chapel to provide adequate interior and exterior lighting. The Chapel's leaking roof was repaired, and all the stucco was repainted. We held an opening dedication ceremony with Alice Taylor's daughter Doree as an honored guest.

Susan Lander had begun her work as Executive Director in January of 2003. She managed the staff and service operations very well. She also worked well with board members. Susan did a great job pulling together the multiple use of our facilities by the growing number of disparate groups who were renting La Foret.

We had a board member who was an advocate of the Carver Model of Board Governance. In substance, what this meant was that the Board would set limitations on what the Executive Director would be authorized to do. Instead of making lists of what an ED <u>should</u> do, a Board creates a list of things an Executive Director could <u>not</u> do without getting expressed board approval.

The board adopted use of the Carver Model, then spent two years creating the boundaries for an Executive Directors work. This intensive effort led to adoption of amended corporate By-Laws in 2006. Susan Lander was very helpful in supporting this whole culture shift.

Way too soon, Susan left us to open an art studio in western Colorado, having decided personnel management was not her bag. Another Director search led to the hiring of Ralph Townsend who had had extensive conference center management experience in eastern Pennsylvania. His references were good. We hired him and even upgraded the Gate House to accommodate his family.

The Townsend's arrived and Ralph started work early in November 2005. Susan had worked remotely beginning in September, so I had plenty to do on-site to keep operations moving until Ralph got there.

He inventively hired a national trucking firm which parked a trailer in front of his house in Pennsylvania for him to load, then hauled the trailer to La Foret's Gate House where his family was to live. Upon its arrival, Ralph unloaded it, saving La Foret a good deal in moving expenses. We thought he would be great. He got off to a good start, revamping the camp staff and forming good relationships with the guests.

In Susan's window, the board member with whom I had done the electrical service update for the Chapel and I did two other infrastructure projects. First, we hired contractors to drill a new well and rebuild the water tower. Then we ran new and fresh-water pipes throughout the camp and repaired all the sewer lines leading to a large wastewater recycling lagoon. This brought the Center into the Twenty First Century.

Then, with the onset of internet usage, and the need for an automated fire alarm system for Inglis Hall, we found an old trenching machine and installed underground phone cables throughout the camp. Using the worn-out machine whose control levers were insensitive, while standing next to it, I could not stop it as it ran over my foot breaking several bones. Oh well!

I continued to direct the work of the Board until my second five-year term expired in December 2007.

A New Conference Office

Somehow, I seemed to be the person in the UCC Rocky Mountain Conference who was the office space guy. Having found five previous office locations, I worked a deal with David Nestor in which we moved the Conference office again. This time was into a large warehouse David owned just south of downtown Denver. He agreed to rent an office space for which we had to create a city-required second exit in case of fire.

This office had a large meeting room in which many Conference Boards and Committees conveniently held their work sessions. The space also worked very efficiently for staff members.

Creating the Rocky Mountain Conference Endowment Fund

A third Conference non-profit affiliate began when the Conference Minister asked me to be part of a small group that was to explore formation of a conference endowment fund. In 2007 and 2008 the team formed The Endowment Fund of the Rocky Mountain Conference of the UCC, Inc. as a separate 501(c)(3). I agreed to serve as president after its incorporation. It soon had over $2,500,000 in managed endowment funds. The Beneficiaries included Conference Operations, Children & Youth Ministries, New Church Starts and Renewals, La Foret, Iliff School of Theology, Chicago Theological Seminary, RMHDC, the Laramie (WY) community mission, and the Gunnison (CO) UCC church.

Chicago Theological Seminary

President Dr. Susan Thistlethwaite's and my remodeling of dorms into office space that was eagerly leased by the University of Chicago eventually led to a huge change in CTS's future!

When I retired as an active CTS Trustee, I was celebrated with a plaque that featured a bronzed hammer, and was inscribed, "Robb, You Always Hit the Nail on the Head!" It was Susan Thistlethwaite's salutation. I served as an active member of the Board until May 5, 2006 at which time I was honored with being named a Life Trustee.

After my regular Board participation ended, Dr. Thistlethwaite led an effort that resulted in the sale of the seminary's academic and residential buildings, except for the President's House, to the University of Chicago. A very efficient single building housing educational, administrative, worship and assembly facilities was built at 60th and Dorchester on the south edge of Hyde Park, just south of the Midway. None of this would have happened without Susan's vision and practical hard work, and the support of a particularly pragmatic Board.

In its new location, and with new financial stability, CTS was on the forefront of equipping students for leadership in many Twenty First Century social, theological, and future-of-the-church issues. This included the sincere recognition of LGBTQ folk both in ministry and in Christian communities. The seminary also is on the forefront of training people of faith to how to confront white privilege, systemic racism, and economic injustices in many cultures and societies.

An evidence of the authentic character of its progressive stance, in 2009, CTS became the first free-standing Protestant seminary to endow a chair in Jewish Studies, this one named after *Rabbi Herman E. Schaalman.* A Jewish Rabbi, Dr. Rachel Mikva, became *Associate Professor of Jewish Studies,* advancing interfaith engagement and multi-faith education. I was able to contribute to this endowment. The next year, CTS founded the Center for Jewish, Christian, and Islamic Studies (JCIS), the first American program of its kind in a Christian theological seminary. This Center offers resources to students who concentrate in theology, ethics, and human sciences that enable scholars to experientially and theoretically integrate Jewish, Christian, and Muslim theology with these topics.

Following an endowment gift Jan and I gave CTS for its new building we were honored with the naming of the seminary library as the LAPP LEARNING COMMONS.

As I reflect on my life and style, my work as a CTS Trustee is a microcosm of the person I have continued to become. I am acutely aware of the God who infuses all of life with a spirit of hope and expectation. Brokenness, incompleteness, tragedy, and death are inherent in the fabric of both individual and communal life. But so are beauty, love, wholeness, and hope. God does not promise escape from moments or even eternities of pain and injustice. In the evolution of continuing creation there is glorious possibility. And, when one contributes a whit or a ton to making another's life more whole and just, it helps fulfil the Holy's vision. My soul is refreshed by that energy.

Chapter 53

⌢⌢⌢

No Day Is Simple –
Even for Seniors

What's This With Jan?

JAN WAS VERY sweet with Aubrey, particularly at bedtime. Jan handled the nightly bath, then read story after story to Aubrey, while embracing her on their treasured rocker. Aubrey was in great need for a caring touch and 100% attention from someone who loved her unequivocally.

As we had gone through three years of Montessori, Jan had done a very credible job as a loving Great-Grandmother and a boundary-setting Mother. But Jan was losing track of details. I had to make most family decisions and handle communications with the school. I also had to manage Aubrey's medical care and do most of the evening meal preparation. Jan started walking impatiently around the house looking for things …her watch…a recipe…an earring…a grocery list…her car keys…

It soon made sense to move Jan's bed out of Aubrey's room, as there was increasing confusion with both Jan and Aubrey in the same room. But Jan continued to very lovingly rock and read to Aubrey at bedtime.

Though our adult kids and I knew Jan's functionality was deteriorating, we did not know what was causing it. At first, we simply attributed these time-consuming moments to attributes of her accumulating birthdays. Though she was becoming increasingly compulsive in the managing of her daily round, I tried to be patient and uncritical.

Karen often stopped by, both to see how we were doing and to help with errands. She also helped me cope with Jan in her mental decline. She and Joel were the "nearby kids", so they helped in many ways, including bolstering our morale.

Aubrey Confronted By a Chronic Emotional Challenge

Shortly after Aubrey began First Grade at West Woods, the Principal called and asked me to come to the office. When I arrived, the School Counselor joined us. They told me Aubrey was having significant difficulty focusing and that she was hyperactive. They recommended that we take Aubrey to her Pediatrician for an evaluation. Aubrey was quickly diagnosed as having Attention Deficit/Hyperactivity Disorder (ADHD). ADHD can contribute to low self-esteem, troubled relationships, and difficulty at school or work. Symptoms include limited attention and hyperactivity.

Various meds were prescribed. They seemed to help. During the next five years I was a constant visitor at the school, dropping off the meds with the Counselor. Jan and I often met with Aubrey's teachers through these years to hear of their concerns and suggestions. Aubrey was able to do quite well as a student and liked going to school.

In her grade school years, we enrolled Aubrey in the summer School Age Enrichment ("SAE") program at a Jeffco grade school.

Aubrey was very analytical. She could figure out how various devices worked and how things were put together. One day we bought a computer table for her room. As we took items out of the box, she looked at each piece and then showed me how they all fit together.

She also was quite good at analyzing what made other kids and adults tick.

When the weather allowed, we would walk about a half mile from the house to a city playground. She loved both the walk and playing on the equipment.

While Aubrey was still in grade school, she made a beautiful Father's Day card for me. On the front she drew colorful feathers with the gold-decorated word, "Papa." Inside she had carefully inscribed: "Dear Papa. Thank you for being the fighter that I can look up to and love. I love you. Happy Fathers' Day! Love. Aubrey."

This card still sits in a prominent place on my desk. To me, it symbolizes Aubrey's emerging self-awareness and affirms her sense of being in a holy relationship.

Jan and I gained a new insight about child development and parenting, a vision we did not see clearly when we had had our three kids fifty some years earlier. We then, as most parents do, thought of our children as blank tablets upon which almost any characteristic could be written. Parents create boundaries and expectations. They decide what experiences, like music, sports and extracurricular activities, kids should have. They even try to guide career choices, as had my father. They have visions of what their kids will do and be like when they are grown.

But Aubrey taught us that the process of moving through the pre-teen years was one of self-discovery. As she gradually emerged, as a butterfly does from a cocoon, Jan and I enjoyed and affirmed the person who was being discovered. It was as much a surprise for Aubrey as it was for us.

Life at its most authentic draws one into sacrificial depths. Taking responsibility for Aubrey was another of the Holy moments I have experienced through time. I was now confronted with conflicting challenges. One was the opportunity to commit to a long-term run with Aubrey and, alternatively, the other was to manage the stuff that comes with the closing years of a lifetime. Once again, the ageless call inherent in the human experience cried out: "Choose life, not death." The heavens opened and embraced our decision. Old age anxiety fell into perspective. This translated into giving Aubrey a continuing chance. We knew we were doing the right thing, regardless of the emotional stress. The Holy had come near.

Just What I Needed!

On a Friday afternoon in the summer of 2011 Aubrey and I went bike riding. On a paved path about a mile from home, we stopped at Ralston Creek so she could watch bugs in an irrigation canal that passed under the creek through a large concrete box culvert. I sat on my bike to get some shade from an overhead Cottonwood. But I was too close to the creek bank, and went backward down an embankment, landing head-first on the concrete culvert. My helmet undoubtedly saved my life, but I broke my pelvis and tore muscles in my left leg and arm. Eight-year-old Aubrey kept her cool. She was able to catch the attention of a passing runner who turned out to be a recently retired Kaiser physician. He helped me out of the creek bed, and because I could move, said he did not think I had broken anything. I was able to get back on my bike and pedal home with one foot, the other leg just hanging. Aubrey was very concerned as she pedaled along home with me. She ran into the house shouting, "Nana, Nana, Papa is hurt!"

I needed to go to the hospital. Jan called a neighbor who took me to Presbyterian/St. Luke's. I had broken my pelvic bone in the left hip socket. Aubrey was very solicitous that night, and again on both Saturday and Sunday, when she came with Jan to visit me.

While I was lying there in bed, the Orthopedic Surgeon told me that people my age (I was 78) with my kind of pelvic injury are often dead within six months, mostly because of lung failure or dysfunction of internal organs resulting from inactivity. Sure enough, shortly thereafter, a friend and two long-term acquaintances broke their pelvises and subsequently expired.

Because nurses were having to help me do almost everything, on Sunday the Hospitalist physician insisted that I go to a rehab center for "a couple of weeks" to get special care and to begin physical therapy. Having had an unhappy experience in that rehab center after my heart surgery, I strongly resisted that suggestion, apparently frustrating the Hospitalist. He discharged me on the spot, even after having earlier said I should remain in his care for a couple more days.

The Holy call would not let me give up. So, equipped with a walker and best wishes, I left Presbyterian/St. Luke's and went home. With fantastic hands and great skill, a Physical Therapist worked with me for seven months while I returned to walking normally, able to get in my daily two-mile exercises.

Alzheimer's

Finally, one day in 2012 I became fully aware that something truly serious was wrong with Jan when she reported that she had gotten lost while driving home. That was the last time she drove her car. In keeping with her style, she did not complain.

When I shared this moment with our kids, they urged me to take Jan to our Primary Care Physician who started a series of tests that led to a diagnosis of Alzheimer's or similar dementia. This led to many life-changing steps for all of us.

We took deep breaths as we became familiar with Alzheimer's and learned that it is a very cruel disease, with no apparent successful medicating.

Shortly after receiving the formal diagnosis, I enrolled Jan in a national Alzheimer's clinical drug trial which involved the taking of an experimental drug and frequent visits to a Denver physician's office. After well more than a year, during which I watched Jan's ability to focus and follow sequences continually decline, the drug being tested was found to be ineffective. We interviewed for another clinical study, but Jan was unable to participate because of possible damage to some of her vital internal organs that might be caused by the next trial drug.

Dr. Bill Leaves Us

In October 2012, Jan joined me in being the last family survivor among ancestors and siblings, when her brother Dr. Bill came to his end after eleven years in the Concord nursing home with Parkinson's. His memorial service in the Contoocook United Methodist Church was an unforgettable reunion for all the Wallaces and most of the Lapps including Aubrey. There was a palpable sense of relief that Bill had finally been relieved of the cruel disease he had bravely endured for so long. We all celebrated a very well-lived life. Jan was now the only Wallace family survivor of her generation. I knew how she felt.

Reflection

Just because I was nearing eighty, I could not stand back from humanity's complex challenges. From family issues to church and community needs, all the way down to a body that sometimes wanted to fall apart, the Holy gave me courage to persevere. I was quite aware that I was still alive and still able to do things for the good of the human order. I was amazed, as I had earlier imagined that I would not live past 65. As I turned 80, I could hear the Holy saying, "Stay the course. I need you." It gave meaning to my life, and a reason to keep fighting the good fight. Such a blessing!

SECTION IX

2013 – 2021

DON'T EVER QUIT!

Chapter 54

~~

Choosing Life Over Death

The Holy's Call is to Persevere, not Give Up.

I APPEAR TO have found a productive way to keep going. When, as an older person, you are continuing to care for your neighbor, you are also saving your own life. Just because you are beyond your prime, the Holy has not stopped calling. Continuing to make life work for others is a force that keeps one's soul and body functional. Life is a gift. It is given as an opportunity and an energy to make the world a better place. One is free to choose. But when you quit the struggle for good, your soul dies before your body does.

This truth manifested itself again in 2013, when I had pneumonia and a sinus infection that would not quit. In early February, a physician at a drive-up ER facility prescribed a heavy Sulfa sequence. Less than a week later, after going to bed, I awoke hardly able to breathe. My chest hurt. Jan called 911. Nine firefighters/paramedics came bursting into the house, five crowding by my bedside. My pulse was more than 250 bpm. Pausing not at all, they rushed me, siren blazing, to Lutheran Hospital in Wheat Ridge. A doctor told me they would anesthetize me, stop my heart, and restart it. Then I lost consciousness. About six hours later I regained consciousness with a defibrillator and pacemaker implanted over my upper left rib cage. I was moved to an ICU where I stayed for five days, enduring a variety of heart tests. A cardiac team concluded I probably had suffered a major allergic reaction to the Sulfa which had caused my heart to race.

Two weeks later I wrote a poem about invisible hands that had kept me going. Jan, Aubrey, and I took it to the Fire Department and were met by a Paramedic. I recognized her as the person who had cut off my pajama top and detected my racing heart. Her jaw dropped. She said, "Robinson?" I could not believe she called me by name!

"My God! You are standing up! You are walking! I did not think anyone would ever see you again. We thought we had lost you!"

I simply smiled and showed her my poem. Tears in her eyes, she asked if she could hug me. "Sure," I said. "Hugs are very healing." Then she asked, "Would it be okay if I gave your poem to our supervisor. I would also like to hang it on our bulletin board. She added, "You know, it was so good of you to come thank us. Hardly anyone ever does. And you're alive!" Before we left, she hugged me again.

The poem:

Whose Hands?

It began with thrashing in my sleep.
Moments later – 911!
I never saw them before.
But with scissors in sure fingers,
They cut off my pajama tops.

They were the hands of one of nine paramedics and EMT's,
This one a reassuring woman named Brooke,
Who came within four minutes,
And scared poor Aubrey
As they paraded silently through the front door to my bedside.
Within minutes, siren blazing, an ambulance full of hands
Rushed toward Lutheran Hospital,
One pair of hands steering,
One pair inserting intravenous tubes into my veins,
A third pair holding a radio connected to an emergency room doc,
Hands of three guys who had never seen me, nor I them,
None of us knowing the outcome of these precious moments.
Bounce, bounce over ER door thresholds.
More hands, I know not whose,
Grabbed the stretcher and steered it behind white curtains.
On my left a woman's hands tried to stick
A fourth or fifth needle into my arm.
Mostly, those hands made a bloody mess,
And quickly withdrew from the effort.
Hands whose face I couldn't see,
As I was beginning to lose consciousness,
A hand held a stethoscope to my chest.
"Pulse 200" said the hand's voice.
A voice said, almost breathlessly,
"We'll have to use anesthesia, put him out,
And use the shock paddles, maybe as many as three times."
The only way I know of other hands that plied my body that night
Is from the bills coming to 6733 Kilmer Court.
Radiologist hands, Cardiologist hands, Nurse hands, Anesthetist
hands,
Surgeon hands.
I never saw those hands. Their eyes had never seen me before.
All nameless, they kept touching me.

Hands doing their skilled best to rescue my body,
Which, in the end, refused to quit.
The anonymity of intimacy was never more poignant!
When I began to emerge from the induced fog
I saw two more sets of hands.
Were they familiar?
More fog.
Yes, maybe Jan's hands,
That have been holding mine for sixty years.
And…
And…perhaps…Karen's hands…
Karen, who will do anything to help her folks.
Their hands found me in the ER and stayed 'til dawn
When I finally could make them out.
Thank God for all these hands,
That knew just what to do!

As we drove away from the fire station, I smiled quietly to myself. I was still alive.

Open-Heart Surgery

But that was not the end of the precariousness. Already wearing Nitro patches and consuming bottles of Nitro-glycerin pills, toward the end of 2015 I began noticing that I could no longer walk as fast or as far, and that I was experiencing shortness of breath and chest pain. An Echo Cardiogram in November revealed that my aortic valve was severely blocked with stenosis. Three hospitalizations later, on January 21, 2016, I had open-heart surgery for replacement of the dysfunctional valve with a cow valve. During the surgery I was stricken with a severe C.-Diff. intestinal infection, then with a pulmonary embolism.

My recovery was the longest and most frustrating I ever have experienced. During that window I went to an emergency room seven times and was hospitalized three times. Along the way, I participated in a 24-session cardiac rehab program at Lutheran, my favorite hospital. Having a dysfunctional heart is an experience I could not wish on anyone. But, amazingly, I have not lost hope. Nor have I become depressed, though there has been good reason to do so. God still calls me to persevere. This gives me courage to weather the down days.

Less than a week after completing the 24 cardiac rehab sessions, a horrible abdominal pain evolved. Back to Lutheran at 3:00 a.m. It turned out to be an adhesion in my small intestine that resulted from the surgery that had taken my large intestine years earlier. It took eight days to get "opened up." Continuing GI issues led to three more days in Lutheran in mid-2017. Then I learned that some of my abdominal difficulty was the result of dehydration. Funny thing, how plain water is still one of today's best medications!

Despite these abdominal problems, my weight has stabilized in the 150's after dropping to 120. Simultaneously, due to the same osteoporosis that sidelined my mother, I have shrunk four inches in height. Guess stuff like this happens when one gets old.

However, I continue to be upbeat, and feel incredibly grateful to be alive! I think my survival, in no small part, comes from a vigorous will to live.

I can say I deeply believe God does not choose whether a person lives or dies. We are, of course, mortal, finite creatures, and do not live forever. But I think God hopes that each of us will be responsive and accountable in ways that carry us into old age. There are many people who think they are living out a "Plan" outlined by God specifically for them. They think that when they have survived a crisis God has intentionally intervened to rescue them. The downside of this perception is the premature death of so many millions of good people of all faiths through all the millennia of history. I do not believe in a God who arbitrarily chooses when one will live and when one will die.

Rather, I think God's role in a person's survival and life surely has to do with the spiritual energy God offers all people, energy to choose life, not death, and energy to respond to God's call for sacrificial self-giving.

With so many things that can go wrong, plague, disease, injury, demise at the hands of others, unfortunate personal judgment, survival until the normal end of one's earthly pilgrimage truly is a matter of luck, as well as courageous perseverance.

The Holy keeps saying, "Don't Ever Just Quit!"

Chapter 55

❧❧

RMHDC Becomes Archway Housing and Services

THE HOLY WOULD not let me even slow down. I was helping Rocky Mountain HDC, Inc. become a significant faith-based player in the Colorado affordable housing arena.

David Nestor and I continued to give leadership to the organization and its creation and management of housing and social services for ill-housed folks. Paul Herskowitz, with whom I had worked on HUD-financed low-income housing in Florida, now living in Colorado, agreed to join the Archway Board in 2013. Having decades of experience as a developer of assisted housing in the west, he is a very helpful member of the Board team.

RMHDC added Greenleaf, a run-down 55-unit single building, to its affordable housing portfolio in 2013, and immediately had to undertake a major rehabilitation. We arranged for grants from the Colorado Division of Housing and the City of Aurora Development Division.

This work included repairing internal wastewater piping, adding a community activity room, replacing kitchen and bathroom appliances and fixtures, and rebuilding the elevator. This reconstruction work had to be done with residents already living in each apartment.

GREENLEAF

We were pleased that many of the existing residents were immigrants from Nepal. But the first thing we had to do was to check existing resident's visas, as illegal immigrants could not live in Greenleaf under governmental loan terms.

Three years later the City of Aurora asked us to replace all the exterior access stairs and walkways. This required relocation of tenants to temporary housing as construction progressed. We also added a children's playground and an attractive gardening space.

In July of 2016, we had a grand reopening ceremony that was attended both by residents and by State and City officials.

After the original Greenleaf acquisition was completed, RMHDC seemed to fall into a difficult malaise. Expenses were exceeding revenues. We did not see any prospects for additional housing for the financially distressed and under-employed populace. There was frustration and turnover among staff members. The Board took this time to evaluate our operation and concluded that the big negative driving issue was the competition for governmental dollars in a down economy.

A strengthening emerged as two things occurred. The economy began waking up. And we were able to get a new loan for Foothills Green which we had owned long enough to refinance it. In the refinancing, we were able to net cash from unpaid developer fees owed by the project to Archway from the outset. This gave us much needed new development capital.

As we worked on Greenleaf, a corporate restructuring seemed appropriate. Our operation was two almost separate businesses. On the one hand we were an apartment management and resident social services operation. On the other hand, we were a development entity that built new projects and acquired existing affordable properties.

We first renamed RMHDC in a reimaging effort. Thinking that "Rocky Mountain HDC, Inc." sounded too much like a for-profit corp., and potentially uninviting to future residents, we changed our name to "Archway Housing and Services, Inc." Our new logo was an inviting archway with a house-shaped roof and a family standing in the opening. Because of our intense Family Services social programs, we added a slogan, "Building Communities, Changing Lives." which we then used in all publicity, advertising, and communications. Going forward, Archway Housing and Services, Inc. was to be the property management and services entity.

Simultaneously we created a sister 501(c)(3) non-profit and called it Archway Investment Corp. It became the building development and owner corporation. One of its functions was to serve as the Managing General Partner of our ownership partnerships, other partners being government entities and tax credit lenders.

In doing this corporate restructuring we continued our commitment to having resident representatives serve on our Boards.

40 West

The next project had been five years in the making. A multiple parcel tract on Colfax Avenue, the main east-west highway through Denver, located in Lakewood, had been purchased in 2012. HUD Tax Credit financing was awarded by the Colorado Housing Finance Authority in 2016, and the 60-unit apartment project had its grand opening in 2017. A wonderful feature of this building is a very large rooftop solar garden that provides a substantial amount of the electrical power for the facility.

40 West is located just north of the new light-rail route from downtown to Golden, giving residents access to jobs throughout the region. 25% of the residential units are occupied by disabled American military veterans. 40 WEST brought our total number of units to 423. The United Church of Christ was beginning to make a difference in community service ministries!

Villa Verde

In 2017 the Aurora Housing Authority asked us if we would purchase a 29-unit property they owned almost immediately adjacent to Greenleaf. It was a small enough property that they needed only part time management for Villa Verde. We bought it with the idea that our property management and Family Service staff members at Greenleaf could also cover Villa Verde. Subsequently, we have refinanced both facilities in a single loan package, which is working out quite well.

Fountain Ridge

As 2017 ended, Archway completed the acquisition of two properties in the village of Fountain, south of Colorado Springs. They are adjacent properties which have an outdoor community space that our Family Services staff uses for work with both adults and children. Fountain Ridge has 36 units and Fountain Ridge South has 75. We have had to do some handicapped access construction at Fountain Ridge South. This has been our first attempt to reach out beyond the Denver Metropolitan area.

The Flats at Two Creeks

FLATS AT TWO CREEKS

In 2018 Archway built The Flats at Two Creeks, a 78 unit building immediately adjacent to 40 West in Lakewood on land that was filled with abandoned and vandalized rental units. We also have a sizable group of disabled American military veterans in this facility. The U.S. Veterans Administration provides support social services here as well as at 40

West. This project opened in 2019 and achieved full lease up in 2020. It also has a large rooftop solar garden.

So, our volunteer-led church non-profit reached 641 affordable apartments, remarkable for a Conference of the United Church of Christ!

Dramatic Transformation of Archway

We had a new challenge when Joyce Alms Ransford announced her resignation in 2019. I was Chair of the Archway Board. Lots of work ahead! Our search for a new corporate CEO led to our hiring Sebastian Corradino, a nationally known leader of organizations that develop and finance tax-credit affordable housing for struggling families. Sebastian started his leadership of the Archway staff in March of 2020.

It did not take him long to begin making changes that created an opportunity for Archway to rethink its strategies for developing additional affordable housing.

Sebastian substantially reorganized Archway's senior staff, adding key senior positions particularly in areas of corporate financial management. But most of all, he expanded our vision of how Archway could develop significantly more units of affordable housing across Colorado.

In this transition we strengthened our significant family-services program which helps people take control of their own lives in face of life's heavy duty domestic, parenting and employment challenges.

KIDS LOVE FIELD TRIPS

There are now five Archway Board persons who are members of UCC churches in the Rocky Mountain Conference. Dr. Jody Huntington is Professor of Counseling and Family Therapy at Regis University. The Rev. Dr. Lee Berg is a UCC minister in Denver who has decades of experience managing educational Non-Profit organizations. Austin Hamre is a public services attorney. David Nestor and I are the other two. Church work is increasingly outside its doors.

New Projects

Prior to Sebastian's arrival, Archway had purchased a tract in Lakewood for another family project. For a variety of reasons, including neighbor opposition, Tax Credit funding was not awarded. Sebastian's new team has reworked the plan for this project, turning it into apartments for low-income seniors. There will be 67 apartments in the Morse Park facility.

Then, in a turn of events that should have occurred years earlier, Archway began working with the Rocky Mountain Conference United Church of Christ on partnership mission ventures that will create housing for low-income persons on declining membership and vacated local church properties.

Using a closed UCC church site, a project in south Denver is slated to create modest affordable modular homes for sale to people who are seeking to move up the housing ladder as they get their lives together.

UCC Churches, one in Colorado Springs and one in Pueblo, that can no longer afford the ownership costs of their buildings, began working on mission joint ventures with Archway. Both congregations are passionate about housing low-income folks. New structures on each property would provide apartments for those in need along with multi-use community space in which church people can hold church activities as well as provide services for their residents. This could lead to another 100 or so Archway units.

Sebastian and the Board also are reaching out to UCC churches across the Rocky Mountain Conference to find congregations that wish to become advocates for housing the underhoused in their communities.

Another new step in Archway's work is the initiation of major philanthropic activities with the goal of raising significant funds for housing development and resident services.

Reflection

Archway's mission is to provide safe decent housing for the marginalized while the nation struggles with the need for economic and racial justice for all in a world that is systemically unholy.

In a very complex and even convoluted life that has focused primarily on an ordained secular ministry totally outside the structure of the church, there is a sense that I have been "counter-cultural" ever since ordination in 1957. My volunteer spearheading of the development of affordable housing opportunities for the economically marginalized is now in its twenty fifth year. Though this work has been done as a volunteer in my retirement years, it may be the most significant church leadership role of my entire ministry. Through such co-conspiracies with the Holy, life creeps toward wholeness.

In 1965, without much forethought, but with an inner conviction that I had been claimed by a Holy Spirit that transcends all religions, a life force that calls out justice and mercy as its highest human priority, I had gone to Selma. And, here I was, toward the end of my life, still challenging the fruits of empire, neither defeated nor sorry that revolutionary transformation has been the story of my life. Jesus' community ministry outside the Temple has been a compelling model.

Chapter 56

~~

A Second La Foret Rescue

Bank Loan Default

IN 2013, WHEN I was no longer serving on La Foret Conference Center's Board, Executive Director Ralph Townsend called me for help. When we met, he started out by saying he felt he was not getting support from the current Board members. I suggested several options through which he could restore the Board's confidence in his leadership. But the dysfunction quickly became severe. Among other things, he had never learned how to work with the Carver Model of Board Governance.

Jan and I learned of the crisis on a Tuesday in September of 2013. We had gone to the RMC-UCC office to greet The Rev. Sue Artt, the Conference's brand new Acting Interim Minister who had begun her work the week before. On the prior Thursday, she had attended a La Foret Board meeting at the retreat center. At that meeting Ralph had told the Board that a commercial bank in Colorado Springs to which La Foret owed some $700,000 would foreclose on the camp within a week. The Director had failed to tell the Board that the bank had initiated foreclosure proceedings six months earlier. In addition, Ralph also had forbidden the camp bookkeeper from telling anyone during the intervening months. The Board fired him on the spot.

This news came shortly after Jan and I introduced ourselves to Sue. A casual meeting suddenly turned serious. Taking a deep breath, I recommended to Sue that we form a Task Force to deal with this crisis. I suggested the team include Sue, Tom Huxtable, already a La Foret Board member, Larry McCulloch, the new President of The Endowment Fund of the RMC-UCC, and myself. In broad terms the mission was to save La Foret once again. Sue agreed to the Task Force idea, and we recruited Tom and Larry within a day. The team assumed I would serve as Chair. We took drastic steps. First was to recommend to the La Foret Board that it step back and let the Task Force run the camp while working out a financial solution to the foreclosure. They readily agreed.

Next, we went to the Board of RMC-UCC, which conveniently happened to be having a meeting that weekend. The Conference had $153,000 in its reserve funds which it loaned the La Foret Task Force. We then offered the Colorado Springs bank an immediate payment of $50,000 and promised to find another lender for the balance in return for cancellation of the foreclosure Sue and I both had working experience with the President and CEO of the National UCC Cornerstone Fund, an entity that makes loans to churches and other UCC institutions. We arranged for a loan of $1,175,000, pledging the entire retreat center property as collateral, to which the La Foret Board agreed at a special meeting. Some of this was used to pay $665,000 to the Colorado Springs bank in return for its release of lien. We repaid the $153,000 Conference loan. We then set aside $293,000 to cover deferred maintenance and major structure stabilization. Finally, we kept $150,000 for an operating reserve for the next two years. For several months, the Task Force met several times a week to save La Foret.

After several weeks, Larry McCulloch, a retired Hewlett Packard officer, took me aside and offered to serve as Interim Director of La Foret Conference and Retreat Center. I was delighted. We soon dropped the "Interim" part of the title.

With his leadership, La Foret returned to being a vital ministry of the Rocky Mountain Conference.

La Foret is a sanctuary where people of all walks find themselves considering the transcendent issues of life, a meaningful spiritual exercise in which they know with ever greater certainty that they are claimed by God, no matter what words, contemporary secular, or historic Christian, they are using. In a new century of human existence, there is a growing emergence of spiritual journeying, that is, listening for the Holy, using secular, not sacred, themes. La Foret is a place where this happens.

Since that first senior high youth camp back in 1962, La Foret has played a pivotal role in my listening for the Holy.

Funny thing, in 2020, I was asked to serve on the Board again, this time as a Member Emeritus. Currently, the retreat center is wrestling with the negative impact of state orders limiting group gatherings during the Covid crisis.

Chapter 57

~~

MAJOR FAMILY TRANSITIONS

Ronzheimers Adopt Aubrey

IN OUR FIRST eight years of raising Aubrey, both Karen and Joel assisted greatly in supporting us. At the beginning of the summer which followed her fifth grade year, Aubrey moved into the Ronzheimer's Coal Creek Canyon home, as Jan was becoming increasingly dysfunctional.

By then, Aubrey had become very comfortable with the Ronzheimers, having spent many overnights and weekends with them. The decision to have Aubrey leave our home felt like the right thing to do. Karen and Joel became legal guardians of Aubrey.

One of the challenges at summer's end was that Aubrey had to be driven 15 miles each way from Coal Creek Canyon to West Woods Elementary for sixth grade. Aubrey was then accepted in a Talented and Gifted program at Excel Academy, a Jefferson County School

District Charter School, for seventh and eighth grades. More 15-mile trips up and down the Canyon!

We all decided while she was in Jr. High that it would be best for the Ronzheimers to have full legal authority and responsibility for Aubrey. This was so that Aubrey would have the continuing support and protection of a loving family as she moved through her teen years into adulthood. During her 8th grade year, the Ronzheimers adopted Aubrey. Not many kids have been adopted twice. And, as an acknowledgement of her family heritage, Aubrey's surname is still Gurkin.

Aubrey is an amazing child. She has several strong suits. She can remember precise details of events that occurred months and even years earlier. She is exceedingly canny, able to piece together patterns of why things happen the way they do. She has accurate insights into the behavior of others, both children and adults. She is a consummate tease, with a subtle sense of humor.

As 8th grade came to an end, Aubrey played a significant role in a school musical, both singing and acting. Then, at church, with another girl, she beautifully sang a duet. The next week she "Continued" from Excel.

60th Wedding Anniversary

As 2015 began, Eve organized a celebration of Jan's and my 60th Anniversary. Doing it from 1,000 miles away was a trick. It was to be held on a Sunday in the community space at First United Church of Arvada. Friends were invited, and family members came from around the country. The plan was for there to be a special family gathering hosted by Joel and Karen at their mountain home on the Saturday before the big Sunday event.

Brittany had not been invited for any of the weekend events because of her many prior outbursts in connection with our having adopted Aubrey. Brittany's modus operandi was that of continually claiming what was happening in her life was the fault of others, not her own.

Robyn called Stuart saying she would not fly in from Kauai if Brittany was left out. Stuart and Robyn agreed to a plan in which Brittany's attendance and participation would be limited and controlled.

Nevertheless, Brittany was very disruptive.

These negative family dynamics made both Saturday's and Sunday's Anniversary celebrations very uncomfortable. It was a lovely party on Sunday, which was also Jan's birthday, but because of the disruptive behavior none of us family members feel totally good about the weekend. After all her work, Eve was most upset.

Appreciating great daily support from both Karen and Stuart, I have had to learn to live with the reality that Jan's and my reaching out to Aubrey has been tough on the family. I have heard the Holy saying, "Family life sometimes requires painful decisions. Do what is right, not what avoids conflict."

Nevertheless, I continue to work hard at maintaining a functional loving relationship with Robyn, which seems to be working. We now talk regularly.

Painfully for me, Brittany has totally cut me out of her life.

Jan's Struggles

After Aubrey had gone to live with Joel and Karen, I knew things were getting worse when one day, while taking a short walk without me, Jan had to borrow a bystander's cell phone to call me, saying she was lost. I told her to tell me what she could see, and she described a gas station several blocks south from our neighborhood walking trail. I told her not to leave the spot where she was standing, and, gratefully, she was there when I arrived, still holding the borrowed phone!

With Stuart and Karen's increasing involvement, we next took two steps to handle Jan's future. The first was to begin some in-home care, needed in part because I was being distracted by severe heart issues. So early in 2016 we tried two different national franchise agencies to help with personal care and elemental housekeeping. The problem with each of them was that they sent different caregivers almost every day. Thus, no one ever developed a functional working relationship with Jan, and Jan was uncomfortable with differing daily routines. Jan quickly became resentful about having "baby-sitters."

Early in this in-home care sequence, Stuart, and Karen, looking at the road ahead, took a second step by arranging for a series of visits to senior care facilities. On one weekend, with Stuart in town to guide us, we visited six independent and assisted living facilities. Stuart and Karen thought that, at least, we should be on a waiting list or two. And so, we signed up at a couple of places, one of them being Springwood in Arvada where, coincidentally, my mother had been a resident 25 years earlier.

However, as the Holy kept whispering, "Love another more than self," I felt that staying in our house would be far more comfortable for Jan. She needed familiar surroundings and a routine with which she was comfortable.

With our experience with home care agencies growing thin, we came across a unique care program based in metro Denver. Called "Out and About," its visionary owner-manager created daily excursions to various museums, Active Minds presentations, historical sites, libraries, and other interesting places. The Out and About program had one caregiver for each three or four patients, with 9 to 12 patients being the case load on any given day. It was a wonderful program which Jan enjoyed very much.

At an Out and About holiday social event which family care givers attended with their spouses, I recognized a man who was there with his ailing wife. He was the Jefferson County Court Magistrate who had awarded us full custody of Aubrey. After hearing how she was doing now, ten years later, he put his arm around me, exclaiming, "You saved that girl's life!"

Because of the long distance the Out and About drivers had to travel to pick up Jan, we were reduced from three to two days a week.

The Out and About owner-director recommended that we hire a local independent caregiver she knew, who had twenty years' experience as a Medical Assistant. An unbelievably caring and loving person, this woman came for 6 hours on the three weekdays that Jan was not with Out and About. She did a few things at the house with Jan, but primarily took her to many of the same kinds of places that she visited with Out and About. Jan's favorite was to go to the local library where moms with preschool kids gathered for educational programs and games. Jan absolutely loved the kids, and the children were very responsive to her.

When the Out and About program dropped Jan down to one day a week, I looked for a second private duty caregiver. Unexpectedly, Springwood's Independent Living Activity Director became a candidate. With flexibility offered by her supervisor, our second aide was able to take six hours two days a week, giving us coverage for every weekday. She was a native Hawaiian, very warm and innovative. Her 3-year-old granddaughter became one of Jan's most special little friends.

So, here I was, running a home care program! Each caregiver received my full hourly payment, rather than having half of it go to one of the nationally franchised companies used by most families. No wonder we had such high-quality support and care!

As soon as the five-day schedule with these two caregivers was operational, it was clear to me that keeping Jan at home was way more desirable than having her go to a memory care facility. One of the elements of this was that Jan was very dependent on my daily affirmations and emotional support. At any Memory Care facility, she would have had to live alone in a small apartment. Further, she reacted very poorly to being in settings with which she was unfamiliar. Karen felt that such an option would have caused a premature demise for her.

An amusing highlight of our daily lives was that Jan very frequently asked me while we both were dressing for the day, "What day is today?" Sometimes she asked me this several times while looking at the calendar we had placed near her sink. On Sundays, she would ask me on the way to our church in Boulder, "Where are we? Where are we going?"

It took me a while to figure out how to respond to Jan in her forgetfulness and confusion. I learned that she was much more comfortable if I did not remind her when she asked something that I had already answered more than once. I just tried to roll with the punches when she did something irrational or unexpected.

It even got to the point where each night she "heard" me calling or answering the phone or speaking with others who were imaginarily in our house. I learned how to comfort her and help her back to bed without exclaiming that she couldn't have heard me because I was sleeping.

She also became quite unstable on her feet and would fall on our walking path when she lost her balance.

Perhaps my most important learning was that she responded very well to my holding and hugging her frequently during the day. In being embraced she felt safe and affirmed.

This caregiving role took increasing amounts of my energy, time, and patience. I did the cooking and the housekeeping. I was present for her when our caregivers were not there. I did the shopping. I arranged her doctor's appointments.

We got to the point where I had to install keyed locks on the interior side of the entrance doors so that Jan could not go outside at night, which she often tried to do, "because there are people out there coming to see us."

On Easter Sunday of 2018, we learned that the Wallace Farm had burned to ground, leaving two of her cousins with no place to live and no way to continue raising dairy cattle. Even in her Alzheimer's haze, Jan was quite distressed.

Then, in August of 2018, both our caregivers and I noticed that Jan's behavior had suddenly become much more erratic. She wasn't excited about day-outings. She started wandering through the house every night. Neither her caregivers nor I could figure it out. A major change was occurring, but we did not know what it was.

On September 13, 2018, Jan awoke well before daylight and walked out of her bedroom. I have no idea where she thought she was going, perhaps to the bathroom, but she flipped uncontrollably down the stairs to the basement. What woke me was her thumping on the stairs on the way down. I found her motionless on the basement floor, bleeding profusely from her mouth and nose. Following the ambulance to the Saint Anthony Hospital ER, I learned that she had a brain injury, a cracked neck vertebra, a broken wrist, and severe facial injuries.

We had a mutual understanding that neither of us would allow heroic medical efforts to extend the other's life. Not ever really understanding what had happened or where she now was, Jan lived four days in St. Anthony Hospital and two more in the Lutheran Hospital Collier Hospice before quietly taking her leave on the 19th, waiting until all but Stuart had left the room.

To accommodate our children and Jan's brother's family members, we waited four weeks to hold a memorial service. There was an overflow crowd at Community United Church of Christ, our church in Boulder. The three adult kids spoke of their memories of Mom. When Aubrey sang "You Are My Flashlight" there was not a dry eye in the church. I did the Eulogy. Among other things, I said:

> "Standing in front of you this morning is one of the luckiest men in the world. Jan was a true gift who came into my life when we both were 18. A most self-giving person, she made our lives work. I could not be more grateful nor more loved!

> "An early advocate for LGBT social justice within the church, Jan supported Julian Rush, a gay Methodist minister who was Executive Director of the Colorado Aids Project, and composer. Jan learned of a hymn he had written. She promoted its inclusion in the UCC New Century Hymnal as it was being assembled in Cleveland in the early 90s. In a few minutes, we will sing Hymn No. 391, "In the Midst of New Dimensions.

> "Looking back, Jan was a very understated person. She never created drama or showed off when reaching out to others. She hardly ever talked, even with me, about her religious beliefs or faith commitments. She just

lived her religion, often sacrificially, at significant cost to herself. And the world is a better place because of her. Her influence in human history did not end with her death. She's very alive to many people."

JAN – 2016

Jan taught me how to love a mate. She uncritically and uncomplainingly loved and supported me no matter what. I quickly learned from her that even a marriage is about someone else, not yourself. A key learning was that trying to change another person to make your life better is unloving. Trying to change your own life to make someone else's work better is much more appropriate. One cannot blame one's own life failures on the behavior of another. Thus saith the Holy.

She never said, "I'll love you more if you …" She would say, "Do you think WE should have no more children? Do you think WE should move back to Colorado? Do you think WE should learn to balance two professional careers?"

What does one say about the woman he has known and cherished for more than 67 years? For people whose personalities are quite different, but whose intelligence, political and world outlook, vocational and social interests are quite similar, we were very much in love the day she died. We cared to a fault about each other's welfare. We each were wounded when the other was struggling with injury or illness.

We always had similar opinions about our children, their mates, our friends, and public figures.

Even in her death, she continues to lovingly support all her family survivors. But I miss her with all my heart and soul!

Jan's adult life had two fascinating interwoven halves. On the one hand, typical of the cultural family model into which she was born, when we were married in 1955, Jan saw her role as mother, lead homemaker, caregiver and parent, and supporter of her husband in his ministry. Life went on this way for her until our children were in their early teenage years.

Then, Jan literally bridged the gap between generations of women in our culture, those who were predominantly homemakers, and those who were employed outside the home. After her life as an at-home family caregiver, a liberated Jan joined the workforce as a professional while two of our three children were still at home. She became one of a growing group of women who learned in the '70s to balance career and family life. It happened that this transition was a time of learning for both of us. A key outcome was her emergence as a proficient professional in social justice and in the care of home bound, often indigent, adults. Jan's entry into the professional work force made a huge difference to both her self-esteem and her identity.

There is another strand of Jan's life which one needs to understand to know her fully. From the day she arrived at Ohio Wesleyan, there was no question that "church" would be a major framework for her life. At Ohio Wesleyan I had learned that if I were to date her, I would be attending Asbury Methodist Church with her each Sunday morning.

She became an ardent participant in the churches I served in Illinois and Michigan. Then she became the "church mother" of the Arvada church. Subsequently, she has fully participated in UCC churches in Rochester, Texas, Evergreen, CO, Denver's Park Hill neighborhood, Florida, and, finally, Boulder. Not going to church was ever discussed in our house. More importantly, the call to sacrificial living that brought meaning to Jan's life for 80-plus years was central to her beliefs and mode of living. One just cannot understand Jan without knowing she did "church" with conviction and commitment.

Such a Blessing!

Before she died, Jan and I deeded to the Rocky Mountain Conference Endowment Fund a 70-acre tract of land in Coal Creek Canyon that we had owned since building our mountain house. It had been on the market for ten years. It suddenly occurred to me that there would be no income tax if we gave the land as a charitable gift, rather than waiting until after it sold to make the gift. Amazingly, the property sold immediately after we gave it to the RMC Endowment Fund for various United Church of Christ missions to which she and I were committed!

After Jan died, she and I were honored by the Rocky Mountain Conference and La Foret Boards. In a ceremony at La Foret, a site for a new adult residential facility to be called LAPP LODGE was dedicated. One of the speakers was our great granddaughter Aubrey, who spoke of her love for La Foret and shared her gratitude and respect for the work we had done to make it a special haven for kids.

A Collier Hospice grief counselor told me that it would take me at least fifteen months simply to get used to the fact that Jan was gone. That turned out to be very true. But I had another discovery. So many older people have been crushed and disabled by the death of their mate that I expected the same emotion. However, for some Holy reason I have experienced deep gratefulness for the time Jan and I had together. And

I have been able to go on with my life, now living alone in a cottage in the senior facility to which I would not send her. None of this means that I do not cry a bit when I think of her or hear her voice in the still of the night.

Jan was a huge influence in my nontraditional ministry. I absolutely could not have made it, had I not been married to a woman who, even though she thought she was marrying a parish minister, learned to heal my wounds and inspire my courage. We saw ourselves in a family joint venture in which we each had mutual voice and a common mission.

After she was gone, as I listened to the world's cries for help, the Holy was saying to me, "Stay the course.!" I cannot think of anything better to be doing as I approach 90.

Our kids and I are experiencing Jan's death as a blessing that spared her from sinking further and more deeply into total disability.

Chapter 58

≈≈

FAMILY MEMBERS DO
THEIR THINGS

Robyn

HAVING MOVED TO Anchorage early in 2013, Robyn soon found living there to be a challenge. While she enjoyed some of the nearby wilderness parks and thought the native culture was fascinating, she did not particularly like either the snowy weather or her job. She lived in a large apartment building across the street from a large sports complex where both amateurs and professionals played almost daily. It was noisy.

Robyn continued to work as a scheduler for the Anchorage Orthopedic Clinic for four years. Not liking what she thought was the unethical behavior of one of the clinic managers at her hospital, Robyn quit and moved again, this time to Santa Fe, NM both to be near her daughter Chelsea who had moved there in 2012, and to take yet another medical job, this time in a hospital. She lives in a rural rental shared by Chelsea, and by ex-husband William Gorman who rejoined the entourage after several years of living back home in Buffalo, NY.

William soon developed physical difficulties, which led to Robyn's having to care for him. Chelsea is often in and out, spending time with her boyfriend at his family's home.

Robyn was temporarily laid off during early in the 2020 Corona Virus pandemic, but went back on the job, expecting to work at least another year and a half before retirement. She is an early recipient of the Covid vaccine.

After Robyn left Kauai, Brittany, who had been living with her, moved to Honolulu and married Jay Thornton, a U.S. Navy sailor. They bought a house and settled there. Brittany began working in the elder care field. While Robyn was still in Anchorage, Jay was transferred to Virginia and assigned to active duty on a ship in the Middle East. Brittany joined him there and is continuing her work in the medical field.

Stuart and Eve

Over time, Stuart grew restless and impatient in working with PWI. He was having to handle corporate management issues for the company that were not specifically drawing on his legal skills. At 57, in 2015, partly because of the many leadership roles he was playing in the Montgomery County Economic Development Partnership and the Chamber of Commerce in The Woodlands, he was invited to join Stibbs and Co., a private law firm in The Woodlands, as Partner. As half-owner, he became manager of the firm which specializes in corporate business law. He is growing the firm, which has opened a second office, this one in College Station, TX.

Stepdaughter Neele continues to work in corporate advertising and marketing. After a long courtship, she and Raquel Cifelli were married in January of 2018 in a fancy ceremony aboard a cruise ship in the Gulf of Mexico. They have purchased a house just south of The Woodlands. Raquel gave birth to their daughter Everly, our fourth Great Granddaughter, on September 29, 2020. In December 2020, Neele earned a Master of Science Degree in Digital Audience Strategy from Arizona State University.

Stepdaughter Nellaine graduated from Lone Star College in May 2015 with an Associate Degree in Criminal Justice. She then graduated from Sam Houston State University in December 2017 with a B.S in Criminal Justice. In March 2019 she graduated from the Houston Police Academy. Now a certified Houston Police Officer, she is facing the challenges of being a peace officer in a health pandemic.

Stuart's and Eve's "adopted" daughter Ruth Mulkey and granddaughter Erin also live south of The Woodlands where Ruth has worked for an auto repair shop for years. I consider Erin to be my third Great Granddaughter.

Eve put together a very successful surprise 60th birthday gathering for Stuart in 2018, held in St. Anthony the Great Church near The Woodlands. Karen, Joel, Jan, Aubrey, and I all flew down. When Stuart walked into the room thinking he was attending a church meeting, he was totally shocked when he saw the crowd of church friends, then spotted us.

Karen, Joel & Aubrey

Our relationship with Karen and Joel has been very close. We do many things together, whether it has been cutting trees for firewood, enjoying meals and holiday celebrations, running to the airport, shopping or just socializing. When it became time for Aubrey to attend High School, she was accepted for entrance into New Vista, a Boulder School District academy-type school. This gave Joel and Karen only 80 miles a day of trips to Boulder. A third of the way through her Junior Year, Aubrey started riding the Regional Transportation District bus part of each way to school. But two-thirds of the way through her Junior Year the Covid 19 virus closed New Vista so Aubrey had to finish her school semester as an online student. This arrangement continued through her Senior year.

Through all of this, Joel continued his employment with the City of Arvada at the West Woods Golf Course.

Karen's employment with AT&T continued with spin-offs into Lucent Technologies and, later, Avaya. In each setting she was responsible for managing inventory required for repairing, maintaining, and replacing complicated commercial phone systems and networks throughout North America. Avaya eventually contracted with a newly formed Boston corporation, On Process Technologies, to handle this inventory management. Karen was hired by On Process Technologies where she continued to do work like that for which she was hired by AT&T thirty-one years earlier. Karen soon began working from home, using the internet to conduct her inventory management work. She was stunned when Avaya ended its contract with On Process in 2017 and hired an offshore company to manage the inventory. She did not even get a termination package much less any retirement benefits!

Karen became the family hostess for holiday and special day events at their house. She also spent many hours supporting Jan and me as we coped with Jan's growing disability.

Since being terminated from On Process, Karen has not had time to look for another job.

Loving dogs, Aubrey plans to attend Colorado State University and become a Veterinarian. She is also very artistic in singing, drawing, and writing.

Chapter 59

～～～

SEMINARY STUDENT - AGAIN

An ST/M Degree 60 Years Later

I RECEIVED A graduate Bachelor of Divinity degree awarded jointly by the University of Chicago and Chicago Theological Seminary (CTS) in June of 1957. What I began to learn about the ultimate meaning of human existence has never been far from my innermost thoughts. Perhaps that is why continuing to listen for the Holy inspired me, only sixty years after that first degree, to earn a Master of Sacred Theology degree in 2017. I became the oldest graduate in the seminary's history. When Jan and I flew to Chicago for the graduation ceremony, David Nestor accompanied us. Stuart flew in from Houston to join us. My heart was warmed by the cheering ovation I received as I walked across the graduation stage in the service held in Trinity United Church of Christ. People knew that my graduate thesis had been *"Hitting the Streets with Jesus – A Spiritual Journey."*

I was not at all theologically sophisticated upon my arrival at CTS the first time. But my approach to contemporary theology has its roots in those first three seminary years. There I began to understand that God is to be found, seen, and experienced in the pithy everyday swaths of personal life, in the challenges and rewards of human relationships which are necessary for discipleship, in the tides of history, and in brave historic attempts at reconstruction of government, society, and culture to provide justice for all humankind. The ancients had narratives, images, and doctrines to describe the characteristics of positive human behavior. Those experiences led to the emergence of the world's religions.

During my first CTS degree journey I gained a Christian vocabulary for the human experiencing of God's justice and mercy. This would become the basic reality on which all my subsequent metaphors have been built and checked. This methodology has really helped me understand the human wrestling for ultimate meaning that composes virtually the entire Holy Bible.

Sixty years later, in taking "New Social Gospel," my first course, from Professor Susan Thistlethwaite, I realized what a gift I was receiving in doing formal study, analysis, and reflection toward the end of a career as a non-traditional minister. In the process of taking courses and writing a thesis, Susan was my faculty advisor. I came to realize that three beliefs had been the faith structure of my lifetime walk with the Holy.

The first is that, for me, the pre-Easter Jesus reveals much more clearly the nature of human relationships with the Holy than does an image of a miraculously Resurrected Christ who, if one "accepts" him, will guarantee a safe afterlife, a belief that leads to serving one's self-interest, to the neglect of carrying lovingly for others.

Jesus worked outside of the boundaries of both Temple and Roman law, confronting the moral value inconsistencies in each realm. He knew that there is a transcendent life-giving power calling forth the best behavior humans can manifest. Jesus knew that, yes, God is real! And he made it so clear to others that they came to call him the Son of God.

Jesus was spiritually driven in absolute covenant with this Holy to have a revolutionary's passion for making human life what it ought to be. His point of beginning was his sensitivity to the damage done to human souls and bodies, and to life itself, by the various manifestations of sin that characterize the lives of every single human being as we seek more for ourselves. He was not afraid to step outside of the traditions of his faith and to meet people in the street. He asked why Israelites hated Samaritans. He wondered why the Prodigal was being punished after he came to his senses. He challenged a rich man to sell all that he had and give to the poor. He overturned the tables of the money changers in the Temple. He sat and talked lovingly with the lost and hurt. And he died for doing what the Holy asked of him. To be a follower of Jesus is serious business.

My second, and equally heretical theological insight has to do with God. Though there are many differing religious traditions in the world, there is only one God. Religious and ritualistic differences are simply the result of differing mythical and metaphorical interpretations of the Holy.

Christianity, as do most other religions, tends to imagine its God to be all-powerful, supernatural, and capable of intervening for good or for ill in the lives of individuals and communities of people. This is a God who capriciously rewards and punishes human creatures. People pray to this God for miraculous rescue from predicaments without exerting themselves sacrificially.

I do not get comfort or energy from such an image. I think God is the transcendent Holy that calls all of humanity to care for, and to love, others more than self. There is, in the fabric of human existence, a pull toward making life work for everyone, despite the human propensity to do just the opposite. That pull is a transcendent holy call. Responding to it is what strengthens one's soul and saves one's life. And, having been created with the ability to make choices, humans, despite their good commitments, inevitably "sin" in their self-interested moments of seeking power over others. But God still loves them.

My sense of God is that God, or the Holy, does not have supernatural powers that allow a breaking of the rules of the natural order, thus is not omnipotent in the sense of being magical. Rather, the Holy's spiritual appeal to all humans, despite their religious beliefs, rituals, and traditions, is to call them into loving all people into the community of making life work for everyone. And, when doing this one feels the energizing and restorative love of God.

My third insight is that no religion is perfect. No gathering of people is perfect. No individual is perfect. So, while I have participated fully and vigorously in Christianity, I have learned to take it as a human construct that offers glimpses of the Holy's divine calling. And, in this spiritual journey, I have learned that human biases often taint what the Holy is saying. So, it is with the Judeo-Christian holy book.

As we move into an Interfaith era, Chicago Theological Seminary is helping students explore future institutional manifestations of the church, questioning the historical myths of both Christian ritual and dogma, and of the Bible itself. Systemic racism is now shaping much of the seminary's academic structuring. And, finally, in a world in which sexism remains a powerful force, CTS is committed to fostering leadership for gender justice, including developing a more mature masculine spirituality and engaging feminist and womanist spiritualities. Christian theology and ministry in the future will be to help people restate these deepest truths about life in contemporary idioms.

Dramatically different from my first go-round in the fifties, most of my classmates and professors this time were women, which, in truth, I found both refreshing and challenging.

The prophetic witnessing of many at CTS was the mirror in which I examined myself in pursuit of this second degree. This self-reflecting brought into focus the meaning of my life.

Lapp Learning Commons Named

As I pursued my first degree, the most hallowed space in the CTS building compound was a beautiful arch-covered interior brick walkway that connected offices and classrooms with Graham Taylor Chapel. Called the Cloisters, it was close to one hundred and fifty feet long. I made it a point to walk through the Cloisters several times each day. I often stopped and reflected on my life, my past, my future, my faith, and my relationship with Jan, and eventually, with our first child. Even after I became a Trustee of CTS, I found myself visiting the Cloisters on a regular basis. It is the Cloisters that I miss the most now that the seminary has moved to its new single unit building.

At the dedication ceremony for the new building, I discovered that the long open stairways offered much the same opportunity for prayer and reflective contemplation, but Jan and I gave an endowment for the library.

We were honored by the naming of its electronic and hard-book library, the *"Robinson and Janet Lapp Learning Commons"* in celebration of my long and supportive relationship with CTS. It is always a bit of a shock to open the CTS online web site and see a drop down for the Lapp Learning Commons. I am excited that the current Library Director is Yasmine Abou-el Kheir, a delightful Muslim woman. Aubrey, who went with us to Chicago for the dedication of the Learning Commons, was both awed and pleased.

CTS LAPP LEARNING COMMONS

I shall be eternally grateful for my relationship with the seminary. There is much that might not have happened in my life had I not matriculated there. At CTS I have been forced to think critically, to live at the boundaries, to question ecclesiastical authority, to cope with the unexpected, to laugh at my uncertainties, and to see all religions as metaphorical responses to the Holy.

Back to the Judeo-Christian Holy Book

The rich Judeo-Christian Holy Book passages that have shaped my understanding of the Holy's claim on my life include several that I repeat to myself every day, particularly when the going is tough. I share them here.

Isaiah 6: 8-9 – responding to the call:

8 And I heard the voice of the Lord saying, "Whom shall I send, and who will go for us?" **9** Then I said, "Here I am! Send me." [5]

Each time I have come to a new challenge for change in the secular world, this passage is the one that has thrown me off the dock into unknown waters, as it did the first time at a church camp when I was 16. Though not from the New Testament, this verse clearly represents Jesus' response to God as a secular teacher who unintentionally led the institutional transition from Judaism to Christianity.

Matthew 26:36-50 - the cost of discipleship:

36 Then Jesus went with them to a place called Gethsemane; and he said to his disciples, "Sit here while I go over there and pray." **37** He took with him Peter and the two sons of Zebedee and began to be grieved and agitated. **38** Then he said to them, "I am deeply grieved, even to death; remain here, and stay awake with me." **39** And going a little farther, he threw himself on the ground and prayed, "My Father, if it is possible, let this cup pass from me; yet not what I want but what you want." **40** Then he came to the disciples and found them sleeping; and he said to Peter, "So, could you not stay awake with me one hour? **41** Stay awake and pray

---

5   p.715. The Holy Bible. Revised Standard Version. Thomas Nelson and Sons New York City. 1952

that you may not come into the time of trial; the spirit indeed is willing, but the flesh is weak." **42** Again he went away for the second time and prayed, "My Father, if this cannot pass unless I drink it, your will be done." **43** Again he came and found them sleeping, for their eyes were heavy. **44** So leaving them again, he went away and prayed for the third time, saying the same words. **45** Then he came to the disciples and said to them, "Are you still sleeping and taking your rest? See, the hour is at hand, and the Son of Man is betrayed into the hands of sinners. **46** Get up, let us be going. See, my betrayer is at hand." **47** While he was still speaking, Judas, one of the twelve, arrived; with him was a large crowd with swords and clubs, from the chief priests and the elders of the people. **48** Now the betrayer had given them a sign, saying, "The one I will kiss is the man; arrest him." **49** At once he came up to Jesus and said, "Greetings, Rabbi!" and kissed him. **50** Jesus said to him, "Friend, do what you are here to do." Then they came and laid hands-on Jesus and arrested him. [6]

This scene is what faithfulness is all about. Jesus was not afraid to die. It takes my breath away. Jesus strength came from an unseen spiritual covenant with the Most Holy, God, to do what was right in spite of the cost. That spiritual bond led to his being called the Son of God, the one with whom people are called to walk through life's disparities.

Micah 6:8 – and then, what does life seek from one?

8 He has told you, O mortal, what is good; and what

---

6   p. 34. The Holy Bible. Revised Standard Version. Thomas Nelson and Sons New York City. 1952

does the Lord require of you but to do justice, and to love kindness, and to walk humbly with your God? [7]

This Hebrew Bible description of God's ultimate life assignment has become my job description.

Matthew 22:34-40 – heart of the teaching of the Pre-Easter Jesus:

34 When the Pharisees heard that he had silenced Sadducees, they gathered together, **35** and one of them, a lawyer, asked him a question to test him. **36** "Teacher, which commandment in the law is the greatest?" **37** He said to him, "You shall love the Lord your God with all your heart, and with all your soul, and with all your mind.' **38** This is the greatest and first commandment. **39** And a second is like it: "You shall love your neighbor as yourself.' **40** On these two commandments hang all the law and the prophets." [8]

It is this simple, no matter how often I fail.

---

7   p.969 Ibid. -
8   p. 28 Ibid. –

Chapter 60

WOULD I DO MY LIFE
OVER AGAIN?

I Would Do It Again!

IN TRUTH, WHEN one passes 80 one starts thinking about how nice it would be to do anything again.

However, going against the deeply rooted cultural self-serving flow is the only way to do it.

This is to say that through it all I appear to have kept my sanity, my soul, my sense of humor, and an appreciation for new tomorrows.

This memoir has been an exploration of spiritual survival in a world of unforeseen events. Whether my challenges were perpetrated by accident or self-chosen, I have had many opportunities to grow pessimistic, even defeated, certainly worn down. However, for some reason, life has been an adventure for which I have been ready to get out of bed every day.

This blessing comes from God. My life's deal with the Holy has been: "Robb, if you seek to love the most unlovable, live with courage, do justice, walk humbly, and if, you die while seeking to do what the Holy is whispering, my benediction for you will be: 'Well done, good and faithful servant.'" How spiritually energizing! I think this confidence about life and God has been most existential for me. Whether it was surviving the tragic death of a little brother, saving my father's and daughter's lives, the challenge of a new church-start in an age of spiritual doubt, housing the marginalized, sustaining a life-long marriage commitment, risking everything for racial and social justice, shaping a new community, saving a church camp, or supporting the seminary from which I graduated twice, I have had the sense that I was changing history and life around me for the better, no matter the risk in challenging the status quo.

No matter how unfair or painful some of the consequences have been, I have marched forward in the confidence that the sun would shine tomorrow. This is spiritual strength that comes both from within and without, especially in the times of heavy challenge. It is God's greatest gift. It sustains a pilgrim in the march through life. Being able to do what life cries out for is the deepest blessing one could ever receive!

CPSIA information can be obtained
at www.ICGtesting.com
Printed in the USA
LVHW081901100421
683998LV00057B/1002